A COMPANION TO SHAKESPEARE STUDIES

Edited by

HARLEY GRANVILLE-BARKER

AND

G. B. HARRISON

CAMBRIDGE UNIVERSITY PRESS

CAMBRIDGE

LONDON · NEW YORK · MELBOURNE

Published by the Syndics of the Cambridge University Press
The Pitt Building, Trumpington Street, Cambridge CB2 1RP
Bentley House, 200 Euston Road, London NW1 2DB
32 East 57th Street, New York, NY 10022, USA
296 Beaconsfield Parade, Middle Park, Melbourne 3206, Australia

First Published 1934
Reprinted 1941, 1944, 1945, 1946, 1949,
1955, 1959, 1962, 1964, 1966, 1977

PRINTED IN GREAT BRITAIN
AT THE UNIVERSITY PRESS, CAMBRIDGE

ISBN 0 521 05132 0

A COMPANION TO SHAKESPEARE STUDIES

CONTENTS

ILLUSTRATIONS

PLATES

TEXT-FIGURES

PREFACE

THE purpose of this book was first formulated in discussions between the editors in their capacities of President and Secretary of the Shakespeare Association. They were in search of a programme. The question was: what avenues of Shakespeare scholarship now most needed exploring? That led to a consideration of recent work, its sufficiency or its prospects, and that to the assembling of the present material.

During the last thirty years or so there has been not only an increase and extension of Shakespearian study, but a notable 'transvaluation of its values'. The extension is reflected in the fourteen-fold division of this book. Not that the student of 1900, or even 1800, would find the subjects new to him, but the apparent estimate of the importance of some of them might well surprise him a little. Here, he might even say, is no study of Shakespeare at all, but a hundred thousand words or more, as much sometimes about our ignorance as our knowledge of the man, about the wretched theatre he had to work for, the clumsy habits of his printers, about his contemporaries and the circumstances, near and remote, in which the work was done; of the transcendental genius itself, no more than an echo or recounting of what has already been said. It is so. But just in this lies the present transvaluing of critical values; the latest, though it may not be the last, as Mr Eliot warns us.

The student's approach to Shakespeare, as the work of the last thirty years has planned it, will be something like a *contemporary* approach. He will try to make himself one with the audience at the Globe or Blackfriars. Certainly, this is only a first step; and beyond it a wide prospect opens out. If the plays have survived their age and the circumstances of their production it will be because of certain innate qualities in them; he will want to know why and how they have survived. If they have entered into an existence apart from the theatre altogether, he must look into that process too. Not, in fact, till he appreciates the history and extent of the phenomenon of Shakespeare can he hope quite fruitfully to approach the thing itself. Then he may do so guideless or guided; and if he still prefer the acted play before him or the critic at his side, he can at least have learned to estimate the quality of his guide. The editors, incidentally, have made no attempt to reconcile the opinions of their collaborators (if these seem to differ it is better for the reader to observe it); and, as it happens, there has hardly been a dispute about facts. The utmost agreement desired was upon this way of approach.

It may be noticed—and objected—that the extension of Shakespearian study has been even wider than here appears, either by record or contribution. The omissions are deliberate. There is no discussion of the personal problem of the sonnets, and Dr Mackail's chapter on the Life is confined to the bare facts. We are concerned with the poet-dramatist, apparent in the work he left us; nothing more.

It remains for us to thank our collaborators, not only for their work but for the patience and goodwill with which they have responded to the occasional need there was for us to do what they naturally could not themselves do—clear away certain redundancies and weld the book into something like a whole. It was this foreseen need, let us add, which prevented our seeking collaboration farther afield; and that we could not avail ourselves of American scholarship has been a matter of particular regret. But the wider the divergencies of the study, the greater the importance of reconciling them to what unity is possible, of producing, in short, a *book*, not a mere assemblage of discourses.

For, finally, we hope that the book may make a wider appeal than to the specialist student. It should be able to bring the keener among the spectators or readers of the plays, whose only care is enjoyment, to a more familiar and a far livelier contact with them.

H. G.-B.
1934
G. B. H.

THE LIFE OF SHAKESPEARE

BY

J. W. MACKAIL

Of the life of Shakespeare little is known. No biography of him was attempted until nearly a century after his death. Floating traditions then collected, partly at Stratford and in the neighbourhood, partly from theatrical circles in London, clothed the bare facts for which there was documentary evidence with some amount of flesh and blood. The portrait of Shakespeare thus produced remains substantially unchanged by the laborious research of two centuries more. Most modern Lives expand their contents partly by accumulation of details however minute and bearing however remotely on Shakespeare himself; and much more largely by inference and conjecture based on treatment of the plays and the sonnets as veiled or unconscious autobiography.

The known facts may be summarised as follows.

The traditional date of Shakespeare's birth is April 23rd, 1564. He was christened in Stratford Church on the 26th: the date assigned for his birth is probable enough, but its acceptance is mainly due to its being the day of St George, the patron saint of England, and also the day, fifty-two years later, of his own death. His father, John Shakespeare, was a prosperous burgess and tradesman of Stratford, described as a glover, or more largely as a dealer in wool and leather, and living at the house in Henley Street now known as the Shakespeare birthplace. His mother, Mary Arden, was the daughter of a family of small land-owners in the neighbourhood. They were married soon before the accession of Queen Elizabeth in 1558, and had eight children, William being the third child and eldest son.

Of his childhood and boyhood no facts are known. There is no reason to doubt that he was educated at the town Grammar School; it was one of good repute, and like other grammar schools provided a liberal education for boys up to the age of about sixteen, in a preparatory department under an usher, and in the main school under the master. For the sons of burgesses this education was free.

The next certain fact in his life is the licence, issued November 27th, 1582, for his marriage to Anne (or Agnes) Hathaway, daughter of a yeoman-farmer in the hamlet of Shottery in the parish of Old Stratford; she was, if the dates given on her tombstone are correct, eight years his senior. The date and place of the actual marriage remain undiscovered. A daughter, Susanna, was christened May 26th, 1583, and twins, Hamnet and Judith, February 2nd, 1585, at Stratford; the entries are extant in the parish register. Until then it may be, as it generally has been, assumed that Stratford remained Shakespeare's home. This it continued in some sense to be. There is nothing to indicate that his wife and children ever lived elsewhere. But his own continuous residence there, both before and after his marriage, until the unknown date when he went to London and became connected with the stage, is matter of pure conjecture. Nor is there any distinct evidence to indicate what induced him to make the theatre his profession. Some acquaintance of his with the stage before he went to London may be taken as certain. Travelling companies of actors came to Stratford now and then; there is a record of performances by two, the Queen's Men and the Earl of Worcester's Men, in 1568–9 at the Guildhall, where they were entertained by John Shakespeare, then alderman and bailiff; Shakespeare himself was then a child of between four and five. But for the years 1585–92 (his own 21st–28th years) there are no first-hand facts at all.

The attack on Shakespeare in Greene's *Groatsworth of Wit* (September 1592) and the apology made for it soon after by Chettle, who had prepared Greene's MS. for publication, give clear proof that he had then gained a well-established position and a growing reputation in the theatrical world, as a dramatic author and adapter, as the handy man, the *Johannes Factotum*, of his company, and apparently also, though the words used are ambiguous, as an actor. Special stress is laid by Chettle on his 'upright dealing' and on his 'facetious grace in writing'. The early jealousy of the 'upstart' had already faded away. Such facts as are known with regard to the plays which he wrote or remodelled about this period—produced at the Theatre in Shoreditch from 1594 to 1597 under Burbage, at the Rose on the Bankside when reopened in 1592, and perhaps also at other houses public or private—go to suggest that for a considerable time he was not attached exclusively to any company, and perhaps was not acting himself, but was fully engaged in being a provider of plays, original or adapted, for several companies of players, including Burbage's and Alleyn's. To this period belong his two poems, the only works he ever published himself, *Venus and Adonis* (1593) and *Lucrece* (1594). Both were dedicated to the young Earl of Southampton. The terms of the dedications do not warrant the assumption of any relation between them other than that of author and patron. The former, 'the first heir of my invention'—the first book, that is, issued by the author under his own name—had wide and long popularity. It allowed him a rank among authors: plays, even when printed, hardly then counted as literature.

In 1594 the Lord Chamberlain's Company was formed, and Shakespeare became a regular member of it. His connexion with it remained unbroken up to his retirement from active theatrical life and probably, though not certainly, up to his death. In the letters patent of 1603 under which it was reconstituted under the title of the King's Servants, with the Globe theatre as their principal place of performance, nine actors are named as shareholders, Shakespeare being the second on the list. They ranked as Grooms of the Chamber, and might be called on for duty as ushers at Court. For this they received red liveries, and were paid regular salaries, besides occasional gifts, some of large sums, for performances at Court.

In 1596, his only son Hamnet died at the age of eleven. About this time Shakespeare simultaneously quickened up the pace of his dramatic output and began to pick up the threads of his connexion with Stratford. In 1596, a grant of family arms was applied for at the Heralds' Office. This was in the name of John Shakespeare, but as he had been going down in the world, and was by this time technically if not actually insolvent, it seems safe to assume that the action was taken by Shakespeare himself in his father's name. Of a later application for leave to impale the arms of Arden with his own, the result is not known. In May 1597 he established himself as a burgess of Stratford by the purchase of New Place, the largest house in the town. Further freehold property in the neighbourhood was acquired by him later, after his father's death in 1601. But for eight or nine years longer he himself remained a Londoner: to these years belongs the series of his great tragedies. In 1597 he is rated for a house in St Helen's, Bishopsgate. Before and after this, he is traced in records as living in Southwark: near the Bear-Garden in 1596; afterwards, from 1599 to 1608, in the Clink on the Bankside; and (1604) as a lodger in the house of one Mountjoy in Cripplegate. In a deposition taken in a lawsuit in 1612, he is described as 'of Stratford on Avon, gentleman'; he had presumably therefore no London residence then. During the last eight years of his life, various entries in Stratford records and diaries show him settled at New Place and taking some part in local affairs. The purchase by him in 1613 of more property in London shows that he was in easy and even affluent circumstances.

His elder daughter Susanna was married, June 5th, 1607, to Dr John Hall, a physician in Stratford: a daughter was born to them in February 1608. His younger daughter Judith was married, February 10th, 1616, to Thomas Quiney, the son of a Stratford friend and neighbour. This is the last known incident in Shakespeare's life. His will, drafted a few days earlier, was executed on March 25th, on an interlineated draft of which no fair copy was made. This is reasonably held to indicate that the matter was urgent; and though the will follows the common form of stating the testator to be 'in perfect health and memory', the illness to which he succumbed a month later may be assumed to be the reason for haste. He died on April 23rd.

The provisions of the will are quite normal. The bulk of his estate went to Susanna and her issue, with liberal provision also for Judith and for his own sister Joan Hart. His wife was secured in her life-interest by common and customary law. The interlineated bequest to her of the second-best bed—doubtless the one they had shared, for the best bed would be in the principal guest-chamber—may be taken as a kindly afterthought. Various bequests to friends at Stratford, and to three of his colleagues in the King's Company, indicate his local and professional attachments.

The elaborate monument in Stratford Church, executed in London by Gerard Janssen or Johnson, was put up a few years later. The verses engraved on it lay stress on his eminence as a writer. The First Folio was already in preparation. The process of his canonisation was beginning. The first note in it is nobly struck in Jonson's lines prefixed to the Folio. But in the literary and theatrical circles of London, so swiftly had the world been moving since Shakespeare's retirement, the news of his death seems hardly to have caused a ripple on the surface. During his life, though Meres in 1598 already singles him out as 'the most excellent in both kinds' (tragedy and comedy) 'among the English', references to him, even when laudatory, nearly all mention him only as one in a group of dramatists or poets. It is not a little remarkable that, in that copiously elegiac age, there is no trace of the decease of the greatest English dramatist and the foremost figure in English literature having called forth at the time a single line of elegy. The Latin distich on the funeral monument ascribes to him, in the pedantic language customary for such tributes, the wisdom of Nestor, the inspiration of Socrates, and the art of Virgil. This may remind one that as little is known of Virgil's life as of Shakespeare's: in both cases we have only such scraps of mingled fact and legend as could be gathered by the research of a biographer something like a century after the poet's death. However far additional knowledge might go in satisfying curiosity, its absence is not greatly to be deplored. The life of an artist survives not in his biography, but in the products of his art.

The only two portraits of Shakespeare which are of established authenticity are both posthumous: the bust, of unknown authorship, on his funeral monument, and the engraving by Droeshout prefixed to the First Folio and there praised by Jonson for its likeness. On what material Droeshout worked is unknown; but the first state of the engraving gives what is certainly a plausible, and probably a faithful, portrait of the living man.

Curiosity about Shakespeare's life only began to arise when the means of satisfying it were already disappearing. The first serious attempt to collect materials was made by Rowe for a Life which he prefixed to his edition (1709) of the plays. What he had to go upon was partly occasional references to Shakespeare in books or MSS. to which he had access, but mainly such tradition as he could pick up, whether theatrical or local. For the former, he had the material collected by D'Avenant and handed on by him to Betterton, the leading London actor of the Restoration period. Both were Shakespearian enthusiasts; and Betterton visited Stratford for the purpose of collecting what might be gathered there. It had already become a place of occasional pilgrimages; as these increased, the manufacture of local legend also did. Such of these additional scraps as are of special interest or have obtained wide currency may be briefly mentioned.

The story of Shakespeare and Burbage recorded by Manningham in his extant diary (March 13th, 1601/2) may be true; it is the only anecdote of Shakespeare which is known to have been recorded during his life. The 'wit-combats' between Shakespeare and Jonson mentioned by Fuller (1662) are only matter of hearsay embroidered by fancy. The note-books of Ward, Vicar of Stratford 1662–81, contain some entries of interest: according to the local tradition which he records, Shakespeare 'spent at the rate of £1000 a year' in his later life at Stratford, and died of a fever contracted by too hard drinking at a merry meeting with Drayton and Jonson.

Reminiscences were collected by Aubrey a little later from an actor, W. Beeston, whose father had been in the Lord Chamberlain's Company in the last years of Elizabeth's reign. According to these second-hand but not negligible reminiscences, Shakespeare had been in his younger years a schoolmaster in the country: he 'came to London, I guess, about 18'; he 'did act exceedingly well'; he was 'a handsome well-shaped man' and 'very good company'. From this source apparently came the first mention of the floating scandal about Shakespeare's relations with the wife of John D'Avenant, the Oxford vintner at whose house 'he did commonly lie' on annual journeys between London and Stratford. If any credit be attached to this scandal, the date of the alleged intimacy would be about 1605.

The local tradition of youthful deer-poaching at Charlecote and consequent flight to London fixed itself indelibly in the popular mind as soon as it became widely known. The earliest mention of it is in notes made by Richard Davies, rector of Sapperton, on papers which came into his hands at the death, in 1688, of W. Fulman, Rector of Meysey Hampton in Gloucestershire. Another version, communicated in 1693 by the aged clerk of Stratford church to one John Dowdall, of whom nothing seems to be known, agrees so far as saying that while still an apprentice to a butcher in Stratford he ran away to London, and was there received into the playhouse as a servitor. In a much later account comes the additional anecdote of his first job in London having been to hold horses for gentlemen who came to the playhouse, and his first employment in the theatre having been as an under-prompter.

These stories have, in their main lines, no inherent improbability. But at the best they are confused and uncertain, and still leave the earlier London years, no less than those previous to them, an almost complete blank.

There is little record of Shakespeare as an actor. Beeston's commendation of his acting has already been noted. But according to the author of the *Historia Histrionica* (1699) he was 'a much better poet than player'; and in the *Roscius Anglicanus* (1708) he appears more as a driller of actors than as an actor himself. Rowe had been told that he took the part of the Ghost in *Hamlet*: another and later story, of very doubtful authenticity, is that a brother of his, in extreme old age, recollected having been in London as a young man and having there seen Shakespeare taking the part of Adam in a performance of *As You Like It*. It seems fairly certain that he never played principal parts; his name occurs only twice in the lists of actors prefixed to printed plays, his own or those of others.

It may be added finally, that in a note appended to the Fulman MSS. by R. Davies, Rector of Sapperton, into whose hands they had come, is the brief sentence 'He died a Papist'. On what information his allegation is made, or what if any credit can be attached to it, is unknown. But seventeenth-century Puritanism, which closed the theatres, was ready to invent or accept anything that was to their discredit, or to the discredit of anyone connected with them.

The inverted pyramids of purely conjectural biography which have been and still are piled up on the slender basis of ascertained fact, and on the slight additions of legend which may be accepted as authentic or highly probable, may be dismissed here without notice. Many of them are of extreme ingenuity. But they are exercises of fancy and do not belong to serious biography. Nor can any fabric woven of plausible guesses and precarious inferences be regarded as reconstituting either the outward incidents or the spiritual experiences of Shakespeare's life. In the volume of his plays and poems, as was admirably said by W. H. Page, in a remarkable speech at Stratford-on-Avon when he was American Ambassador in England, 'each of us finds the whole world of action and emotion mirrored. Especially does he find all his own moods and potentialities, his own dangers, audacities, escapes, failures and triumphs. He could write his own innermost biography from Shakespeare'. His own, yes; but not Shakespeare's.

THE THEATRES AND COMPANIES

BY

C. J. SISSON

THE CONDITIONS OF SHAKESPEARE'S ART

DR JOHNSON never mentioned Garrick in his *Preface* to Shakespeare, and thought that 'many of his plays are the worse for being acted'. Such a view has its dangers. Every artist has to work in his chosen medium. And drama, the most complex of all arts, proceeds by a triple process to its completion. It involves creation by the dramatist, re-creation by a company of actors on the boards of a stage, and a third incarnation in the illusion of the spectators. All three are essential, inseparable, indispensable. The closet-drama is an ignoble retreat from the proper conditions of the art. The hurly-burly of actor, stage and audience is the proper element of true drama.

It is right to think of Shakespeare, therefore, in terms of the stage as well as of literary categories. He worked in his medium, and there is evidence enough that he was content to do so. A good workman does not quarrel with his tools. And Shakespeare was no less craftsman than artist—words that the Elizabethan joined together and that modern confusions have divorced. His drama was rooted in his own age and in the conditions of his art, in the stage and its habits, in the audience and its tastes, as well as in the drama of earlier generations in England. What he learned of others, what was imposed upon him by the conditions of his occupation, as well as what he gave of his own, has come down to us blended together in his plays. And by his genius and prestige he has dwarfed his contemporaries, obscured his background, and polarised all thought about the drama.

It is therefore of the utmost importance to seek to know under what conditions Shakespeare worked, subdued to his medium, yet not enslaved by it. We shall understand his genius the better when we know more about these actors, their theatres, and their audiences, and consequently about the opportunity, the stimulus, the freedom of his task, as also its limitations and bondages. To neglect such considerations is in effect to turn Shakespeare into closet-drama and to deprive him of much of his great glory.

THE ACTORS' COMPANIES AND THE THEATRES

Shakespeare was an actor himself, and both he and the company of which he was a member shared the accumulated traditions and experience of some three hundred years of continuous acting. For the drama was already an ancient art in England. The corporate resources of the great provincial towns had developed in the Middle Ages not only elaborate productions of miracle plays, not only literary drama for such productions, but also trained groups of competent citizen actors. And they had fostered the natural taste for dramatic entertainments. So also the folk play, in its many forms, of unknown but great antiquity, bred both actors and audiences throughout the country. The nucleus for the professional practice of the art of acting was found in the houses of the nobility, who maintained small groups of entertainers, the descendants of the epic singers and jesters of earlier days. Such organisations may be seen to-day in native states in India, the actors being also skilled fencers, swordsmen, wrestlers, dancers, musicians and singers, experts in the various arts of entertainment. Such were also the members of these early English companies of actors, and the Elizabethan stage inherited their traditions of miscellaneous expertness, as well as the tradition of service to a patron.

The play of *Sir Thomas More* gives a picture of such a group of actors, Cardinal Wolsey's Men, called in to perform in More's house in London about 1529. This illustrates the transition from the purely domestic group of actors to the travelling group, available for hire when invited. With the Tudor settlement of England life became freer, fuller, and more mobile. The nobles allowed their actors to go round exercising their trade. They ceased to be mere retainers, and maintained themselves. And gradually they became independent organisations, though still protected by the name of their master and still owing service to him when called upon. And when they had theatres the 'lord's room' was at their patron's disposal.

The deciding factor in the further development of the actors' companies was the growth of London and of the Court under the Tudors. The actors were quick to see here a steady market for their entertainments and the possibility of regular employment and a settled life. When we first hear of theatres in London we find them in the form of inn-yards adapted with a stage. And the inns thus used as theatres were advantageously sited. Some, probably the earliest, lay in the outskirts upon the main roads leading into the City, the Saracen's Head in Islington upon the North Road, the Boar's Head and the Red Lion in Whitechapel in the east, the Tabard in Southwark to the south, tapping the traffic in all directions. Others were situated in the heart of the City, in Bishopsgate, Gracechurch Street or Ludgate, the Bell, the Bull, the Cross Keys, the Bel Savage. Here were the homes of the professional Elizabethan drama before the days of Shakespeare, during the first twenty years of the reign of Elizabeth. A group of actors, having made its way to London with its waggon of costumes and properties, and its play-books, would seek its pitch in some such inn. It would come to an agreement with the landlord, generally to pay him some share of the takings, and the yard would be reserved for their use after midday dinner. The arrangement suited both parties, for the plays brought custom to the inn and added to its attractions, while the inn was a convenient home for the players with a ready-made audience and a ready-made playhouse.

The next step, there is good reason to believe, was the entire occupation of an inn, converted to the sole use of the actors.[1] So it was, apparently, with the Red Lion and Boar's Head in Whitechapel and possibly the Cross Keys in Gracechurch Street, with permanent stages and 'scaffolds' or stands for spectators. From this it was a short way to the erection of a new building for the especial purpose of a theatre. This was the happy thought, probably, of one of the many small financiers who began to see the possibilities of the new industry of the stage. John Brayne was financing the building of a stage and seats in the Red Lion in 1567. And in 1576 we find him providing the money for the erection of the Theatre in Shoreditch, in co-operation with his brother-in-law James Burbage the actor, then manager of Leicester's Men. The decisive step was taken. With the provision of a permanent theatre the way was open for the development of both the trade and the art of the actor. The experience of generations guided the builders of this and of other theatres which soon sprang up in London. The drama, hitherto subject to the conditions of its temporary homes, now had a say concerning its demands of its vehicle, the stage.

In the main, however, the new theatres followed traditional lines in their structure. The inn-yard surrounded by a gallery leading to guest-chambers was the foundation of its plan. The circular shape of the Globe in Southwark was the obvious improvement suggested by the bull-baiting ring, with its greater convenience for seating spectators, giving all a fair view of the stage.

The sites of the new theatres were determined by two factors. First, there was the opposition of the City, in fear of plague of body and soul alike, to theatres within its walls, which relegated them to the suburbs. Second, there was the need to keep the theatres, nevertheless, as accessible as possible to the City and to seat them within districts of growing population. The Theatre and the Curtain lay in Moorfields close to Shoreditch. The Rose, the Swan, the Globe and the Hope exploited the south bank of the Thames, in the heart of Southwark and with easy access by

[1] In 1578 I find Brayne, Burbage's partner in the Theatre, purchasing the George Inn in Whitechapel in order to use it as a theatre. He was, however, forbidden to establish a theatre there.

London Bridge or by boat to Westminster and the City. The Fortune was set in the area just outside Cripplegate, in Golden Lane, and the Red Bull served the needs of the dense population of Clerkenwell, in St John's Street.[1] The instant success of Burbage and Brayne in the Theatre led to these other ventures, with the result that during the last quarter of the sixteenth century London became amply provided with permanent theatres, large and solid structures which aroused the wonder and admiration of foreign visitors to London, as well as the indignant dismay of Puritan preachers against the stage, and which were a visible sign of the great prosperity of the industry of the theatre.

Most of these theatres were owned by investors like Francis Langley, who built the Swan, or Philip Henslowe, who built the Rose and the Fortune. The companies of actors who used them had much the same relations with the owners as they had had with the landlords of the inns, and were merely his tenants during such time as they could agree together, an unsatisfactory arrangement. Usually the landlord received for his share one-half of the gallery takings. Sometimes he acted also as financier to the company, when improvident actors and playwrights tended to fall into perpetual debt to him and into virtual servitude, which was even more unsatisfactory. Such was the case with those companies which dealt with Henslowe, at whose theatres Marlowe's great plays were produced, the famous Edward Alleyn playing their heroes, Faustus or Tamburlaine. Alleyn was Henslowe's son-in-law and, alone of the Admiral's Men, made a fortune out of his acting and his share of the profits, retiring thereafter, Lord of the Manor of Dulwich and founder of Dulwich College.

But it was otherwise with the company to which Shakespeare belonged during the greater part of his career, after some years spent as actor and dramatist at the Theatre with Lord Strange's Men. The members of his company, patronised successively by Lord Hunsdon, then Lord Chamberlain, by his son, who held the

[1] The Theatre and the Curtain in 1576, the Rose in 1587, the Swan in 1595, the Globe in 1598, the Fortune in 1599, the Red Bull about 1605, and the Hope in 1613.

same office, and by King James himself, during most of the time of Shakespeare's connexion with them, had their theatres to themselves and more or less in their own hands and ownership. Among their number was Richard Burbage, their leading tragic actor, the son of James Burbage who built the Theatre, John Heminge and Henry Condell, the editors-to-be of the First Folio edition of Shakespeare's plays, and William Kempe, the great comic actor. In 1598 they decided to leave Shoreditch and move to Southwark, where they erected the Globe theatre on the Bankside at the joint expense of the chief members of the company, including Shakespeare. It was their own theatre, and for the first time we have the actors masters in their own house. No wonder that the history of the Globe theatre is one of glory as well as of prosperity, that its company was the most solidly organised of all, in the highest repute, attracting to itself the best actors and the finest dramatic work of the age, and was fittingly chosen, when James came to the throne, to be the King's Men. Shakespeare was working, as actor and dramatist, under the fairest and most stimulating conditions that the time could afford.

From 1608 onwards the company had two theatres. In that year they obtained a lease of a theatre in the Blackfriars, consisting of a hall and adjacent rooms converted to that purpose.[1] The Globe, unroofed and open to the sky, was more suitable for summer use, while the Blackfriars, an indoor theatre, was better adapted for winter playing.[2] It was in these two theatres that the plays of Shakespeare's maturity were performed. And to them the comfort and dignity of the houses, the quality of the plays, and the excellence of the acting, attracted all that was best in Elizabethan audiences. The evidence is clear that Shakespeare's relations with his fellow-actors were intimate and happy, and that all conspired to draw from him the highest and completest art that his great genius could beget.

[1] For the history of the Blackfriars theatre, see below, pp. 15–16, 18–20.

[2] There is some evidence that the audience at the Blackfriars was likely to be more select than that at the Globe. In the earlier years of the use of the two theatres, the company possibly allowed for this in their provision for both. In time, the Globe sank definitely to second place.

THE BOYS' COMPANIES

The acting of plays seems to have been a regular feature of Tudor education both in schools and in universities. In 1567, for example, I find the guardian of a boy, anxious to prove that he had had him brought up in learning and 'like a gentleman child', bringing evidence of his proficiency in the part he was to take in a play at his Blackfriars school. The boy also sang in St Faith's choir. He was then under twelve years of age.[1] Here was the material of which a number of boys' companies were composed. The Boys of St Paul's took part in the public performance of a miracle play in 1378. The Children of the Chapel Royal, under their master, from furnishing music to the Court of Henry IV, came to be trained also for dramatic performances at Court under Henry VIII. The Boys of St Paul's similarly presented interludes before Henry VIII, led by John Heywood, the writer of their plays, and Sebastian Westcott their master. Other great schools and chapels contributed to such activities. Such boys' companies shared the patronage of the Court with professional adult companies, and in the end some of them came to be professionally organised for public performances. In 1576 we find the Children of the Chapel performing at a theatre opened in Blackfriars, in part of the buildings of the dissolved monastery, by Richard Farrant, who had come to some financial agreement with their master, William Hunnis. And a few years later the Paul's Boys, under Thomas Giles, joined them there, acting Lyly's plays publicly in 1584. The Paul's Boys continued later as a separate organisation in their own theatre near St Paul's, for the profit of Giles and Lyly, until about 1590. The company was revived again ten years later, managed by Edward Peers and Thomas Woodford, with plays by Marston, Chapman and Middleton, but came to an end about 1606. So also the Children of the Chapel are found again at Blackfriars after an interval, in 1600, under Nathaniel Giles, their master, and his financial partner Henry Evans, acting plays of Ben Jonson, Chapman, Marston and

[1] P.R.O. c. 24/80.

Day. They were reorganised as Children of the Queen's Revels, indicating how far the process of professionalisation had taken them from their ancient status, and continued under varying names and managers, moving to a Whitefriars theatre in 1609, until about 1615. The adult companies had, in the end, beaten the boys out of the field.

In the early history of the Elizabethan stage the literary quality of the boys' plays, as well as the weight of custom, gave them an advantage. They could furnish the grace of music, too. But the men's companies, as they developed, allied to themselves scholar-writers and produced their own dramatists of genius. Moreover, they attracted into their ranks the best boy actors as they grew up, and trained their own boy apprentices. So they could offer to the Court as to the public all the qualities of the boys' performances and in addition the deeper passion, realism and humanity of adult acting. But there is no doubt that the Blackfriars Children were formidable rivals even to Shakespeare's company at the Globe at the end of the sixteenth century.

COURT AND PRIVATE PERFORMANCES

The evidence of the repute in which his company was held may well be found in the frequency with which they were invited to perform away from their theatres in places where it was an honour to provide such entertainment. It was, moreover, a source of profit of great importance in a company's budget. £10 was the price paid by Queen Elizabeth and King James for the performance of a play at Court.[1] And when plague closed the theatres and deprived the King's Men of their ordinary sources of revenue in London, they were kept in being and in practice for Court plays by gifts amounting to as much as £40 in one year from their royal patron. The Master of the Revels at

[1] In 1595 Henslowe was drawing up to £3 a day as landlord of the Rose, though his average share was no more than 30*s.* He took as his share half the receipts for the galleries. But we cannot with certainty deduce the whole 'house' from this. About 1616 the Red Bull, at its very best, took in £8 or £9 a day. When after 1628 Sir Henry Herbert, then Master of the Revels, took 'benefits', they amounted to about £7 at the Globe and £16 at the Blackfriars.

Court chose plays and companies for the Queen's or the King's amusement, especially at the Christmas season, the performances being given at the royal palaces. The Inns of Court also celebrated great occasions with dramatic entertainments. The fledgling lawyers were especial lovers of the theatre. They gave their own shows, and they also brought in the professionals, as on the famous occasion when Shakespeare's *Comedy of Errors* was performed, as part of the revels, on a Grand Night at Gray's Inn in 1594. Finally, it was the fashion for the nobility to present plays for the amusement of their guests in their own houses, in celebration of a wedding, for example, or in honour of some notable visitor. So we see, in the play of *Sir Thomas More*, how More sends for the Cardinal's Men to act before his guests. And Shakespeare himself gives pictures of similar performances in private houses, as in *Hamlet* or *A Midsummer Night's Dream*. It is a matter of great interest to consider how far plays were actually written for such occasions, and there is much to be said for the belief that some of Shakespeare's own plays were so devised. It may well be that *A Midsummer Night's Dream* was written and first acted for the celebration of some noble wedding, and that *The Merry Wives of Windsor* was in fact written by royal command for a special Court performance. There can be no manner of doubt that the name and fame of Shakespeare were known to all interested in the theatre and drama, and that he and his fellows bore constantly in mind the needs and tastes of those higher circles before whom it was their pride to be chosen to perform. For the most part, however, plays selected for Court performance were taken from among those tried and proven by public performance. Thus intimately was the Court theatre bound up with the public theatre. The same drama and the same actors ministered to the delight of both, in the main. And this was a happy omen. For if the Court elevated the drama by its critical or special demands, the general audience ensured the sturdy health and varied appeal of a drama that was bound to be truly national to satisfy it. It says much for both that Shakespeare was able to gratify both equally with the same poetry, the same wit and humour, and the same stories in dramatic form.

THE 'PRIVATE' THEATRES

It is obvious, however, that the stage at Court or in a private house differed from that in a 'public' theatre. In the former the plays were acted indoors, in a hall, and by artificial light. The main features of such performances were paralleled in the 'private' theatres of the Elizabethan age. In them we have the third category of professional London theatres, to add to the inn-yard theatres and the new 'public' theatres.

We have seen that Shakespeare's company used such a theatre in the Blackfriars from 1608 onwards. The refectory of the monastery had long before served the same purpose, when Lyly wrote plays adapted to this stage and to the capabilities of the Children of the Chapel and the Children of Paul's. The Paul's house was evidently of the same type as the Blackfriars, save that it was circular in shape instead of rectangular. It may well be that in Lyly's day both houses catered especially for a select audience. But when they were revived towards the end of the century both were more popular. St Paul's at any rate thrived then on topical plays of local interest to the citizens in the heart of the City.

The first Blackfriars theatre was closed when the owner of the property retook possession of it from the managers of the Children of the Chapel. But in 1596 James Burbage bought a lease of a part of it and reconstructed the theatre. Local opposition prevented its re-establishment for four years. Burbage died in 1597, and in 1600 his sons Richard and Cuthbert let it to Evans to house the reorganised Children, who were dangerous competitors with Shakespeare's company at the Globe, and are referred to in *Hamlet* as 'little eyases' who spoil the art and business of their betters. They were troubled by plague, by the censorship, and by quarrels among the partners, and in the end Evans surrendered his lease. In 1608 a new lease was made at a fixed rent of £40 to a syndicate which included Shakespeare and his fellows Heminge, Condell and Sly. Thus the competition of the Blackfriars children was eliminated, and the theatre now came into the possession of the company which already owned the Globe.

The King's Men also took over the best of the boy actors, by whom the company was materially strengthened.

Such theatres were known as 'private' theatres as distinct from 'public' theatres. The term had little real meaning, for they were used precisely as were the others. They were open to all who would pay for entry, though the charges were higher.[1] In structure, it is true, they resembled the halls of private houses, though galleries were added in the course of reconstruction as theatres, and permanent seats, probably on a raised incline in the body of the hall. These differences in structure and stage conditions make the term a useful one in discussions of the Elizabethan stage.

It is of importance to realise, however, that Shakespeare's latest plays were acted both at a 'public' theatre, the Globe, and at a 'private' theatre, the Blackfriars, and by the same actors. The conclusion is inevitable that by then there was some measure of similarity in methods of production at both. The Blackfriars theatre was remodelled to some extent by Burbage in 1596, twenty years after he had built the Theatre and shortly before the Globe was planned. He can hardly have failed to profit by his experience in the designing of both new theatres, though it is not known what was the nature of his reconstruction of the Blackfriars. The 'private' theatre used more machines than the 'public' theatre, as we shall see. And the style of acting of a boys' company in a 'private' theatre, before a select company, was different. It was more intimate than that of the 'public' theatre, and less life-like of necessity. Such acting would not have served for the heroic drama, built on a larger scale in all things, of Marlowe for example. The children could hardly have acted satisfactorily *Tamburlaine* or Shakespeare's *Richard III*, though we know they did in fact perform *Jeronimo*. When we come to the later 'private' theatres, and above all to the Blackfriars when occupied by adult actors, we have to consider the probable results of some decades of development in the theatre and the drama, and the certainty of the

[1] The charges at the 'public' theatres ran from a penny to a shilling; at the 'private' theatres, which were definitely expensive, from sixpence to half a crown.

mutual influence exerted by the 'private' and 'public' theatres one upon another. The 'public' theatre with its adult actors must have ensured a more natural and convincing presentation of characters of men, though there is no doubt whatever of the excellence of boy actors in women's parts and of their power to give them life. The 'private' theatre, in return, must have toned down the rant and declamation of the 'public' theatre. And this higher conception of the art of acting, to which both 'private' and 'public' theatres contributed, is set forth by Hamlet who, speaking surely for Shakespeare, urges the virtues of moderation and natural acting upon the visiting players, in words which are too often taken to refer to dramaturgy instead of histrionics.

An examination of the plays written for 'public' and 'private' theatres respectively after 1600 gives evidence of such an approximation. In 1604 Marston's *The Malcontent* could be acted 'in folio' at the Globe by Shakespeare's company as well as 'in decimo-sexto' by the Revels Children at the Blackfriars, with a little padding to fill up the time taken by musical interludes, a feature of the 'private' theatres. How far the 'public' and 'private' theatres influenced each other in other respects is a problem of great interest and difficulty to the student of Elizabethan staging.

ELIZABETHAN STAGING

In the matter of Elizabethan staging we have to keep in mind two main threads in its history. First, we have to think of the elementary mother-wit stage of the early professional players making the most of their hall or inn-yard stage, practising the art of improvisation with such properties and costumes as they could carry about with them, innocent of all attempt at scenic illusion or localisation of their scene. Secondly, we have the cultivated stage of the Court, the universities with their academic drama, and the Inns of Court. With them, we find clear traces of the kind of staging that was practised by the Italian Renaissance theatre, which used structural 'houses' and painted back-cloths in perspective as a unified setting for its plays, the action being confined to the limited locality represented. This method of staging was, however, modified by the needs of such romantic plays as the Court rejoiced in early in Elizabeth's reign, with their wider range of locality. The convention of 'multiple' staging, which used juxtaposed 'houses' representing localities distant from one another in turn as the action changed from one place to another, was the traditional method of the miracle plays, and modified the Italian influence at Court.

The first 'private' theatres emulated this Court staging, and Lyly's plays illustrate both 'unified' and 'multiple' setting. In *Alexander and Campaspe* we have the market-place as the unified locality, with structures representing the palace, Apelles' shop, and Diogenes' tub. In *Midas*, on the other hand, the action takes place in a variety of places and is not restricted to even a single country. We may observe that the 'unified' setting would have served for Shakespeare's *Comedy of Errors*, and it was doubtless after this fashion that it was presented at Gray's Inn.

Had the drama continued as an art devised for artificial cultured taste, practised by boys and staged in 'private' theatres, this method of staging might have sufficed, and might have dominated the Elizabethan theatre. But such arrangements could not have been emulated by the professional companies in their early career, even if they had wished to do so. Such productions needed a permanent theatre, or a permanent storehouse and workshop like that of the Office of the Revels, and demanded financial resources beyond small corporate purses. By the time the permanent theatres were available for the men's companies, in a more prosperous season for the profession, these methods were unsuitable for other reasons. For the drama had developed the scope of its action far beyond the classical limits of a unified place. The romantic drama was the staple entertainment provided by the professional stage, confirming the wavering taste of the early Elizabethan Court-stage. But the 'multiple' setting provided by the Revels at Court for some play of chivalric romance, or for Lyly's *Midas*, was not followed by the 'public' theatre. It fell back upon the freer, less limited, if cruder methods of the wandering players, who used no 'houses' and whose stage, or any given part of it, could represent successively several places in any one play. Whatever 'houses', as distinct from specific 'properties', the 'public' stage used in its later development, were of a stock type, convertible to various uses for various plays or for various parts of a play. An admitted convention, moreover, allowed parts of the action to take place in an indefinite locality when in passage from one main centre of the story to another. Such was the basis of the method of staging which met the needs of the great Elizabethan drama in its highest development. But it had learned some lessons from the Court or 'private' stage.

It had learned, above all, to aim at some measure of stage realism. In particular, it sought to use all the resources at its command to aid the process of illusion. It used the physical structure of the 'public' theatre; it used properties; and it used dialogue. It did not use the art of the scene-painter or the scene-builder, nor, consequently, did it ever change the scene in the modern sense of the term. But, within these limits, it did all in its power to suggest locality and atmosphere for the action of the play. The Elizabethan play, moreover, was decorated by handsome and expensive dressing, the costumes being in the main Elizabethan, though modified where necessary by fancy and symbolism, and occasional historical suggestion.

It is easy to realise the principal advantage of such methods of production, namely the supple freedom of scope and rapidity of movement in a drama thus loosed from the bondage of time and space. The drama could rival the epic. It kept a liberty of action which has been regained to-day only in the theatre of the screen, though the revolving stage does what it can to multiply scenes and free action from immobility, in the stage proper.

THE TYPICAL STRUCTURE OF THE 'PUBLIC' THEATRE

A summary of the main features of the typical structure of the Elizabethan 'public' theatre may serve to illustrate the means by which dramatic illusion was furthered. It is certain that the theatres differed from one another in detail, and that the later theatres must have modified the structure of the earlier theatres,

THE SWAN THEATRE, BANKSIDE.

in the light of experience gained. For example, a drawing of the Swan theatre which has survived shows no central opening at the back of the stage, an essential feature of the Globe.[1] But the

[1] The accuracy of this drawing, it is true, is suspect.

main outlines of the Shakespearian stage are clear enough, though there will always be obscure points of detail open to conjecture and debate. The evidence is more complete than one might expect to have come down to us. We have this contemporary sketch of the Swan stage, contemporary specifications for the builders of the Fortune and the Hope, and the whole

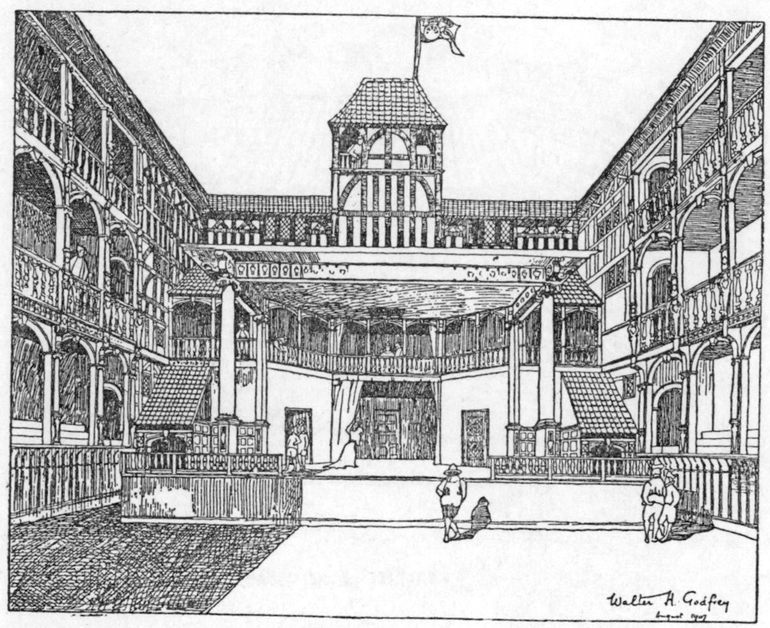

THE FORTUNE THEATRE[1]

body of stage directions of Elizabethan plays, together with hints in their dialogue. The structure was the logical development of the inn-yard plan modified by experience and by the influence of the Court or 'private' stages. The screen and side-doors of the hall of a great house may well have furnished the model for the stage-wall, and possibly for the gallery or balcony above the stage. There was a raised stage jutting out into a 'yard' or pit.

[1] See Note on p. 43.

The audience stood in the pit into which it projected, or sat in the galleries built around the theatre walls and fronting the stage. A few even purchased stools on the stage itself or sat on the rushes with which it was strewed. One gallery was, as it were, continued behind the stage, which it probably overhung, and to which it formed an adjunct as an upper stage. Behind the stage were the tiring-rooms of the actors, in which they dressed and kept their properties, costumes and play-books, from which they emerged upon the stage and into which they entered upon their exits. In the wall of the stage, which was hung with arras or tapestry, were three openings, one door on each side, and a larger opening in the centre curtained off and revealing, when the curtain was drawn, a space behind the stage, being part of the tiring-room area. This space furnished a second adjunct to the main stage, an inner stage. All three openings were at the back of the stage and communicated with the tiring-rooms, which were built in three stories, so that the upper stage could be entered directly from them, as well as from the front by occasional scaling-ladders. An active man could, indeed, safely jump down from it on to the main stage. Over the whole stage-structure projected the 'heavens' or canopy, also accessible apparently from the third-story tiring-room. It stood upon posts resting on the stage and protected it from the weather. The spectators' galleries were roofed, but the pit or yard was open to the sky. Finally, the tiring-rooms communicated also with the space underneath the stage, which was boarded off, in communication with trap-doors constructed in the stage-floor, which afforded a further means of entrance and exit. Such were the structural resources of the stage in Shakespeare's day, summarily stated on the balance of evidence.[1] The actor and the dramatist could also count upon a considerable provision of properties. No doubt elementary erections of a common-form type supplemented the structure of the stage. But the especial needs of any one play were met by the use of properties which could be got on or off the stage, moved or wheeled through the

[1] It has been argued that there is evidence of side-doors also projecting at an angle to the stage-wall, with further balconies above each.

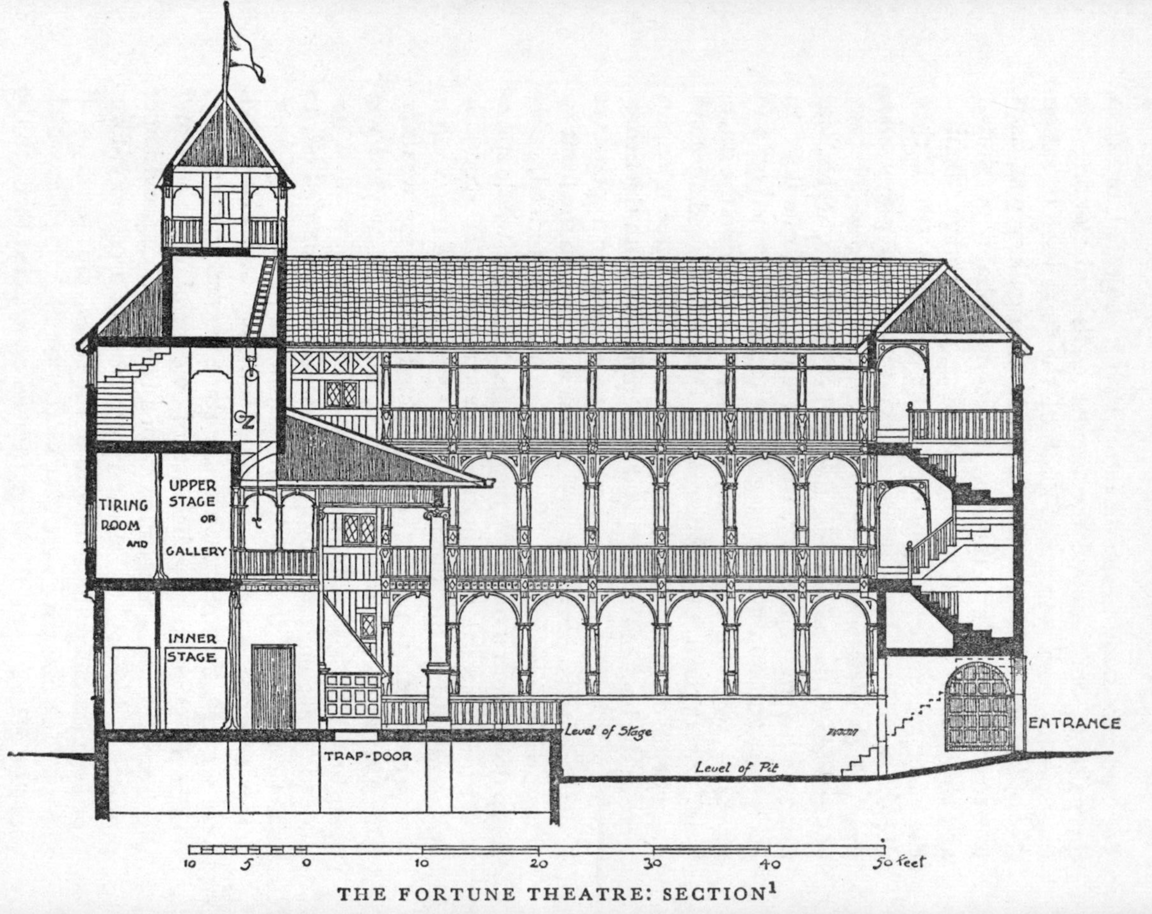

THE FORTUNE THEATRE: SECTION[1]

1 See Note on p. 43.

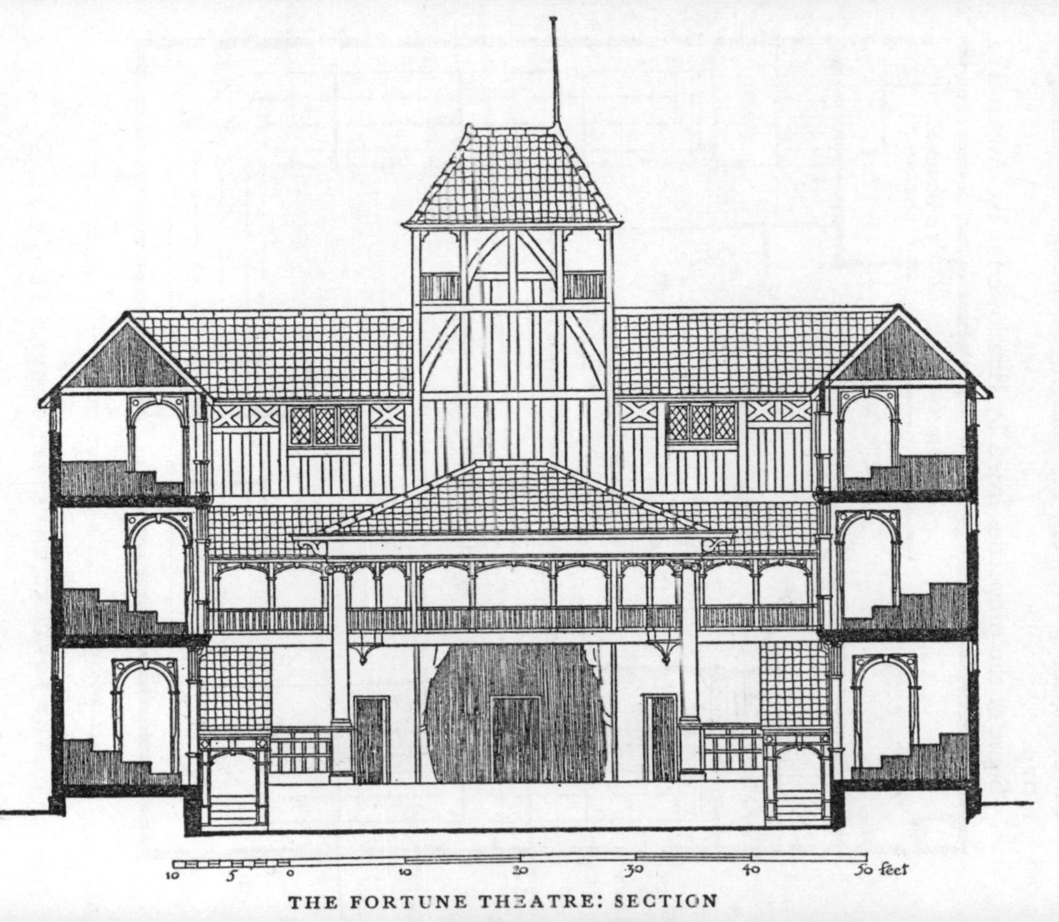

THE FORTUNE THEATRE: SECTION

entrances, let down from the heavens, or brought up through a trap.

Some of the properties listed by Henslowe for the Admiral's

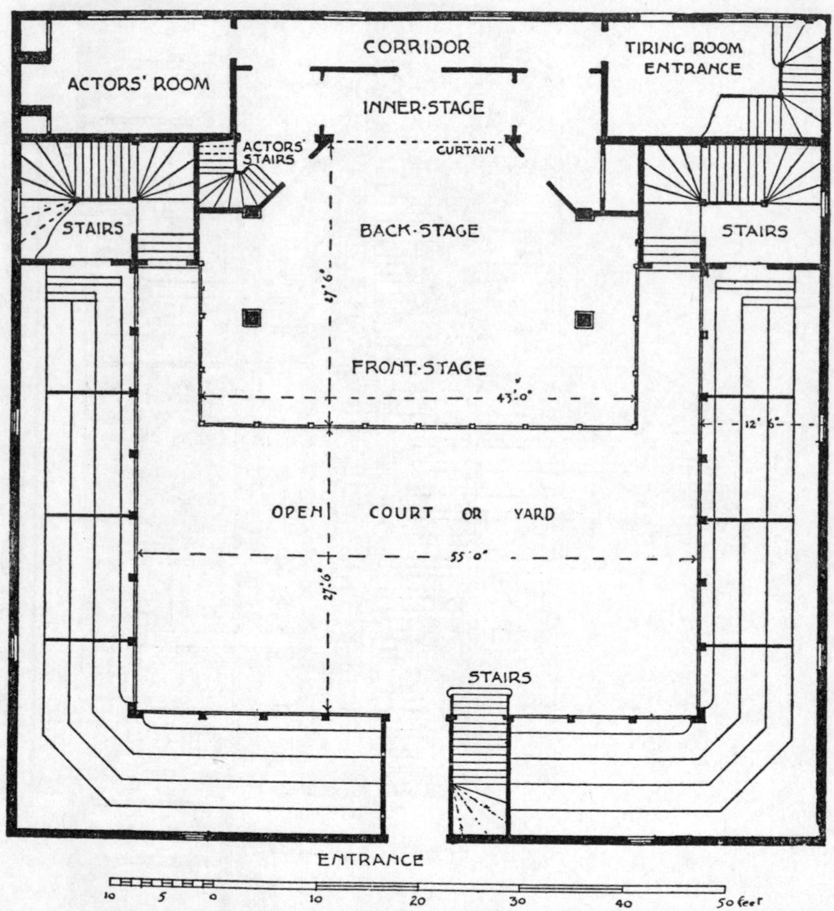

THE FORTUNE THEATRE: GROUND FLOOR PLAN[1]

Men indicate the extent of the material available. There are not only beds, trees, benches, tables or thrones and simpler properties. There is machinery to draw on and off a structural

[1] See Note on p. 43.

wall, for example. Or a gibbet can be set up. There is a cauldron for Barabas to fall into in *The Jew of Malta*, a 'great horse' for a Troy play, a Hell Mouth (a survival of miracle-play effects,

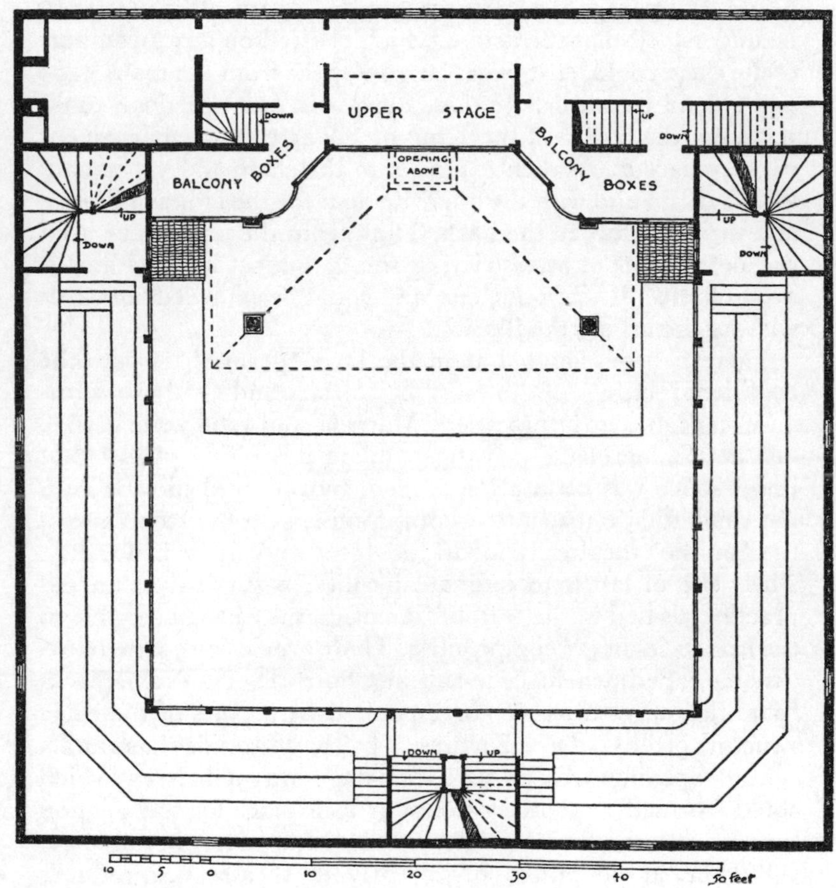

THE FORTUNE THEATRE: FIRST FLOOR PLAN

and a practicable structure), a tree of golden apples, and even a 'cloth of the Sun and Moon' and a 'city of Rome', probably the nearest approaches in a 'public' theatre to the painted canvases of the Court productions. It was the business of the theatre craftsman to make the utmost and most ingenious use of these resources to further dramatic purposes. Properties used in the inner stage could be removed after closing the curtain, before that part of the stage was needed again. It is always to be understood that the action which centred on any given part of the stage could, as it were, borrow space from the main stage and spread outwards. In *Love's Labour's Lost* one door could represent the palace of the King of Navarre. The environment of the palace could then extend into the stage and yet remain localised. So also with the opposite door for the ladies of France and their territory in the Park. Thus again the inner stage need not be thought of as restricting the action set in it within its actual limits. It was a nucleus, and could be extended outwards without disturbing the illusion.

There is little doubt that in the later 'private' theatres the traditional settings of the early Blackfriars and Court performances continued to be practised. Marston could still write in 1606 of 'the fashion of the private stage' in presenting plays.[1] But the practice was certainly modified, by the need to cope with the romantic drama, into a compromise with the technique of the 'public' theatres, allowing for greater variety in locality. Their use of labels to indicate locality, a survival of an old practice disused in the 'public' theatres, may have been due to the exigencies of the compromise. There are, indeed, signs of occasional experiment in scene-shifting. Both at St Paul's and Blackfriars the stage-structure corresponded with parts of the basic structure of the Globe or Fortune. They had two side-doors and a central opening. And above the stage was a balcony which could be used as a music-room or as a place for stage-action 'above' on a small scale. And they had trap-doors in the stage.

Whether at the 'public' or the 'private' theatre, the producer did his share to aid the illusion. The actors made it easy to accept the illusion. The poet stimulated and suggested by his creative art. And the audience co-operated with their entertainers, susceptible of illusion and desirous of enjoying it. In a later chapter we shall see with what skill, ingenuity and tact

[1] In *Sophonisba*.

Shakespeare used the means at his disposal, how closely he was in touch with the practical craft of the theatre, how he progressed in his craft, and how he reconciled the increasing demands of his dramatic art with the conditions of his medium. It is evident that the Elizabethan theatre, far from hampering a competent dramatist, could furnish a satisfactory medium even for the dramatist of genius. Shakespeare occasionally calls attention to the deficiencies of the 'unworthy scaffold' of his 'wooden O', as in *Henry V* and *Pericles*. But by no stage could the vast sea or the epic battle of Agincourt be presented 'in their huge and proper life'. It is the medium itself, and not his Curtain or Globe stage, that lacks capacity for such great matters. And this is the thought underlying such particular appeals to the imagination of his audience. D'Avenant had exactly the same apology to make in 1656 for even the elaborate scenery of his *Siege of Rhodes*.

THE MASQUE AND THE STAGE

The later years of Shakespeare's career pointed the way, however, to a theatre in which spectacle began to develop at the expense of drama. In the greatest days of the Elizabethan drama spectacle was in the main confined to such effects as can be obtained by splendour of costume, upon which the actors spared no expense, and which served to dress the stage to the admiration of the spectators. But with the reign of James came the vogue of the Court masque, which joined the dance and music with symbolic costume and also with increasingly elaborate scenic and architectural display, and machines, designed by such men as Inigo Jones, and carried out at enormous expense to the King. With this the King entertained his Court and himself, as well as foreign visitors whom it was desired to impress. Such displays had their inevitable repercussion on the professional stage, and could best be emulated in the 'private' houses, in enclosed rooms and by artificial light, before a more select audience. Shakespeare's later plays betray the influence of the masque and by their strong masque element show how he and his company catered for the new taste. The masque in due time led not only to the opera in England, as devised by D'Avenant in the latter years of the Commonwealth, but also set the example for the elaborate *décors* and machinery of the back stage in the Restoration theatre, which carried still further the development of scenery in the 'private' houses under masque influences. For the rest, the Restoration theatre continued to use the 'apron' of the Elizabethan theatre, jutting out from the main stage, for its principal action, and inherited from the Globe and the Blackfriars alike the tradition of the platform stage.

The new trend of the stage at the end of the Elizabethan period is evident from the supremacy of the Blackfriars 'private' house, which, like other 'private' theatres, the Cockpit or Salisbury Court, emulated the Court masque as an added attraction to their patrons.[1] Both the Cockpit and Salisbury Court theatres were revived at the Restoration. And D'Avenant, author of masques under Charles I and of spectacular operas in the Commonwealth, was also dramatist and theatre manager under Charles II.

The theatre was still far from the ultimate logical development of these tendencies into the complete picture stage of later times, with its use of a front curtain opening to reveal a set scene, with its devices for changing scenery by mechanical means, and with its action restricted to a limited artificial world of canvas and painted wood. But the trend towards scenic illusion was hastened by the masque, which helped towards the gradual subjection of the drama to its medium. With Kemble, Macready, Irving or Tree the drama was frozen into comparative immobility, and forgot the bright speed it had when Shakespeare planned plays of action, wide-ranging, vivified by poetic atmosphere and incarnate in powerful acting, for the framework of the Elizabethan theatre. A taper or two burning, a 'sleepy tune', and Shakespeare distilling night in words, imagery and thought, these things shut out all daylight from the Globe

[1] The capital examples of the growth of scenery before the Restoration are Suckling's *Aglaura* in 1637, Habington's *Queene of Arragon* in 1640, both at Blackfriars and at Court, Nabbes' masque, *Microcosmus*, at Salisbury Court in 1637, and D'Avenant's *Siege of Rhodes* at Rutland House in 1656.

theatre as darkness slowly descends, compelled by the art of the dramatist and actor, in *Julius Caesar*.

THE REPERTORY OF PLAYS

The plays themselves came to the actors' companies both from actor-playwrights, members of the company which used them, and from free-lance dramatists from whom the company purchased a play outright. Or a company in financial straits might sell a play in its repertory to another company, or to a publisher, when, if printed, it became common property. A play once in the repertory might be revised, brought up to date, and rewritten, either by its author or, failing him, one of the company's 'poets'. All play-books were in charge of an officer of the company called the book-keeper, who also served as prompter. Henslowe's *Diary* gives us interesting details of the financier's dealings for his companies with dramatists bringing their goods to market, selling plays sometimes an act at a time, joining often with from two to four brother dramatists to hasten production in collaboration. The price of a play varied from a mere £4 to four or five times the amount in later years or if provided by a popular dramatist. It is Henslowe also who gives us facts about the run of a play at one of his theatres. A new play would be repeated, at short intervals, from six to seventeen afternoons according to its success with the audience. One play at the Rose had as many as thirty-two performances in three years. The average run of a play was about ten performances. And there were old plays that were constantly being revived, like Marlowe's *Dr Faustus* or Kyd's *Spanish Tragedy*. The Admiral's Men bought as many as twenty-one new plays in one year to add to their accumulated repertory at the Rose, and the total number at their disposal must have been very great. But few plays survived after their first run to become tried favourites. The Elizabethans desired novelty. Henslowe's *Diary* always notes the performance of a 'new' play, which drew more spectators and takings. This involved notably intense activity during the acting season for both actors and dramatists.

THE PERFORMANCE

Performances took place in the afternoon, after dinner, beginning at two o'clock and lasting generally two hours. Bills were printed and set up on convenient posts or distributed to advertise the performance. The entrance money was taken by 'gatherers' who stood at the main entrance and at entrances to stairs leading from the 'yard' to the galleries, taking the higher prices by instalments, as it were. The stage-hangings, if black, would be premonitory of a tragedy, if gay with mythological tapestry, of a comedy. Behind the curtain of the inner stage stood some actor peeping out to estimate the audience as it gathered. There might be the poet too in the tiring-room awaiting the fate of his play. The 'platt' or synopsis of the play was hung up on a peg for the actors to consult. 'Stage-keepers' were there to give mechanical help. And the 'book-holder' or prompter sat there with his prompt-copy, close to the inner stage. The actors were dressed and ready when a trumpet was sounded to give warning. Upon the third sounding the performance began. The play was introduced by a Prologue, dressed in a black cloak, to pray for favourable reception. Then followed the play proper. In the early days of the 'public' theatre it was probably acted straight through. But the practice of having intervals grew up with the development of music given by the boys of the 'private' theatres as an overture and between the acts, and spread to the 'public' theatres in later years. There are frequent indications of 'Musique' at the end of acts in Stuart times. And two intervals in a public theatre play of 1631[1] are marked by the prompter as 'Long' in a manuscript prompt-copy, at the end of Acts I and III. This may well have been the established custom of the theatre by then.

The Epilogue followed, generally some character in the play, to beg applause. The audience was apt to give clear indications of its views during the play. And it was a fashionable thing for a gallant to arrive late for his seat upon the stage, to pay no attention to the play, to mark his disapproval and to leave before

[1] Massinger's *Believe as you List*.

it ended. But a good response to the Epilogue would reassure the actors. It was followed in the 'public' theatres by an afterpiece, called a jig. The jig was originally an individual song and dance, but it developed into a more elaborate affair, with three or more players and something of a plot, in fact into an elementary comic opera, generally on a theme that was anything but edifying. With this the entertainment concluded, and the audience dispersed in merry mood. The stage-keepers came out to take down the arras hangings, and the actor-sharers remained behind to count the takings,[1] or adjourned with the poet or with friends among the audience to a tavern for refreshment. For acquaintance with a Burbage, a Shakespeare, or a Ben Jonson, was a feather in the cap of an Elizabethan gallant, and cherished by some of the graver sort.

THE ACTORS

The actors who acted in *Hamlet* were also competent, at any rate in the earlier stage of their career, to perform the lowly jig, to sing and dance expertly as well as with comic verve. They could, indeed, take charge of what we should now call 'variety' as well as 'legitimate' performances. A wrestling match in *As You Like It*, a fencing match in *Hamlet*, Sir Andrew Aguecheek's illustration of dancing feats in *Twelfth Night*, all would be genuine skilled exhibitions by trained experts. But we are not to think of the Elizabethan actor the more meanly for this. On the contrary. He was in every respect, as far as we can judge, better qualified for his profession than the generality of actors of to-day. Far too much, moreover, has been written upon the theme that the actor was then classed with vagabonds in the eyes of the law. Most of this is due to the excited enmity of Puritan opponents of the stage. The fact is that the actor's profession established itself as a legitimate occupation before Shakespeare joined it. It was recognised by royal letters patent as early as in 1574, and regulated ten years after by a royal officer, the

[1] This was certainly done, and the division made, after each day's performance, at Evans' Blackfriars theatre at any rate.

Master of the Revels. The Queen herself patronised a company from 1583 onwards, and Shakespeare and his fellows, on the accession of King James, were not only the King's Men, but Grooms of the King's Chamber. Edward Alleyn, of the Admiral's Men, as we have seen, died rich, lord of a manor, founder of a great school, and husband of the daughter of a famous Dean of St Paul's, Constance Donne. Heminge and Condell, fellows and friends of Shakespeare, were prominent parishioners of Aldermanbury and held office in the parish. Shakespeare himself was held in the highest esteem in Stratford as one of its worthiest and wealthiest citizens, bearing arms. They were all acceptably described in Courts of Law as 'gentlemen'. And when Richard Burbage, the great tragic actor, died, no less a person than the Earl of Pembroke grieved so much for his 'old acquaintance' that he refused to go to a play given at a great entertainment to the French Ambassador. It was a profession that a father might fairly put a boy to, though not a girl, for there were no women on the stage. It recruited itself with apprentices who served a leading actor or 'sharer', received a training, and graduated in due course from singing and from women's parts, and from tutelage, to man's estate and independent status.[1] A share in a company might be the reward of a good apprentice turned good journeyman in a company. Or a share might be purchased. For shares were as much permanent, saleable assets as any other kind of stock, as long as the company held together. A share in Queen Anne's Men was valued at £80 under James I, and could be bought and sold by actors entering or leaving the company.

It is true that not all companies had the solidity of that to which Shakespeare belonged, and most of them had chequered careers. But at its best the actor's profession was of settled dignity. We need not be surprised to find Shakespeare, in *Hamlet*, writing critically of the actor's art, with much contempt for its inferior professors. He knew what his plays owed to the acting

[1] The adult companies profited greatly by the recruitment of young actors from the boys' companies, in which they had had a thorough training and a fair education. Thus Shakespeare's company in 1608 had notable accessions from the Revels Children.

of his great fellows, just as the dramatist Webster knew what *The White Devil* owed to the genius of Richard Perkins at the Red Bull, where his tragedy was acted by Queen Anne's Men to his great satisfaction. Nor must we underrate the skill of the boy actors who acted women's parts, for there is contemporary evidence enough of their powers. The poorer companies, it is true, even in Shakespeare's day, had a leavening of less qualified, sometimes almost illiterate, journeymen or 'hirelings', who were paid from six to ten shillings a week for their services and even, if the week's takings were not satisfactory, as little as half a crown. But the profession was very much as it is to-day in this respect. And Shakespeare's plays were acted by the cream of Elizabethan actors.

His company was a stock company. And there are clear signs that there was some specialisation in their parts and that Shakespeare had to consider this in his work for them. At least, he certainly made the most of their especial gifts or peculiarities. I do not think we should read in *Hamlet* the words 'for he is fat and scant of breath' to refer to a portly Burbage but only to mean 'out of condition', as we should say to-day. For one thing, no leading man would consent to have these words said of him, if they bore that sense, lest ill-timed laughter should extinguish his heroic career for ever, and Falstaff remain the only part feasible for him to play. He could hardly have acted Othello, as we know he did. We may well believe that Edward Alleyn's parts,[1] as written by Marlowe for him at the Rose, suited his technique, an earlier technique of robust declamation and grandiose gesture, and even that Marlowe was influenced in his writing by this knowledge. Certainly it is true that when Joseph Taylor succeeded Burbage in the King's Men, and John Lowin was second leading man, the whole business of acting must have been toned down, made less individual, passion giving place to dignity or pathos, declamation to eloquence, in Shakespeare's last plays and in such plays as his successors provided for them. Shakespeare himself, in *Hamlet*, condemns on the one

[1] A large fragment of the manuscript of his part in *Orlando Furioso* has survived, at Dulwich College.

hand robustious exaggerated dealings in tragedy, and on the other immoderate and ill-regulated comic acting and licence in gagging and 'business'. He may well have had in mind the old comic 'star', Richard Tarlton, of an earlier generation, or his own fellow the famous William Kempe, the creator probably of his own Justice Shallow and certainly of Dogberry, who had left the company in 1600 to go on his morris dance all the way to Norwich and subsequently to repeat his dancing venture over the Alps to Rome, and was now a member of a rival company. Kempe was of the older school of comic acting, and it is probable that the disappearance of the formal clown or jester from Shakespeare's plays marks the end of the Kempe tradition in this company. Robert Armin, himself an author of plays, took his place as principal comic actor, followed later by Thomas Pollard, who excelled in literally 'fat' parts.

Well stocked as was the Chamberlain's-King's Company, it had to consider economy in the use of actors. And the large repertory necessary to an Elizabethan theatre forbade word perfection on the part of all members of the company in all its current plays. Parts were therefore extensively doubled, as we may see from certain surviving summaries of the action of a play, called 'platts', used by the prompter and containing the names of the actors playing each part, as also from the study of such a manuscript prompt-copy as that of Massinger's *Believe as you List*. Even so, the number of the cast increased rapidly from the four or five necessary for an old interlude to the minimum of nine or ten men with three or four boys required for most of Shakespeare's plays. The doubling, in the main, affected the minor parts. But it is clear enough that larger secondary parts also allowed doubling. There is no more interesting pastime than the attempt to cast an Elizabethan play, given the known names of the company, the characteristic parts generally allotted to each, and the possibilities of doubling. Once more, Shakespeare had to know his business. There was little place on the Elizabethan stage for 'native woodnotes wild' sung even by a great natural genius. Acting was a serious art, and justly demanded a skilled craftsman for its dramatist. Shakespeare knew this, and so did another great dramatist, Webster, who gave high praise to Queen Anne's Men

for the true imitation of life, without striving to make nature a monster, the best that ever became them.

THE AUDIENCE

Far from being miraculous flowers growing out of place in a field of thistles, Shakespeare's plays stand out in their proper setting, in harmony with their medium and their vehicle, and by no means wanting

that which is the onely grace and setting out of a Tragedy, a full and understanding Auditory,

as Webster put it. Many dramatists, it is true, gird at the pit or groundlings, and appeal to more cultivated taste. Even Shakespeare has his fling, in *Hamlet.* But we must beware of such evidence. There was something of a fashion in this, something of desire to flatter the gentry. It still goes on to-day, and plays and actors are accused of 'playing to the gallery', though the gallery (the 'groundlings' of to-day) now houses, we are told, the soundest and most unprejudiced critical taste. Shakespeare could not play only to his high-priced balcony, or to the gallants smoking on the stage, or to the Court, and write up to them. It is true that there were differences in theatres and in audiences, between Shoreditch and Blackfriars. But *Romeo and Juliet* was written for Shoreditch. And the Globe was never an aristocratic theatre. His 'Prince Hamlet' pleased all, said a contemporary. The fact is that Shakespeare found fit hearers among all classes of London citizens. If they had a fault, it was that of uncritical catholicity of taste. It was the pit that above all demanded the poetic drama as well as mirth. It was they who rejoiced in patriotic historical plays and knew too little of the Court to be disillusioned. They saved the Elizabethan drama from becoming over-educated and urbanised, and preserved its strength and universality, despite theorisers, men of wit and fashion, and experimenters like Ben Jonson. Incurably romantic and emotional, they longed for romance even if they did, while in the theatre, crack nuts, buy and drink bottled ale, and occasionally fall to riot.[1] And Shakespeare, at heart in full sympathy with men of his own make, wrote at least as much for them as for their betters, and reconciled all in one delight.

THE ENEMIES OF THE STAGE

The only discordant note was struck by two militant companies of dissidents. There were those who brought moral and theological argument to bear against the stage. They were unable to agree with the classical view, which Sir Philip Sidney pressed in defence of the stage (though he satirised the stage of his own day), that the drama was as morally profitable as it was delightful. Nor would they bow to the authority of the schools and universities, which used the play for educational purposes and gave their pupils the taste for it. Even within Oxford University there was dissension among heads of colleges, the Puritan John Rainoldes against the academic dramatist William Gager. And in London the battle of printed controversy was long and hot from 1577, a year after the Theatre was built, onwards. 'Vain Plays' were classed with dancing and dicing as evils by Northbrooke, and Stubbes in 1583 elaborated his *Anatomy of Abuses*. Gosson, once a writer of plays, turned and rent the stage in books. And from the pulpit at Paul's Cross notable preachers inveighed against plays as pagan entertainments, as schools of sin, as taking young and old away from divine service, as showing boys in female dress in despite of canon law, as socially dangerous. When, in 1583, a bear-baiting house in Paris Garden fell upon its spectators, the case was held to be proved by this judgment of God. In reply to these fulminations the young poet and dramatist Thomas Lodge wrote *Honest Excuses* in 1579, and Sir Philip Sidney later defended poetry in general and with it the stage and drama, in his *Apologie for Poetrie*, as did Nashe in his *Piers Penniless* in 1592. The drama

[1] We may remember that Bishop Latimer complained of the unruliness of distinguished audiences at sermons preached before the King, under Edward VI. And Dekker, in *The Gull's Hornbook*, is most severe on the gallants on the stage

had for its function the presentation of moral lessons by example. And some modern critics have assiduously sought to vindicate Shakespeare on such grounds. The debate was profoundly irrelevant, and inconclusive.

But the second group of opponents, closely allied to the Puritans, not only talked, but acted. The Puritan campaign died down by the end of the century, but the simultaneous assaults of the City authorities upon the theatres, though overborne again and again, were never stifled. The theatre, as they saw it, was a centre of disturbance, a menace to good order within the City, and a pit of infection in days when the dreaded plague was endemic in London. It took apprentices from their work and brought them into evil company. The remedy was to close the theatres and banish the players, or, failing that, to remove the theatres from within the City walls to the suburbs. Against the City stood the noble patrons of the players, and the whole influence of the Court. It was a convenient fiction that the players' real function was to present their plays before the Queen, and they must be allowed to exercise themselves and rehearse their plays to that end. To forbid them to play publicly was therefore to interfere with their duty to the Queen and, worse still, with the Queen's pleasures. The Privy Council thus naturally interposed between the City and the players oppressed by their ordinances. Attempts were made to arrive at a compromise by regulations, from 1574 onwards. Their first result was the foundation of the suburban permanent theatres. The City succeeded, with the entire agreement of the Council, in enforcing temporary closures of all theatres during severe outbreaks of plague. This occurred from time to time throughout the Elizabethan period, and was a constant hazard of the actors' trade. But when the City authorities pressed their case too far, and challenged the Council more firmly in 1584, they were obliged to yield.

The final result of the conflict was that the supervision and licensing of plays, players, and theatres were taken out of their hands and put in charge of the Master of the Revels, a royal officer under the Lord Chamberlain, who had long supervised performances at Court. To this day the Lord Chamberlain holds some of these powers in relation to the stage. The City took toll of the players in the form of contributions to their poor funds. But the Master of the Revels proceeded to develop a system of fees for licences which brought him in a handsome income. So the position of the players was increasingly strengthened by the support of a powerful vested interest.[1] There were still alarms and excursions. But during Shakespeare's time the only potent enemy of the theatres was the plague, which closed them for long periods both in 1592–4 and in 1603–4. During such closures, as also in summer, the companies could resort to provincial tours and travel, as in the days of their predecessors, with their waggon, their books and their costumes. In such circumstances, as well as in the great London theatres, were Shakespeare's plays performed. A wandering company of Yorkshire actors, in 1609, included the newly printed *King Lear* and *Pericles* in their repertory. A play, once printed, was at their disposal for sixpence, the price of the book. And the earliest texts of many Elizabethan plays bear the indications of the shortening and simplification which adapted them for representation 'on the road'. The King's Men often took Oxford in their circuit, and Cambridge too, less frequently. The title-page of the First Quarto of *Hamlet*, published in 1603, is our authority that they had performed Shakespeare's greatest play in both the university towns. There is a pleasant picture in a Cambridge University play of Burbage and Kempe among the students giving a lesson in the art of acting to some young aspirants to the theatre. This scene in *The Return from Parnassus* is surely a reminiscence of this or some other visit of Shakespeare and his fellows to the university. Hamlet, after all, had studied at Wittenberg, and would be at home in Oxford and Cambridge. So, we may be sure, would Shakespeare himself, though no university man.[2]

[1] Edmund Tilney, Master of the Revels during most of Shakespeare's career, was a relative of the Lord Admiral, the patron of the Admiral's Men, who indeed procured the post for him, and said so in a Court of Law.

[2] His *Venus and Adonis* found its place, we are told, under the pillows of undergraduate enthusiasts.

The moral is clear. *Hamlet*, most famous of all stage-plays, met with success and acceptance in 'public' and 'private' theatres alike in Elizabethan days, as also in the hall of a university town, or at Court, on a great variety of stages, before all manner of audiences. In 1607 it was even acted on board an India-bound ship, the *Dragon*, by its officers and men, off Sierra Leone, with waist and poop and companion for its stage. The play continues to this day to exercise its power, with undiminished vitality, on the stage as in the study, even when it is forced into the Procrustes bed of a theatre for which it was not written. But it must have air, speed, continuity, and the sequence native to it. So with other plays of Shakespeare, all married to the Elizabethan medium in which Shakespeare worked and was at home, and which he helped to develop and modify. When scholarship, freed from mere antiquarianism, is allied to theatrical craftsmanship in the service of these plays with their essential dramatic stuff, we can still find them triumphant over time and fashion, not only as literature, but as plays.

NOTE

The reconstruction of the 'Fortune' on p. 24, and the sections and plans on pp. 26–9, were prepared by Mr W. H. Godfrey, in consultation with the late William Archer and Dr W. J. Lawrence in 1907, from the details given in the Agreement, now at Dulwich (*Henslowe Papers*, ed. W. W. Greg, p. 4). This contract gives the exact measurements of the ground plan (p. 28) but declares that the stage is to be 'Contryved and fashioned like vnto the Stadge of the saide Plaie howse Called the Globe'. The plan of the stage is chiefly justified by study of the text and the stage directions of the plays it accommodated. Upon its main features there is fairly general agreement, but certain details are still subjects of dispute;—the exact disposition of the side doors, the dimensions of the inner stage and of the spaces behind, and the existence of the public staircases at the sides.

EDD.

SHAKESPEARE'S DRAMATIC ART

BY

HARLEY GRANVILLE-BARKER

THE THEATRE AS HE FOUND IT

WE cannot say certainly when or how Shakespeare's connexion with the theatre began. But by 1592 he is known both as actor and playwright, and *Venus and Adonis* will be published in 1593. He is twenty-eight years old.

There is now sufficient agreement as to which of the plays in the First Folio may be called early work, but discussion still as to whether the earliest of these are wholly or only partly or merely nominally Shakespeare's. The question is unanswerable in exact terms; but the discussion will be enlightening if it lets us divine even dimly the processes of the work, the ways of the workshop, and the dramatist himself in the making.

In Greene's detraction of him—of the upstart crow beautified with our feathers...his tiger's heart wrapped in a player's hide...who supposes himself as well able to bombast out a blank verse as the best of you...who is in his own conceit the only Shake-scene in a country—we discover, as one often may in such detraction, the very reasons of his success. He is actor and playwright both. He is at home in the theatre, that is to say, as Greene and his fellows, for all their 'rare wits', have never been. A third advantage, still unperceived, is to carry him to something better than success. His blank verse is as good as another man's, and better; the music of *Venus and Adonis* and *Lucrece* charms us; so does the fine flow of rhythm and rhyme in *The Comedy of Errors* and *Love's Labour's Lost*. But the secret is not here. It lies—and he has yet to discover it himself—far deeper; in the very conception and genesis of whatever idea is to find pervasive expression in the play. A poetic idea, dramatically conceived. The fruit of it, therefore, will be not drama written in the form of poetry, but something we can truly call poetic drama—which is a very different thing.

This triple combination of actor, playwright and authentic poet had not been found in the theatre before; and it was just such a combination that was now needed for the development of the art of the theatre as a whole.

The theatre to which Shakespeare came was dominated by its actors. They were the proprietors, the paymasters of its poets, and (as ever) the great attraction to the audience.[1] They had, indeed, within the last few years, *made* the theatre; had taken the old miming and mumming, the old moral declamation, something even of the derelict pageantry of the 'old' religion, and roughly moulded them into a coherent whole, endowed with fresh life and given new direction. It was, in its small way, a part of the typical Tudor achievement of organising, consolidating and laicising the realm. There was opportunity in the laicising of the drama, though discretion alone must have dictated it. For the new learning opened enchanting vistas of antiquity and romance, and the new patriotism could recall glories nearer home. So David and Bethsabe give place to Lady Salisbury and King Edward (who reforms and goes to the wars for, alas, a much inferior second half of the play), and Herod to Tamburlaine. The Church lost much in losing the drama, though it has waited three hundred years and more to discover that. The drama lost much too. But the immediate gain was great; in adventurous freedom, in the new demands made both on dramatist and actor. State control narrowed its field, certainly. Puritan rule exchanged whips for scorpions a little later. Still later came a combination of both; no part, however, of our present story.

It had not been, quite inevitably, an actor's task, all this. If

[1] Hence while we know positively that Alleyn acted Tamburlaine, Marlowe's authorship has still to be inferred.

Farrant and Lyly—merely to imagine it!—could have kept their boys on to act as grown men instead of letting them pass to other callings or into the men's companies we might now be effectively dating the English drama from Paul's, not from the inn-yards, the Theatre, the Curtain and the Rose; and this would have been a drama cut rather to the dramatist's taste than the actor's. A far more correct affair, doubtless; yet it must have lacked the vigour, the unruly passion and abounding vitality, which made the Elizabethan theatre at its worst a quite exciting place, and at its best, the theatre for which *Hamlet* and *Othello* and *King Lear* could be written.

Shakespeare came, then, to a theatre which was at least full of life, but with the heart of its new being, seemingly, in the actors and their acting. The poets are needed, of course; and a *Tamburlaine* or a *Spanish Tragedy*, not to mention a certain lost play in which a ghost cried 'Hamlet, Revenge!', will be valuable assets. But was there never to be anything more to drama and acting than this bombasting out of blank verse, with the clown's fooling for variety? Alleyn might rest content with it, since he made the bombast his own so magnificently. We are in the region of surmise. Still, these are questions which may well have germinated, somewhere about 1590, in the mind of a sensitive young man; poet at heart, rathe if not ripe; lately turned actor and ready to turn playwright.

THE ESSENTIAL BEGINNING

It would not be too much to say that Shakespeare created a new art of acting. He did this incidentally, but of necessity; it was the instrument of his drama, part of the medium in which he worked. Methods of acting have changed since his time; they have to accord with another sort of theatre and drama now. Little has finally been added to the actor's opportunity; gains in refinement have meant loss both in scope and power. A glance at the art as he found it and left it will throw some light upon his own art and its development.

Compare, simply from this point of view, *Tamburlaine* and

Hamlet. When the actors have posed and moved and spoken their lines magnificently they will have done about all Marlowe asks of them. What actor ever feels that he has fully and finally interpreted Hamlet? Where does the difference of opportunity lie? It is easier to trace than to define. It is not always in the difference between a good and a bad play, but it does distinguish a live from a dead one. *Tamburlaine* is dramatically crude; granted! But it might be impeccably constructed, the plot worked out with clarity and point; suspense, surprise, all the well-recommended ingredients might be there; the characters could even be solidly conceived and legitimately developed, and it would still lack life. By many good rules *Hamlet* should be counted a bad play. But the force of its dramatic idea sweeps such rules into limbo, and in every scene, in almost every speech, it is alive. With art as with life itself the essential finally defies analysis. In *Hamlet* the secret abides in a conception of character so vital as to irradiate even the unsloughed dead matter of the older story. But quite simple plays may have something of this quality of life in them. There it can exist mainly in the idea; familiar enough, this will probably be, for us to be able to enrich it from our own imagination. The actors will enrich it with theirs, and as much by what they are as by what they do. But though vivid, this is transient; the actors gone, the play perishes. Hamlet and Ophelia, Laertes, Polonius, Gertrude, Claudius—these live on, as spirits that dwell in the bodies of generation after generation of actors, who themselves die and are forgotten.

It is in this peculiar vitality, I fancy, rather than by external marks of style, that we shall most safely distinguish even the first touches of his enfranchised hand. Among duller stuff, some speech seems to leap from the pages at you; or a single phrase forced from a character at a significant moment—while characters around him may be elaborately explaining themselves—will send its light to the unconscious depths of his being. In the earliest plays these revealing phrases spring oftenest from some simple soul; no convention of verse or fine writing set up for a barrier. Is not Christopher Sly, if only in virtue of his

'Tis an excellent piece of work, madam lady: would 'twere done!

a more actual figure than any in the play which he and we have to watch? Does not Costard, begun as the conventional word-juggling clown, suddenly in the last scene of *Love's Labour's Lost*, not only take on life himself but confer it upon poor Sir Nathaniel, by stepping out from the pageant of the Nine Worthies, with his

> There an't shall please you: a foolish mild man; an honest man, look you, and soon dashed! He is a marvellous neighbour, in sooth, and a very good bowler; but for Alisander—alas, you see how 'tis—a little o'erparted.

And whatever we may question in *The Two Gentlemen of Verona*, it will not be Launce and his dog.

But verse, for the Elizabethan dramatist, was more than a convention. Upon a stage where all illusion centred in the actor, there was nothing like it for capturing and holding the attention of the audience and for swaying emotion. It had the advantage over prose that song has over speech.

To make it your vehicle for a seemingly spontaneous expression of character—there may be a problem. Shakespeare is soon ready to reject much that has been dear to Greene, Peele, Nashe and the rest; the Latin tag (evidence that they really were university wits); the too deliberately set speech; the long repetitive passages, line echoing line; the long drawn out line for line exchanges, the presenters, the dumb show. In principle he has nothing against such things. He does not seem to have let principles as principles bother him; if he can vivify their use, well and good; but if not, they must go.[1] We find him making all sorts of experiments in metre. The question is a very practical one. He gives even the old 'fourteener' its chance (in *The Comedy of Errors* and *Love's Labour's Lost*); but the long lolloping gait of it is monotonous; and, with emotion heightening the stress of our already heavily stressed English, it exhausts the speaker—and becomes more monotonous still. The five-foot couplet makes gentler going, and his natural bent may well have been towards the grace of rhyme. He gives this ample trial, varies it by quatrains, even by a sonnet occasionally; and he never quite

[1] To the end we may find him turning old conventions to account. There is, for instance, a long passage of stichomythia in *Antony and Cleopatra*.

abandons the rhymed couplet. But blank verse proves to be the best. It is the most malleable and adaptable of forms; open, as no other is, to variety and individuality of expression. It has correspondent drawbacks and dangers. No metre so easily becomes mechanical and dull or can slacken to such formlessness. Shakespeare himself, matured in experience, could still write long lifeless screeds of it; his successors debauched it; and re-discipline only turned it to ritual, which has at last gone the way of all ritual of forgotten purpose. But once let him be possessed by some creature of his imagination and the freedom is not too large; the intensity of the possession keeps the form itself tense and strong.[1]

THE FIRST DEVELOPMENTS

For a sight of him, authentically himself, but still adolescent in his art, experimenting impulsively with couplet, quatrain, blank verse, prose, passing from convention to spontaneity and back to convention, for a very epitome of this first stage of his development look into *Romeo and Juliet*. The verse at the beginning is smooth and swift; too smooth and swift to cut out character as it flows. The music of it is descriptive; in tune as well as words the Prince's speech is stern authority incarnate, yet he himself is nobody. Montague and Benvolio paint for us the lovesick Romeo more vividly than they paint themselves. Romeo takes up the painting; and here is youthful character so far realised that we have him self-consciously picturing himself as he wishes to be seen. But we are also conscious of the dramatist at work, and of his verse and its charm. Then, in the third scene:

Enter Lady Capulet and Nurse.

Lady C. Nurse, where's my daughter? Call her forth to me.
Nurse. Now, by my maidenhead at twelve year old,
I bade her come. What, lamb! What, ladybird!
God forbid! Where's this girl? What, Juliet!...

[1] The purely poetic qualities of Shakespeare's verse are dealt with by Mr Rylands, and are subject enough for a chapter. I confine myself, as closely as I may, to its dramatic value.

—and, suddenly (who, watching the play, has not felt it?) the barriers of artifice drop, and beside *this* reality, the very stage and the solid theatre become unreal. We do not note for the moment whether it is rhyme, blank verse or prose that is being spoken; vivid character has made the whole dramatic medium incandescent.

These speeches of the Nurse are Shakespeare's first unequivocal triumph in the moulding of the blank verse convention to the seemingly spontaneous expression of character. Analyse them; every accent, every pause and fresh impulse to the rhythm has its revealing purpose. Yet he seems to be working in perfect freedom. Yet, again, he keeps all the compelling power which the music of verse can give him.

With *Romeo and Juliet*, we find Shakespeare definitely set towards his end—which is, indeed, the end of all drama—the projection of character in action. And his advance will be to an ever deeper, richer, subtler conception and expression of character; finally also, to reflection in a man's expression of himself of the world in which he spiritually dwells. That last step, however, is still far ahead with the great tragedies. He is searching now for appropriate form; never content to take this ready-made. Turn to Mercutio and mark the change from the verse of the 'Queen Mab' speech—charming, but expressive of anybody and nobody—to the prose of the death scene; the man is himself by then. Mark the development in the expression of Romeo with the development of his character; from the self-conscious lover making conventional complaint, through the pure emotion of the love-making and the passion bred from Mercutio's death and Tybalt's, to the achievement of tragic simplicity in his answer to the fatal news:

> Is it even so? Then I defy you, stars!

its acceptance with

> Well, Juliet, I will lie with thee to-night.

He turns convention to dramatic account when he enshrines the first meeting of the lovers in a sonnet; it gives him the very touch of delicate shy formality that he needs. The method of the 'balcony' scene is as apt. It abounds in conventional imagery, made fresh again by the music of the setting, but it comes at last to the quietude of

Juliet. Romeo!
Romeo. My dear!
Juliet. At what o'clock to-morrow
Shall I send to thee?
Romeo. By the hour of nine.
Juliet. I will not fail; 'tis twenty years till then.
I have forgot why I did call thee back.
Romeo. Let me stand here till thou remember it.
Juliet. I shall forget, to have thee still stand there;
Remembering how I love thy company.
Romeo. And I'll still stay to have thee still forget,
Forgetting any other home but this.

Part of the effect is gained by the resolution from picturesque phrase to commonplace. Beauty of words can add nothing to their love, and its beauty makes the simplest—the silliest!—things beautiful. Shakespeare clarifies his medium here to entire transparency; yet (again) none of the value of the medium itself is lost. Anyone, surely, could write as simply! Perhaps. But to wed simplicity to poetic and dramatic power, that is another matter.

We may find less to praise in the spasmodic return to convention—to the extreme of artifice, indeed—when, a few scenes later, Juliet has to meet the news of Tybalt's death. This, for distraction and rage:

O serpent heart, hid with a flowering face!
Did ever dragon keep so fair a cave?
Beautiful tyrant, fiend angelical!
Dove feathered raven! wolfish ravening lamb!...

might have been lifted entire from *Henry VI.* And the cascade of puns upon 'I', 'ay' and 'eye' which follows (and which no actress of Juliet is nowadays asked to face) may seem, for the moment, to destroy the dramatic illusion altogether.

It will not have done so for Elizabethan audiences. Shakespeare, it is true, soon and finally abandoned such polyonymous apostrophes. He never abandoned the pun itself, though he grew thrifty in his use of it. But the pun was not then necessarily comic. We may think of the Elizabethans as so in love with their language and its new-found strength that even play with it delighted them and did not seem ridiculous. In

> Now is it Rome indeed and room enough
> When there is in it but one only man,

and in

> I'll gild the faces of the grooms withal
> For it must seem their guilt,

there was the stimulus of surprise, and an added power of emphasis, to which we no longer so readily respond. And Juliet's seven lines of threefold punning, as brilliantly spoken as the boy actor would be trained to speak them, will have come, not as mere word juggling, but about as a piece of *coloratura* singing (for there is a convention we still accept) sounds to us in an opera house to-day. Even now, if we can learn to listen, the verbal music—the 'I', 'ay', 'eye' repeated on varying notes—has its dramatic appeal.

For the apparent retrogression from spontaneity to verbal convention of whatever kind (and Shakespeare does this with Romeo too; also, notably, in the concerted scene of the mourning over Juliet's supposed dead body) we shall see the excuse if we remember that he is not composing and perfecting a poem, but preparing a play to be acted; and that, besides, he may well be in something of a hurry. He has to tell his story dramatically and provide his actors with the means of making certain effects. No difficulty if the characters are alive in his mind and will rise to each occasion, spontaneously expressive! But suppose one of them suddenly will not. You cannot shirk the occasion and its effect; your play requires just this. At this precise moment you need a Juliet in a passion, a Romeo in despair, or a chorus of grief. So if passion, despair or grief will not spring spontaneously and expressively, you fall back upon a convention, a formula. And you do so because it is a thing the actor understands, and *you can trust him to do the rest.* You have at least provided him with material for the effect.

THE BOY AS WOMAN

The practical playwright is at pains rather to exploit convention than to change it; the creative artist sets himself to turn its very limitations into strength. Shakespeare has been commiserated upon his boy heroines, upon a gawky Juliet, a husky Rosalind, a squeaking Cleopatra. We have no hint that the custom ever irked him, and he could have made good occasion for one when he lashed the 'robustious periwig pated fellow' and shook a finger at the clown.[1] He exploits the boy, turned girl, turning boy again, in comedy after comedy, from *The Two Gentlemen of Verona* to *Cymbeline*. It was the most popular of devices, and the fact itself sheds a light upon the disposition of Elizabethan audiences. They liked make-believe for its own sake (here, indeed, does lie the unsophisticated fun of drama), liked it so much that they could enjoy this double dose of it. Accept young Ned So-and-so as Rosalind; it will add a spice to your enjoyment to see Orlando accept Rosalind as Ganymede.

But mark how Shakespeare both safeguards the device of the boy as woman and draws profit from it. He safeguards it by never setting the boy to do anything ridiculous or embarrassing. For all the theme's passion, there is next to no physical love-making in *Romeo and Juliet*. The two are left alone together only for the less than forty lines of their tragic parting, for her yet more tragic waking to find him dead, and for the balcony scene. This is the play's pre-eminent love scene (it is, I suppose, the first passionate love scene in Elizabethan drama, and may well have been the making of the play's success), and in it the lovers are carefully kept out of physical touch. Even when he comes to treat *Antony and Cleopatra*—of all subjects in the world!—Shakespeare can escape the obvious dangers; can miss what would seem to the dramatist of to-day his likeliest opportunities! Of Cleopatra's sensuous charms we hear chiefly from the miso-

[1] The 'squeaking Cleopatra', coming as and when it does from Cleopatra herself, is certainly no such hint. And we should remember Coryat's comment when, in Venice, he '...saw women act, a thing I never saw before...and they performed it with as good a grace...as ever I saw any masculine actor'. This is his fashion of praising them.

gynist Enobarbus (and if he who detests and distrusts her can glow into praise of them, they are potent, we may be sure). She herself—but for a hint or two—is not voluptuous even in speech; when they are together, it is with wit, malice, or subtle mischief that she masters him. Never once throughout the play are they alone together. The dialogue provides for two embraces only; it may be three. The story begins with their parting; when they meet again catastrophe is imminent, and what is sensual in their passion is sublimated by its tragedy. Shakespeare, in fine, asks nothing of his Cleopatra that a boy cannot accomplish. Positively, by painting her in this medium of delicate dialectic, of swift speech, and of the music and colour of words, he puts the skill of the boy actor at a premium. And, in consequence, the charms of the actress of to-day are superfluous, nor has room been left for their exercise. The 'serpent of old Nile', realistic in the flesh, will but obscure Shakespeare's Cleopatra. To tell a woman to begin her study of how to play a woman's part by imagining herself a boy may seem absurd; but this is the right approach nevertheless. It is not a question—let us be clear—of conception of the character, but of its presentation. Shakespeare no more thought of Cleopatra herself so limitedly than he thought that the Senate House at Rome or her palace in Alexandria looked like the stage of the Globe theatre. That stage had to serve his purpose, he devised his play accordingly; and we have come to recognise at last how we betray him by foisting upon it painted pictures which only distract us from the visions his poetry creates. This heritage of the boy-Cleopatra, the boy-Ophelia, the boy-Desdemona, is of much the same nature. We need not in the one case cramp ourselves into a reproduction of the Globe stage, with its petty inconveniences; we have only to recognise wherein it differed from other stages, and why. Nor need we turn the actress out of Shakespeare if she will only recognise that what modern dramatists legitimately ask of her, physical and emotional charm, overt or covert, his plays do not. Let her first achieve the selfless skill and beauty that they do ask. Then, and then only, may charm and the rest, unconsciously given, be perhaps a little to the good. The great comedies reinforce the case. Shakespeare's Rosalind is—very naturally!—not self-conscious in her doublet and hose, his Viola casts no sheep's eye at Orsino, and his Beatrice conquers Benedick by her wit, nothing more primitive.

Given the choice, Shakespeare might not have chosen the single sex theatre—though doubtless it had positive advantages in discipline and equanimity. But he was not given it, and see to what profit he turns his limitation! Cruder phases of the emotional traffic between male and female his audience must take for granted; he can make no effective play with them. But what of true tragedy, or comedy, or even of the finer savour of romance, rests in these? Very little; and in that little still less variety. Shakespeare goes clean to the heart of romance. From a canoodling Romeo and Juliet, from the calf-love for Rosaline on exhibition, God preserve us!—do we not so exclaim if we imagine the sort of thing and compare what we have in its place? And in Hamlet's

> I did love you once....You should not have believed me.
> ...I loved you not....Get thee to a nunnery;
> Why wouldst thou be a breeder of sinners?

—in the sparse, conflicting phrases, in the fact that now he *has* no more to say to her, is the very essence of Ophelia's tragedy and his. It is tragedy of the spirit. As to comedy; that is set in lists where men and women meet on equal terms, where the fighting is above-board, with never a love scene that we are embarrassed to overhear—and the victory to the liveliest!

THE CONVENTION OF PLACE

All Shakespeare's craft and very much of his art is rooted in the needs and peculiar opportunities of his theatre. We praise the speed and comprehensiveness and variety of his action. His cipher of a stage gave him freedom in imagined time and imagined space, and he took full advantage of both. Now to do this he limited his freedom first. An anarchy was no use to him. One cannot speak precisely in such matters, but it is true enough to say that for the inn-yard spectator the actor before him was, to begin with, frankly on the stage, and the character impersonated often nowhere in particular. The playwright felt under no more constant obligation to settle his characters on a definite spot than had he been telling his tale in any other fashion. If the action suddenly demanded a battlement or a city gate, a balcony or an opening was at hand to impersonate it, even as the actors were impersonating their characters. The use over, it relapsed into an ignored anonymity, even as the actors did when they left the stage. A play might run its whole length without any such definite demand. Some hints at locality the story was bound to involve; no story-teller gets through without them. But they could often be of the vaguest; and the playwright might be glad to leave them vague, since it did not help him in his creating of illusion to have to insist on the existence of things, which, insisted on, were obviously not there. What is more, a scheme of consistent movement from place to place would ask careful devising.

For an extreme of carelessness in this kind take Marlowe's *Edward II*. The action begins presumably in London, and presumably continues there for nearly a third of the play's length. Then, without warning, it appears that the King is at 'Tinmouth' to welcome Gaveston from exile. With no more warning, after a hundred lines of the flight of Gaveston from the nobles, we find that everyone concerned is near Cobham. The Queen's journey to France and back is made clear. The King's failure to reach Ireland is only told by a

> We were embarked for Ireland, wretched we...

when he has landed again—we suppose it must be in England (unless the mere '*Enter, with Welsh hookes, Rice ap Howell*...' was eloquent of Wales). We see and hear of his movements between Killingworth and Berkeley; it is not clear where he is killed. Meanwhile the Queen and Mortimer and Prince Edward may be—or not—back in London. As to time, there is nothing to tell us whether it is passing quickly or slowly. If we know our history we know that the action covers the whole reign, but as far as the play is concerned time does not exist.

Turn now, for the limitation of such haphazard freedom, to *Richard II*. The comparison is apt, because the beauties in Marlowe's play had evidently impressed Shakespeare, and he echoes more than one of them. But the stagecraft is of another dispensation. As to place, he may seem at first sight to be as vague about it as Marlowe was; in half a dozen scenes there is no knowing exactly where we are, in most of the others we only know by reference, or can infer it from the action itself. But whenever there is some point in our knowing we find that, by one way or another, we know; moreover, what may be called the geographical scheme of the action is kept very clear indeed. In the first two scenes it matters not much where we are; the editors will have it the King's palace in London and the Duke of Lancaster's; for Shakespeare and his audience it is King Richard in state and John of Gaunt more or less at home. But we have insistent warning that we shall find ourselves in the lists of Coventry very soon, and the moment the next scene opens there very obviously we have arrived. During the scene, however, no more talk of Coventry, for there is nothing now to be gained by it. In the next scene we are again nowhere in particular; what matters is that Henry of Lancaster is off to his banishment, that the King

> ...will make for Ireland presently,

—and, pat upon this, comes the news that John of Gaunt is grievous sick. 'Where lies he?' 'At Ely House.'

> Come, gentlemen, let's all go visit him:
> Pray God we may make haste—and come too late!

The King and his minions go out, and at once John of Gaunt is carried in with

> Will the King come, that I may breathe my last
> In wholesome counsel to his unstaid youth?

The King arrives, and towards the end of the scene tells us again:

> To-morrow next
> We will for Ireland.

In the next scene we are with the Queen, once more nowhere in particular; the important thing now is that Richard is gone to Ireland and that Bolingbroke has returned; then that the Duke of York is for Berkeley Castle, Bushy and Green for the safer retreat of Bristol.

Next we find Bolingbroke and Northumberland on the march. The scene opens with:

Bol. How far is it, my lord, to Berkeley now?
North. Believe me, noble lord,
I am a stranger here in Glostershire:
These high wild hills and rough uneven ways
Draws out our miles, and makes them wearisome.

But if Northumberland does not know, young Percy soon comes to tell us:

There stands the castle by yon tuft of trees,
Manned with three hundred men as I have heard,
And in it are the Lords of York, Berkeley and Seymour....

York appears, and Bolingbroke persuades him to travel on to Bristol

...which they say is held
By Bushy, Bagot and their complices....

But we do not arrive there till the next scene but one. A short scene interposed spares Shakespeare the awkwardness of an *Exeunt Bolingbroke, York and the rest* with a re-entrance to follow after a moment's pause. Such a gap of emptiness—even so small a one—would check the flow of the story. It would involve explanations too; something would have to be done to give us the sense of shifted place and intervening time, which the intervening scene quite naturally, and, so to speak, tacitly gives. And this is put to further use; its twenty-four lines between Salisbury and a Welsh Captain tell us of Richard's fortunes. Again we are nowhere in particular; but the Captain's accent and Salisbury's '...thou trusty Welshman' are informing enough.[1]

[1] Just in that one clinching phrase 'thou trusty Welshman' lies the effective difference between this and Marlowe's Welsh scene.

Bushy and Greene despatched to their death, we hear that Bolingbroke is

To fight with Glendower and his complices,

and we see him depart to do so.

Richard appears with Aumerle. We have

Richard. Barkloughly Castle call they this at hand?
Aumerle. Yea, my good lord. How brooks your grace the air,
After your late tossing on the breaking seas?

and the scene ends with

Go to Flint Castle....

The next scene begins with Bolingbroke's and Northumberland's:

Bol. So that by this intelligence we learn
The Welshmen are dispersed; and Salisbury
Is gone to meet the King, who lately landed
With some few private friends upon this coast.
North. The news is very fair and good, my lord:
Richard not far from hence hath hid his head.

Shakespeare has thus manœuvred Richard to Ireland and back, Bolingbroke home again, and the two to an encounter, and has kept the various journeyings clear enough in our minds.

The technique and its purpose are evident. There is seldom any great gain in insisting at the actual moment upon the exact whereabouts of a scene. The action will show, if need be, the sort of place it is. Description would only distract attention from the action itself, and, elaborated, might even tend to destroy the illusion which the action is creating.

The key to this as to all Shakespeare's stagecraft is in the axiom that *illusion lies in the characters and their action and nowhere else.* Such a mere picturesque hint as

These high wild hills and rough uneven ways...

will, in passing, stir the imagination, and he is to come to much subtler and more elaborate devices of the kind. But he will never shift the burden of drama from person to place. On the other hand it may be important to fix a play's 'geographical scheme' clearly in an audience's mind, and—in this play it particularly is—the itinerary of the characters. For that gives a sense of actuality to the story. Also it will help to give form, which, consciously or unconsciously, all artists seek.

As Shakespeare's editors grow more and more oblivious to the theatre he worked for, so, thinking in terms of their own, they take more trouble to discover or invent a definite whereabouts for each scene. Often enough this can be done, for he will have had, roughly or exactly, a whereabouts in his mind—since somewhere your characters must be. But his stage had, of its own right, no such integrity of place as is conferred on ours by the illusion of a painted scene. He uses it for some room in Ely House, and with less realism for the lists of Coventry. Then, with even less, he uses stage and balcony for Flint Castle and some space beneath its battlements—which space is, to begin with,

here...
Upon the grassy carpet of this plain.

But a hundred and twenty lines later it has become the 'base court' of the castle itself. And as for Salisbury and the Welsh Captain, or the Queen after Richard's departure, he does not have to specify, even to himself, where, within miles, they are, or whether they are indoors or out.

So also he may move the dying Henry IV from one room to another in the middle of a scene, or Julius Caesar from the street to the Senate House, by passing them from the outer stage to the inner. He may have the monument of Cleopatra's refuge now on the upper stage, now on the lower. He may shift Juliet's bedroom from upper stage to lower in the middle of a scene, may let her descend bringing (so to speak) her bedroom with her.[1] And earlier in the play (very much as with Boling-

[1] The complication of the bedroom is, to be exact, both less and greater. When the scene begins the upper stage is the balcony upon which the newly married Romeo and Juliet stand saying farewell, and the lower stage the orchard into which Romeo descends. He being gone and Lady Capulet approaching, Juliet, by an inner staircase, also descends, and the lower stage (perhaps with the curtains drawn back and the inner stage with her bed revealed) becomes her bedchamber. And the scene is continuous. But the device is clumsy, and Shakespeare did not repeat it.

broke before Flint Castle) Mercutio and his companions can '*march about the stage*', and so symbolically proceed from the street into the midst of Capulet's old accustomed feast.

Convention allows him this fluidity; such an increase of it, moreover, as we find in the battle episodes of *Antony and Cleopatra*. This stretch of action the editors commonly parcel into twenty-two scenes, no less; ten of them from only four to twenty-two lines long. And they carefully localise each one: *A plain near Actium*. . . .*Another part of the plain*. . . .*Between the camps*, and so on. But here they very definitely do harm, since they obscure and pervert a masterly piece of stagecraft. What is Shakespeare trying to do? To give us, in terms of drama, a sense of the effect of this three days' battle upon the lives and fortunes of his characters. In terms of drama: he will keep, therefore, as clear as maybe of description, and show us the direct effect upon the characters themselves. He must be economical; he allows himself less than nine hundred lines in which to compass the whole business; and this includes one episode—of Thidias's embassy in between battles—which alone runs to two hundred, and the last, in which Antony stabs himself, of a hundred and fifty. But he must not epitomise too stringently; he wants to give us a panorama of the entire event, since in its quick turns and confusions lie the significance of its tragedy. He must show us his characters in constant action and concentrated upon the action itself; the more specifically because he also needs for them intervals of emotional reaction, if their human aspect is not to be eclipsed. Clearly he will be glad to emancipate himself from all but the essentials of the elaborate coming and going, to minimise the mere surroundings as much as possible. And that is just what this convention of fluid space allows him to do—to present us with the dramatic essentials of his swiftly moving picture; isolated, and the more significantly dramatic, and the swifter moving for that. The whole thing is easier to explain by a comparison. A novelist has something the same privilege. He can describe every detail of a room or a landscape if he chooses, but he need not. He can move his scenes in swift succession when he will. He can abstract his characters from their surroundings altogether, to fix our attention the better upon their thoughts or feelings. The Elizabethan stage likewise could be almost imperceptibly resolved from 'anywhere' to 'anywhere'; and it could be dissolved into as near to 'nowhere' as made no difference.

These effects belong more particularly, of course, to a swift and diversified action. But turn to *Othello* and ask where exactly the scenes take place through which Bianca passes, or how it is that, later, Roderigo can suddenly thrust himself (as, if Shakespeare and his audience were imagining definite locality, he must) into the privacies of Othello's home; Bianca, on her way to Cassio's lodging, must be making a thoroughfare of some part of it too. Editors and critics supply strained explanations; but thus it must incongruously seem to an audience—if their imagination works to that effect at all. The imagination of Shakespeare's audience did not. The Senate chamber at Venice was positively itself because the Duke and the Senators were in council there, and Desdemona's bedroom her bedroom in virtue of the bed, she in it. For the rest, if we look and listen as that early audience did, we shall have a sense of the action passing in some likely place. No *particular* place may be likely. Then, if the action calls for the utilities of none, if it is absorbing, and if it absorbs us in the characters themselves, and in what they are as much as in what they do, we shall ask no inconvenient questions. It is always our sense of the matter which counts; and upon this Shakespeare plays with greater ease and to better advantage than a strict geography would permit. He created out of the dramatic vagueness which he found, nothing so cut and dried as a *system* of diversity as against unity of place, but a supple means to a definitely dramatic end.

The student will be well advised to erase from his book all the localisations of the editors. Even when they do no more harm, they still show him an important aspect of Shakespeare's art from a wrong point of view. And these two last instances of misunderstanding have been taken from two of his maturest, of his greatest, plays.

THE CONVENTION OF TIME

As to treatment of time, the difference between *Edward II* and *Richard II* is yet more remarkable. Marlowe practically left time to take care of itself, kept events in their sequence, no more. Shakespeare sees a need and an opportunity; and sees it as usual from the most practical—which here will be the most essentially dramatic—point of view.

No question of accuracy need arise; and accurate time would in any case assort ill with indeterminate space.[1] But he discovers a primary need for speed. You must at all costs hold the attention of your audience. If you try to do this by constant emphasis and passion both actors and audience will be worn out. Speed—though not haste—is a good substitute, and an even better means of sustaining excitement. Verse by itself can give him speed, or the impression of it; but he will often want a more fully dramatic sense of speed in the event.

He discovers a need also for something of more dramatic import than sequence of incident, for a significant continuity of action. The audience must be made as conscious of its purpose as will keep them expectant, must sometimes be led to the brink of foreknowledge—and then the action must go swiftly forward, leaving them the more interested to follow. Upon a stage which lets him carry his characters where he will, the mere continuity is easily contrived; it is not so easy to give it significance and dramatic value. But as he schemes out the geography of a play, so he provides a time-scheme also; it is another dimension of form.

He frames the entire action of a play in time with no great exactitude (unless, as with *The Merchant of Venice*, a time-scheme is part of the drama), with no more than will give us some sense of actuality; and it is usually towards the end that we are let feel: about so much time has passed. Meanwhile he will have been more concerned to produce impressions of event crowding

[1] Even we to-day, more or less realists in the one matter, allow a large licence in the other. Half an hour's acting in the completest illusion of surroundings may pass for an imaginary hour or more, and we shall not remark the anachronism.

on event, or of suspense while nothing happens, according to the play's current need for excitement or calm, for tense emotion or slack. This is his chief, indeed his only, concern. He will make use of the calendar, so to speak, to give us these impressions (in a world which, though mimic, is mimicking the real world, what but our calendar should he use?); but he does so very arbitrarily, and with no more consistency than will save him from absurdity. And how inconsistent and arbitrary he can afford to be has never ceased to puzzle the commentators, who will try to measure the matter by realities rather than appearance. They involve themselves in futile explanations and in elaborate theories of 'short time' and 'long time' and the rest. This is the wrong approach. Shakespeare is not *directly* concerned with time in that sense at all. For him there will be at most something we can call 'dramatic time', by which he moves his play, now quickly, now slowly, according to his need. He uses, for effect, the vocabulary of the calendar, but he no more feels fettered by the usual laws of it than he does on his 'cipher' stage by the laws of space. His freedom in time and his freedom in space are alike only limited by apparent likelihood and the illusion of the moment.

The time-scheme of *Richard II* is a simple one. The whole action, as we near the end of it, seems to have lasted some few months.[1] But we have had a sense of far swifter movement meanwhile.

The first two scenes are largely summaries of earlier matter; the action really begins to move only in the third, with Bolingbroke's banishment; but from then on it goes swiftly. From start to finish there is no sense of pause. If it is not uninterrupted action, it is like the running of a relay race; as each scene ends the thread of the story is promptly picked up to be carried on in the next. Oftenest there is no need to bring in the calendar to help the illusion. The journeyings of the characters (clearly mapped as we noted), the ground they are covering, give us just about the right impression of the time the events might credibly occupy. But when the two measures, real and imaginary, happen not to fit Shakespeare pays no regard whatever to

[1] In actual history the events took twenty-two months.

the likelihoods of the calendar. Bolingbroke is back in England before, by the calendar, he could even have left it. The business could easily have been made more credible. But for the sake of dramatic effect, which is all he cares about, Shakespeare not merely neglects to do this, he quite deliberately does the opposite. He had only to seem to slow down Richard's journey to the dying John of Gaunt and delay his departure for Ireland. But no; Bolingbroke has hardly left Coventry before we hear that the King is 'for Ireland presently'[1]; and, John of Gaunt dead, twice in a speech we have the start for Ireland to be made 'to-morrow'. And fifty lines later, in the same scene, Northumberland has already heard that Bolingbroke

With eight tall ships, three thousand men of war...

is rebelliously on his way back from France. He cares only for the dramatic effect, and here hardly seems even aware—quite probably was not, nor in the event are we!—that he is sacrificing anything to it. Between John of Gaunt's death and Bolingbroke's return the story contains no useful material; that is what will determine him. And just as he has the play moving with the right impetus (it has taken long enough to get going) he certainly does not want to slow up, pad out the action with irrelevancies or cover the intervening events with a chorus, and then have to work up speed again. For Shakespeare time has its dramatic uses, but no rights of its own.

The matter will not always be so simple, but there is never a sign that its complications troubled him—as they do us when we stop to dissect them. With *The Merchant of Venice* an exact framework of time is a dramatic necessity, and he makes it three months. He has a second story running concurrently, which should hardly spread over three days. If you are to take the calendar seriously here will be a pretty problem. But all he does is to allot the three-day story as many scenes as he can—which at least gives us the sense that a fair number of things are occurring. They fill up the space, and *dramatically* they seem to fill out the time. He leaves them their own calendar value,

[1] *I.e.* immediately.

without insisting on it. Upon the calendar of the Shylock story he must insist. But he only does so at its beginning and its end; and its frequent interruption in favour of affairs at Belmont gives us an impression, whenever we return to it, that time has been passing.

The case of *Othello* is more complex, and subtler issues are involved. He needs impetus and continuity of action, as he always needs it, to help hold his audience under the play's spell. But he has positive dangers to guard against. Lest Iago's reckless trickery should seem too discoverable, more particularly lest Othello himself should seem a fool not to discover it, he satisfies the need for impetus so thoroughly that, by the calendar, the very occasion of the tragedy becomes impossible; Desdemona and Cassio are left no opportunity for adultery at all. But, watching the play, do we notice anything wrong? The use of the calendar is cavalier in the extreme. By references to 'this night' or 'lately' or 'a week away' we are given the impression now of speeding, now of lagging time. And so arbitrarily is it done that in the very same scene one impression is allowed to combine with—and contradict!—another. The impression of speed is left dominant, for this is of primary importance; the impression of delay will be incidental. We benefit by each and are unconscious of the contradiction.

The exceptional instance in which the dominant time impression is of delay is, of course, *Hamlet*—which is the tragedy of delay. Here the necessary swiftness of the action itself is sustained by half a dozen devices: by fresh characters appearing, short scenes, swift-flowing verse, change between verse and prose. How fatally easy—given that subject and that hero—to have made *Hamlet* a tragedy of slack monotony also! Shakespeare runs no risks there.

CHARACTER DOMINANT

As his powers ripen, he turns them more and more to the elucidation of character and develops his stagecraft almost wholly to that end. He took—and left—the mere mechanics of the stage very much as he found them. Its appointments were enriched in his time, but he seldom eked out his work with pageantry.[1] Processions and elaborate dumb-shows were popular enough and easily provided; in his plays they are rather remarkably absent.

The indoor conditions of the Blackfriars, when the King's Men made it their chief centre, doubtless gave a new turn to the technique of play-writing; here is the beginning of our modern drawing-room drama. We may perhaps see this 'indoor' disposition reflected in his latest plays, particularly in the dramatic repose of *The Tempest*; but by then his greatest work was done. He had done it for the glaringly public stage upon which it might well have seemed that magniloquence and arresting action could be the only masters. His capital discovery—if it was innate in earlier work he was properly, I think, the 'discoverer'—is that physical action in itself and by itself is the least effective thing upon that stage or any other. You may kill a man or kiss a woman, and, whatever the interest in this, it is over in a moment. The why and the wherefore, what went before and what is to come after, those are what count. They are the fruitful stuff of drama. From which it soon follows that not rhetoric merely or mainly, nor what may be openly said, but the thing only thought or felt will need to be expressed. But how turn a flagrant publicity—the disillusionary daylight, the platform for a stage, the spectators as aware of each other as of the actor—to such intimate account? Here the discovery is consummate in a seeming paradox. Let all other aid to illusion be absent and the illusion lodged in the actor himself will only grip us the more strongly. Set him in our midst, make him one of ourselves, fix our attention wholly on him, and we shall come to feel so at one with him that not only will the barrier between our actual world and his imagined world the more easily vanish, but the innermost of the character he plays will be just what it will be easiest for him to reveal and for us to respond to. The discovery was the more readily made because,

[1] Quite apart from the masque and its influence, the later resources of the King's Men in this matter may be gauged by the stage directions to *Henry VIII*.

as we saw, all illusion upon the platform stage inevitably centred in the actor. Once made, once this close and unhindered fellowship has been established, it becomes, in Shakespeare's hands, the passport to something like another world of drama. He first enters it, in full confidence, with *Hamlet.*

THE SOLILOQUY

The direct means to self-revelation is, of course, the soliloquy. Shakespeare accepted this as he accepted other conventions; it was a convenience and a freedom. It could be used, even more directly, for the telling of the story; the character turned to something very like a chorus. The function, for instance, of the Scrivener in *Richard III*, with his

> Here is the indictment of the good Lord Hastings;

even of Tyrrel with his description of the murder of the young princes:

> The tyrannous and bloody act is done,
> The most arch deed of piteous massacre
> That ever yet this land was guilty of....
> 'O thus' quoth Dighton 'lay the gentle babes':
> Thus, thus, quoth Forrest...

—the line of distinction between that sort of thing and the direct address of chorus to audience is not easy to draw. These instances are from an early play; but Shakespeare never yields the substance of such freedom. We find Hamlet's

> I'll have these players
> Play something like the murder of my father,

not to mention Iago's many and varied confidences. What he learns to do is so to vivify and dramatise soliloquy that, the convention accepted, the illusion of character will not be broken.

It is, however, such an obvious convenience that its use or abuse may be some measure of a dramatist's skill. Shakespeare, as he advances in mastery, either turns it to significant account or largely does without it. Among the introspective characters and plays it flourishes; with the others it will be subordinate, may be all but eclipsed. In *Hamlet* it is naturally of capital importance, in *Macbeth* too, and (for Iago) in *Othello*; in *King Lear*, *Antony and Cleopatra*, and *Coriolanus*, where the heroes are by nature men of action, it is not.[1] Soliloquies in *The Winter's Tale*, *Cymbeline* and *The Tempest* are frequent; but they partake in a manner of the more conscious artifice which distinguishes the latest plays. There other questions are involved.

CHARACTER REVEALED, AND THE NEW POWER IN POETRY

But however expressed, in dialogue or soliloquy, verse or prose, it is this ever-ripening vitality of created character which marks the main advance. Up to the time (approximately) of the three mature comedies and of *Henry V*, we may best speak of the 'realisation' of character, and note besides that the figures most fully rounded and realised are (in the word's most liberal sense) comic figures; we note, also, and as a probable consequence, the increasing use of prose. *Julius Caesar* marks the change. The subject's grandeur gives verse chief place again; and while Mark Antony is as objectively seen as Hotspur, though far more subtly and elaborately modelled, we have in Brutus the difference of a character 'revealed'. And Brutus leads on to Hamlet, with *Hamlet* the play made one long contrivance for the revelation of Hamlet the character. It is in *Hamlet*, too, that we find the verse charged with a new and peculiar power, for the fresh task demands it.

Shakespeare does not relapse upon plain analysis of thought and emotion, upon such a static drama as that would produce. He must still have action; he must at any rate have movement; but movement itself is now to be made expressive of character or theme.

Witness the picture we have of the excited Hamlet going from the play, past the praying King, to his mother's closet; later

[1] In *Coriolanus* there are but two true soliloquies, both very short: Antony has hardly thirty lines of soliloquy, Cleopatra not one. Nor does Lear soliloquise; the invocation of the storm is not a true soliloquy.

tugging the slain Polonius upstairs; then, through a scene or two, rounded up by Rosencrantz and Guildenstern and the guard with their torches. There is far more dramatic value in this than lies in the mere physical movement. It is eloquent of character and mood. Incidentally, it is expressive as upon a realistically visual stage it could not be; since there the background and its changes would be over-emphasised and the figures to the front diminished in importance. Witness both the diverse movement of the battle scenes in *Antony and Cleopatra* and the terror of her flight from his rage, and the berserk rage itself after his final defeat. Witness the master movement of the action of *King Lear*; his leaving Goneril for Regan, his passage through the storm, his escape and his wanderings, his rescue to the haven of Cordelia's pardon. In no earlier plays, I think, is physical movement—though it may speed and clarify the story—given such emotional significance.

Also he now begins to reflect place and circumstance in and from the characters and their moods. By this means he can give place dramatic value if he wants to and enlarge the sensitiveness of a character besides. These changes of method are, of course, never sudden, nor are they absolute. Even as he will abide by or revive an old method, so the seed of a new one may be found in an earlier play, its sprouting-time not yet come. From the beginning we have found him taking occasion to paint in words the beauty of an imagined scene, and to the end he will be content, if there is no gain in more, with a mere label. Richard II's

> Barkloughly Castle call they this at hand?

has its counterpart in Coriolanus'

> A goodly city is this Antium.

He will also still do without labels and let change of place speak through the identity of the characters and their action. In *Antony and Cleopatra* and *Coriolanus* this is largely so, and for sound dramatic reasons. The story involves much shifting of place; these soldiers will not be over-sensitive to their surroundings, and constant labelling would prove trivial interruption. From the beginning it has been a question of the play's particular need. *Love's Labour's Lost*, with its artificial wit combats, has little picturesque setting. In *Romeo and Juliet* we have, on the one hand, the simple descriptiveness of

> Lady, by yonder blessed moon I swear,
> That tips with silver all these fruit tree tops...

and, on the other, the atmosphere of the tomb more intensely created. There is elaborate painting of the moonlit garden at Belmont. This is to withdraw us from the powerful influence of Shylock and the bond; it is elaborate, but descriptive and sententious still. We ought not to expect to be touched to the tune of Nature herself in that euphuistic Forest of Arden, where she is merely a peg upon which to hang the jests and moralising and balladry of its sophisticated lodgers, a tapestry background to the satire of Jaques and to Rosalind's wit. The description—it is description still—of the lioness with udders all drawn dry and the green and gilded snake strikes the appropriate note of incongruity. In *A Midsummer Night's Dream*, the wood near Athens can almost be called the play's chief character. The fairies but half emerge from it into individuality, the wandering lovers are half absorbed into it.

Now compare the moonlight over Verona and Belmont with the starlit darkness in which the ghost of Hamlet's father walks, or the murk of the night of Duncan's murder; compare treatment, dramatic purpose and effect. Description has gone, or it is merged into the action, or it has become a spontaneous expression of a character's mood. The hour and its darkness when *Hamlet* begins are given us by a quick confused exchange between sentries; and a page of description of the chill, boding, silence would not better

> *Francisco.* For this relief much thanks; 'tis bitter cold,
> And I am sick at heart.
> *Bernardo.* Have you had quiet guard?
> *Francisco.* Not a mouse stirring.

Banquo paints us the blackness of Macbeth's courtyard with the simple

> *Banquo.* How goes the night, boy?
> *Fleance.* The moon is down; I have not heard the clock.

Banquo. And she goes down at twelve.
Fleance. I take't, 'tis later, sir.
Banquo. Hold, take my sword. There's husbandry in heaven;
Their candles are all out...

and Lady Macbeth adds how much more with

Hark! Peace!
It was the owl that shrieked, the fatal bellman,
Which gives the stern'st good night.

Description would indeed not better, it would definitely spoil the dramatic effect of all this, for it would distract us from the matter in hand and the mind and mood of the characters; and upon these, in their new complexity, Shakespeare must, at any cost, keep us concentrated. He has here, for one thing, achieved a very necessary economy.

He need not economise all the time; tension must be relaxed and perspective shown. And he does not altogether reject description, but this will be less than ever an end in itself. He can allow himself the idyll of Duncan's first sight of Inverness:

Duncan. This castle hath a pleasant seat; the air
Nimbly and sweetly recommends itself
Unto our gentle senses.
Banquo. This guest of summer,
The temple-haunting martlet, does approve
By his beloved mansionry, that the heaven's breath
Smells wooingly here: no jutty, frieze,
Buttress nor coigne of vantage, but this bird
Hath made his pendent bed, and procreant cradle:
Where they most breed and haunt, I have observed
The air is delicate.

Descriptive, but turned doubly to dramatic purpose; for it follows swiftly upon

Macbeth. My dearest love,
Duncan comes here to-night.
Lady Macbeth. And when goes hence?
Macbeth. To-morrow as he purposes.
Lady Macbeth. O! never
Shall sun that morrow see!

and is followed by her reappearance, as smooth and soft and smiling in her welcome as is Nature's dressing of her home. She has counselled him

> To beguile the time,
> Look like the time; bear welcome in your eye,
> Your hand, your tongue: look like the innocent flower
> But be the serpent under it.

What could better reinforce the tragic irony than her setting him the example, in this sunset picture of the martins circling and dipping beneath the eaves?[1]

Lastly, as with the storm scenes in *King Lear*, not only can he dramatise place and circumstance, and reflect them in and from character, but he can *identify* these with the inward drama, interpret one in terms of the other and enhance the effect of both. Kent and Gloucester do enough to *describe* the storm. Lear—striving (we are given the hint)

> ...in his little world of man to outscorn
> The to-and-fro conflicting wind and rain,

matching himself against the storm, echoing it in defying it—becomes for us, without ceasing to be himself, a very image of it. He creates it dramatically; but not by detached description, which would merely let us see it through his eyes. He is endued, and he endues us, with the very spirit of it. He, for the crucial moment, is at one with it, and we with him, and he is to us Lear and the storm, too.[2]

Can we now see the scope of the developed task? It ranges from revelation of a man's innermost self to the seizing us—for yet further revelation—with his apprehension of the world without him, in its simplicity or its mystery. As medium there is still only dramatic speech and such action as will not check nor obscure it. We have, to convince us, the actors in their characters physically present; but the revealing speech admits us to an

[1] Needless to add, I hope, that if our *eyes* are distracted by a painted picture of the castle and its nests, the nine lines will have been spoken before our *ears* have well begun to listen, and Shakespeare's whole effect will be lost.

[2] And for a measure of Shakespeare's advance in this particular technique, compare the storm as dramatised for us in *Julius Caesar* by Casca, Cicero and Cassius.

immaterial world of emotion and idea, in which physical action may be no more than a measure of the inner and the true event, a metronome marking of the symphony. Hence it is a world in which the heroes—Othello, Lear, Antony, Macbeth—can grow to colossal dimensions. And they do so the more easily because upon that cipher stage they are set free from many crippling realisms of time and place. Shakespeare is careful to keep them actual in all ordinary aspects, as human of habit as the actors who present them; indeed, the higher they tower the more care he takes to touch in familiar traits and to surround them with the little realities of life. But they have their full being in that world of passion and the spirit, to which poetry in some kind is our only witness; and its bounds are wide.

We find, with the great tragedies, an increasing ease and breadth of treatment in what may be called the outer reaches of his stagecraft. But it is to the inner commerce of the scene that we must now look for his art's essential strength and virtue. It may dwell there in a peculiar power of speech—not easily to be defined. Form apart, here will be words wielding something like absolute power. It is true poetic drama, not merely drama in poetic form, that he is writing now. He can project a character in a single line. When Antony's Octavia says:

> The Jove of power make me most weak, most weak,
> Your reconciler,

sense, tune and rhythm combine to reveal her to us. How much of Hamlet is not already implicit in

> 'Tis not alone my inky cloak, good mother,
> Nor customary suits of solemn black....

All the fine irony and distaste are there; and almost as eloquently, one is tempted to say, in the very vowels and consonants as in the meaning!

The struggle between Lear and Cordelia is joined with:

Lear. But goes thy heart with this?
Cordelia. Ay, my good lord.
Lear. So young, and so untender?
Cordelia. So young, my lord, and true.

With twenty-one words, planned to be spoken just so, and placed precisely in the scene, he states for us the whole tragic issue between the two. Compare this in its strong economy with anything from the earlier plays which can be made comparable. The material of the medium is the same; but the art of the use of it is really a different thing altogether.

Again, for what may be found in the 'inner commerce' of a scene, study their second encounter; when, rescued from his wanderings, he wakes, clothed now in his kingly robes, to find her watching over him.

Cordelia. How does my royal lord? How fares your majesty?
Lear. You do me wrong to take me out o' the grave.
Thou art a soul in bliss; but I am bound
Upon a wheel of fire, that mine own tears
Do scald like molten lead.
Cordelia. Sir! do you know me?
Lear. You are a spirit, I know. When did you die?
Cordelia. Still, still, far wide!
The doctor. He's scarce awake; let him alone awhile.
Lear. Where have I been? Where am I? Fair daylight!
I am mightily abused. I should e'en die with pity
To see another thus. I know not what to say.
I will not swear these are my hands. Let's see:
I feel this pin prick. Would I were assured
Of my condition.
Cordelia. O look upon me, sir,
And hold your hands in benediction o'er me.
No, sir, you must not kneel!
Lear. Pray do not mock me.
I am a very foolish fond old man,
Fourscore and upward, not an hour more or less;
And, to deal plainly,
I fear I am not in my perfect mind.
Methinks I should know you and know this man;
Yet I am doubtful; for I am mainly ignorant
What place this is, and all the skill I have
Remembers not these garments; nor I know not
Where I did lodge last night. Do not laugh at me;
For as I am a man, I think this lady
To be my child, Cordelia.

Cordelia. And so I am, I am.
Lear. Be your tears wet? Yes, faith! I pray, weep not.
If you have poison for me, I will drink it.
I know you do not love me; for your sisters
Have, as I do remember, done me wrong.
You have some cause, they have not.
Cordelia. No cause, no cause!

One is loth to analyse its perfection; but we are talking of mere technique, of the means to the end, not trying to explain in what the great poet is great—and possibly at his greatest when he can achieve such pregnant simplicity. What are the means? The contrast with the Lear that was; the homeliness of the speech, given its one enhancing touch of richness in that 'wheel of fire'; the quiet cadence of the lines, kept from monotony by a short line here and there; the descent from 'You are a spirit, I know' through 'I should e'en die with pity to see another thus' (this from Lear!) to the deliberately commonplace 'Would I were assured of my condition!' Then, for an answer to the gracious beauty of '...hold your hands in benediction o'er me', the sudden sight instead of the old king falling humbly on his knees to her, and Cordelia's compassionate horror at the sight; this picture informing her suspense and ours with the silent question: Will he come to his right senses now? His passing from darkness back to light is told in the opposition of two words: I think this *lady* to be my *child* Cordelia. And at that she falls on her knees, too. We may be as sure she is meant to as if Shakespeare had written the direction; for this was the poignant moment in the old play, and no false pride would stop him taking for his own such a thing of beauty—the two there together, contending in humility as they had contended in pride—when he found it. A daring and unmatchable picture, for it is upon the extreme edge of beauty; one touch further and it might topple over into the absurd. And he can melt Cordelia for us utterly with the simple repetition of 'And so I am, I am'; and can sum up her nobility in two words more, and her generosity in their repeating—in that 'No cause, no cause!' And here is hardly more than the half of these mere means to the scene's end.

Pass from the grandeurs and simplicities of *King Lear* to the stern strength of *Macbeth*. Under our very eyes, so to say, Lady Macbeth is created:

> Come, you spirits
> That tend on mortal thoughts, unsex me here,
> And fill me, from the crown to the toe, top-full
> Of direst cruelty....

Note the ultra-human pitch, hit and sustained. Lower it only a little and some of the matter of these 'creative' scenes would seem ridiculous. But Shakespeare has also relied here on the impersonal method of the boy actress to help him. It is Macbeth who completes the creation for us with his:

> Bring forth men children only!
> For thy undaunted mettle should compose
> Nothing but males.

The phrases and the verse are alike bare almost to crudity. But what is wanted from this act of creation? Not an elaborate picture of the lady in every relation of life; as wife, mother, hostess, friend (which, for one thing, would badly upset the balance of the play); but the suggestion of an almost ultra-human force for evil. It is, with a difference, the Iago theme; a revelation of the deadly power which may reside in ruthless devotion to a single narrowed aim. Simple egoism with Iago; in Lady Macbeth the tragedy reaches both to self-destruction, and to the loss and destruction of him she loves. Here is the dramatic need for ultra-human force; and we credit this image of it the more because it is thus isolated, just because we are left knowing so little else about the woman. It is an added daring which lodges such force in this frail figure, going, for the rest, quietly about her household business. Shakespeare shows us two beings, arrestingly and astonishingly one; the woman that everyone around her may see and the creature of the power of his poetry.

Macbeth's self-creation involves more than this. Not merely is the distraught mind of the man opened to us, the very field of his spiritual conflict is staged. He is imaginative enough, yet not by nature or choice introspective. He sees the conflict as in an apocalyptic vision:

Besides, this Duncan
Hath borne his faculties so meek, hath been
So clear in his great office, that his virtues
Will plead like angels, trumpet-tongued, against
The deep damnation of his taking-off;
And pity, like a naked new-born babe,
Striding the blast, or heaven's cherubin, horsed
Upon the sightless couriers of the air...

And the magnificence of the vision is a measure of the wrecked nobility in the man.

Shakespeare has now to show us the ebbing of the life within these two, their death while they still live; for here is the essential tragedy. He needs a method proper both to the process and the characters. Description will not do, of course; and introspection —even were that in their nature—exhibits spiritual life, not death. With Lady Macbeth the solution of the problem is a simple one, so simple that only a master-hand could have made it effective. Hers has been the ruling will and ruthless spirit. Both are brought to nullity. But for one exhausting flash of the old power, when Macbeth is trembling like a 'baby of a girl' before blood-boltered Banquo; but for the shreds of mother-love she would protectingly fling round him would he let her,[1] all the help she can bring him in his agonising is the dulled:

You must leave this;

the wearied questioning

What's to be done?

He will not tell her, and she dare not ask again. With scarce more matter than this; with a few rhymed couplets swaying to a sort of knell of helplessness, and the sight of her tottering under the splendid weight of her Queen's robes, Shakespeare shows us her downfall.

In the sleep-walking scene we see her already spiritually dead. It was an inspiration; by what other means could the

[1] 'I have given suck, and know how tender 'tis to love the babe that milks me....' She turned that tenderness to iron for him; the remnant memory of it is not much.

thing have been done? The murderous power has crumbled to the pitiful

> ...all the perfumes of Arabia will not sweeten this little hand.

And the Satanic soul with the poetry which painted it to the senseless muttering:

> To bed, to bed; there's knocking at the gate. Come, come, come, come, give me your hand. What's done can't be undone. To bed, to bed, to bed.

The body's death is nothing; it can be dismissed with that distant cry of women and Macbeth's helpless shrug. This is her true end.[1]

To show us Macbeth in spiritual dissolution is not such a simple matter. But for Shakespeare—for any poet—insensitiveness is a sort of death. And the man must harden himself; first against conscience to kill Duncan; later, against the terrible dreams that shake him nightly; then against the patent vision of the murdered Banquo. After which, since there is no going back:

> For mine own good
> All causes shall give way....
> My strange and self-abuse
> Is the initiate fear, that wants hard use....

Harder use, indeed, he gives it. His king; his comrade; and now a woman and her children! From which very naturally follows:

> I have almost forgot the taste of fears.
> The time has been, my senses would have cooled
> To hear a night-shriek, and my fell of hair
> Would at a dismal treatise rouse and stir
> As life were in't. I have supped full with horrors:
> Direness, familiar to my slaughterous thoughts,
> Cannot once start me.

This to be given immediate and bitter proof when, to the news:

> The Queen, my lord, is dead.

he can only answer:

> She should have died hereafter.
> There would have been a time for such a word...

[1] And the actress, who tries to make it one of the 'great' scenes of the play and to fill it full of the tortures of remorse, will defeat, of course, its whole dramatic intention.

and fall to philosophising! It is one of Shakespeare's most daring strokes because it is an effect of *omission*. She has been his very 'outward soul'; she is dead and he can feel nothing.

But there must be, besides, some positive painting of this negative process of the debasement and death of the spirit; and Shakespeare has prepared a means in that vividly 'extraspective' imagination. Macbeth can crush all conscience in himself (though it dies torturing him), yet only to become more conscious of the world without as he has now made it for himself to live in; a sinister world. We have a hint of what is to happen in the tremendously imaginative:

> Will all great Neptune's ocean wash this blood
> Clean from my hand? No, this my hand will rather
> The multitudinous seas incarnadine,
> Making the green one red.

And, the deed done, all nature reflects it for him and is tainted with evil and horror:

> Light thickens; and the crow
> Makes wing to the rooky wood;
> Good things of day begin to droop and drowse,
> While night's black agents to their preys do rouse....

He is obsessed by these images; of scorpions, snakes, bats, of carrion birds, of darkness, and of blood:

> It will have blood; they say, blood will have blood.
> Stones have been known to move and trees to speak.
> Augurs and understood relations have
> By magot-pies, and choughs, and rooks brought forth
> The secret'st man of blood.

He looks for help from this destructive evil, since he now feels himself kin to it. He turns again to the witches, who have power to make

> ...the treasure
> Of Nature's germen tumble all together,
> Even till destruction sicken.

But he begins to be conscious too of the mere mortality of Nature, and of his share in that:

> I have lived long enough; my way of life
> Is fallen into the sere, the yellow leaf....
> I 'gin to be aweary of the sun,
> And wish the estate of the world were now undone.

The spirit in him flags and flags. Nothing will be left of him soon but Nature's fighting beast, to be slaughtered like a beast. And when the Wood of Birnam moves against him to destroy him, it is almost as if Nature were making him a queer, mocking gesture—her last!

The technical and unique achievement in all this lies, I think, in so spending the poetry and its power upon the creation of that sinister world that within it the man's living spirit does seem at last to shrivel to a cipher and to become

> ...a tale
> Told by an idiot, full of sound and fury,
> Signifying nothing.

He, too, is dead before he dies.

Now, for pure contrast in purpose and method, turn for a moment to *Antony and Cleopatra*; and see how she creates herself, vibrant with life, in the verse and its music:

> Nay, pray you, seek no colour for your going,
> But bid farewell, and go. When you, sued staying,
> Then was the time for words. No going then!
> Eternity was in our lips and eyes,
> Bliss in our brows' bent; none our parts so poor
> But was a race of heaven....

And how Antony comes to his full height in the very moment of his fall:

> Unarm Eros, the long day's task is done,
> And we must sleep....
> Off, pluck off!
> The seven-fold shield of Ajax cannot keep
> The battery from my heart. O, cleave my sides!
> Heart, once be stronger than thy continent,
> Crack thy frail case....

I will o'ertake thee, Cleopatra, and
Weep for my pardon....
Eros!—I come, my Queen—Eros!—Stay for me:
Where souls do couch on flowers, we'll hand in hand,
And with our sprightly port make the ghosts gaze:
Dido and her Æneas shall want troops,
And all the haunt be ours.

FIRESIDE *VERSUS* THEATRE

If Shakespeare, as I have contended, not only wrote but thought and felt dramatically, and has given us not merely plays in poetic form but something that is fundamentally and essentially poetic drama, it should follow that only in the theatre, and perhaps only in such a theatre as this for which he wrote them, will they be fully alive. But here is a vexed question, and an array of his greatest critics and truest lovers—those, at least, best able to express their love: it is not always quite the same thing!—refuse assent to its logic. The refusal is not so categorical as it used to be. Research and experiment have shown that the Elizabethan stage was not such a ramshackle contrivance after all; it gave birth, we now admit, to a craft and art of its own. But Shakespeare's art at its greatest—this is the plea—so utterly transcends the material circumstances of its creation that these now can be, and had better be, neglected altogether, and the essential drama somehow isolated in its purity.[1]

[1] The last and not the least cogent statement of this case comes from Mr Logan Pearsall Smith in his wise and witty book *On Reading Shakespeare*, and he challenges an answer.

Perhaps he does wrong in his summary to quote Carlyle's famous lament that, writing for the Globe theatre, Shakespeare's '...great soul had to crush itself, as best it could, into that and no other mould'. For this is really mere rhetoric. All art has to crush itself into some mould or other. Dante's great soul was crushed into the *terza rima* and Michel Angelo's into the ceiling of the Sistine Chapel; but at neither statement do we shake a pitying head. Was the dramatic form to which the Globe gave scope so entirely contemptible? This being the very question, better not begin by begging it!

Here, however, is the gist of his case. 'But though the drama was the instrument which drew forth his gifts, his genius gradually outgrew that instrument, and we can best appreciate that genius when we can emancipate it, as by reading we can emancipate it, from the kind of drama in which his contemporaries delighted, and with which he provided them without stint.

'But true drama, in the highest sense of the word, drama which does not rely on

One should not aim for a merely dialectic victory in the matter. How much of the case must be admitted? How much may rest upon too meagre an idea of the possibilities of the stage? How much upon purely personal preferences for the fireside and its solitude?

Clearly we cannot blame the art of the theatre for bad performances; for maltreated text, misguided staging, or unbridled egotism in the actor. These are corrigible things. We must try and envisage the best performance possible; dogmatise only upon that. Not, however, an ideal performance; this will never be possible, the very use of the human medium forbids it. With much to compensate, the theatre must always be in a sense the most imperfect of the arts.

The ideal, the omnipercipient reader; he, in the course of nature, is not to be looked for either. Strange as it may seem, the dramatist himself will often find a performance of his play bringing excellent things to life that he did not know were there.

But envisage the best possible reader too, and his task. He must, so to speak, perform the whole play in his imagination; as he reads each effect must come home to him; the succession and contrast of scenes, the harmony and clash of the music of the dialogue, the action implied, the mere physical opposition of characters, or the silent figure standing aloof—for that also can be eloquent. Not an easy business even with the simplest play;

histrionic effects, on the weaving and unweaving of plots, and hardly, except in a formal sense, on action, but rather in the presentation of characters and the dramatic clashes between them, or in the conflict of tragic forces in great souls leading to terrible conclusions—it is in this kind of drama that Shakespeare's highest achievement consists. And this can be best appreciated by reading Shakespeare's plays for their texture rather than for their structure.'

But here again are many questions begged, not argued. Is there nothing in the practical stagecraft of *Hamlet*, *Macbeth*, *Othello* except what may be stigmatised as 'the kind of drama in which his contemporaries delighted'? How much does the most 'histrionic' of plays, unfit for anything but performance, rely upon the weaving and unweaving of its plot? Very little, it will be found, in comparison with the presenting of character, whether this be predominantly done by dramatist or actors. And can 'the presentation of characters and the dramatic clashes between them' (there is objectivity in the very phrase) ever be as vividly convincing to the reader as to the spectator? Much behind and beyond them will take shape, perhaps; but will the presentation and the clash themselves be as *convincing*? Nor, surely, are texture and structure in the least mutually exclusive terms. Performed or read, there is certainly more texture apparent than structure in *Hamlet*.

and when it comes to the opulent art of an *Antony and Cleopatra* the most expert of us may feel diffident. But, reasonable excellence on both sides being granted, what upon the balance shall we gain from reading that performance cannot give us, and of what will this rob us that solitude and the armchair bring?

There must be no apologising for the intrusion of the actor. Fear him as at times we well may, this 'foolish Greek' and the gifts he brings, he and they are an integral part of every practical playwright's scheme. And however greater a man Shakespeare became, when did he cease to be this? Even *King Lear* was a contemporary success. Perhaps it ought not to have been, but it was. One may own that the personality of the actor, which in itself adds so much to the poor play, will equally be, as such, inadequate to the great one; may even obscure or deform it, unless, having first let it aggrandise him, he will at last exercise the magnanimity of the interpreter and so suppress himself that the essence of the thing interpreted may shine through. This can be done; it is not an impossible ideal. We, for our part, can learn to listen through as well as to the actor. That we habitually do when it is a question of great music, imperfectly because humanly performed; and of those very few experts who can, still fewer seem to be content to sit at home and read the cryptic score. But what we *ask* of an actor is this very humanity, and to this the quality of imperfection properly belongs. Pursue it to a paradox, the more perfect a play's performance the worse it might be, since this would be lacking. He is asked to use his humanity with force and freedom; and the greater the play the more he can give and the more it will absorb. Not to echo the author's voice, nor count himself a mere moving shadow, but to add to the play his positive and objective self—and that he can do so devotedly and unselfishly is no paradox at all.

But just here and in this lies the true difficulty with our solitary firesider. What he really dislikes is not the failings of the actors but their very virtues. A performance of Shakespeare may be bad, but the best would not please him. He resents any interference whatever between him and the Shakespeare of his own private and particular idea. He by no means relishes, to begin with, the assault on his emotions which it is the business of the actors to deliver. Their triumph will be to make him laugh or cry, to 'take him out of himself', to 'carry him away'. He does not care to be one of a crowd, to have to suspend his judgment, take what is given him and yield himself in return. He prefers to go his own pace; to be critical; to exercise taste, savouring what he likes twice or thrice over, questioning or passing by what he does not; and now and then he may float off upon the wings of some notion of his own, which a telling line will have suggested to him, even though 'some necessary question of the play be then to be considered'—Shakespeare's censure of the clown can serve for the dilettante reader too! Only thus, are we to be told, can great dramatic art be appreciated? Its last refined and ethereal beauties, perhaps! But even those beauties will be less beautiful, too insubstantial and vague altogether, unless they have been reached through the means which the art creating them has provided. The art of the drama makes a primary demand upon us: to leave our armchair throne of judgment and descend into the mellay of contradictory passions—which the action of a play is—and submit for the while to be tossed to and fro in it; and far less of literature or art there will seem to be in the experience than of the vulgar emotions of life. It is so; drama's first aim is to subdue us by submitting us emotionally to the give and take, the rough and tumble, of some illusion of life. In great plays the illusion is raised to the highest pitch of emotional intensity, and out of it their spiritual beauty springs. But the way to this in its fullness and significance, and the only way, is through experience of the emotion so conveyed and commonly shared; there is no short cut. With that experience absorbed, by all means let the reader seek his fireside. The mere structure of the play will then mean how much more to him; and its texture be a far finer, richer and more substantial thing! Acting embodies the drama. When the imperfect human embodiment and the immediate emotion are all, a case can be made against the theatre; artistically, and sometimes morally too. But they need not be all, and they never have been when great dramatists were about. Even the theatre is very much what we make it, and the more we ask of the actor the more he will learn to give. Our cultural Puritans no longer seem to fear the theatre; they deny it instead. And that is worse; it is even foolish. For a bodiless drama is a contradiction in terms, and the demand for one pretty poor humanism besides.

SHAKESPEARE THE POET

BY

GEORGE RYLANDS

One of the three books I have with me is Shakespeare's Poems: I never found so many beauties in the Sonnets—they seem to be full of fine things said unintentionally—in the intensity of working out conceits.

Letter of Keats, November 22nd, 1817.

It may perhaps be doubted whether even he did not sometimes give scope to his faculty of expression to the prejudice of a higher poetic duty.

Matthew Arnold, Preface to *Poems*, 1853.

FROM POET TO DRAMATIST

SHAKESPEARE was a poet before he was a dramatist. To say this is not merely to remind ourselves that he composed the narrative version of the Venus and Adonis theme before his dramatic version of the no less popular story of Titus Andronicus. The *Venus and Adonis* belongs to the same date as *Titus* and *I Henry VI* (if these are Shakespeare's, as I believe), and, although there have been fewer to love than to praise the poem, no one would deny that it is in its kind a finished work of art, and the two dramas the essays of an apprentice.

The question is not only how the poet was transformed into the dramatist. Poetic drama, like opera, is a peculiar *genre* commonly composed of warring elements, and one must ask oneself where poetry ends and drama begins. What distinguishes narrative from dramatic blank verse, dramatic speech from rhetoric, lyrical imagery from rhetorical tropes? These questions of vocabulary and figures of speech, of metre, syntax and word order are all-important, for Shakespeare experienced diverse phases and mastered many styles. In his long development there was much that he discarded and much that he acquired. He was never too old a dog to learn new tricks. These problems are presented at the outset, although this chapter does not allow of their solution, so that my angle of approach may be understood. Examples must serve in lieu of argument and definition.

A simple and clear contrast between dramatic poetry and poetic drama is to be found in the suicide speeches of Romeo and Othello. The prototype of lovers is fertile in epithet and profligate of imagery. Night is a palace; the worms are Juliet's chambermaids; death is an ensign-bearer, an amorous monster, a lawyer, an unsavoury guide. Romeo is leisurely. There is a steady rise of pitch. We foresee the end in the beginning. But Othello weaves no fancies. He sums up his character and fortune, and once more a soldier gives his orders. The colour and decoration in his speech owe nothing to the *murex* of Marlowe and Spenser's Tyrian dye. The base Indian, the Arabian trees, the turbaned Turk revive the peculiar glamour that invests the Moor. We see Othello again as we saw him at his command, 'Put up your bright swords'. And the flash of his dagger takes us completely by surprise.

The first soliloquy of Hamlet is, I will make bold to say, the first piece of essentially dramatic verse in Shakespeare. Before that we can find realism modifying and moulding the verse form, in Juliet's nurse for example; in the great emotional speeches we can find rhetoric or poetry; the poetry of Richard II, Romeo and Titania; the rhetoric of Richard III, Constance, Henry IV and Mark Antony. By a rhetorical speech I mean one in which either the dramatist himself or a particular character is more concerned with working upon the emotions of the audience than with expressing and communicating his own experience. There are anticipations in Brutus and at moments in the earlier heroines, especially Viola, but it is in the soliloquies of the Prince of Denmark that rhetoric is first completely transformed into poetic drama. Dramatic effect depends much upon the emotional pitch. A poem frequently opens at a pitch above the normal by means of a command, a wish, an invocation or a cry, whether it be 'Blow, blow, thou winter wind', or 'Come unto these yellow sands', 'Behold her single in the field', or 'What can ail thee, knight at arms?' And thus it is with Hamlet's, 'That it should come to this...Heaven and earth...Must I remember?...A little month!...But break my heart!' And again, 'What's Hecuba to him?...Am I a coward?...Bloody bawdy villain!' or, 'Have you eyes?...What devil was't?... O shame, where is thy blush?' This is the direct expression of emotion, capable of mounting to an even higher pitch in *King Lear*, where it can be best appreciated by reading aloud Act II, Sc. iv with its reiterated, 'Who stocked my servant?' and, 'Return with her?' The cross-fusillade of Goneril and Regan culminates in Regan's question, 'What need one?' and the answering cry, 'Oh reason not the need!' That is the climax. The method and manner of Hamlet's soliloquies have been expanded and distributed into dramatic dialogue. The last scene of *Othello* shows an intermediate stage. We have travelled far from the denunciations of a Margaret or Constance, from Clarence's dream and the railings of Lucrece. If we seek for anything of quite the same dramatic value before 1599 we shall not find it in verse but in a prose speech; in Shylock's 'Hath not a Jew eyes...?' It is not until the tragedies that the verse, the syntax, the imagery do their part in the presentation of character and in creating a particular dramatic atmosphere. Matter and style 'interinanimate' and flow into one another.

I am suggesting that poetic drama aims at producing a series of situations or moments: these moments result in emotional expression which is more akin to a lyrical poem than to a speech in a novel. Hamlet's 'O what a rogue and peasant slave am I' is more comparable to Donne's 'For God's sake hold your tongue and let me love'; 'To be or not to be', more comparable to 'Break, break, break' than to a soliloquy in Jane Austen or an analysis in Henry James. Hence the utterances of the protagonists of poetic drama will not bear the same kind of psychological investigation and speculation as those of the novelist or of an acquaintance in real life.

The development is the result of metrical innovation and freer grammatical usage. Clauses are shorter, pauses are stronger, transitions more abrupt; commands, questions and interjections abound. The transparent blank verse line of Marlowe has been cracked and starred; it is soon to be shivered into fragments. Every actor and producer knows, or should know, how much these things contribute towards vigour and variety of dramatic effect. The development in the use of imagery is a more complicated affair and deserves closer attention.

In a general survey of Shakespeare's style we might say that he passed through three stages. In the first he is primarily a poet and an Elizabethan poet at that, indebted to Spenser, Marlowe and Lyly. To this period belong the poems, almost all the sonnets, and three very successful plays, a comedy, a history and a tragedy, all of which are as much poems as they are plays. He then undergoes a transitional phase, the second phase common to most great writers, where he learns to select, to restrain, to omit; in a word, the art to blot. He largely abandons verse in favour of prose, for some of his characters demand the new medium, and Marlowe's mighty line proved facile in imitation. The style of the verse, where we have it, is not far removed from that of prose; in the trial scene of *The Merchant of Venice*, for example, neutral, fluent as Heywood, 'well-languaged' as that of Daniel, in conformity with the Wordsworthian ideal. In *Julius Caesar* there is more volume, more emphasis, more organic strength. But it is Roman simplicity. And then a change! In the tragic period Shakespeare is most himself in metre and in diction, but we might still call him a Jacobean although not an Elizabethan poet; his style has affinities with that of Webster and even Sir Thomas Browne. Remarkable in this period are his experiments in vocabulary and his peculiar use of metaphor, his combinations of concrete and abstract, of sensual and intellectual, which link him with that great rebel against Elizabethanism, John Donne. And here the metaphors and imagery are subservient to the main design, now to the atmosphere of the whole and now to the characterisation. Finally in the romances or tragi-comedies we detect signs of a reaction to Elizabethanism; a resurrection of the imagery and mythological allusion of

Spenser, Marlowe and Lyly. But in *Antony and Cleopatra*, *Cymbeline* and *The Winter's Tale*, Shakespeare seems to gather in all the harvest of his poetic and dramatic experience, to hark back and to adventure farther. He has mastered style, but style has become an exacting and imperious mistress. Yet in *The Tempest* she ceases for a moment to be so whimsical, provocative and outrageous. We have the colloquial simplicity of

> They'll take suggestion as a cat laps milk,

or the direct expression of character or situation in

> You taught me language; and my profit on't
> Is, I know how to curse,

or

> I am your wife if you will marry me,
> If not, I'll die your maid; to be your fellow
> You may deny me, but I'll be your servant
> Whether you will or no.

Yet even in *The Tempest* there are such idiomatic things as

> The fringéd curtains of thine eye advance,

or 'earthy and abhorred commands', 'pioned and twilled brims', and 'dark backward and abysm of time', which may be compared with 'the Areopagy and dark tribunal of our hearts' in Sir Thomas Browne. Prospero's great speech 'Ye elves of hills...' looks back in tone and *tempo* to Titania's 'These are the forgeries of jealousy...'.

THE POETIC APPRENTICE

Poets learn from poets. Ben Jonson approves the doctrine of the Ancients that *Imitatio* is the third requisite in a poet: 'Not as a creature that swallows what it takes in, crude, raw and undigested: but that feeds with an appetite and hath a stomach to concoct, divide and turn all into nourishment'. Thus Spenser concocted Chaucer, thus Milton turned Spenser into nourishment. Shakespeare, if we change the metaphor of digestion for one of education, put his head and heart to that Elizabethan school which begins with Wyatt and Surrey and includes Spenser,

Sidney, the singers and sonneteers, the school from which the rebellious Donne played truant. The copy-books of that school were the sonnets of Petrarch, the *Metamorphoses* of Ovid, the odes and lyrics of Ronsard and du Bellay, Vergil's *Fourth Eclogue*, Baptista Mantuanus, *Daphnis and Chloe*, Lyly's *Euphues*. These names are representative; they comprehend much. *The Pléiade*, for example, drew upon the Greek Anthology and the Anacreon. Vergil and Longus are the fathers of a varied and vigorous pastoral tradition. The sophisticated and ingenious Lyly puts mediaeval conventions to new uses and argues his chivalrous and sentimental theme with the aid of unnatural illustrations from Pliny's *Natural History*. Directly and indirectly these diverse influences worked upon the youthful Shakespeare. He was at first an Elizabethan poet and it is of this stuff that Elizabethan poetry was made. In the two following passages there is hardly a distinguishing mark. Both are Elizabethan:

At last the golden Oriental gate
Of greatest heaven gan to open fair,
And Phoebus fresh as bridegroom to his mate
Came dancing forth shaking his dewy hair.

See how the morning opes her golden gates,
And takes her farewell of the glorious sun.
How well resembles it the prime of youth
Trimmed like a younker prancing to his love.

The first is Spenser, the second the young Shakespeare; and although Shakespeare is a little freer in movement and cannot resist transforming Phoebus Apollo into an Elizabethan gallant, the idiom is the same. Similarly we find in Spenser, both in *The Shepheards Calender* and elsewhere, the use of analogy and imagery drawn from the seasons which is so familiar in Shakespeare's *Sonnets*. Time with his sickle, summer's rose, the canker in the bud, the sneaping frost, the sere and yellow leaf, all these are frequent in Spenser and his school (the sonnets of Samuel Daniel, for instance) as they are in Shakespeare. Moreover they provide many parallels between Shakespeare's poems and sonnets and Shakespeare's early plays; the *Two Gentlemen of Verona*,

Love's Labour's Lost and *Romeo and Juliet* in particular. The argument of the *Venus and Adonis*—

> Seeds spring from seeds, and beauty breedeth beauty:
> Thou wast begot: to get it is thy duty—

is the argument both of the first seventeen sonnets and of the third book of *The Faerie Queene*. It is the theme which Spenser's disciple was to celebrate for the last time in the mouth of Comus. On the other hand the influence of Marlowe is to be detected in *Titus Andronicus* and the early history plays, and even in *The Merchant of Venice* we catch the echo of the Zenocrate refrain in a speech of the Prince of Morocco. A poet's Juvenilia (like first novels) are usually to be remarked by his inability to leave anything out. To compare *The Book of the Duchess* with *The Nun's Priest's Tale*, *Comus* with *Paradise Regained*, *Endymion* with the *Odes* is to follow an artist in what Walter Pater believed to be the principle of art, 'the removal of surplusage'. Young writers put all their goods in the shop window. They coin and compound words. They accumulate images for their own sake. Shakespeare is no exception. In his early work there is considerable padding, and he follows Spenser and Sidney (who followed *The Pléiade*) in his employment of the compound epithet. Water-standing eye, earnest-gaping sight, dead-killing news, show this practice at its weakest. Coleridge tells us that in the later editions of his own Juvenilia he pruned the double epithets with no sparing hand and he remarks: 'If a writer, every time a compounded word suggests itself to him, would seek for some other mode of expressing the same sense, the chances are always greatly in favour of his finding a better word'. Shakespeare did discover another mode, an idiomatic one. The compound epithet and the elementary arrangement of, say,

> A joyful mother of two goodly sons

give way to more hardly sought and carefully paired adjectives; scambling and unquiet time, fatal and neglected English, creeping murmur and the poring dark, puff'd and reckless libertine, thin and wholesome blood. Above all they give way to the qualifying substantival phrase where nouns are doing the work of epithets; the morn and liquid dew of youth; the slings and arrows of outrageous fortune; the quick forge and working house of thought; the catastrophe and heel of pastime; the staggers and the careless lapse of youth and ignorance; husks and formless ruin of oblivion. This is a very Shakespearian idiom which is most to be remarked in the *Hamlet* period. Later the examples are more rare and more elaborate.

ELIZABETHAN IMAGERY AND CONCEIT. SHAKESPEARE'S DEVELOPMENT AND INDIVIDUAL PRACTICE

The use of imagery in Shakespeare's first period is now to be considered, and in this connexion it will be convenient to speak of mythological allusion. Two aspects must be kept in mind, the Elizabethan aspect and the poetic aspect. Elizabethan imagery is emblematic. Marlowe, Spenser and Lyly, the singers and sonneteers, all have a stock-in-trade of names and images which are emblems of the ideal. The rose is the emblem of youth, the lily of purity; or alternatively Diana of purity, Helen of beauty and youth. I take the simplest examples. Juno is the emblem of majesty, Pallas Athene of wit, Mercury of swiftness, Hercules of strength, Phaethon of audacity and pride. Marlowe's Zenocrate is lovelier than the love of Jove, comparable with Latona's daughter bent to arms or

> Flora in her morning's pride
> Shaking her silver tresses in the air.

The hair of an Elizabethan mistress is as golden wire; the lily and the rose war in her cheeks; her veins are violet; her teeth are pearl; her lips are cherries charming men to bite; she is white as snow, as ivory, as alabaster, as swan's down. The poets are content to elaborate endless variations upon the same theme. Shakespeare describes the hand-clasp of Venus and Adonis,

> A lily prison'd in a gaol of snow,
> Or ivory in an alabaster band,
> So white a friend engirts so white a foe.

This beauteous combat, wilful and unwilling,
Show'd like two silver doves that sit a-billing.

The two swans of Spenser's *Prothalamion* come softly swimming:

The snow which doth the top of Pindus strew
Did never whiter shew;
Nor Jove himself when he a swan would be
For love of Leda whiter did appear;
Yet Leda was, they say, as white as he,
Yet not so white as these nor nothing near
So purely white they were.

And even the rugged Ben will write more curiously:

Have you seen but a bright lily grow,
  Before rude hands have touch'd it?
Have you mark'd but the fall of the snow,
  Before the soil hath smutch'd it?
Have you felt the wool of beaver,
  Or swan's down ever?
Or have smelt o' the bud o' the brier,
  Or the nard in the fire?
Or have tasted the bag of the bee?
O so white, O so soft, O so sweet is she!

In the *Lucrece*, a 'graver labour' than the *Venus and Adonis*, in which Spenserian lyricism is ousted by rhetoric, this emblematic imagery of flowers and precious stones is still notable. The heraldry of Beauty's red and Virtue's white is in the heroine's face, a silent war of lilies and of roses. Fear makes her colour rise

First red as Roses that on lawn we lay,
Then white as lawn, the Roses took away.

The perfect white of her hand shows like an April daisy on the grass. Her eyes like marigolds have sheathed their light. Her breasts are ivory globes circled with blue. Lucrece and her weeping maid are pretty creatures

Like ivory conduits coral cisterns filling.

And in *A Lover's Complaint* the properties of the diamond, the ruby, the emerald and the pearl are defined.

In the *Sonnets* this Elizabethanism begins to disappear in favour of images drawn from actual experience. Shakespeare reacted against the convention and against the mythological name, although we find even in *Hamlet*—the Prince had a taste for the university wits—

> Hyperion's curls, the front of Jove himself,
> An eye like Mars to threaten and command,
> A station like the herald Mercury
> New lighted on a heaven-kissing hill.

Whether it was the poet or the dramatist or the lover who reacted one cannot say. Queen Elizabeth had made red hair the fashion and we get glimpses of a dark lady in the early plays:

> A wightly wanton with a velvet brow,
> With two pitch balls stuck in her face for eyes.

And there is the sonnet:

> My mistress' eyes are nothing like the sun,
> Coral is far more red than her lips red,
> If snow be white, why then her breasts are dun;
> If hairs be wires, black wires grow on her head;
> I have seen roses damaskt red and white,
> But no such roses see I in her cheeks....

Be that as it may, he gradually discarded mythological allusion and the stock-in-trade of Elizabethan imagery. In *A Midsummer Night's Dream* he is undoubtedly chaffing the Elizabethan lover in a speech of Demetrius. Faulconbridge in *King John* and Hotspur in *I Henry IV* follow suit. Mercutio strikes the same note with the lovesick Romeo, and Benedick laughs at mythology and himself. The new attitude finds clearest expression on the lips of Rosalind:

> Troilus had his brains dashed out with a Grecian club; yet he did what he could to die before and he is one of the patterns of love. Leander, he would have lived many a fair year, though Hero had turned nun, if it had not been for a hot summer night; for good youth he went but forth to wash himself in the Hellespont and being taken with the cramp was drowned; and the foolish coroners of that age found it was Hero of Sestos. But these are all lies; men have died from time to time and worms have eaten them, but not for love.

Is it not conceivable in the light of this that Shakespeare intends the opening of that epilogue of music and moonlight, which mitigates the bitter taste of Shylock's downfall, to be, beautiful though it is and his most careful variation on the old mythological theme, a deliberate presentation of sentimental love; just as lovesickness is treated with affectionate irony in *Twelfth Night*? In the tragedies the mythology has its natural place when the setting is Roman, and it is effectively employed in *King Lear*, to which Shakespeare intentionally gave a pagan and primitive atmosphere. Lear, himself a Titan, swears by the sacred radiance of the sun, by Jupiter and Apollo, by the mysteries of Hecate and the night. Mythology is no longer an ornament. Shakespeare is inspired by the very spirit in which the pagan gods were first conceived. The bluff Kent, however, an elder Faulconbridge or Hotspur, mimics court speech when he swears to Cornwall 'by the wreath of radiant fire on flickering Phoebus' front', and court affectation is severely satirised in the person of the upstart Oswald.

Shakespeare was to make ample amends. He returns to the old Elizabethan idiom, to the currency and coinage in which Spenser and his fellows had trafficked. Coriolanus speaks of Valeria as

Chaste as the icicle
That's curded by the frost from purest snow
And hangs on Dian's temple.

Iachimo whispers by the bed of Imogen

Cytherea!
How bravely thou becom'st thy bed, fresh lily,
And whiter than the sheets.

Posthumus speaks of her 'as Dian had hot dreams and she alone were cold'. The beauties of Italy are described as

For feature laming
The shrine of Venus or straight-pight Minerva,
Postures beyond brief nature.

Marina is 'in pace another Juno'; Perdita 'no shepherdess but Flora peering in April's front'. She speaks of Proserpina, of

Violets dim
But sweeter than the lids of Juno's eyes
Or Cytherea's breath; pale primroses
That die unmarried ere they can behold
Bright Phoebus in his strength.

It is a return to the court poetry of Gloriana, in a sense a recantation. But the artifices of the old mellifluous Ovidian school have become charged with emotional power.

So much then for one of the fashions of Elizabethan diction, the use of images as emblems of the ideal. I turn now to the more extended use of images and to the Elizabethan conceit. A poet such as Shakespeare or Keats, who thinks in images, learns to employ them not for their own sake but as contributing to the harmony of the whole; he learns to control and order and direct them; they must be his servants and not his masters. When Keats writes

> The morn was clouded but no shower fell,
> Though in her lids hung the sweet tears of May,

we see the translation of the thought into poetic idiom take place before our eyes; just as Dr Johnson said of *The Rehearsal*, 'It has not wit enough to keep it sweet' and then dissatisfied, translating into his own idiom, 'It has not vitality enough to preserve it from putrefaction'. Similarly Shakespeare gives us his matter in a single line,

> Small show of man was yet upon his chin,

and then proceeds at leisure to translate and embellish:

> His phoenix down began but to appear
> Like unshorn velvet on his termless skin,
> Whose bare out-bragg'd the web it seem'd to wear:
> Yet show'd his visage by that cost more dear;
> And nice affections wavering stood in doubt
> If best were as it was, or best without.

This passion for either spinning out an image or accumulating diverse images to illustrate a single idea is very dominant in Shakespeare's early work. It is a dangerous passion, for as often as not it dissipates instead of concentrating the emotion. In the narrative poems it is not so fatal. Crabb Robinson once observed acutely, 'To object to the poet a want of progress is as absurd as to object to the dancer that he does not get on. In both alike the object is to give delight by not getting on'. But it mars the Hubert and Arthur scene in *King John* when the boy says

> There is no malice in this burning coal;
> The breath of heaven has blown his spirit out
> And strew'd repentant ashes on his head.

And he does not rest there. It mars some important passages in *Romeo and Juliet*, passages that can only be allowed as an ephemeral convention, for example the line,

> What says
> My concealed lady to my cancelled love?

Matthew Arnold complains of Shakespeare's irritability of fancy and over-curiousness of expression as the preponderating qualities of which all modern poetry has felt the influence, in which composition is sacrificed to detail. And Dr Johnson closes a magnificent indictment with the sentence: 'A quibble was to him the fatal Cleopatra for which he lost the world and was content to lose it'. The passion was, however, a youthful one. Conceit and simile give way to metaphor. Ornament ceases to be calligraphic, to be ornament for ornament's sake: it becomes functional and organic. For example, the sonnet

> That time of year thou may'st in me behold
> When yellow leaves, or none, or few, do hang
> Upon those boughs which shake against the cold

becomes dramatically

> My way of life
> Is fallen into the sere, the yellow leaf,

and the 'Out, out, brief candle' of the same speaker looks back to Gaunt's

> My oil-dried lamp and time-bewasted light
> Shall be extinct with age and endless night,
> My inch of taper shall be burnt and done.

Guizot's statement, which Arnold seems to approve, that Shakespeare tried all styles except simplicity, is utterly discredited by certain carefully prepared moments in the tragedies; moments of which Arnold himself elsewhere realised the secret: 'Poetry gets the privilege of being loosed at its best moments into that perfectly simple limpid style which is the supreme style of all, but the simplicity of which is still not the simplicity of prose'. It is the style of

Do not laugh at me;
For as I am a man, I think this lady
To be my child, Cordelia.
And so I am, I am.

In his last period Shakespeare's style is again complicated in the extreme, but the complication arises from the flexibility and resolution of the metre, the unexpected vocabulary, the rapidity of the thought and the audacity of the syntax. For example,

Sluttery to such neat excellence oppos'd
Should make desire vomit emptiness,
Not so allur'd to feed,

or

Was this taken
By any understanding pate but thine?
For thy conceit is soaking; will draw in
More than the common blocks: not noted, is't,
But of the finer natures? By some severals
Of headpiece extraordinary? lower messes
Perchance are to this business purblind? say.

Or again,

O Queen Emilia,
Fresher than May, sweeter
Than her gold buttons on the boughs, or all
Th'enamell'd knacks o' the mead or garden! Yea,
We challenge too the bank of any nymph,
That makes the stream seem flowers; thou, O jewel
O' the wood, o' the world, hast likewise blessed a place
With thy sole presence! In thy rumination
That I, poor man, might eftsoons come between,
And chop on some cold thought!

These show something more than decoration and accumulation. The over-curiousness of the *Venus and Adonis* is akin to the over-curiousness of Keats and Tennyson; the irritability of fancy in *The Winter's Tale* has affinities with that of Donne; *The Tempest*, as has been indicated, is exceptional in the last period. The style of that little-appreciated Elizabethan masterpiece *A Lover's*

Complaint shows an advance on the lyrical *Venus and Adonis* and the rhetorical *Lucrece*. As in the *Sonnets* the intelligence has more play and the climax, although it at once diverges into Elizabethanism, surpasses any effect in the other two narrative poems:

> O father, what a hell of witchcraft lies
> In the small orb of one particular tear!

It surpasses Donne's *Witchcraft by a Picture.*

THE POEMS. INFLUENCE OF LYLY

We have not done with Shakespeare's imagery. We must distinguish between two processes of the poetic imagination; a fine but profound distinction which earlier criticism has attempted to define as the difference between the fancy and the imagination. This means something more than a difference of intensity; it involves a difference of purpose. The difference between the conceits of the poems or early plays and the metaphors of the mature style is comparable with that between the conceits of Cowley and the conceits of Donne, or between the similes of *Sohrab and Rustum* and the similes of *Paradise Lost*; the difference is between something employed for its own sake and something employed as a means to an end. There is such a thing as a logic of imagery. Shelley's *Music when soft voices die* is a logical poem, although the logic is not that of prose and the reasoning is intuitive. Coleridge is the first man to explore the processes of the imagination, and it is interesting here that one of his most illuminating passages arises from a consideration of the *Venus and Adonis*:

> It has been before observed that images however beautiful, though faithfully copied from nature and as accurately represented in words, do not of themselves characterise a poet. They become proofs of original genius only as far as they are modified by a predominant passion or by associated thoughts or images awakened by that passion; or when they have the effect of reducing multitude to unity or succession to an instant, or lastly when a human and intellectual life is transferred to them from the poet's own spirit.

Coleridge goes on to remark that it is this particular excellence in which Shakespeare even in his earliest and in his latest work transcends all other poets. As a generalisation this will be allowed. And it is true that in the *Venus and Adonis* Shakespeare, by the predominant melody and consistency of style, by the perfect sweetness of versification and the sense of musical delight on which Coleridge insists, succeeds in unifying the copious imagery, but the imagery has the effect of dissipating rather than intensifying the emotion. For those who find the theme distasteful, this may be an advantage. It strikes different readers very differently. The Elizabethans, if we are to credit Harebrain in *A Mad World My Masters*, paired it with *Hero and Leander*; 'two luscious marrowbone pies for a young married wife'; while Hazlitt found the *Venus* and *Lucrece* as cold and glittering as ice-houses.

The *Venus and Adonis* is a masterpiece of decoration. Of the nature of the decoration something has already been said. The abundant imagery, often conventional and euphuistic, but as often actual and vivid, is unified by the regularity of the versification and the studied conduct of vowels and consonants. The content is adequate to the style and sufficiently varied; there is description and some action; disquisitions on the 'idle overhandled theme' of 'Gather ye Rosebuds while ye may'; the supplication of Death; the distinction drawn between love and lust; and the concluding prophecy on the nature of human love thereafter. The poem has form. Indeed, it is nearer to Milton's *Ode on the Nativity* than to the early work of Keats. The rural images of horse and hawk and hound, of sky and field, are particularly attractive to those who like to fancy Shakespeare fresh from Stratford with the poem in his pocket: the dive-dapper peering through the wave, the tender horns of the snail, the fisher who spares the small fry, the hunted hare. Such images as these are in the plays rarer than one would expect, even though the subject-matter does not often suggest them, and they are here happily combined with more bookish instances and imitations, such as the birds deceived with painted grapes or the protracted description of the boar, indebted to Ovid. The personification of Jealousy as a sour unwelcome guest and later as a sentinel giving a false alarm, as an informer, a spy, a carry-tale, is an early example of the Shakespearian method to be examined later.

But in the *Venus and Adonis* there is no drama and no characterisation. We find signs of these in the less popular *Lucrece*. Here Shakespeare strives to realise and analyse the sensations of the two protagonists—the conflict in Tarquin which foreshadows that of Brutus and Macbeth. When Tarquin prays to the heavens to countenance his sin and reflects

> The powers to whom I pray abhor this fact,
> How can they then assist me in the act?

one looks forward to Claudius

> O what form of prayer
> Can serve my turn?

The style of the *Lucrece* is burdened with saws, fables and unnatural history; all the euphuism of the earlier history plays and *Romeo and Juliet*. More interesting are the great rhetorical *tirades* on Time, Death and Opportunity which prepare the way for some of the full-length soliloquies of King Henry VI and Richard II and the railings of Constance. Time is a favourite Shakespearian theme. Lucrece's magnificent amplification on the activities of the 'ceaseless lackey to Eternity' anticipates many sonnets similar in tone on the bloody tyrant, the suborned Informer; and the same theme inspires the central passage in *Troilus and Cressida*. The consciousness of death characterises the Middle Ages, the sense of time is the dominating note of the Renaissance.

Elizabethan imagery owes a vast debt to euphuism. And in Lyly we find imagery of two kinds. Sometimes the idea is only valuable for the images it suggests. Sometimes the images are intended to argue the idea. Thus, as an example of poetic logic we might take the words of Venus:

> Torches are made to light, jewels to wear,
> Dainties to taste, fresh beauty for the use,
> Herbs for their smell and sappy plants to bear,
> Things growing to themselves are growth's abuse.

Seeds spring from seeds, and beauty breedeth beauty:
Thou wast begot: to get it is thy duty,

or of Lucrece:

Why should the worm intrude the maiden bud?
Or hateful cuckoos hatch in sparrows' nests?
Or toads infect fair founts with venom mud?
Or tyrant folly lurk in gentle breasts?

and in the *Sonnets*:

No more be grieved at that which thou hast done.
Roses have thorns and silver fountains mud;
Clouds and eclipses stain both sun and moon
And loathsome canker lives in sweetest bud.

This is the method of Lyly's madness:

For as the Bee that gathereth Honny out of the weede, when she espyeth the faire flower flyeth to the sweetest: or as the kynde spanyell though he hunt after Byrdes, yet forsakes them to retryue the Partridge, or as we commonly feede on beefe hungerly at the first, yet seing the Quayle more dayntie, chaunge our dyet: So I, although I loued *Philautus* for his good properties, yet seeing *Euphues* to excel him, I ought by Nature to lyke him better.

We may find *Euphues* merely quaint but it left its mark on every Elizabethan, and on Shakespeare as much as any, although he reacted against it, as he reacted against Marlowe's versification. And Lyly's sequences of images are a crude form of what I have called 'poetic logic' which at its best is illustrated by Shelley's lyric already named or his *Love's Philosophy* or

When the lamp is shatter'd,
  The light in the dust lies dead;
When the cloud is scatter'd,
  The rainbow's glory is shed;
  When the lute is broken,
Sweet tones are remember'd not;
  When the lips have spoken,
Loved accents are soon forgot.

FROM CONCEIT TO METAPHOR. SHAKESPEARIAN STRENGTH ISSUES FROM ELIZABETHAN SWEETNESS

Now Shakespeare himself developed from the more elementary sequences of images of his Elizabethan period a far more subtle and profound use of imagery which is very near to that of the great poets of the romantic revival and not unlike the finest conceits of the metaphysicals. From the sweetness of his euphuisms came forth the strength of his metaphors. And metaphor, Aristotle tells us, is the poet's greatest gift, for it implies an eye for resemblances. Such an eye or such a wit Lyly possessed. But Shelley's interpretation of this faculty is more profound; 'Metaphorical language marks the before unapprehended relations of things'; which may fairly be connected with Johnson's definition of wit as 'the discovery of occult resemblances in things apparently unlike'. In Donne there is a fusion of scholastic, chemical, physiological, astronomical, geographical, legal and sensuous images. In him they are modified by a predominant passion. His intellect reduced multitude to unity. Shakespeare drew his illustrations from life and not from learning, but the variety of his experience and the nimbleness of his brain enabled him to achieve a similar unity. Shakespeare thinks of falsity in friendship; it suggests flattery; flattery suggests a fawning dog begging for sweetmeats, and then his mind makes an unaccountable leap—or were Elizabethan candies formed to represent flowers?—from the dinner table to a peeled and stripped forest tree:

> The hearts
> That spaniel'd me at heels, to whom I gave
> Their wishes, do discandy, melt their sweets
> On blossoming Caesar; and this pine is bark'd
> That overtopped them all.

But more important than the complexity and rapidity of the associations, the convolutions and evolutions of style in such a play as *Macbeth*, are those moments where Shakespeare 'marks the before unapprehended relations of things'; where, that is to say, it is not the image, it is not the idea: it is the scarcely realised relation between the image and the idea which is intended. That is the secret of the old ballad snatch:

> Western wind, when will thou blow,
> The small rain down can rain!
> Christ, if my love were in my arms
> And I in my bed again!

W. B. Yeats writes of two lines of Burns:

> The wan moon is setting ayont the white wave
> And Time is setting with me, O!

Take from them the whiteness of the moon, the wave, whose relation to the setting of time is too subtle for the intellect, and you take from them their beauty. But when all are together, moon and wave and whiteness and the last melancholy cry, they evoke an emotion which can be evoked by no other arrangement of colours and sounds and forms. We may call this metaphorical writing, but it is better to call it symbolical writing.

In Shakespeare we find such symbolical writing. The lines of Burns or those of Donne to his mistress

> O more than Moone,
> Draw not up seas to drowne me in thy spheare

may be compared with the effect of Othello's words when Emilia breaks into the bedchamber with news of foul murders done:

> It is the very error of the moon;
> She comes more near the earth than she was wont
> And makes men mad,

and Cleopatra's words as Antony dies:

> O wither'd is the garland of the war,
> The soldier's pole is fall'n; young boys and girls
> Are level now with men; the odds is gone,
> And there is nothing left remarkable
> Beneath the visiting moon.

Or again, the still small voice of Iras as Cleopatra whispers to Charmian

> Finish, good lady; the bright day is done,
> And we are for the dark.

This is more than metaphorical, it is symbolical writing.

THE *SONNETS*

The *Sonnets* have this in common with the *Venus and Adonis*, that artificial and natural imagery are felicitously combined, but actual imagery predominates and is more diverse than in the poem. It is drawn from husbandry, medicine, navigation; from the court, from music and painting, from usury and law; from the stage, military life, astronomy and alchemy. Analogies from the seasons are very frequent, and these are more realistically expressed than in the poetry of Spenser and his school. Euphuism also is becoming naturalised. The diversity of imagery is only to be paralleled in Donne, and Dr Johnson's objection to the use of technical words in poetry, which is disproved by most Elizabethan poets, is completely exploded by such a sonnet as Shakespeare's fourth. It is of Donne that we think when we seek for Shakespeare's peer as a love-poet. These two poets before all others have expressed the many different shades of feeling, the varied and complex experiences and attitudes of the lover; the idealism and realism, the *Odi et Amo*, the constancy and jealousy, the daydreams and disillusion, the selfless dedication and the torments of lust. In the *Sonnets* there are direct statements, 'moral ideas', in Arnold's words, such as

> Love is not love
> Which alters when it alteration finds,

or

> They that have power to hurt, and will do none,
> They do not do the thing they most do show,

or

> till action, lust
> Is perjur'd, murd'rous, bloody, full of blame.

In the plays general truths abound. In the *Sonnets* the truths are more frequently particular and extremely personal in expression, the fruit of individual experience. But, as Gibbon remarked, a love-tale is much the same in Babylon and Putney, and Shakespeare's experiences and intense feelings find an echo in the heart. We read them with all the pleasure of recognition. Our whole being is reorganised. What was faint, confused and half-realised becomes precise, acute, ordered, permanent. Our five senses, and our five wits, our own actions and sufferings approve the evidence, and in the *Sonnets* a personality is revealed as real and as admirable as in the *Letters* of Keats. For the style also they can be read innumerable times and never without fresh shocks of surprise. The imagery is as rich as in the narrative poems and richer; but style and content are no longer separable. The metaphors are no longer decorative; like the conceits of Donne, they are the poem. Only in *A Lover's Complaint* is there something of the same maturity and intelligence. And besides a use of metaphor now concentrated, now extended, which is so happy that we seem to see the English tongue as we know it forming and evolving itself before our eyes, there is a *curiosa felicitas* in single words and short phrases; as, for example, 'Siren tears', 'adder's sense', 'ambush of young days', 'tender inward of the hand', 'Nature beggar'd of blood', 'affable familiar ghost', 'sin lace itself with his society', 'what freezings have I felt', 'chopp'd with tann'd antiquity', 'I have frequent been with unknown minds'.

The opening sonnets are in a sense exercises on an Elizabethan theme, and throughout the sequence we light from time to time upon a phrase or image which can be paralleled in other Elizabethan sequences, or in Ronsard and du Bellay, whose pockets the sonneteers picked so dexterously. Towards the end of the collection we find sonnets more powerful and more austere than the 'sugred sonnets' referred to by Meres in 1598, sonnets in which imagery is more rare, the expression more intellectual than sensual and the vocabulary, as Beeching indicated, more Latinised. These are to be associated with *Hamlet* and *Troilus and Cressida* rather than with *Romeo and Juliet* and *Love's Labour's Lost*. Sir Philip Sidney alone among the sonneteers is comparable in power of expression and in the value of the experiences communicated; he, like Shakespeare, is at once personal and permanent, and in him there is, although to a less degree, the necessary separation between 'the man who suffers and the mind which creates'.

One word about form. Shakespeare, like his fellows, departs

from the Italian pattern; but behind the three quatrains and the couplet which is variously employed sometimes as climax, sometimes as comment, sometimes as a dying fall, sometimes—it must be confessed—as a lame and impotent conclusion, there may frequently be discerned the double movement, the octave and sestet division of the true Petrarchan form. Shakespeare's experience as a sonneteer had some effect on the versification and paragraphing in the earlier plays. The influence of the form is to be detected in parts of *Love's Labour's Lost*, *The Two Gentlemen of Verona*, and *Romeo and Juliet*.

THE PHOENIX AND THE TURTLE. THE SONGS

Many are the manifestations of the passion of love in the plays and poems of Shakespeare; in man, woman and child; in the young, the middle aged, the senile; in Constance the mother, in Hotspur the soldier, in Isabella the saint; the lovesickness of Orsino, the appetite of Cleopatra, the jealousy of Leontes, the burnt-out desires of Falstaff. But in *The Phoenix and the Turtle* Shakespeare celebrates love of yet another kind, selfless, sexless, 'interinanimating', as Donne puts it—not the marriage of two minds but the union of two souls:

So they loved, as love in twain
Had the essence but in one;
Two distincts, division none,
Number there in love was slain.

Shakespeare's own adventure in the metaphysical style combines at once the quality of a proposition in Euclid and of a piece of music. It is pure, abstract, symbolical and complete.

Shakespeare's songs are so familiar to us that we feel they are individual in style; and their familiarity makes them as difficult to assess as Hamlet's 'To be or not to be'; but they have the peculiarly anonymous tone of all the Elizabethan song-books and are indeed less individual than much of Breton and less full of matter than the songs of Campion which are more definitely poems. They are so written as to give plenty of freedom to the composer and at the same time to be relevant to their contexts and to contribute to the dramatic effect, as Richmond Noble has, perhaps too emphatically, insisted. *Twelfth Night* shows the dramatic use of song at its happiest, with the love-melancholy of 'Come Away, Death', and the ironic setting of 'O Mistress Mine' in a supper party of an old rake and a poor ninny. Both in *The Tempest* and in *Cymbeline* we have a song more thoughtful and mature; a song which is also a poem and can stand alone. The Elizabethan anonymity of Shakespeare's songs is enhanced by his fondness for reviving and echoing traditional ballad snatches and earlier airs, whether it be on the lips of Ophelia or a Fool or (as has been lately shown) in 'It was a Lover and his Lass'.

The secret of his success indeed lies in a fusion of the natural with the artificial; of the traditional English singing of tavern and field and cloister with the delicate artifice and charming affectation of euphuism and the Petrarch-Pléiade school. There is the same fusion in the *Sonnets*; in the *Venus and Adonis* it is not fully achieved. The songs serve as a touchstone of Elizabethan lyric. Shakespeare's note rings truer than that of many of the courtiers, scholars and wits. There is a rustic simpleness, a more natural air. The populous city and the painted chamber dissolve. We breathe

> The smell of Grain, or tedded Grass, or Kine,
> Or Dairie, each rural sight, each rural sound.

And if we miss the passion of 'Follow your Saint', of Bethsabe's song, of Nashe's Dirge, we are more than compensated by a 'native woodnote wild'; by a purity of diction which A. E. Housman holds is matched only in Blake. The Elizabethan lyric Muse had a decided taste for silks and fine array, foreign modes and pastoral *simplesse*:

> My Love in her attire doth show her wit,
>   It doth so well become her:
> For every season she hath dressings fit,
>   For winter, spring, and summer.

We admire the liquefaction of her clothes. Shakespeare was wiser and less sophisticated:

> No beauty she doth miss,
>   When all her robes are on;
> But Beauty's self she is,
>   When all her robes are gone.

CHIEF SECRET OF THE MATURE STYLE

One of Shakespeare's most frequent and successful devices remains to be examined. Coleridge tells us that the imaginative faculty reveals itself in the reconcilement of the general with the concrete, the idea with the image. Mediaeval literature employed personification and allegory to communicate intellectual concepts and states of mind. They thought in pictures: their books were frescoes, illuminated missals and stained glass. And for the Elizabethans the Cardinal Virtues, the Seven Deadly Sins, the Ages of Man, Death and Time were still pictorial figures. Graunde Amoure, False Report, Constrained Abstinence were as the lords and ladies of mediaeval chivalry. The mantle of Mercy is white, of Righteousness red, of Truth a sad green. As in Bunyan the abstract has the interest and vividness of the concrete. The mediaeval practice survives to some extent in Shakespeare; in his 'tickling Commodity' or 'the devil Luxury with his fat rump and potato finger' or, more submerged, in his fond use of the epithet 'envious'. But it is characteristic that Death the skeleton, so familiar in mediaeval art, is found in the history plays but is superseded by an Elizabethan bailiff; 'that fell sergeant death is strict in his arrest'. Personification is an artificial device and Shakespeare's method is more rapid and subtle. It is no longer a question of an abstract word with a capital letter and conventional attributes; the effect is obtained by a qualifying phrase, a verb or epithet. In Shakespeare, desire vomits, concealment feeds, corruption bubbles, fate hides in an auger hole, accident is shackled, description beggared, reason furs gloves, distinction puffs, liberty plucks justice by the nose, ambition shrinks through bad weaving, friendship's milky heart turns in less than two nights, valour preys on reason, impatience becomes a mad dog, injury is pity's gaoler, emulation hath a thousand sons. In the lines: 'And silken dalliance in the wardrobe lies' or 'To lie in cold obstruction and to rot' we have the required reconcilement of the general with the concrete, of the idea with the image.

We can detect in this practice the influence of the Bible. The Old Testament, like Shakespeare, is full of images, metaphors and similes drawn from everyday life, and there are the same combinations of abstract and concrete. In the Bible, health is a faithful ambassador, poverty comes as one that travelleth, iniquity stops her mouth, transgression is sealed up in a bag, truth is fallen in the street, righteousness is a girdle, 'I wash mine hands in innocency', 'wisdom hath mingled her wine and furnished her table'.

We must keep in mind also the terrific influx of Latinisms into the language about 1600 with which every writer was experimenting. In Shakespeare, as in Sir Thomas Browne, we have the Latinism and the native word, often a synonym, paired together, the first with intellectual, the second with physical associations; for example, exsufflicate and blown surmises, exterior and outward, inestimable and unvalued, malignant and turbaned Turk, the voice of occupation and the breath of garlic eaters, the inaudible and noiseless foot of time, catastrophe and heel of pastime, infinite and endless liar, earthy and abhorred commands. We frequently receive a treble effect. The Latin element is united with the Anglo-Saxon; the polysyllable with the monosyllable; the abstract with the concrete. Moral ideas, in which Shakespeare abounds, are visualised for the man in the street. Thus the thought that there is one justice for the rich and another for the poor becomes

> Plate sin with gold,
> And the strong lance of justice hurtless breaks;
> Arm it in rags, a pigmy's straw does pierce it,

and the simple truth, that 'the present eye praises the present object', is elaborated and varied by Ulysses, in thirty-five lines of personification and concrete imagery. Shakespeare's abstract words are neither the lords and ladies of mediaeval allegory nor the bogus deities of the eighteenth-century ode. *Nihil in intellectu quod non fuit prius in sensu.* One might indeed say that Shakespeare's body thought. It is to this simultaneous and harmonious working of all human faculties that the style of Shakespeare's greatest plays owes its strength.

Disparity of space and subject has made generalisation in this chapter inevitable; and, as Blake warns us, to generalise is to be an idiot. Generalisations as to certain aspects of Shakespeare's style before 1599 and after 1607 are venial, but the four tragedies which are by common consent his highest achievement would demand individual treatment, if this were not a chapter but a book. In recent years far closer attention has been paid to the nature and importance of the style. Witness an illuminating essay by Middleton Murry on Shakespeare's use of a single word, 'dedication'. As regards the four great tragedies where style contributes so much to the atmosphere and characterisation, Bradley noted the recurrence of allusions to the brute creation in *King Lear*, Wilson Knight has written of 'the Othello music', and Miss Spurgeon has remarked the fondness for the imagery of disease in *Hamlet*. At Shakespeare's best, an exquisite equilibrium is sustained between the characterisation, the dramatic theme, and the vocabulary. In *Coriolanus* and *The Winter's Tale*, style, as Strachey has insisted, has the upper hand of drama.

Shakespeare's plays are plays. That aspect must come first, although the food for psychological speculation which they provide has sometimes proved too appetising. But an analysis of the style serves to illuminate the English genius in poetry, both in the Elizabethan idiom and in that of the Romantic Revival and its aftermath. Indeed in contrast and comparison with the poetry of the ancient and the modern world, from Sophocles to Gerard Hopkins, such a study enables us to get half glimpses of the true nature of poetry itself.

SHAKESPEARE AND ELIZABETHAN ENGLISH

BY

G. D. WILLCOCK

ELIZABETHAN ENGLISH IN GENERAL; THE LANGUAGE OF THE COURT AND OF THE STAGE

Any well-annotated edition of a Shakespeare play introduces one to some of the types of linguistic change which, together with alterations in customs and thought, make a veil or barrier between the sixteenth century and ourselves. Some of the commonest Shakespearian tags—for example, 'Thus conscience does make cowards of us all'—require a linguistic note of some kind to enable the beginner to understand their original, Elizabethan, meaning. The points which play the maximum part in ordinary language notes on Shakespeare are concerned with lexicography (additions and losses in vocabulary), semantics (alterations in the meanings and associations of words), accidence and syntax (changes in inflexion and construction). In addition there are equally far-reaching phonological changes. Our phonetic equivalents for vowel and consonant symbols are not the same as the Elizabethan: the symbols *ee* (as in *meet*) and *ea* (as in *beat*) have now only one phonetic value and the words can rhyme; in the late sixteenth century the two symbols still denoted two distinct vowel sounds. There have as well been countless alterations in the pronunciations of individual words, of which the most prolific cause has been the desire to make the pronunciation fit a traditional spelling. This tendency, growing with the growth of the reading population, has been responsible for the restoration of *e* for *a* before *r* (as in *servant*, pronounced and frequently written in Shakespeare's day *sarvent*) and of initial *h* in words of Romance origin like *humour* (contrast *hour*); innumerable single words like *soldier* and *somewhat* have been phonetically remade by this modern distrust of oral tradition—*sojer* and *summat* were in Shakespeare's day not vulgarisms but good enough for royalty. These phonological changes play an inconspicuous part in ordinary annotation, and it may therefore be forgotten that Shakespeare's English did not sound like ours. If we could recall Richard Burbage to speak a passage for us in good London English of his time, we should, if we had any phonetic training or were reasonably quick of ear, have little difficulty in understanding, but it would sound to us like 'dialect'; we should be able to spot resemblances to modern Cockney (particularly in some of the diphthongs) or to some Midland pronunciations or even to American or Scots. We should probably admit that the general weakening and partial loss of *r* in modern 'Received Standard' has resulted in a lack of acoustic richness and energy in our speech as compared with Shakespeare's.

Some acquaintance with these and other ascertained facts concerning contemporary speech habits is necessary before we can distinguish between the liberties in language which Shakespeare *finds* and those which he *takes*. Purists from Dryden onwards have sometimes accused Shakespeare of taking liberties with 'correct' usage when he is merely being Elizabethan and availing himself of a natural and legitimate flexibility which the language has since lost. His accentuation repeatedly differs from ours (as in *canónize* for our *cánonize*) and many words appear with a variable stress (as in *cómplete* beside *compléte*), because late Tudor English was passing through a transitional phase in the accenting of Romance words and recent polysyllables. Over-modernised editions sometimes by spelling or punctuation suggest a 'liberty' where none exists: in Portia's last speech in *The Merchant of Venice* we find the line

And charge us there upon inter'gatories

which suggests that Shakespeare has by 'poetic licence' shortened, and changed the stress of, *interrógatory*. But reference to Henslowe's Diary and other documents where the spelling is 'phonetic' shows that the word (a well-established legal term) was current in some form like *intérget(e)ry*—there has been no 'licence', poetic or otherwise. A very detailed knowledge of the contemporary spoken language is sometimes necessary for the judging of Shakespeare's puns by the standards that should prevail in punning circles, especially as these puns are also frequently disguised or distorted in modern editions. In the play-scene in *Hamlet* (Act III, Sc. ii, l. 249) Hamlet (nowadays) replies to the King's request for the title of the play: 'The Mouse-trap. Marry, how? Tropically' (*i.e.* by a figure of speech or trope). From the evidence of Q 1 the actor probably said at one time: 'Mouse-trap...trapically', availing himself of a change from *o* to *a* in certain words of which other examples are *stap* (for *stop*) and *Gad* (for *God*). This *a*-pronunciation was originally a south-westernism,[1] and was probably brought to town by Raleigh and other Devonians. In the next line (still in Q 1) the unexpected location of the murder in 'guyana' prompts (if it be not a mere blunder) the speculation whether the knowing in the audience were not expected to see more than a somewhat affected pun.[2]

Though Elizabethan English was characterised by much liberty of usage, the idea of a Standard Language was well above the horizon by Shakespeare's time. The most conclusive evidence for this is provided by the critic 'Puttenham' in his *Arte of English Poesie*, 1589.[3] Here the young poet is advised to take the 'vsuall speach of the Court and that of London and the shires lying about London within LX myles and not much aboue'. The desirable form of speech is definitely identified with southern

[1] H. C. Wyld, *History of Modern Colloquial English*, Ch. IV.

[2] In Q 1 the relevant lines run:

Mouse-trap: mary how trapically: this play is
The image of a murder done in guyana.

The *Discouerie of Guiana* (describing Raleigh's voyages) had been published in 1596 and re-issued (by Hakluyt) in 1598.

[3] Bk. III, Ch. 4, *Of Language*. The identity of the author is still under dispute.

and not northern, and the novice is as strongly warned against the usage of the universities as he is against archaism and rusticity. In the matter of standardisation distinctions must always be drawn between the printed, the written and the spoken forms of the language. Thanks to the tidying efforts of the compositors, Elizabethan printed books show practically all writers as using the same general brand of English. Their MSS., when extant, reveal far more personal caprice as well as linguistic variations; nevertheless, as Puttenham notes, the written language had proceeded much further towards unification than the spoken. Some speakers, as again Puttenham notes, acquired two dialects by adding the courtly norm to their own home-grown local speech. Others, like Sir Walter Raleigh, brought their broad Devon to Court and kept it there.

It is very generally held that in the late Elizabethan period a specially close connexion existed between good colloquial and written language. The more tortuous forms of prose rhetoric must always have taken shape on paper, but it is possible to find works which owe their peculiar quality to a harmony between the language of books and the living voices of men. Both Sidney's *Defence of Poesie* and Puttenham's *Arte of English Poesie* suggest the transference to paper of a trained but not artificial capacity to speak well and at length; they have the lightness and urbanity of cultivated discourse. Puttenham's sentences, indeed, sometimes need the inflexions of the living voice to prevent ambiguity. This ease of interchange between a dignified spoken, and a flexible written, word was, for the dramatist, all to the good. He is perhaps hampered at the present day by a wider gulf between the literary and the colloquial.

From such works as these, from letters, despatches and recorded sayings of statesmen and wits, it is possible to guess at the scope of the best Elizabethan speech. But this is not to arrive at the native speech of Shakespeare, a 'bourgeois' from those 'far western parts' beyond the radius of Puttenham's courtly circle. Attempts to find traces of Shakespeare's Warwickshire origin in his language have proved inconclusive. Shakespeare in London shows no sign of surviving local patriotism. When he has occasion to use dialect in his plays (as in the Tom o' Bedlam scenes in *King Lear*) he is content with the conventional stage 'southern'. A number of dialect words (some of them traceable to Warwickshire) have been collected from his works, but the contexts in which they occur (notably the Witches' scenes in *Macbeth*) have mostly the effect of detaching the poet from them. For the accents of his workaday speech we have no evidence at all. As an actor he had to speak as was required of him. It is not possible to imagine him inflexible of mind or insensitive of ear. Though he had served no boyhood apprenticeship to the stage, he must have acquired the tones and delivery which would make his speech current with City and Court.

Of the language of the accepted body of Shakespeare's work as preserved in 'good' Quartos and the Folio it is possible to speak more positively. It is based on Elizabethan speech at its best. The popular side of Shakespeare's art has been so much stressed in recent years that it may seem startling thus to claim, in effect, courtly affinities for his language. Shakespeare possessed, however, genius, professional flexibility and noble patrons; he belonged to a Company which, like other companies and more so, was a link between City and Court. It had to keep in its repertory plays suitable for production at Court at short notice and to provide actors proficient enough to avoid disgrace before an audience not only critical but brutally frank. This quality of courtly audiences was so much in Shakespeare's mind during the first part of his career that we can be sure he had learnt his lesson or watched others learning theirs. Few people can witness the last act of *Love's Labour's Lost* without wishing for the Nine Worthies, however o'er-parted, a more friendly and patient hearing. Athens has a kindlier atmosphere than Navarre, but in the final scene of *A Midsummer Night's Dream* the joking comments of the 'polite' audience are not 'asides' conventionally inaudible to the victims; they are heard and sometimes replied to. In both these cases the poet, as professional, is acquiescing genially in the fun poked at amateur performances. When the professional players come to Elsinore they meet, in private, a courteous but discriminating host; in public, however,

Hamlet, pursuing his antic disposition, assimilates his manners to those of the young blood of the Court: 'pox, leave thy damnable faces, and begin'.[1]

ELIZABETHAN TASTES, STANDARDS AND TRAINING IN LANGUAGE. INFLUENCES ON LANGUAGE, ACADEMIC AND NON-ACADEMIC

The tendency to standardisation must not be over-stressed. Richard Carew,[2] writing about 1596, glories in the diversity of dialects ('all right Englishe') as evidence of the 'copiousnesse' of the language, and in recent times it has been declared: 'In the rankness and wildness of the language he [Shakespeare] found his opportunity'.[3] Though ideas of 'true' pronunciation, orthography and usage were beginning to occupy men's minds, the analogies of modern 'Received Standard' (as vouched for by the B.B.C.) and 'Public School English' are misleading. Those who were helping to build up the courtly standard were less obsessed than we are by 'correctness' and uniformity in spelling or pronunciation, by 'accent' and all that it connotes to-day. They had other tests as well for a man's quality or breeding as expressed in language. The features that impressed them most were (in words culled from their own vocabulary): 'copie', 'sentence', 'pressness', loftiness of 'conceit', 'mellifluousness', 'readiness', 'fullness' of illustration and allusion.

They thought of this language as acquired, not taught. Here we touch an important difference between that age and ours. Neither schoolmaster nor don had as yet done his best or worst upon the language. The schools at the beginning of Elizabeth's reign were the depleted heritage of the Middle Ages, when all ecclesiastical institutions from the large and highly organised monastery to the single chantry-priest had held a potential connexion with education. Since the services of the Church were in Latin, since the bulk of religious and serious literature was in

[1] *Hamlet*, Act III, Sc. ii, ll. 266–7.

[2] *The Excellency of the English Tongue*, printed 1614; see Gregory Smith, *Elizabethan Critical Essays*, II, 292.

[3] Prof. G. S. Gordon, *Shakespeare's English*, S.P.E. Tracts, No. 29, 1928.

Latin and even business records were sometimes kept in the same language, this ecclesiastical education had been almost entirely in and for Latin. That the Reformation, substituting an English prayer-book and English Bible, did not bring about an educational revolution is due to the coincident 'Revival of Learning', to the hereditary and international prestige of Latin and to conservative inertia. Only the acuter minds like Mulcaster, Spenser's master at Merchant Taylors', saw or admitted that the chief grounds for the complete Latinisation of education had been swept away.

In later Tudor times, apart from the choir schools which existed to train choristers for the Cathedrals and Royal Chapels, there were two main classes of schools—the Pettie schools for little children (Fr. *petit*) and the Grammar schools. These last concerned themselves (in theory) solely with Latin grammar and a varying amount of Greek. They resented having to waste time and talent in teaching English reading and writing to make up for widespread deficiencies in the 'Elementarie' course. Only in this last did any study of the mother tongue find a place. The inadequacy of the English basis appears incredible to us; in the Pettie school the child was expected to learn to read and write English, to begin to spell out Latin, to get some practice with figures and to be grounded in the principles of the Christian religion. This narrow curriculum was still further straitened by ignorant teaching with the help of horn-books, ABC's and Primers. ABC's consisting of the alphabet, some simple words, and the Lord's Prayer or Catechism were sold for one penny. This and some Psalms or verses made the bulk of the child's 'reading', which he thus economically combined with his religious instruction. The more scholarly the Grammar school to which he proceeded, the more 'Humanist' the master, the less attention did he pay to his mother tongue from that time forth, and the more was he encouraged, not only to write, but to think in Latin, and to find in 'the Ancients' a complete code for the ordering of life, literature and language.

Education must have been, moreover, especially in mid-Tudor times, deficient in quantity as well as quality. As a result of the destruction of the old institutions, the engrossing of Church lands, and the transference of many refounded schools from a land endowment to a money endowment (with consequent depreciation), there was for a period a sort of school famine. The mediaeval world had always thought of education as a free gift of the Church to those who could profit by it, and this, in secular terms, remained the Tudor conception. In the absence of a capitalist notion of money-making schools, it was necessary to found and endow them. The lead given by the King Edward VI Grammar schools was followed up by the Queen Elizabeth Grammar schools and the Guild schools such as Merchant Taylors' and the Stratford Grammar School itself. The earlier school famine led to a high proportion of illiteracy in older people at the time of Shakespeare's coming to London; moreover, the entanglement of education with the results of the economic revolution (which was one consequence of the Reformation) and the absorption of vigorous minds in ecclesiastical polemic were prime causes of a Philistine bleakness in the pre-Armada period which is as clearly reflected in the literary language as in any other field. Except when the lilt of a tune enfranchises mind and ear, the diction, the rhymes and rhythms of the mid-century poets between the *Songs and Sonnets* (1557) and *The Shepheards Calender* (1579) are meagre and obvious. Barnabe Googe, author of *Eglogs, Epytaphes and Sonettes* (1563), will provide a representative specimen of the sort of language that could earn a man a reputation in those days:

Whan thou doste hym forget I wysh,
  all mischifes on the lyght,
And after death, the Fendes of Hell,
  torment thy lyuyng spryght.[1]

Even the swashbuckling Gascoigne rarely, if ever, escapes from the contemporary blight:

And thereupon I have presumed yet,
To take in hande this Poeme now begonne:
Wherin I meane to tell what race they ronne,

[1] *Egloga Septima.*

Who followe Drummes before they knowe the dubbe,
And brag of *Mars* before they feele his clubbe.[1]

It is clear that a new spirit was wanted and poets of a very different breed, whom this unschooled and little-considered language should call to adventure and experiment.

The concentration in Public and Grammar schools on the *literae humaniores* of Latin and Greek long out-lasted the so-called Revival of Learning. The English language has not been very long directly under the ferrule of the schoolmaster. Indirectly, however, it has been subjected to a continual pressure from the classical languages (particularly Latin), and this pressure was already being exerted in Shakespeare's youth. Of this Shakespeare shows himself well aware through Holofernes, whose absurdities will, if carefully studied, be found to provide pointers to all its most important results. In himself both product and active supporter of the Tudor school system, Holofernes not only thinks in grammar but in the Latin order: 'A soul feminine saluteth us'.[2] This reminds us that there was a danger to the language in Renaissance times which had not threatened during the Middle Ages. Then—though the familiar use of Latin led to embellishing vernacular composition with all sorts of schemes, tropes and allusions drawn from classical and pseudo-classical writers—Latin itself had been used as a living language, and the actual structure and substance of the native language had been safe. At the Renaissance rhetoric replaced logic as the principal subject of study at the universities, and 'style' became an end in itself. There were scholars in Italy who could not sleep o' nights if they had lapsed from pure Ciceronianism during the day. The doctrine of Imitation as expounded by Ascham (an English Ciceronian) in the *Scholemaster* (1570) led inevitably from the Latin imitation of Greek to the English imitation of Latin, and the pedants soon began to busy themselves with the task of making the native language less native. A series of 'Orthoepists', among them Ascham's friend Sir Thomas Smith, set themselves to 'reform' English pronunciation and orthography.

[1] Gascoigne, *Posies*, 1575; *Dulce bellum inexpertis*.
[2] *Love's Labour's Lost*, Act IV, Sc. ii, l. 75.

Spelling reform must have been sufficiently prominent to make it worth while to raise a laugh at it in *Love's Labour's Lost*; that the reformer is Holofernes leaves us in no doubt as to Shakespeare's standpoint. Holofernes' 'ab*h*ominable'[1] has indeed long since been laughed out of court, but his *debt* (replacing *dette*) has secured a partial victory (we write it but do not say it), while of other inventions and pedantic corrections made by his tribe (such as *perfect* for *parfit*, *adventure* for *auntyr* and *aventure*) the triumph is complete.

Syntax, sentence structure and vocabulary offered equally accessible fields for interference. A process of Latinisation set in which reached its climax in the seventeenth century with Sir Thomas Browne in prose and Milton in verse. On the whole Elizabethan verse resists invasion better than the prose, and Shakespeare's mature verse-sentences, even when (as they often are) complex, have, unlike Chapman's in his *Iliad* and Milton's in *Paradise Lost*, an individual and native complexity. All the figures of classical rhetoric were becoming yearly more popularised by the publication of useful text-books in the vernacular applying to the adornment of written and spoken English all the devices of Tully's eloquence and the rules and examples of Quintilian. The influence of this rhetoric is omnipresent in more studied Elizabethan work. It makes a very large part, according to Puttenham, of the Art of English poesy. He devotes eleven chapters of Book III of the *Arte* to a delighted exposition of the 'figures'. Though they are minutely distinguished and classified, the bulk of them (and all that were commonly used) resolve themselves into variations of two principles—balance (including antithesis) and repetition. They thus naturally exert a potent influence on the shape and design of English sentences. These figures are pervasive in Spenser and rife in the drama of the University Wits. They were thus a part of Shakespeare's heritage, as can be seen in early plays like *Richard II* and *King John*. Not only figures but ornate and pedantic words were disseminated by the arts of rhetoric. Puttenham's amusing and sometimes delightful Englishings of the Greek terms (rendering,

[1] *Love's Labour's Lost*, Act V, Sc. i, l. 23.

for example, *Epizeuxis* by 'Underlay or Coockoo-spel') were a spirited attempt to resist undue classical invasion of the vocabulary. The books of rhetoric were perhaps the most prolific sources of the much-decried Inkhorn terms, many of which, however, usefully filled gaps and soon ceased to be mere 'terms of Art'. Holofernes here once more appropriately enters the field with his 'insinuation, as it were *in via*, in way of explication'.[1] *Insinuate* was (though not exclusively) a technical rhetorician's word.

There was another respect in which the early Elizabethan language was, as compared with the literary language of to-day, unschooled. Far more pervasive than any pedagogical influence is tradition. In the mid-sixteenth century many of the links with the past had broken or worn thin. Phonetic change had rendered Chaucer's technique (as distinct from his spirit and narrative power) incapable of appreciation. Mediaeval prose had been far less developed than the verse and could offer the Elizabethans little guidance. The change of faith, the spread of 'Humanism' and new tendencies in social life, all tended to cut the Elizabethan off from his English past. He was taught far more about the classical past than his own. The result was a certain impoverishment of language (again in the mid-Tudor period) as well as one-sidedness of culture and imagination.

The position of the Tuscan language in the period of Ariosto offers an illuminating contrast. It was overshadowed by the cult of pure Latinity, but it enjoyed an unbroken literary tradition stretching back through Boccaccio and Petrarch to Dante. A poet who took it up knew where he was in it; he had masters to whom to turn. The Elizabethans, though they acknowledged the rights of custom, had no comparable support in their own language. There was a phase of uncertainty, even timidity. Most of the better-known sixteenth-century writers were men of stout heart who refused to be daunted, but their words often betray an atmosphere of doubt all round them. Ascham asserts that it would have been, not only more creditable, but *easier*, to have written his *Toxophilus* (1545) in Latin (for there would

[1] *Love's Labour's Lost*, Act IV, Sc. ii, l. 13.

then have been a model to imitate). Sidney, in his *Apologie*, finds it necessary to rally to the defence of the language against two current accusations: that it is a 'mingled' (*i.e.* impure) language and that 'it wanteth grammar'. Mulcaster in his *Elementarie* (1580) makes the matter very plain. He refers in detail (though not by name) to contemporary writers who find various causes of complaint with English: it is not 'certain', and therefore makes an unstable foundation for any composition, it is impossible to know how to spell it (Mulcaster deals thoroughly with that), it has not been subdued by 'Art', it carries no credit, and it is a waste of time to write 'anie philosophicall argument' in it because the 'vnlearned vnderstand it not, the learned esteme it not'. All this Mulcaster triumphantly refutes.

The critical movements, too, of the same period from Ascham to Mulcaster could only have perpetuated this diffident and chilly spirit had the later writers given way to them. One of these movements—the attempt to impose classical metres on English verse—proceeded by forcing English words and syllables into alien moulds with a complete disregard of native speech habits and would, if successful, have cut English poetic speech off from its roots. The crusade against the importation of foreign words (which emanated from the same Cambridge circle led by Sir John Cheke and Ascham) has something more to be said for it, but it was singularly ill-timed. The language needed enrichment, not curtailment. The drab 'Saxon' colouring given to the poems of Googe and Gascoigne by the prevalence of words like *brats*, *trudge*, *trot*, *doleful dumps* and *carking care* shows that a poet of singular tact as well as conviction was required to recover for the literary language the lost treasures of Chaucer's English.

Spenser had been through Mulcaster's hands and doubtless absorbed from his beatings some additional courage and enterprise, though he does not elect to follow Mulcaster's modernising way. Coming immediately after the mid-century poets and recognising the 'winter-starved' condition of the language he turned to the native past for new linguistic material as well as for subject-matter. From the emergence of Spenser onwards a new spirit begins to manifest itself. A gathering of energy and confidence is one of the most striking features of the years 1580–96. It shows itself in every department of life, art and thought, and is expressed in language with even less hesitation than elsewhere. Shakespeare, younger than Spenser by some dozen years, was born free of the inhibitions of the mid-century. Acquisition was now in the air; there was a buccaneering spirit abroad in language as well as on the high seas. The part of Shakespeare as language-maker has naturally been more closely studied than that of any other Elizabethan author. Our debt to him in new words, new adaptations, new phrases, which by their vividness of metaphor or aptness and pregnancy of gnomic expression have become current coin, has been assessed and estimated again and again, and the tale is not yet told. But the making of language was going on all around him. It has been calculated that Chapman actually invented more new words than Shakespeare, though they have never come home to men's business and bosoms in the same way. Among the prose writers, Nashe excellently corroborates and endorses the work of the poets. He glories in language; no word, learned or popular, comes amiss provided it be vigorous and expressive. He grows impatient with the 'Saxon' monosyllabic small change of which the native part of our language so largely consists and takes no small credit to himself for acclimatising a new brand of foreign word—'Italianate' long verbs in *-ise*. The nature and quality of this late-Elizabethan achievement cannot be appreciated apart from the whole Tudor evolution in language of which it forms the second great phase. It is the thaw succeeding the frost. Though mid-Tudor barriers were now everywhere overflowed they were not entirely swept away. During the period 'of long-choosing and beginning late' English literary criticism was born. The educated Englishman became critically and linguistically self-conscious; he acquired standards and power of comparison. He was compelled to consider England's place in the Republic of Letters. In the phase of expansion, fine words, racy phrases, exuberant sentences appealed not only through novelty and contrast, but also as ammunition; it was as patriot that the Elizabethan developed his linguistic sense.

Shakespeare's plays not only harvest the linguistic wealth of this period of expansion, but reveal also, especially the comedies, a linguistic consciousness. This prompts the speculation whether it is possible to trace among the late Elizabethans, as well as a rich sense of language, some unacademic factors at work, reaching even the more or less illiterate and uniting them in a common interest. One such factor must have been the widely diffused love of music, especially of singing. John Dowland's and other song-books demonstrate a capacity for lyrical composition far outside the ranks of identifiable poets, and in addition there was the whole body of genuinely popular folk-song and ballad. Any one who had by heart half-a-dozen representative songs had the root of the matter in him; he had a touchstone by which to gauge poetic rhythm and speech. But, above all, the Elizabethan had to be a good listener; the more illiterate he was, the more he was forced to train his ear. There was little cheap print, and even the broadside was useless to the man who could not read. He absorbed the grisly details of the latest murder or the progress of some popular agitation from the lips of someone better informed or more imaginative than himself. There must have been much derangement of epitaphs among the Dogberry and Dame Quickly class in town and country. It is the inevitable result of hearing long words and never seeing them. Malapropism in characters like Dogberry and the clown or yokel in *Love's Labour's Lost* is not a mere stage trick; it rests upon a difference in literacy between those days and these. The eager manner in which words were picked up shows the same acquisitiveness in the clowns as in their betters. Though they lived mainly upon the almsbasket of other people's words, if they found themselves at a feast of languages they stole the scraps:

> Remuneration! O, that's the Latin word for three farthings... why, it is a fairer name than French crown. I will never buy and sell out of this word.[1]

Punning and verbal acrobatics show the same eager attention to words on the part of all classes. According to Feste one of the functions of high-class clowning was the corruption of words—

[1] *Love's Labour's Lost*, Act III, Sc. i, ll. 130–5.

i.e. the audacious or humorous abuse of them—and the turning of sentences inside-out like 'cheveril gloves'. The trained jester had to keep his society jargon up-to-date and to know when *welkin* came in and *element* went out. He had to be ready with every sort of quip or quibble. In the theatres, too, the same sort of verbal wit passed current; otherwise dramatists would hardly have toiled so painfully at

> ...a practice
> As full of labour as a wise man's art.[1]

People loved, then, to follow words; they were also trained to listen strenuously. There is no comparison between their listening and our short-flighted 'listening-in'. Large numbers stood in the open air for two hours or more listening in the theatres; they also stood listening to sermons at Paul's Cross and elsewhere; if they sat, they sat on stools or hard benches in unheated churches while coughing drowned the parson's saw. In many schools and homes young people were required to recapitulate on Monday Sunday's discourse. A conscientious and eloquent preacher would expect to hold his congregation for an hour. There were homely preachers like Latimer in mid-Tudor times, whose successors were the Puritan orators of the Martin Marprelate period, in whom militant earnestness was valued more than learning. At the other end of the scale was a courtly, scholarly divine like Lancelot Andrewes. Even Latimer makes more demands upon his hearers than do preachers at the present day. Modern university lectures, though delivered to presumably trained audiences, offer more concessions to the frailty of easily-dulled minds than does the sermon of any sixteenth-century preacher of standing. The sermons of Henry Smith, a moderate Puritan who became minister of St Clement Danes' in 1587, provide excellent examples of preaching for the plain man, undertaken at first with no thought of literary form. There are extant numerous 'pirated' examples of Smith's preaching, compiled from notes taken during delivery, and representing approximately, therefore, the sermons as they reached the listener. Smith uses a natural, middle diction, with plenty

[1] *Twelfth Night*, Act III, Sc. i, ll. 69–70.

of homely, striking illustration, but the style is never as 'open', the connexions are never as easy as would be those of a modern speaker appealing to an audience of 'tired business men'. It requires a little imagination when reading at leisure and in comfort to gauge the effect upon ear and attention of the more intricate and sustained passages, such as this sentence from the sermon on 'The Restitution of Nabuchadnezzar':[1]

As Daniel noted the time of his pride, when he walked in his pallace, to shewe howe pride growes out of buildings, and wealth, and apparel, and such rootes: so he noteth the time of his fall, while the words were in his mouth, to shewe that he was punished for his pride and ignorance, that he might know where to begin his conuersion, and abate his pride, and when he had taken away the cause, then God would take away the punishment, so likewise he noteth the time of his restitution, *At the ende of these dayes*, that is, after seuen yeares were expired; to shewe how long the sicknesse of pride is in curing, and to shewe how euerie thing was fulfilled which was prophesied, euen to the poynt of time, for it was tolde him by Daniel that he should be like a beast seuen yeares, therefore Nabuchadnezzar is prompt as it were to confesse the trueth, and saith as the prophet sayth *At the ende of these dayes*, that is, at the ende of seuen yeares, I Nabuchadnezzar was restored to my Kingdome....

Educated Elizabethans, as well, must have retained attentive listening habits, and, if they had any gift of expression, a corresponding range and dignity in speech. Books were restricted in their circulation and were only gradually becoming *pastime*. Newspapers as drugs, and barricades between man and man, had not been invented. There was more reading aloud, especially to women as they worked. A great man's table was expected to be a conversational feast; children were sent to be 'educated' in great houses by keeping their ears open while they made themselves useful. Elizabethan lighting must have restricted evening employments at home and out-of-doors. The eye must have been compelled to rest while the ear and tongue were busy. Lyly is not a realist, but in *Euphues and his England* (1580) he is

[1] *The Sermons of Master Henrie Smith, gathered into one volume*, 1592. The pirated versions, though differing in numerous details from the above and from each other, offer on the whole a remarkable tribute to accuracy of oral attention.

undoubtedly describing a phase of courtly sophisticated life which fascinated him. The dinner-time symposia, the capping of stories, the fireside debates, are not in their high-flown, over-disciplined euphuism transcripts from life, but they are based upon a contemporary zest for extempore expatiation on topics of love and sentiment which was fostered by the growth of a new convention of *amour courtois* at Court. To the interest and importance of this as a novelty Lyly refers again and again.

THE AUDIENCE

Shakespeare could count, then, on an audience of good listeners. It was an audience, too, far more ready than we are to think of speech as an art, to accept conventions, and quick to note and appreciate distinctions and changes of key, for all family and social life was more strictly governed by these then than now. There was more difference between the modes of address reserved for one's superiors and one's inferiors, between the tones and phrases used to the old and the young. Sir Toby Belch, who, though he may find congenial company below-stairs, is a man of spirit and knows the ways of his world, advises Sir Andrew in composing his challenge to 'thou' his opponent some thrice;[1] such a use of the familiar form by a comparative stranger would constitute an unforgivable insult. In *Lear* there is something peculiarly horrible in the manner in which Goneril and Regan preserve hollow forms of filial respect:

> O Sir, you are old....

If we can judge from the long stage-history of a genuinely popular piece like the *Spanish Tragedy*, the audience was more ready to stretch mind and ear then than now. It relished the sweep from epic *tirade* to euphuistic lovers' debate, or from:

> O eyes! no eyes, but fountains fraught with tears;
> O life! no life, but lively form of death

[1] *Twelfth Night*, Act III, Sc. ii, l. 46.

to the macabre prose dialogue between the hangman and Pedringano:

> Ay, truly; come, are you ready? I pray, sir, despatch; the day grows away.
>
> What, do you hang by the hour?...

There was far less distrust of fine language and direct appeal to the emotions. Now the word *rhetorical*, like the word *artificial*, has acquired a pejorative meaning. The Elizabethan was afraid of neither. The modern dramatist or novelist who subscribes to the canons of 'realism' strives by broken sentences, reproduction of clichés, current colloquialisms and even by devices of punctuation such as dots and dashes, to represent the short-breathed incoherencies of an age grown careless of speech. The Elizabethan could savour the quality of 'language such as men do use', but he also expected the dramatist to recall by his diction the divinity that hedged a king and to do his duty by all the great common-places—Death the Skeleton and Time the Shadow. The actor expected it likewise and would have thought poorly of a play which offered no such opportunities for the display of virtuosity as: 'Have at you then, affection's men-at-arms', 'All the World's a stage', 'Farewell, a long farewell to all my greatness'.

It is no derogation to the reputation of Shakespeare to point out that he turned dramatist at (linguistically as well as otherwise) a singularly fortunate time. Ten years earlier or ten years later would have made significant differences. The interaction of his early work and that of the University Wits and the changes in his latest plays which have been ascribed to the influence of Beaumont and Fletcher, preclude us from claiming that he would or could have remained Olympically unmoved by the *Zeitgeist*. Shakespeare grew to maturity under Elizabeth, and catered for an Elizabethan Court and an Elizabethan City. Pedant and Puritan were as yet kept in their place—the latter with increasing difficulty. Elizabeth herself made a royal and penetrating use of language and had the same tastes in style and jokes as her full-blooded citizens. Under her the genius of the language could combine a centralising, stabilising tendency with individual liberty. Excellence was admired, the right and the wrong were debated, but there was no worship of uniformity—except in church-going. The Court of James was to prove no substitute for the Court of Elizabeth, and, owing to far-reaching religious, social and political changes, the Jacobean audience was to prove a far less catholic collaborator in language.

Shakespeare exercised a unique power over language; at the same time his 'normality' can be most definitely and concretely illustrated from this field. He had an instinct for the heart or centre of language. There is comparatively little in his works of the more ephemeral, though vigorous, Elizabethan linguistic activities. Though, as in *Love's Labour's Lost*, *Henry IV* and *Twelfth Night*, he enjoyed a laugh at learned, fashionable or popular affectations, he was unwilling to waste much energy on any form of speech which lay far from the sufficiently abundant Elizabethan core. He prefers to *suggest*, rather than *reproduce*, the speech of those classes or individuals who were, linguistically, on the fringe. He allows rustics, for example, to reveal themselves by homely phrases, vain repetitions, simplicity of ideas and connexions, rather than by set rusticisms or dialect,[1] and he makes a temperate use of the canting phrases, thieves' jargon and out-of-the-way professional terms so robustly exploited by the conny-catchers, and judiciously used by Ben Jonson to buttress his careful realism. He exercised his boldness and felicity not, of course, on a language which was actually used by all classes in his audience, but on one for which all had an affinity once he had illumined it to their imaginations.

From this Shakespeare drew his potency as a language-maker. His words went home. At the same time he kept the most flexible speech ever used by Englishmen linked to great issues and bathed in the light and shadow of imagination. He was the master of

> ...the multitudinous seas incarnadine

and

> Pray you, undo this button.

[1] For Shakespeare's use of dialect, see above, p. 121.

While his plays remain the common study of English people he will, it can be hoped, continue to exercise a centripetal, unifying influence on language. As a 'tradition' he will prevent our speech from suffering from a repetition of the mid-Tudor rootlessness. He keeps a certain amount of vivid Elizabethan word and phrase in popular circulation to-day. In his mature plays he kept the dramatic and the poetic together, just as he kept together king and clown. At the least, he may be expected to exert a certain pull against the narrower interpretations of 'realism'; in language, as in action and character, the reputation of Shakespeare, especially when compared with that of Ben Jonson, has shown that what counts after a hundred years or so is life and power, not a day-to-day verisimilitude.

SHAKESPEARE AND MUSIC

BY

EDWARD J. DENT

The age of Shakespeare was one in which music, both in England and in other countries, reached an extraordinarily high artistic level. Not merely is it an age of great composers all over Europe, but it is an age in which music was widely cultivated and appreciated. In mediaeval days music had been centred mainly in the courts of princes, in the cathedrals and the monasteries. Outside these environments domestic life had been neither secure nor comfortable enough to permit of any serious and continuous cultivation of the art by ordinary people. The English, it is true, had always been a music-loving nation since the twelfth century, if not before; but in days when no music was printed and comparatively little written down, musical education apart from professional circles (in which we can include both the wandering minstrels and the church musicians) must have been very irregular. During the whole of the fifteenth century there was a very large production of ecclesiastical music, but our records of secular music during that period are of the scantiest. Church music was written down and preserved for regular use; secular music, composed for the entertainment of people who had few books and comparatively little occasion for either reading or writing, was learned largely by ear. There was no reason to preserve it in writing; when audiences were tired of one song or dance musicians were always ready to provide new ones. Church music was required for regularly recurring ceremonies; secular music, whether courtly or popular, served the needs of the moment.

With the beginning of the Renaissance and the simultaneous invention of printing, musical culture spread to much wider circles. At the various Courts there was more occasion for secular ceremonial, and in lower social circles life became generally more leisured and cultivated, so that there was much more opportunity for the domestic practice of music. Music had been printed as early as 1465; but the real beginning of music printing and publishing as an industry dates from 1501, when Petrucci started printing music at Venice. The printing of secular music in England began with Wynkyn de Worde in 1530. In Castiglione's famous book *The Courtier*, first translated into English in 1561, there is much discourse of music, and it is considered to be an indispensable accomplishment for a gentleman. In early mediaeval days it had been regarded as disgraceful and effeminate except for those trained for the priesthood; but in Castiglione's book a gentleman who takes this view is very sharply reprimanded by the lady who is the supreme authority on good breeding. Italy set the example to all the Courts of Europe, and the English Court, from the time of Henry VIII to that of Elizabeth, took an active interest in music. Henry VIII was himself a composer; Edward VI played the lute well, and his sisters Mary and Elizabeth were both accomplished performers on the virginals.

The English have always been singers rather than instrumentalists, and at all periods vocal music has been England's chief contribution to the art. Wynkyn de Worde's first musical publication, apart from ecclesiastical music, was a book of songs. The word *song* in those days generally signified vocal part-music rather than songs for a single voice with instrumental accompaniment; but although most of the secular vocal music of the sixteenth century has survived in the form of part-music we have abundant evidence to show that this music was very often performed in actual practice by one voice with instruments.

The favourite type of vocal music in the sixteenth century is often said to have been the madrigal, and that word is often used very loosely to describe all sorts of vocal part-music. Strictly speaking the madrigal is an Italian form cultivated in Italy throughout the century, but mainly in the first half of it. The leaders of music from about 1450 to 1550 were the Netherlanders, and Italy in those days was overrun with Netherlandish musicians who were employed at the Italian Courts. The Italian madrigal was the joint product of Netherlandish music and Italian poetry. England naturally maintained a close connexion with the Netherlands, and it was indeed from England that the Netherlanders had learned their musical style in the fifteenth century, a style which in the fourteenth century seems to have arisen from contact between England and Italy. During the first half of the sixteenth century England possessed a flourishing school of its own, closely allied to that of the Netherlands, but characteristically English and showing no signs of Italian musical influence. Italian music did not reach England until at least half-way through the century, and its influence was not markedly felt until after the publication of *Musica Transalpina*, a collection of Italian madrigals with English words, in 1588. It is from this date that the great school of English madrigal composers begins, going on into the reign of James I.

The Italian madrigal, especially in these later years, was cultivated mainly at the small Courts, where professional singers and instrumentalists were engaged. In England the madrigal was much more performed in amateur circles, especially in the houses of the great families, whether in London or in the country. Many English composers were regularly employed as domestic music-masters in great houses, as for example Wilbye at Hengrave Hall. If Morley is to be believed, it was the usual custom to hand round part-books after supper for family singing, and when any unfortunate guest was unable to sing his part at sight he was considered unfit for polite society. One may suspect, however, that Morley may have been guilty of some slight exaggeration; it would naturally be to his interest as a professional musician to put the case for the urgency of musical education as vigorously as possible. There is at the same time considerable evidence to show that instrumental music, especially for viols and recorders, was very generally cultivated by amateurs. The lute was the most popular instrument of the time, along with various other instruments of similar type. It has often been asserted that the lute was an exceedingly difficult instrument to play; but the same thing may be said to-day of the pianoforte, if the attainments of a Liszt or a Busoni are taken as the normal standard. There certainly were, in Shakespeare's days and later, lute-players of exceptional virtuosity; but one may safely suppose that most Elizabethans played the lute no better than the average amateur plays the pianoforte now. It was always in demand for dance music and for simple accompaniments, and 'vamping' was probably even commoner then than it is in our own day.

There was a simplified form of lute called the cittern, which had only four strings, and was easy to play; its widespread popularity is shown by the fact that it was to be found in every barber's shop for customers to amuse themselves with while waiting to be shaved.[1] The virginal was also sometimes to be seen at the barber's, and this fact gives us a characteristic view of the general enthusiasm for music in Elizabethan England. The love of music was certainly not confined to the educated classes, although these naturally pursued a higher standard of knowledge and performance. Apart from the musicians employed by the Court and by official bodies such as municipal corporations there were innumerable performers of a lower class who picked up a living as best they could. They were to be seen wandering about the streets waiting for casual engagements to play at weddings or other festivities; they played for the entertainment of people in taverns and in houses of ill fame. Like the actors, they were legally regarded as rogues and vagabonds if they were not definitely in the service of some prince or nobleman, but this did not diminish their general popularity.

This last seems to be the music which County Paris brings to his wedding with Juliet, and it is *not* the music which a great nobleman would have already at his command. Here, then, whether by error or design, Shakespeare is writing in terms of

[1] See Ben Jonson's *The Alchemist* and *Epicoene*.

another social class; and, indeed, Capulet's household throughout has been more a burgess's than a nobleman's.[1] The names of Simon Catling, Hugh Rebeck and James Soundpost suggest that they were players of stringed instruments, but as one of them says:

> Faith, we may put up our pipes and be gone,

it is clear that they enter playing on wind instruments, either shawms or recorders, and these too would sound more effective than strings when played behind the scenes.

Compare this with the Count Orsino's music in *Twelfth Night*; a very different business and, dramatically, far more correct. He has his musicians in permanent attendance, to play when he will. And almost certainly these are stringed instruments, for they accompany not only a song, but very quiet speech.

Not more than a summary account can be given here of the various instruments played in Elizabethan England. The flute in general use was not the modern cross-blown flute (called in the eighteenth century the German flute) but the recorder, blown from the end like the flageolet or penny whistle, which are merely varieties of the same instrument. The recorder was made in several sizes, treble, tenor and bass, and used for music in parts. Its tone was sweet and melancholy. The fife was used for military purposes, and the pipe (a small flageolet) used with the tabor (a small drum) for country dancing.

Feste, the clown in *Twelfth Night*, plays the pipe and tabor in combination; something of a step dance being included too. This asked for a good deal of skill,[2] and Ariel in *The Tempest* is directed to play a tune on the tabor and pipe. Folk dancers of to-day will be perfectly familiar with the pipe and tabor played by one man simultaneously.

The hautboy was the universal reed instrument. Its tone was more shrill and harsh than that of the hautboy used in modern

[1] See p. 189.

[2] There is extant a portrait of Richard Tarlton playing on pipe and tabor and one of William Kempe dancing a Morris from London to Norwich, while a man walks beside him playing a pipe and tabor too. Both Tarlton and Kempe were actors in Shakespeare's company.

orchestras. The hautboy, like the recorder, was made in several sizes; its bass variety is the bassoon. Hautboys were also called shawms or waits. The word *wait* originally signified a sentinel or watchman who gave signals by blowing a horn; early in the fifteenth century it was applied to municipal watchmen who were also employed as musicians; later the word came to be applied both to their instruments (shawms or hautboys) and sometimes to the pieces of music played on them.

Horns were used only for hunting music. They are employed in *A Midsummer Night's Dream* when Theseus bids the huntsmen wake the sleeping lovers with their horns. The instrument called a cornet was not the modern cornet-à-piston, but an instrument (now quite obsolete) with a cupped mouthpiece, blown like a horn or trumpet. It was generally made of wood covered with leather; it had finger-holes, so that it could play a chromatic scale, which the horn and trumpet could not. The cornet was also made in various sizes; its bass is the serpent, which survived well into the nineteenth century. The tone of the cornet was something like that of a trumpet, but softer; and in the 'private' or indoor theatres it seems—probably for this reason—to have replaced the louder instrument.[1]

The trumpet was pre-eminently a military instrument, and therefore traditionally associated with royalty. In Germany trumpeters were regarded as the aristocrats of the musical profession. They enjoyed certain social privileges, and the music of trumpets at weddings and so forth was forbidden to be employed by persons under a certain rank of nobility. Trumpeters do not seem to have been such important personages in England, but the instrument none the less stood apart from the others as expressive of special dignity. Trumpets were almost always associated with drums.

The sackbut or trombone, on the other hand, was more associated with religious ceremonies. Cornets and sackbuts were often used in English cathedrals and churches to support the organs, which were weak and small as compared to ours, or indeed to replace them altogether. The sackbuts were not

[1] See W. J. Lawrence, *Shakespeare's Workshop*, 1928, p. 48.

exclusively reserved for church music, but they were always employed for music of solemn and ceremonial character.

Of stringed instruments played with the bow the viols were the most important. The earlier mediaeval rebec was almost obsolete in Shakespeare's day (but we find an indirect allusion to it in the name—Hugh Rebeck—of one of the musicians in *Romeo and Juliet*). The more modern violin had been introduced from Italy in Henry VIII's reign, and enjoyed the patronage of royalty, but none the less it was considered in cultured circles to be a coarse and aggressive instrument suited only to country folk.[1] Viols, like recorders, were made in various sizes. A 'chest of viols' generally consisted of two trebles, two tenors and two basses. The viol had a flat back and six strings; its tone was soft and reedy.

In *Pericles* it is to the sound of viols that Thaisa is brought back to consciousness after the shipwreck.

> The rough and woeful music that we have,
> Cause it to sound, beseech you;
> The viol once more....

We may presume their use, too, for the music which stirs the statue of Hermione, and for that to which King Lear wakes to sanity.

Any gentleman of education might be expected to play upon the viol—upon the viol-da-gamba, at least. Though we do not see him put to the test, Sir Toby Belch boasts that Sir Andrew Aguecheek

> ...plays o' the viol de gamboys.

In Jonson's *Every Man out of His Humour* the actor of Sir Fastidious Brisk is positively called upon to play one.

The lute and cittern have already been mentioned. There

[1] The use of the violin in Tudor times has been disputed by Mr Jeffrey Pulver (*Dictionary of Old English Music*, London, 1923), who maintains that the words *violin* and *violon* in English documents of the sixteenth century can only refer to treble and tenor viols. Mr Pulver holds that the violin was not much known in England before 1638, when Charles I paid £12 for a Cremona violin. If violins cost so much as that they were hardly likely to have been used by country fiddlers as Anthony Wood says they were. It may be noted that the word *violin* does not occur in Shakespeare.

were other varieties of the lute, but they cannot be described here.

Upon one sort of lute or another a dramatist could be sure that some of the actors—of the boy actors in particular—would be reasonably skilled. Ophelia (by a stage direction in the First Quarto of *Hamlet*) enters, *playing on a lute*; and in *Henry VIII* the Queen tells her waiting-woman

Take thy lute, wench: my soul grows sad with troubles;
Sing and disperse 'em, if thou canst: leave working

—which is the signal for the singing of

Orpheus with his lute made trees....[1]

And, in *Julius Caesar*, the 'instrument' over which Lucius playing a 'sleepy tune' falls asleep, is pretty certainly a lute. Brutus takes it from his lap, saying:

If thou dost nod, thou break'st thy instrument.

The virginal, an ancestor of the pianoforte, in which, however, the strings were not struck by hammers but plucked by quills actuated by a keyboard, was played mainly by ladies. Queen Elizabeth was an accomplished performer on it, and the Elizabethan composers wrote for it with a skill and ingenuity quite unparalleled in any other country. From a Shakespearian point of view, however, it is of slight importance, except for the fact that the collections of virginal music of the period are a most valuable source for the popular tunes and other pieces of music alluded to by name in Shakespeare and his contemporaries. It does not seem to have been in use in the theatres, either public or 'private', and, indeed, could hardly have been effective there.

The organ, on the other hand, was certainly used in the theatre; it is expressly mentioned in Marston's *Sophonisba*, combined with various other instruments. The word *organ* at this period generally signifies an instrument with flue-pipes; there was also the regal, a small instrument with beating reeds, something like a diminutive harmonium, but decidedly harsher in

[1] The scene is Fletcher's, certainly.

tone, if one may judge from the surviving specimens. It must be borne in mind that the organ in Shakespeare's day was not exclusively a church instrument; small chamber organs were often to be found in private houses, and as they were easily moved about, often more easily than a modern grand pianoforte, they could be used in theatres without practical difficulty. The regal was even more obviously portable.

The regal was often associated with melancholy situations; it was used thus by Monteverdi in his *Orfeo*. Probably the 'infernal music' of *Sophonisba* was played on the regal. The organ, with its brighter tone, was quite often used for dance music, and its employment does not necessarily signify any solemnity. A quartet of recorders sounds exactly like a small chamber organ, and indeed the obvious function of an organ was to save labour, since one player at the keyboard could do the work of four or more instrumentalists.

In modern music, whether serious or frivolous, public or domestic, we may notice four instruments, the tone of which is generally prevalent to our ears—pianoforte, violin, clarinet and horn. These four qualities of tone were entirely absent from Elizabethan music. The Elizabethans had no idea of combining instruments into anything like the modern orchestra or even like the orchestra of Haydn and Mozart. They had a strong sense of what we call instrumental colour, and of the possibilities of using it for dramatic effect; but their method was to group the instruments in families, not to use them all together, although they often made use of small mixed combinations of three or four instruments with or without voices. Such combinations were called 'broken consort' or 'broken music'. In domestic performance 'broken music' was inevitable, as parts had to be played by such instruments as were available at the moment, and this must certainly have often been the practice in the theatres as well when resources were limited.

The mediaeval mysteries had made plentiful use of music, but it consisted for the most part of Latin hymns and antiphons. There are, however, occasional English lyrics interspersed, such as carols and folk-songs, as well as directions for instrumental music. During the sixteenth century, as the religious plays gradually gave place to plays of purely secular character, the use of songs and instrumental dances was continued and further developed; the Latin hymns and canticles naturally disappeared. A characteristic feature of the plays produced after 1560 was the dumb-show, which was always accompanied by instrumental music. In *Gorboduc* (1562) each act is preceded by a dumb-show, and for each of these different instruments are specified in order to enhance the dramatic effect by appropriate instrumental colour. Violins accompany the first, introducing six wild men clothed in leaves; cornets play for the second, flutes for the third, hautboys for the fourth, drums and flutes for the fifth, which illustrates a battle. This idea must certainly have been derived from the Italian theatre.

We have no record of the actual pieces played in these dramas, but we can at least note the elaborateness of the incidental music. Plays of this kind were acted before cultured audiences, and on special occasions for which money could be spent with some freedom.

Music played an important part in the plays acted by the choristers of the Chapel Royal and other ecclesiastical establishments. The Children of St Paul's Cathedral were also actors; they performed a play before Elizabeth at Hatfield in 1552 and also entertained her, soon after her accession to the throne, in 1559. The Children of Windsor and of Westminster too were greatly encouraged by Elizabeth, and the efficiency of the choirs —incidentally, therefore, of the performance of the plays, their subsidiary occupation—belonging to the Chapel Royal, Windsor and St Paul's was assured by the privilege granted by her of 'taking up'—*i.e.* forcibly impressing—boys from other choirs and schools.

The plays written for his choristers by Richard Edwards, who became Master of the Children of the Chapel Royal in 1561, are of great interest in this respect, owing to the songs which are introduced into them. These songs generally occur in death scenes or other moments of emotional tension; they are intended as the spontaneous personal expression of the character that sings them, just as in an opera. Their alliterative verse and their frequent repetitions of words and phrases often seem ridiculous to the modern reader who looks at the words alone; but alliterative verse gains a certain force by being set to music, and the repetition of phrases has continued as a common musical device down to our own times, because repetition is a characteristic feature of musical form and can produce an intensification of the emotional effect.

Several of these songs have been discovered in various libraries. They were composed by the leading church musicians of the time, such as Richard Farrant and William Byrd, and as might be expected they often show great musical beauty and expressiveness as well as accomplished craftsmanship. They are generally set with an accompaniment of four viols. Mr Arkwright, who first discovered these songs and pointed out their importance, suggested that possibly some of the songs in Byrd's *Songs of Sadnes and Pietie* may also have been composed for chorister plays.

As the choirs possessed considerable musical establishments it was natural that music should be a conspicuous feature of their plays; and when we look at the songs which have survived, it may be wondered that England never developed out of them something analogous to the opera which was at this very period just beginning to take shape in Italy.

But whatever might have been favourable to this, a variety of things combined to nullify the opportunity. In the 1580's the great vogue of the men's companies of actors began; and, though the skill of the boys in singing, speaking, and even in acting would be great, quite obviously Alleyn, Burbage and their fellows could make a robustly emotional appeal to audiences that boys could not. Moreover, the men's companies, besides having their own apprentices, recruited boys from the choirs and must have profited much by their training.[1]

Not that the boys did not retain a reputation of their own,

[1] Indeed, in 1607–8 the King's Men (as Shakespeare's company had then become) took over the Blackfriars theatre, where a boys' company was playing, largely that they might inherit the best of the talent it contained. See Chambers, *Elizabethan Stage*, II, 215.

and the standard of their skill must have been high when, for some years after 1583, John Lyly was writing plays for them.[1] These plays, rather formally and delicately written (as was to be expected from the author of *Euphues*), must have suited their capacities to a nicety. Edwards with his *Damon and Pithias* may have served in some sort as a model; but Lyly improved upon it vastly. And he certainly gave ample scope for music. *Galathea* provides 'fairies dauncing and playing'; *Endimion*, more fairies and a long dumb-show to be done to music. In *Midas*, Apollo sings to his lute and Pan to his pipe, and in *Mother Bombie* 'three fiddlers' are brought on to play, who must be actors also. And in the eight plays altogether there are at least thirty-two songs. Some of them are directly dramatic—might be called operatic—in their tenor; two in *Sapho and Phao*, more particularly, the concerted

Arme, arme, the foe comes on apace...,

and Vulcan's song, labelled

...in making of the arrowes.

But we note no further development in this direction. The boys found other dramatists, who wrote for them very much the same sort of plays as those provided at the men's theatres. They had their periods of great success; once, at least, as we know from *Hamlet*, they again seemed seriously to be rivalling the men. But in the end, after a complexity of difficulties between their 'masters' and with the authorities (they found themselves involved in the dangerous Marprelate controversy), they ceased to count, and their influence upon the drama evaporated. Of their musical aptitude the men's companies absorbed what they conveniently could, but they did nothing to develop it.

Lyly's delicate art, after an interval, is next manifest, rather—though with changed tendencies—in the masque. This had some decorative influence on the theatre, but its music was too costly and elaborate to be transported there. For Campion's masque 'in honour of Lord Hay' (1607) we have directions for four groups of musicians; in the gallery a consort of hautboys, lower

[1] 'For them' must stand for various companies, the history of which, their amalgamations and divisions, is still obscure, though much study has been given to it.

down, on the right of the stage, a group of six voices and six cornets, on the left a group of twelve in which bowed instruments predominated, and lastly, nearer the audience, a group of ten, two violins, a harpsichord and lutes, with a trombone as bass. These groups were employed separately for different parts of the masque. There were also singers who accompanied themselves on lutes on the stage; and at the climax of the masque, when the chief dancers made their appearance, Campion utilises his entire orchestra simultaneously, together with groups of five 'voices' on each side of the stage.

Nothing done upon this scale could become a popular entertainment in the economic sense; but here, if anywhere, is the line of descent to opera.

The boys' companies provided music apart from the songs and dance accompaniments and the incidental music in the plays. While the public theatres had their jigs for a finish to the entertainment, at the Blackfriars, when the boys were acting there, one could find music between the acts and as much as an hour of it before the play began.[1]

The Duke of Stettin-Pomerania, on his travels, visited the Blackfriars in September 1602; and he records in his diary an excellent performance upon 'Orgeln, Lauten, Pandoren, Mandoren, Geigen und Pfeiffen', and a boy singing 'cum voce tremula', so delightfully that unless perhaps from the nuns in Milan he had heard nothing on his journey to excel it.

The men's companies in their public, open-air theatres could neither make music so effective nor—at any rate in their earlier days—so well command it, either in quality or quantity (though when, in 1608, the King's Men took over the Blackfriars, it is likely that they took over at least part of its music-customs too and saw to it that the standard was kept up).[2] But music they

[1] For the jig and its music see pp. 35, 160. The custom of inter-act music did not apparently obtain at the public theatres, where conditions would, indeed, have been very unfavourable to its enjoyment. For that reason it is doubtful whether there were more than formal intervals between the acts, or (often) any intervals at all.

[2] Sir Bulstrode Whitelocke, writing of the year 1634, speaks of 'the Blackfryers Musicke, who were then esteemed the best of common (*i.e.* professional) musitians in London'.

had to have. There were the fanfares blown from the turret upon trumpet or sackbut to announce the beginning of the play. If it were a 'History', or brought kings or any great personages upon the stage, the trumpeter would find employment throughout it, in blowing 'flourishes', 'retreats' and the rest, and taking his share with the drummer in 'alarums' and other such 'effects'. A drummer would be needed for the 'marches', for which, as for the alarums, there are a variety of directions. The alarum may be 'loud', 'low', 'short'—and the march may be 'afar off', may be a dead march, or, as in *Hamlet*, a Danish march may be specifically noted. It is evident that quite a variety of definite 'effects' of this sort were obtained, probable that the audience recognised the significance of the particular 'flourish' or 'retreat' they heard—though when we come to the stage direction in *Antony and Cleopatra*, 'alarum far off, as at a sea-fight', we may feel more doubtful of this. The trumpeter and drummer might also be expected to appear upon the stage in character. In *King Lear*, Edgar, to take up Edmund's challenge, enters 'armed, with a trumpet before him', and a drummer was often, if not invariably, a part of the symbolic 'army' which makes so many entrances in Elizabethan drama. Neither trumpeter nor drummer might be actors in the usually accepted sense; but the musicians were generally capable of at least a few lines if necessary, and, as we have seen, certain of the actors—besides the clowns, who must be expert upon the pipe and tabor at least—would be reasonably skilled upon an instrument or so.

Besides all this, however, there would very often be more elaborate music demanded; a consort of viols, or recorders, or hautboys, or a 'broken consort'. And, whichever for that particular play it might be, they could certainly be hired for the occasion. The airs themselves would be well known. There is no evidence that special music was composed for plays; the signs are rather that the dramatist wrote his lyrics (if he did write and not merely import them) to existing tunes—a custom which, indeed, in large part survived until the mid-nineteenth-century copyright acts put a stop to it. And we definitely know that, for inter-act music in the 'private' theatres, the audience would call out for their favourite tunes. Musicians of various sorts could be hired. These might be 'Sneak's Noise' itself (if Falstaff did lose his voice with hulloing and singing of anthems, some taste for good music may have been left him!); it may well have been Sneak whom County Paris hired (so inappropriately) for his wedding.[1] But this would seem not to have been quite what was required by Thurio in *The Two Gentlemen of Verona*, when, for a serenade to Silvia, he speaks of going

> ...into the city presently
> To sort some gentlemen well skilled in music,

nor to be what Cloten employs for the aubade in *Cymbeline*. Possibly the theatre had to 'make do'; but music of another quality was certainly available. There would be the musicians attached to the households of the companies' own patrons, the Lord Admiral or the Lord Chamberlain, or some other great lord. These were never forbidden to take 'outside engagements'. It may have been a question of cost, as to which, in general, account-books of the time show a wide divergency. In 1561–2, for instance, we have the Dowager Duchess of Suffolk at Grimsthorpe paying the 'Waits' of Lincoln 3*s.* 4*d.* 'in rewards for playing'. But the Queen's Trumpeters had had 20*s.*, and so had the Queen's 'violens at New yerestyde'. And 'my lord of Rutland's man who plaied uppon the lute' had, to his own account, received 6*s.* Such musicians were obtainable, evidently.

The evidence for what happened in these matters at the public theatres while their fortunes were still none too sure is conjectural only. It is worth noting that the stage directions of *Coriolanus* and *Henry VIII*, both late plays, call for wood-wind, brass, drums, and almost certainly for string music too. *Henry VIII*,

[1] *II Henry IV*, Act II, Sc. iv:

'*First Drawer:* ...see if thou canst find out Sneak's noise; Mistress Doll Tearsheet would fain hear some music'.

This 'noise', or small band, of Master Sneak's is again referred to in Heywood's *The Iron Age*, the writing of which Chambers dates about fifteen years later. It had more than a passing reputation, then. And these two references even suggest that it may have been employed in the theatre. See Naylor's *Shakespeare and Music*, and the *Arden Shakespeare* (*II Henry IV*), p. 75 n.

indeed, specifically requires hautboys, drum and trumpets, cornets, lute, not to mention a solo song, and 'four Quirristers singing'. But we do reach some certainty in 1624, with a reference to twenty-one 'Musitions and other necessary attendants' upon the King's Men, the company to which Shakespeare had belonged. By then at least—and presumably for some while before—an orchestra made a part of a theatre's permanent establishment.[1] In general, however, the public theatres could not have provided as good music as the choristers' theatres did. A consort of viols, pre-eminently suited to performance in private houses, would still make its due effect in an indoor theatre, whereas its gentle and delicate tone might easily be lost in the theatres open to the air.

In the public theatres, and almost certainly in the private ones, the normal place for the music was a curtained box called 'the music-room'; a part of the gallery which ran at the back, and, in the later theatres, probably turned to enclose part of the side of the stage. But the musicians were often required to play on the stage itself; and there are instances (as in *Antony and Cleopatra*) where they play under the stage. The 'music-room' survives into the Restoration theatres (which were recognisably like modern ones); and it is not until quite late in the seventeenth century that the orchestra is placed in front of the stage as it is in the theatre of to-day.

Add the undoubted fact that from the beginning music was always considered an attraction, and that as much of it, if not of one kind then another, would be provided as possible; that certain of the actors themselves were evidently capable of playing some instrument when required, and that most professional musicians were capable of playing two or more different instruments, and we have a not inaccurate outline of the part played by music in the Elizabethan drama, undocumented as this has remained.

There can be no doubt whatever that Shakespeare himself had a very considerable knowledge of music. His poems and

[1] See T. W. Baldwin's *Organisation and Personnel of the Shakespearian Company*, p. 10. The document referred to is a 'Protection' from the Master of the Revels.

plays are full of allusions to the art; not only does he speak of music plainly and directly, but he very often mentions technical musical terms in a metaphorical sense. But whereas writers of the nineteenth century seldom mention music without committing some ridiculous error, Shakespeare never makes a mistake, even when he alludes to theoretical details of a difficult and obscure kind.[1] How Shakespeare acquired his knowledge of music can only be conjectured. He would probably have learned the rudiments of music, including sight-singing, at school at Stratford; it is also quite probable that he might have found someone there to teach him to play the lute and possibly the virginals, if not the recorder. We have, however, no evidence as to his abilities as a performer, either instrumental or vocal. It should, however, be noted that although Shakespeare's characters talk more about music than those of his contemporaries, they do not give us as much useful information about the practical details of stage music as some of the other comedies do, and there are various plays by other authors, such as Marston, which have much more copious and elaborate stage directions as to the performance of music.[2]

The music employed in Shakespeare's plays may be classed in three groups—fanfares, dances and songs. The first category includes all the indications of trumpet calls, such as alarms, retreats and tuckets, as well as marches for drums. Music of this type is naturally associated with battles; otherwise the trumpets are reserved for situations connected with kings and princes or other persons of high degree. The very obscure term *sennet* has never been satisfactorily explained, but it is evident that it must have been a long piece of music, as compared with flourishes, etc. Under the heading of dances we may conveniently class all indications of purely instrumental music, whether required for dancing or not, for in Shakespeare's time most of the serious instrumental music composed was written in forms derived from the dance. The Pavan and the Galliard were still in fashion as dances, but the musicians had already begun to treat them as

[1] See Naylor's *Shakespeare and Music*.

[2] *Antonio and Mellida* in particular. Malone Society Reprint, 1921.

pure music, employing their forms for the kind of serious music that later composers would put into string quartets and symphonies. The only other kind of artistic music written at this period is based on the principle of fugue, and is generally given the name of *fantasia* or *fancy*. Music of this type was eminently suited to private performance, but it is hardly likely that it was much used in the theatre, except perhaps in the 'private' theatres, where it may well have been played before the performance—or during entr'actes.

There is no evidence extant as to the actual pieces of music played at the original performances of Shakespeare's dramas. Dr Naylor gives a number of useful suggestions for trumpet flourishes, etc., but they are all of later date and mostly from continental sources. For the dance music of the period there is abundant choice of material, but care must be taken to distinguish between music written definitely for dancing and music which utilises the conventional dance forms for purely artistic purposes. For all details as regards the dances and their steps the reader must be referred to Dr Naylor's book *Shakespeare and Music*.

Shakespeare's use of songs in the plays varies considerably, and it is one of the many, though uncertain, indications of the circumstances of a play's production and the resources at the moment of his company.

In *Love's Labour's Lost* the small boy who played Moth sang, it seems, what was probably an Irish song, its title in the text corrupted to 'Concolinel'.[1] In *I Henry IV*, written a very few years later, the boy who played Glendower's daughter had to sing a song in Welsh. The association of the two things may not be accidental. The songs at the end of *Love's Labour's Lost*, not specifically given to any of the characters, are likely to have been sung by Moth and another boy. In *The Two Gentlemen of Verona* and *The Merchant of Venice* solo singers (in the first certainly adult, in the second probably) come on for the occasion only. We infer—but we must not be too certain—that they were engaged for the particular purpose and occasion. In *The Mer-*

[1] See note in the *Love's Labour's Lost* volume of *The New Shakespeare*.

chant of Venice some of the minor actors and attendants 'bear the burden', *i.e.* sing the chorus. But very few Elizabethans, on the stage or off, would not have been able to do that respectably. In *A Midsummer Night's Dream* and *The Merry Wives of Windsor* the singers (and dancers) seem to be children, and a fair number of them would be needed. But these two plays, it is agreed, were written for special occasions—there is indeed no evidence that they were ever seen upon the public stage at all—and for such occasions children could easily be recruited.[1]

In *Much Ado About Nothing* and *As You Like It* the (obviously adult) solo singer is a character in the play; a quite unimportant one, but his few lines would need speaking well. There is, it is possible to argue, a hint in *Much Ado About Nothing* that he was not even a very expert singer. But music abounds in these two comedies. There are two dances in *Much Ado About Nothing*, and in *As You Like It* two boy singers besides Amiens. Touchstone can sing also; and there is a masque, which demands 'still music'. It has been suggested that Shakespeare was thus lavish because the competition of the 'Children of the Chapel'—of the little eyases who so plagued Hamlet's actor-visitors—was beginning to be felt. Be that as it may these two comedies are made for the help of music, and may need it the more because they are largely written in prose. *Twelfth Night* follows close upon them, and again abounds in music. There is the music played to the moody Count Orsino; there are the catches sung by Sir Toby and Sir Andrew; there are above all Feste's songs, three of them. Nor was this the actor who sang as Balthazar and Amiens, but (we may almost be sure) Robert Armin, the company's new clown. Armin would appear to have been a very different sort of person from Tarlton or Kempe (who were always apt to speak more than was set down for them), and it is thought that later Shakespeare fitted him with the Fool in *King Lear*, who had indeed to be singer and actor too.[2] But the music in *Twelfth Night* shows

[1] One sees, in fact, the choristers' schools contributing their strength to the adult company.

[2] Into the text of the Fool's part in *King Lear*, however, have crept one or two matters, one bawdy passage in particular, which may, one fears, have been Armin's.

signs of rearrangement. Viola, who, when she urges the sea-captain to present her in disguise to Orsino, says

> ...I can sing
> And speak to him in many sorts of music...,

was obviously to be allowed to sing; and there are patent signs in the text that 'Come away, death' was originally her song.[1] A boy's singing voice will crack; yet, if he can act Viola well one will not be quick to divest him of the entire part. There had been a boy who could both sing and act in *Julius Caesar*, written a year or so earlier; there is a boy to sing 'Take, oh take those lips away' in *Measure for Measure*, though no acting is asked of him. Ophelia has

> ...chanted snatches of old tunes...

and soon after the boy Desdemona must sing the Willow Song and sing it well; and acting enough is also asked of him.

We are now in the period of the great tragedies, and while the songs are few they have acquired a very definite dramatic function.[2] They are associated with abnormal states of mind, as with Ophelia and—since he is pretending to be mad—with Edgar in *King Lear*. No originality, of course, can be claimed for Shakespeare in this. Mad people sing snatches of song in other plays, and so, very often, do people when they are distraught in real life. He uses music as one of the means of restoring the suffering King Lear to sanity. This is a trifle more remarkable; but from the days of David and Saul music has been held to have something of that power. He uses music to hold Leontes spell-bound while the statue of Hermione comes to life; but it has always played its part, on the stage and off, when any sort of magic is working. With far subtler art he uses Desdemona's song, both to show us her suffering wrought at the moment to a point beyond all normal expression, and to insert, for contrast, a touch of quiet beauty before the brutal horror of her murder comes.

Music has its share in the comedies of the last period too. In

[1] See the new Cambridge *Shakespeare*, *Twelfth Night*, p. 100.

[2] For a full study of this see Richmond Noble's *Shakespeare's Use of Song*.

The Winter's Tale, Autolycus, the itinerant ballad-vendor (the type still survives) and thief, who must sing his songs to sell them, demands an actor who can sing, and sing well. Robert Armin may have played this part too. In *Cymbeline*, besides the aubade, we have the curious touch of the 'ingenious instrument' in Belisarius's cave, which will play music if you 'give it motion'.

Mechanical instruments already existed in Shakespeare's time. The inventory of Henry VIII's musical instruments (British Museum, Harl. 1419) includes 'a virginall that goethe with a whele without playing uppon', and Athanasius Kircher (*Musurgia Universalis*, Rome, 1650) describes various elaborate mechanical instruments which were probably existing at least 20 years before his book was printed. Mechanical carillons are of still earlier date. It is highly improbable that a mechanical instrument was actually used in the theatre; it could be simulated by an organ or indeed by any kind of music.

What Shakespeare mainly wanted was an accompaniment to the speaking of the threnody

Fear no more the heat o' the sun

which the consort of viols, or whatever had gone with the aubade, could provide. The 'ingenious instrument' gave a dramatic excuse for it.

The Tempest, last of the plays, and half masque in spirit and form, naturally abounds in music. Nor has Shakespeare ever used it more dramatically. But never once does it dominate the play. As Prospero holds Ariel captive, so does Shakespeare keep music the servant of his drama still.

There has been much discussion of the relation of Shakespeare's songs to what is called folk-music, especially since folk-music has been made a special object of study and almost a religious cult. The literature and the music (printed or manuscript) of the sixteenth and seventeenth centuries in England show us clearly that there were a large number of simple tunes which enjoyed a very widespread popularity. Their authorship is for the most part unknown, and it is impossible to guess at the actual date of their composition on the internal evidence of style. These melodies are generally spoken of as traditional folk-tunes, and recently there has been a tendency to invest them with a kind of halo of sanctity, as if they were the fruits of a special inspiration denied to the composers of serious music. All we can truthfully say of them is that they were the popular tunes of their day. They are frequently to be found in the works of the serious composers, used for instance as themes for elaborate sets of variations for the virginals. In the theatre such tunes as 'Brave Lord Willoughby' and 'Fortune my foe' were used as musical settings of the jigs that were the delight of popular audiences. It is obvious that the popular theatre always makes use of popular tunes, and equally obvious that a tune is likely to become popular if it is heard in the theatre.

The question has often been raised how far Shakespeare was indebted to traditional music and to the words of traditional songs, but it is one which cannot be answered with any satisfactory degree of certainty. There are in the plays many allusions to the words of songs and ballads older than Shakespeare's time, and for many of these the music is extant; but these songs are seldom actually sung in the plays, or sung only in snatches. And not all of these musical allusions refer to traditional ballads; Dr Naylor points out that 'Farewell, dear heart' (*Twelfth Night*) was a song composed by Robert Jones and published in 1600, the year before the appearance of the play. As regards the complete songs in the plays, the difficulty of discovering the truth about them is complicated by possible corruption of the text in printing. Modern criticism assigns some to Shakespeare and some to other writers; a further difficulty arises from the fact that, when a tune is found that seems to belong to a Shakespeare song, the melody will not always fit the words ascribed to Shakespeare. It is still a matter of uncertainty, for instance, whether 'It was a lover and his lass' (*As You Like It*) and 'O mistress mine' (*Twelfth Night*) were written by Shakespeare and set to music afterwards by Morley, or whether Morley's settings were in existence before Shakespeare wrote his plays; in any case Morley's music and Shakespeare's words do not agree as satisfactorily as one would expect if Morley had composed the music for the actual first performance. It is further uncertain whether the tunes are Morley's own composition or whether he did no more than arrange tunes already well known.

Apart from these two songs of Morley the only other settings of Shakespeare's songs that are anywhere near contemporary are Dr John Wilson's settings of 'Lawn as white as driven snow' (*The Winter's Tale*) and 'Take, oh take those lips away', and Robert Johnson's of 'Full fathom five' and 'Where the bee sucks'. But it is considered improbable that any of these are the settings of the original performances; Johnson's music may have been written for a revival of *The Tempest* in 1613;[1] Wilson's settings must date from considerably later, as he was not born until 1594.[2] It has been suggested that many of Shakespeare's songs were written to tunes already in existence, although those tunes may not be known to us now; but it is difficult to see how convincing proof of this theory can be established, even if its plausibility be admitted.

The influence of the masque on Shakespeare's plays is a subject more appropriate to some other chapter of this book; but it must be mentioned here because it is also a question of musical interest. The influence of the masque is most strikingly apparent in *A Midsummer Night's Dream* and *The Tempest*; and these two plays, together with the Carolan masques, are the direct ancestors of Purcell's English operas. The masque, as a stage form, was deficient in dramatic interest, but it offered opportunity for music in large quantities—for long stretches of continuous music which enabled a composer to group movements together so as to build up an extended musical construction. That is its chief contribution to the development of English opera. The Elizabethan chorister plays, as we have seen, if they had been further developed, might ultimately have led to real opera, for they admitted the basic principle of opera, the use of song as the direct expression of feeling in a character represented at a moment of emotional crisis.

[1] It is likely that the play had been first produced only in 1611.

[2] But see Baldwin's *Organisation and Personnel of the Shakespearian Company*, p. 420.

The jigs, with which the performances at the public theatres used commonly to end, may be considered as a very primitive form of comic opera, for in these the whole drama was written in a ballad metre and sung to well-known ballad tunes repeated over and over again for each stanza. But the jig was too primitive and coarse an entertainment to attract the interest of serious musicians; it made its very natural appeal to audiences by its humorous situations and by the pleasure which ordinary people obtain from hearing a simple popular tune many times repeated.

Shakespeare, for all his knowledge of music and sensitiveness to the theatrical value of music, never adopts the principle of opera. Mr Percy Scholes, starting from the very reasonable basis that music in Shakespeare was often associated with magic and the supernatural, worked out an ingenious theory that Shakespeare's use of music was invariably intended to signify some abnormal psychological state. This theory, however, has not found favour with Shakespearian scholars. The association of music with the supernatural goes back, it need hardly be said, to very ancient times, and in this case Shakespeare did no more than follow a tradition ready to hand. Music was obviously an attraction to Elizabethan audiences, and it has been shown that the Shakespearian theatre eventually became sufficiently prosperous to be able to hire as many musicians as might be wanted. The musical element is most conspicuous in *The Tempest*, and *The Tempest* is a play abounding in effects of magic. Whether Shakespeare wrote the play in order to make copious use of music, or whether he employed music because it was appropriate to that particular dramatic idea, is a question which can only be answered by conjectural speculation. The function of the songs in the part of Ariel would seem to be to distinguish him as a supernatural character from the ordinary mortals; this at any rate was the view of Dryden. If Shakespeare had had any conception of the Italian operatic principle he would have made Hamlet or Othello burst into melody at moments of crisis. Those of his characters who are generally provided with songs are intended to represent persons who, if they had existed as real people, would have learned music as an accomplishment and have been ready to sing when occasion required, either as a social entertainer like Feste, or a vendor of ballads like Autolycus.

From the operatic point of view music is the normal language in which human intercourse is carried on; Shakespeare, however, except perhaps in the case of Ariel, and the fairies in *A Midsummer Night's Dream*, gets no nearer to this principle than the adoption of poetry as a normal language. Music is for him always something extraneous, as it is in ordinary daily life. A composer of opera regards his characters as creating the music which they sing out of their own emotions; Shakespeare is concerned only with the effect of music on those who listen to it. His listeners are not his audience alone, but in all cases the characters on the stage as well. We may include among the listeners even those who sing, for they sing (as many people habitually do, unless they are professional musicians) for the pleasure of singing. It is an attitude of reception, not of creation.

THE NATIONAL BACKGROUND

BY

G. B. HARRISON

I

TENNYSON in one of his less happy phrases sang of 'the spacious times of great Elizabeth', and panegyrists of the age of Shakespeare have ever since been at pains to stress its gay colours and sombre contrasts, as if the men of that generation differed from all others. Even Lytton Strachey, who was hardly to be reckoned among the romantics, wrote:

by what art are we to worm our way into those strange spirits, those even stranger bodies? The more clearly we perceive it, the more remote that singular universe becomes. With very few exceptions—possibly with the single exception of Shakespeare—the creatures in it meet us without intimacy; they are exterior visions, which we know but do not truly understand. It is, above all, the contradictions of the age that baffle our imagination and perplex our intelligence. Human beings, no doubt, would cease to be human beings unless they were inconsistent; but the inconsistency of the Elizabethans exceeds the limits permitted to man. Their elements fly off from one another wildly; we seize them; we struggle hard to shake them together into a single compound, and the retort bursts. How is it possible to give a coherent account of their subtlety and their *naïveté*, their delicacy and their brutality, their piety and their lust?[1]

Such romantic exaggeration arises from the easy mistake of judging a generation by its exceptional men and books, and not by the average. Sir Philip Sidney was the pattern of perfect knighthood, but his contemporaries admired him because he

[1] *Elizabeth and Essex*, pp. 8–9.

was so different from themselves; *The Faerie Queene*, *Tamburlaine*, *Hamlet*, Bacon's *Essays*, Hooker's *Laws of Ecclesiastical Polity* are not everyday specimens of Elizabethan literature but the museum pieces of an epoch. It will, in like manner, be possible for the superficial historian in another age to stress the glories of the Georgian era by evoking as typical of its spirit the attack on Zeebrugge, Rupert Brooke's poems, *St Joan*, *The Dynasts* or *The Testament of Beauty*.

For the serious student of any period, the average is more important than the conspicuous exception. Most Elizabethan books—poetry, drama or prose—are cumbersome and tedious to read, and when the common man in his actions and motives is considered, it will be seen that the character of the Englishman has changed very little in its essentials. Shakespeare's England, far from being spacious, was in many ways narrowly confined, and not least in the means of exchanging ideas.

It is difficult for moderns to realise a world in which news and opinions could not be rapidly disseminated in newspapers or periodicals. The newspaper tends to make men unsociable; when one can read at home there is less need to go abroad to tavern or ordinary to learn the latest rumour, so that, except at times of emergency and censorship, the newsmonger in public places is regarded as a nuisance. Shakespeare's contemporaries, lacking regular newspapers, had of necessity to exchange views by word of mouth. In towns, and especially in London, they lived more in public, frequenting the Court, the Paul's Cross sermon, or the law courts at Westminster, ordinaries and playhouses; they existed therefore in a state of perpetual gossip and scandal, often of rumour and alarm. Moreover, no free discussion of State matters was tolerated; criticism of the Government was easily magnified into sedition or high treason. Even in Parliament, which was only summoned at intervals of four or five years, members were forbidden to debate matters of high policy. In 1593, for instance, Queen Elizabeth forbade the question of her successor to be brought up, and when one Peter Wentworth presented a petition on the subject, he was sent to the Tower, where he remained till he died three years later.

In such conditions men were naturally more excitable and emotional than they are to-day, and more subject to sudden panic and prevailing moods; and, as there were always apprentices and masterless men eager for a riot on the least provocation, the crowd-scenes in *II Henry VI*, *Romeo and Juliet*, *Julius Caesar* and *Coriolanus* were very near to common experience.

Shakespeare has several times depicted the effects of rumour, notably in *King John* (IV, ii, 186) and in the prologue to *II Henry IV*, which is spoken by 'Rumour, painted full of tongues'. There was no exaggeration here. In the news-letters and diaries of the time there are constant references to the wildest gossip and alarms. One notable instance is described in a letter written by John Chamberlain on August 9th, 1599, at the time of the false report of a Spanish invasion:

> Upon Monday, toward evening, came news (yet false) that the Spaniards were landed in the Isle of Wight, which bred such a fear and consternation in this town as I would little have looked for, with such a cry of women, chaining of streets, and shutting of the gates, as though the enemy had been at Blackwall.

The panic subsided, and when it was clear that all the preparations for defence had been due to false alarm, another crop of sensational rumours was soon flourishing. A fortnight later Chamberlain wrote:

> The vulgar sort cannot be persuaded but that there was some great mystery in the assembling of these forces, and because they cannot find the reason of it many make wild conjectures, and cast beyond the moon; as sometimes that the Queen was dangerously sick, otherwhile that it was to show some that are absent that others can be followed as well as they, and that if occasion be, military services can be as well and readily ordered and directed as if they were present, with many other as varied and frivolous imaginations as these.[1]

Even more sensational was the sudden rumour which spread round London in the morning of March 22nd, 1606, that King James had been assassinated at Woking. The train-bands were at once paraded; the palace guards doubled, the gates of

[1] *Letters written by John Chamberlain during the reign of Queen Elizabeth*, Camden Society, 1861, pp. 59, 62.

the Tower shut, and the cannon loaded. This rumour began about 6.30 in the morning, and spread (with many circumstantial details) until after 9, when a proclamation was made that the report was false.

The theatres occupied a peculiar position in the life of London. Sober business men avoided them as injurious to public morals, because the plays often presented unseemly themes, and as a hindrance to trade, because the apprentices were tempted to waste their afternoons. They were too a general meeting place for young gentlemen of means and leisure, and the disreputable characters who follow such. Moreover when free speech was repressed, men found in drama a speaking commentary upon life which existed nowhere else. Many plays directly criticised or presented recent events. In July 1597, for instance, all theatres were closed for three months because of *The Isle of Dogs*, a play written by Nashe and Jonson, which contained 'very seditious and slanderous matter'. In October 1599 the Battle of Turnhout (fought in January 1597) was enacted and living worthies were introduced on the stage, particularly Sir Francis Vere; it was noted that the player taking the part was carefully made up to represent the original, who was actually in London at the time. In May 1601 the Privy Council directed the magistrates of Middlesex to take action upon a complaint

> that certain players that use to recite their plays at the Curtain in Moorfields do represent upon the stage in their interludes the persons of some gentlemen of good desert and quality that are yet alive under obscure manner, but yet in such sort as all the hearers may take notice both of the matter and the persons that are meant thereby.

In December 1604 Chamberlain notes:

> The tragedy of *Gowry*,[1] with all the action and actors, hath been twice represented by the King's Players, with exceeding concourse of all sorts of people. But whether the matter or manner be not well handled, or that it be thought unfit that Princes should be played on the Stage in their lifetime, I hear that some great Councillors are much displeased with it, and so 'tis thought shall be forbidden.

[1] *Winwood's Memorials*, II, 41. The Gowry affair, when James narrowly missed assassination, occurred in 1600.

The nuisance was more common in the private theatres, where dramatists, through the mouths of the boy players, were at times very impudent and constantly in trouble. In 1605 Jonson, Chapman and Marston were imprisoned for some disrespectful remarks concerning the Scots and King James's new 'forty pound knights' in their play *Eastward Hoe*; and in 1608 the Children's Company at the Blackfriars was suppressed and disbanded because they acted, contrary to express orders, *The Conspiracy of Biron*, a play dealing with French history of six years before, and introducing the reigning French king, with his wife and mistress in an unseemly bickering.

Players did not confine their commenting to national or local affairs; they attacked each other. Different theatres had their own local supporters; competition was keen; and there was considerable feeling between rival companies, which led in 1600 and 1601 to the 'war of the theatres'.

Though plays dealing directly with recent events were only a small proportion of the whole, audiences instinctively took notice 'both of the matter and the persons'; and not only in dramas but in all kinds of literary work. History, in particular, was studied because of the parallels it offered to modern times: one of the most telling passages in Bacon's Speech for the prosecution of Essex was his apt comparison of Essex with Pisistratus: Ben Jonson, in the margin of his copy of Greenaway's translation of *The Annals* of Tacitus, noted opposite the account of the fall of Sejanus 'The Earl of Essex'.

A good example of the way in which a double meaning was frequently read, and often intended, is the case of Dr John Hayward's unfortunate *History of Henry the Fourth*. For some curious reason the followers of Essex found a satisfactory parallel between Queen Elizabeth and the story of Richard the Second and his deposition; and it was probably for this cause that when Shakespeare's play was published in 1597 it went rapidly into three editions. Early in 1599 Hayward published a book on the *History of Henry the Fourth*, which related in some detail, and with considerable imagination, the events leading up to the deposition of Richard. He dedicated the book to Essex in a somewhat equivocal Latin Epistle. Immediately the Council suspected that the book was seditious, and at intervals during the next two years Hayward was closely cross-examined, and at length imprisoned in the Tower. Moreover, the Essex conspirators confirmed the suspicions of the Council when, three days before the rising, they bribed the Chamberlain's players to act *Richard II* at the Globe. The significance of the book and of the historical parallel was one of the points which the preachers were commanded to stress in their sermons after the rebellion.

It follows, therefore, that to comprehend what Shakespeare wrote, his plays must be seen against the national background, which can only be built up by a close study of those events, great and small, which were likely to have excited the minds of the first spectators of a new play.

II

The background of Elizabethan drama from Marlowe's *Tamburlaine* (*c.* 1587) to *Hamlet* (published in 1603) was a great war.

The most spectacular of the early engagements was the coming of the great Spanish Armada and its destruction by tempest in the late summer of 1588. In the following year a combined naval and military force was despatched to Portugal with the object of setting the pretender, Don Antonio, on the throne. The 'Portugal voyage' was not a success, for, although Corunna and Lisbon were entered and destroyed, there were great losses by sickness, and on their return the demobilised soldiers and sailors for some weeks terrorised the City of London. In the autumn a force was despatched under Peregrine Bertie, Lord Willoughby, to aid Henri de Navarre against the Catholic League and their Spanish allies. The next year English soldiers were helping the Dutch in the Low Countries. By the end of 1590 the Spaniards began to penetrate Brittany, and in 1591 two English expeditions were sent over; Sir Roger Williams was in command of a small army in Normandy, and Sir John Norris entered Brittany. In the autumn, the Earl of Essex took over a larger force to Normandy and assisted Henri in the siege of

Rouen; his troops included a company of gentlemen from the City as well as a considerable body of personal followers. The siege, however, was hurriedly abandoned in the spring of 1592; it was during these months that the heroic speeches of brave Talbot in *I Henry VI* aroused such enthusiasm amongst Bankside audiences. For the next year Henri fought a losing war, until in 1593 he came to terms with the League and was admitted into the Catholic Church. There was some natural alarm in England, as it seemed likely that with a change of faith he might also change sides; but when it was clear that Henri would continue the war against Spain, another English expedition under Norris and Frobisher drove the Spaniards out of Brest; but Frobisher died of his wounds.

No important engagements by land occurred in 1595, but persistent reports came from Spain that a new and greater armada was preparing. In the summer Hawkins and Drake set out on a combined voyage to South America from which they never returned. In many quarters there was a feeling of panic. Anger with the French was growing; it was suspected that Henri was about to desert his allies and that the Catholics in England might rise when the enemy appeared. It was decided therefore to carry the war into the enemy's country, and in the autumn orders went out that a great fleet was to be assembled in the spring.

The next year (1596) was full of excitement. In April news came that the Spaniards from the Low Countries had suddenly invested Calais. Men were hastily demanded from the train-bands of the City of London, and, by order from the Lord Mayor, the constables shut the people in their parish churches as they were making their Easter Communion until 1000 men had been impressed. Meanwhile Essex and Lord Charles Howard, the Lord Admiral, hurried down to Dover to collect as many ships and men as possible for the relief force. All the next day the sound of cannon could be heard in London, but as the fleet was ready to sail news came that Calais had fallen. The great fleet set sail in June, and on the 20th appeared before Cadiz, which was captured after a heroic naval action. The city was occupied, sacked and burnt, and many Spanish ships were destroyed. It was a gallant, flamboyant success, and brought back good plunder. With the expedition went out many young men of fashion, of the same kind as accompanied King John in the play—

And all the unsettled humours of the land,
With ladies' faces and fierce dragons' spleens,
Have sold their fortunes at their native homes,
Bearing their birthrights proudly on their backs,
To make a hazard of new fortunes here.

The Cadiz Voyage of 1596 was succeeded by the Islands Voyage of 1597. This time Essex was in sole command. The expedition on the whole was a failure. Its start was long delayed by the bad weather in the summer, so that, instead of raiding the coasts of Spain, the fleet made for the Azores, where some ships were taken, but much booty was lost through the incompetence of Essex. In October, before the fleet had returned, there was a general alarm of a Spanish invasion, and the forces in the southern counties were partially mobilised. The new armada had indeed set sail, but was scattered by a storm when two days' sail from Land's End.

The war with Spain languished somewhat in 1598. Peace negotiations were opened, during which the French, contrary to their treaty with England, secretly made a peace with the Spaniards, leaving England and the Low Countries to carry on the war alone. In the summer England was occupied with a war in Ireland, which soon proved more costly than any foreign expeditions. For some years rebellion had been growing, largely owing to the corruption of the services, civil and military. In August 1598 Tyrone defeated the main English force near Armagh, with a loss of some 2000 out of a total of 3500, and by the end of the year it looked as if the English would be driven out of the country. In the following March Essex was sent over as Lord Deputy with a large army of 16,000 men, well found and equipped.[1]

[1] This Irish Expedition—comparing population and national finances—was a greater military effort than the despatch of the Expeditionary Force in 1914. Moreover, an army which varied from 12,000 to 16,000 was maintained in Ireland until the end of the reign, being fed and paid from England.

The great war with Spain evoked a whole gamut of national emotions. In 1592, when expeditions to the continent were still popular, the fire-eating patriotism of Talbot coincided with general feeling. Later, in the anxious times of 1595 and 1596, a deeper feeling of patriotism was prevalent, and the saying passed current 'If we be true within ourselves, we need not care or fear the enemy'; it was reflected in dying Gaunt's speech on England, and the closing lines of *King John*:

> This England never did, nor never shall,
> Lie at the proud foot of a conqueror,
> But when it first did help to wound itself.
> Now these her princes are come home again,
> Come the three corners of the world in arms,
> And we shall shock them. Nought shall make us rue,
> If England to itself do rest but true.

Eighteen months later, after the sordid controversies arising from the Islands Voyage, military glory seemed to have grown somewhat fusty. Shakespeare reflects a prevalent feeling in Falstaff's cruel parody of Hotspur's worship of bright honour. In *II Henry IV* the cynicism is even more pronounced, and the heroic exaltation of 'this other Eden, demi-paradise' has degenerated to 'it was always a trick of our English nation, if they have a good thing to make it too common'; whilst the scene of Falstaff's abuse of his commission, when he accepted bribes to release the best recruits, was a dramatising of a common scandal. Twelve months afterwards, the spectacular departure of Essex to Ireland aroused a general spirit of patriotism which is directly mentioned in the chorus before Act v of *Henry V* and constantly reflected in the heroic speeches in the play.

Essex accomplished nothing effective. The army was frittered away by disease, and in September he made a truce with Tyrone. Then, contrary to his express orders, with most of his staff and many of his regimental commanders, he left his post and appeared without warning before the Queen. During his absence there had been another alarm of a Spanish invasion, and a general mobilisation of the home forces was ordered to concentrate at London, where training proceeded for some weeks.

Essex was succeeded in Ireland by Charles Blount, Lord Mountjoy, who rapidly changed the situation. He planted large garrisons in strategic points, and with a mobile force continually harried the rebels. In the late summer of 1601, however, the Spaniards sent a force of 3000 men to Tyrone's assistance, which occupied Kinsale. Mountjoy was thus faced with a winter campaign with sickly troops. He had to contain the Spaniards and at the same time prevent Tyrone from uniting with them.

Meanwhile the Spaniards had become very active in the Low Countries, where there had been intermittent fighting for the last ten years, and in July 1601 the Archduke of Austria, who had married the Infanta of Spain, began to invest Ostend. Sir Francis Vere was put in command of the combined English and Dutch forces, and for the next nine months defended the town against great odds. The fiercest attacks were made at Christmastide 1601, when an assault by 10,000 Spanish troops was repulsed with enormous slaughter after an all-night battle. The enormous cost and the superb gallantry shown by both sides in the three years' siege of Ostend moved Camden to comment: 'the stoutest and bravest soldiers of the Low Countries, Spain, England, France, Scotland and Italy, whilst they eagerly contended for a barren plot of sand, found here as it were one common sepulchre, though withal it were an eternal monument of their valour'. Hamlet likewise cried pity and admiration upon

> The imminent death of twenty thousand men,
> That, for a fantasy and trick of fame,
> Go to their graves like beds, fight for a plot
> Whereon the numbers cannot try the cause,
> Which is not tomb enough and continent
> To hide the slain.

The news of Vere's success reached London early in January 1602; a few days later it was learnt that Mountjoy had utterly defeated Tyrone, and that the Spaniards in Kinsale had surrendered. The war in Ireland lasted for another year, but the rebellion was completely subdued, and Tyrone finally submitted a few days after the Queen's death on March 24th, 1603.

For the first twelve years the burden of the war had not been too serious, and the number of men demanded from the counties was comparatively small. After 1598, however, the burden became excessive, and the drain of men was heavy and continuous; in July 1601 alone 8000 men were demanded to reinforce the armies at Ostend and in Ireland.

Englishmen were thus very familiar with war, and many of them had seen active service. Of literary men, for instance, Spenser took an active part in Irish affairs and his house was burnt by the rebels; Lodge went on Cavendish's expedition; Donne was present at Cadiz; and Jonson was a volunteer in the Low Countries. Unfortunately so little is recorded of Shakespeare's early life that the source of his intimate familiarity with soldiers and the details of campaigning is unknown. Soldiers and warfare are in varying degrees the theme in the majority of his plays, and in Fluellen, Gower, and Falstaff he created permanent monuments of different types of Elizabethan officer.

III

Many other events occupied the tongues of gossips during these years. A long and costly war, as always, provoked much social unrest; it took various forms, frequently religious. Political parties had not yet come into existence, but since the theory of the state was based upon the interpretation of Christian doctrine it followed that the three principal forms of religion—Catholic, Established Church and Puritan—to a considerable extent expressed different views of the social order. In the accepted theory the Queen was supreme head of Church and State, and she constantly insisted in her speeches and public documents that she was directly under God's special blessing and His Vicegerent in the realm. The Church, through the bishops and other officers and clergy, had many and important functions and obligations in the State. The censorship of books, for instance, was in the hands of the Archbishop of Canterbury and the Bishop of London; in the parishes the churchwardens were responsible for the relief of the poor and impotent; whilst public morals were (in theory) safeguarded in the ecclesiastical courts. To rebel against the established order was thus, in the eyes of its supporters, to defy God. The position was emphatically put in the play of *Sir Thomas More*—in the scene attributed to Shakespeare himself—when More harangued the mob of London rioters:

> For to the King God hath His office lent
> Of dread, of justice, power and command,
> Hath bid him rule, and will'd you to obey;
> And, to add ampler majesty to this,
> He hath not only lent the King His figure,
> His throne and sword, but given him His own Name,
> Calls him a god on earth. What do you then
> Rising 'gainst him that God Himself installs,
> But rise 'gainst God?

Both Puritans and Catholics accepted the doctrine that the social order must be founded on the will of God, but regarded the established State as anti-Christian.

The Catholics were, by the State, regarded as the greater danger, for when Pope Pius V excommunicated Queen Elizabeth in 1570 he absolved Catholics from their duties of allegiance, and it was a matter of great anxiety whether, in the event of an invasion, Catholics would fight for or against the Queen. It was difficult too to know who were Catholics in secret, for, although the compromise in doctrine and ritual made at the beginning of the reign was generally accepted, there were many, especially amongst the upper classes, who would have welcomed a restoration of the old faith.

A man's religion was thus something more than an intellectual acceptance or refusal of certain dogmas. Not only was he influenced by family and sentimental loyalties, but his material comfort, perhaps even life, depended on his choice. Two factors went against Catholicism: those who had received a large share of the immense plunder of the dissolved monasteries were firmly for the Established Church; and, as of old, when the quarrel lay between an English sovereign and a foreign pope, national sentiment was stronger than religious, so that the disloyal efforts of the English Jesuits did immense harm to the Catholic cause, and especially after the Gunpowder Plot. Most of the better known writers passed through trials of faith. Donne's family was Catholic and had suffered for its religion; and he made his choice of the Establishment only after considerable hesitation; Jonson was converted to Catholicism whilst in prison in 1597; Lodge turned Catholic, and probably also Campion. Marlowe, having apparently gone up to Cambridge to train for ordination, became agnostic. Marston, after a period of agnosticism, turned churchman. Shakespeare's family was apparently Catholic, and his father was thereby obliged to abandon his public offices at Stratford during the zealous efforts of Bishop Whitgift in the 1570's; it follows that Shakespeare was brought up in the old faith, though there is no evidence of his practice in manhood.

More ardent Catholics kept closely in touch with Rome. Colleges for English youths of good family to be educated under Catholic fathers were established at Rome, Rheims, Douay and Valladolid, and many of these afterwards returned to England as missionaries, principally as members of the Jesuit Order. By law it was treason for a Catholic priest to enter the kingdom, and many of them were executed as traitors. The Jesuits were particularly active in the years immediately before and after the Armada, and in 1591 a stern proclamation was set out denouncing all who should harbour priests as maintainers of traitors.

The fanaticism of the Jesuits did much harm to the Catholic cause in England, and from 1599 to the end of the reign there was an open and undignified feud between the secular priests and the Jesuits. It started at Wisbech Castle (which was used as a place of internment for Catholic prisoners), when a Fr. Blackwell was appointed from Rome to be archpriest of the Catholics in England; though not a Jesuit he was much under the influence of the Order, and being a tactless, tyrannical man he was soon cordially disliked by his fellow-prisoners. The dispute grew so bitter that both sides began to justify themselves by putting out pamphlets and manifestos. Before long Dr Bancroft, Bishop of London, took a hand in the controversy, for he saw a fine opportunity of creating ill-feeling between English and foreign Catholics. He took the Secular pamphleteers under his protection, and arranged for the printing of their books against the Jesuits. At least forty pamphlets were issued during these months, and the controversy excited considerable feeling. The greatest complaints made by the Seculars were that the Jesuits brought odium on the Catholic religion by openly supporting the Queen's enemies, and by their avowed practice of equivocation, which was too Machiavellian for the Protestant conscience; your absolute Englishman must speak by the card, or equivocation will undo him.

The Seculars indeed hoped that if Jesuits could be separated from Catholics some toleration in religion might be allowed; but in this they were disappointed, for in November 1602 a proclamation was published, banishing the Jesuits from the realm forthwith, but allowing the Seculars two months' grace to submit themselves, and stating emphatically that two religions would not be tolerated in the State.

Whilst the Catholics were believed to be in league with the Queen's enemies abroad, the danger anticipated from the Puritans was rather a social revolution at home. Extreme Puritans claimed that the Bible alone was the expression of God's will, and thence deduced violent and alarming theories of the State. They proposed a kind of democracy whereby their Church was to be organised in local elderships, and thence to district Conferences, Provincial Synods and finally a National Synod which should have supreme power, even over the sovereign. They proposed also that weighty matters affecting the commonwealth should be controlled by Parliament. As for the Church of England, it was an unchristian body, intolerable to a good Englishman. They agreed, however, with the other sects in a rigid determination that the spiritual and material benefits of their religion should be confined to their own members. It was to meet the Puritan view that in the Bible alone was to be found rule of life and salvation that Richard Hooker published his work *Of the Laws of Ecclesiastical Polity*.

Though such extreme views were held by a small, but rigorous, minority, a more moderate Puritanism appealed largely to the merchant classes. Moreover, the best of the Puritan leaders and preachers were zealous and austere in their lives, contrasting favourably with the worldlier clergy of the Church of England; and austerity of life was good for business. The sympathies of the merchant classes were very naturally with the Protestants in the Low Countries, who were their best customers, and against the Spaniards, who oppressed them and interfered with trade.

Although in general the merchants inclined towards Puritanism and the professional classes towards the Church or Catholicism, there was as yet no distinct cleavage, nor usually was there any clash of interest between the Court and the City. Younger sons of good family went into business, and elder sons married the daughters of wealthy aldermen. Players, however, were a cause of frequent irritation; whilst the Privy Council considered plays a reasonable amusement, approved and patronised by the Queen, the Common Council of the City regarded theatres as immoral in themselves, a constant temptation to idleness, a rendezvous for rioters, and a likely source for the spread of infection whenever there was any risk of plague. It is not surprising, therefore, that the Puritan was treated unsympathetically by Elizabethan playwrights.

IV

Another cause of deep and continuous anxiety was the succession. The memory of the Wars of the Roses and more recently of the troubles that followed Henry VIII's death, with the violent changes from reformation to reaction under Edward VI and Mary, was still vivid. When it was at last obvious that the Queen would never marry and bear children the problem of succession became acute. Catholics supported the claims of Mary Queen of Scots, but after her execution in 1587 there was no obvious heir, and civil war between various claimants, none possessing general support, seemed inevitable. The Queen forbade the matter to be debated, knowing from her own early experience that if the crown was entailed there would be a general movement to desert her in favour of her successor. In 1595 the problem was very generally discussed, when Fr. Parsons, the leader of the English Jesuits on the continent, produced a book called *A Conference about the next Succession.* Parsons considered the various claimants; they ranged from King James of Scotland and Lady Arabella Stuart, who had claims by descent, to a member of one of the noble families nearly related to the Queen, and, if any foreign prince were considered, to the Infanta of Spain. He concluded that the matter would not be settled without civil war; the soliloquy of the Bastard over Arthur's body (*King John*, IV, iii, 140–59) expressed a parallel foreboding. Parsons maliciously dedicated his book to the Earl of Essex, and in the next five years there were many who favoured Essex himself.

Robert Devereux, Earl of Essex, began his career at Court as a protégé of his stepfather, the great Earl of Leicester. After Leicester's death in 1588 Essex, who was then in his early twenties, soon became conspicuous for his romantic ambitions. In defiance of the Queen's orders he joined the Portugal Voyage in 1589. Two years later he was in nominal support of the English force assisting Henri IV; at the early age of twenty-six he was made a member of the Privy Council. His greatest triumph was on the Cadiz Voyage, where he shared the command with Lord Charles Howard, who was thirty years his senior. In action Essex was conspicuously heroic, and his chivalry to the enemy was greatly applauded. Thereafter his fortunes declined as steadily as they had ascended. He came back to Court expecting praise from the Queen, and was bitterly irritated when she began to inquire into the balance sheet of the expedition. The best explanation of his career is to be found in the clear-sighted advice which Bacon offered him at the peak of his career. Bacon warned him of the danger of military greatness and ambition, neglect of punctilious behaviour towards the Queen, and excessive popularity. The advice was ignored, and Essex soon found himself in the dangerous position of being regarded as the natural patron of malcontents. His reputation was still further damaged in the Islands Voyage of 1597. It was indeed obvious, even to his supporters, that he was not born to command. His romantic desire for military glory degenerated into vanity, and it was easy for his less scrupulous followers to inflame his jealousies by the mere suggestion that his honour was being touched. He came back from the Islands Voyage to find that his enemies at Court had made full use of their chances. From this time onwards he was a menace in the State; for he was dangerously popular in the City of London, with the Puritans and the professional captains; he was, moreover, suspected by his enemies of aiming at the crown.

Essex's relations with the Queen were always uneasy. At times she loaded him with favours and rewards, but he was quick to resent criticism and openly showed his resentment. The most sensational of many incidents occurred in July 1598. Essex wished his own nominee to be sent to Ireland; when the Queen rejected his advice he contemptuously turned his back on her, and received a box on the ear. Essex withdrew from Court in passion, and did not return for ten weeks. Essex's criticisms of the mismanagement of the Irish affair were so strong that early in 1599 he was selected to be Lord Deputy. His departure from London was spectacular. After his sudden return in the autumn he was for many months confined to the house of the Lord Keeper. In June 1600 he was brought before the Star Chamber, when his actions in Ireland were publicly condemned. Soon after he was released and allowed to go free, but he was not permitted to enter the Court. It was still uncertain whether the Queen would restore him to favour. In October, however, the farm of sweet wines, which was the most lucrative of his sources of income, lapsed, and the Queen did not renew it. Essex's fortunes were now precarious; he owed large sums of money; his more desperate followers told him that his honour was smirched, and urged him to make an attempt to force an entry into the palace so that he might personally lay his grievances before the Queen.

Hitherto Essex had lived very privately. Now his house was crowded with gallants and unemployed captains, and Puritan preachers held forth to large audiences, to whom they proclaimed that there were circumstances which might justify the deposition of a sovereign. The Council were alarmed at the reports from Essex House. On February 7th, 1601, Essex was summoned to Court to explain the meetings, but he refused to come, alleging that his life was in danger. Next day (which was Sunday) the Lord Keeper Egerton, the Earl of Worcester, Sir William Knollys and the Lord Chief Justice appeared before Essex House and demanded admission. When they entered the courtyard they were surrounded by an excited crowd, almost three hundred strong. Essex conducted them into the house and kept them as prisoners. Then, without further preparation, he led his followers, the Earl of Southampton amongst them, into the City, proclaiming that his life was in danger. The citizens, however, though sympathetic, did not join him. He entered the house of Sheriff Smith, who—so he imagined—would aid with a thousand men of the train-bands, but the sheriff withdrew and warned the Lord Mayor. When at length Essex and his followers emerged, they learnt that the Bishop of London had collected some of the train-bands to resist him. There was fighting at Ludgate Circus, and then Essex made his way down to the river and returned to Essex House by water. The house was prepared for defence. Gradually the little army which had been collected by the Lord Admiral closed round the landward side. There was some sniping and a few casualties. By nine in the evening cannon had been brought from the Tower, and all was in readiness for a bombardment. About ten, Essex and his party surrendered.

Both sides had been taken by surprise, and it was some days before the Council had sifted the evidence enough to discover that no vast conspiracy had been organised. Essex and Southampton were brought to trial on February 19th, and both condemned to death. Essex was executed on February 25th; Southampton was reprieved, but remained a prisoner in the Tower. The conspirators were, on the whole, treated leniently. Only five of Essex's immediate followers were executed; the rest were fined, and after a few months released.

For more than three years the fortunes of Essex caused continuous excitement, which is abundantly reflected in Shakespeare's plays. During the last phase, when the whole problem of loyalty to the established order was bitterly in controversy, Shakespeare in *Troilus and Cressida* gave Ulysses a speech on 'Degree' which was an obvious comment on the anxieties of the time. Nor could an audience in the months immediately following the Essex rising have failed to notice a parallel in the situation in *Hamlet* where Laertes at the head of a rabble of Danes breaks into the royal presence, to be abashed by the kingly dignity of Claudius—

> Let him go, Gertrude; do not fear our person:
> There's such divinity doth hedge a king,
> That treason can but peep to what it would,
> Acts little of his will.

Kingship and loyalty were indeed constant themes in Shakespeare's plays, and he stressed especially the awful responsibility and loneliness of the sovereign in phrases which Queen Elizabeth herself echoed in a speech to the members of her last Parliament of 1601: 'To be a King', she said, 'and wear a crown is more glorious to them that see it than it is pleasure to them that wear it'. It is noticeable, moreover, that such speeches are most common when they were peculiarly significant to the times; the theme of kingship and its responsibility does not recur after the death of Queen Elizabeth.

The emotions engendered by the fall of Essex produced a bitterness and disillusion very conspicuous in the last years of the reign; Englishmen had to choose between resignation to 'the whips and scorns of time' or disloyalty to the established order and ensuing discord. The causes of this pervading mood of melancholy are complex and difficult to analyse. The mood appears in many forms and few writers of any importance escaped it. Its most prominent expression in literature is in the satires which began with the publication of the first three books of Hall's *Virgidemiarum* in the spring of 1597; in the next two years there followed such collections as Marston's *Scourge of Villanie*, Guilpin's *Skialetheia*, and Donne's unpublished Satires. The movement, however, was suddenly checked when in June

1599 the Archbishop of Canterbury and the Bishop of London summoned the Wardens of the Stationers' Company and ordered them to gather and burn all copies of a number of the offending collections. On the stage the vogue was transmuted into drama in such plays as Chapman's *Humerous Dayes Myrth*, Jonson's Comedies of the 'humours' and Marston's *What You Will*. *Hamlet* is the greatest expression of the melancholy of the age.

The problem of the succession had been almost forgotten during the alarms of the last years of Essex's career. After his death the air was cleared. Neither Catholics nor Puritans had any strong candidate for the throne, nor did any of the noblemen who had claims through their descent take any action to dispute the right of King James of Scotland. Those who stood to gain by the change secretly began to open communication with the Scottish Court and to extract unwritten promises from the King. The matter had, however, already been arranged. Sir Robert Cecil, the Queen's secretary (who was almost in complete control of English policy after the death of his father, the great Lord Burghley, in 1598) had compacted with the King that he should be proclaimed on the Queen's death. By the end of 1602 it was obvious that the Queen's health was failing; she died after a few days' illness in the early hours of March 24th, 1603. King James was immediately accepted as King, without dispute, and there was a very general feeling of relief that this dangerous problem had been settled without bloodshed or anarchy.

V

Many changes came in with the new sovereign. King James was on friendly terms both with the pope and the Spanish King, so that—since wars were still regarded as the personal quarrel of princes—the war came to a sudden end, to the general relief of all but the professional captains and privateers. The reaction, however, from the first enthusiasm was swift. Sober observers were disgusted by the blatant scrambling for the many offices and emoluments which were now vacant. Court officials took bribes to introduce dubious candidates for the knighthoods so lavishly bestowed. In his first year the King knighted more than nine hundred, and it was a Court joke that an usher had pushed aside the knights to make room for the gentlemen. Before the summer was over the old Queen was very generally regretted, for those very qualities which had seemed irksome were soon magnified into virtues. Thus Sir Roger Wilbraham, compiling a journal of observations for the use of his children, noted that the King was

> most bountiful, seldom denying any suit; the Queen strict in giving, which age and her sex inclined her unto: the one often complained of for sparing; the other so benign that his people fear his over-readiness in giving. The Queen slow to resolution and seldom to be retracted: His Majesty quick in concluding and more variable in subsisting. The Queen solemn and ceremonious, and requiring decent and disparent order to be kept convenient in each degree: and though she bare a greater majesty yet would she labour to entertain strangers, suitors and her people with more courtly courtesy and favourable speeches than the King useth: who although he be indeed of a more true benignity and ingenuous nature, yet the neglect of these ordinary ceremonies, which his variable and quick wit cannot attend, makes common people judge otherwise of him.

Wilbraham's notes were written when the King had been on the throne but three months.

There were other details which Wilbraham had not yet had time to observe. The Queen loved the public acclamations of the crowd; she professed, and genuinely, that nothing was so dear to her as the love of her people: James disliked crowds; he tolerated them for the first few weeks, but afterwards he drove them away with abuse. The Queen had an enormous capacity for hard work. She remained, up to the last, the managing director of her kingdom. King James soon tired of State business, spent much of his time in hunting and gave order that he was not to be troubled except with the most urgent of State affairs. The result was a noticeable falling off in the general discipline of the State, which was soon reflected on the stage. The players, it was noted in March 1605, 'do not forbear to present upon their stage the whole course of this present time, not sparing either King, State, or Religion, in so great absurdity and with such liberty, that any would be afraid to hear them'.

For the first time since the death of Henry VIII there was now a royal family, with the vastly increased expenses of the household. The new Queen was not on the best of terms with her husband, and she liked expensive amusements, so that Court entertainments and pageants were magnificently extravagant. At Christmas 1604 £3000 was expended on the Queen's masque and it was disapprovingly noted that the costumes were more suited to courtesans than to great ladies.

The dignified Court life under Queen Elizabeth soon vanished, and fashionable manners rapidly degenerated. In July 1606 the Danish King paid a state visit to the Court, upon which Sir John Harington (who was no kill-joy) commented 'I think the Dane hath strangely wrought on our good English nobles; for those whom I never could get to taste good liquor now follow the fashion and wallow in beastly delights. The ladies abandon their sobriety and are seen to roll about in intoxication'. Harington went on to describe a masque of Solomon and the Queen of Sheba which was devised for the royal entertainment, but ended disastrously because both the performers and the royal spectators were prostrated by drink. It is small wonder that Hamlet's denunciation of the drunken manners of the Danes should have disappeared from the text of the Folio, or that in the last comedies there should be a pervading sense of disgust at the sordid intrigues of Court life.

At the coming of the King, all who had grievances crowded optimistically to the Court, and in a short time general disappointment set in. The Puritans found that the King had nothing for them; indeed at the Conference held at Hampton Court he rated them soundly. Catholics, who had been led to expect some kind of toleration, were told that the King had said in public audience that he would rather fight in blood to the knees than give toleration of religion. Courtiers of such great standing as Raleigh were put from their posts. Troubles soon began. Raleigh was tried and condemned for the plot to depose the King in favour of the Lady Arabella Stuart in November 1603, and in 1605 the Gunpowder Plot was only discovered on the night before its execution. It was a stupendous plan whereby the whole executive government of the country would have been destroyed at one clap. The players, however, benefited greatly by the changes, and the various companies now became royal servants. The Lord Chamberlain's Company became the King's Men, the Admirals were taken over by the Prince of Wales, the Children of Blackfriars became the Children of the Queen's Revels.

VI

In the new reign Shakespeare wrote fewer plays, and the stories which he chose gave less opportunity for significant parallels of situation and emotion. The remarks of Malcolm in *Macbeth* upon the English king's powers of healing 'the Evil' are a topical and, in their context, not particularly happy compliment to King James. In *King Lear* (performed at Court at Christmas, 1606) the words of Gloucester echoed the disgust at the general deterioration of society and the particular abhorrence of the intrigues and plots of the first four years of the new reign:

> These late eclipses in the sun and moon portend no good to us: though the wisdom of nature can reason it thus and thus, yet nature finds itself scourged by the sequent effects. Love cools, friendship falls off, brothers divide; in cities, mutinies; in countries, discord; in palaces, treason; and the bond cracked between son and father.[1]

Although such speeches bore a special significance for the first hearers, they are not 'topical allusions'; for it was rather Shakespeare's method to see old stories in the light of modern instance than to season his plays with passing references. Nevertheless there are quite a number of direct references which have been generally accepted. Titania's speech of the nine men's morris 'fill'd up with mud'[2] is a reminder of the vile summer of 1594; Gratiano probably referred to the case of Dr Lopez in cursing Shylock.[3] *Hamlet* is full of topicalities of various kinds.

[1] *King Lear*, I, ii, 114–22.
[2] *A Midsummer Night's Dream*, II, i, 82–114.
[3] *The Merchant of Venice*, IV, i, 132.

Rosencrantz's comments on the 'aery of children, little eyases' obviously refer to the stage war, whilst Hamlet's strictures on ranting tragedians and extemporising clowns were probably directed against Edward Alleyn and Will Kempe. In *Twelfth Night* there are well-known references to the new map of the Indies, and a pension to be paid from the Sophy, reminding the audience of the recent doings of Sir Anthony Shirley, who, having made his way from Aleppo to Persia, was appointed the Shah's Ambassador Extraordinary to the Russian Court. There are a number of others. Many remarks too which are obviously topical have not yet been explained; such as Hamlet's cryptic observation 'By the Lord, Horatio, these three years I have taken note of it; the age is grown so picked that the toe of the peasant comes near the heel of the courtier, he galls his kibe'; or Mistress Mall's picture that was like to take dust; or the exact meaning of Feste's remark that 'words are very rascals since bonds disgraced them'. *Love's Labour's Lost*, in particular, is full of quips which have become quite inexplicable.

A serious student of Shakespeare's plays cannot neglect the national background, for in an age that was in so many ways cribbed and confined the problems of the individual were inseparable from the problems of the State. The picture of a Shakespeare magnificently aloof from life may be pleasing to romantic critics, but it does not square either with the facts, or with Shakespeare's own comment upon his art. 'Players', said Hamlet to Polonius, 'are the abstract and brief chronicles of the time; after your death you were better have a bad epitaph than their ill report while you live.' Besides, the purpose and end of playing, 'both at the first and now, was and is, to hold, as 'twere, the mirror up to nature; to show virtue her own feature, scorn her own image, and the very age and body of the time his form and pressure'.

THE SOCIAL BACKGROUND

BY

M. St CLARE BYRNE

Many of the Elizabethan writers are too true to be good. They have given us so faithful a picture of the men and manners of the day that their value as artists is distinctly second to their value as social documents. For the detail that enables us to recreate the Elizabethan scene we go to a dozen other writers rather than Shakespeare. The student who consults such books as Professor Dover Wilson's *Life in Shakespeare's England*, or the present writer's *Elizabethan Life in Town and Country*, finds at once that for the purposes of illustrative quotation Shakespeare figures hardly at all, in comparison to the minor writer. Where the ordinary Elizabethan writer is topical in the situation, characterisation and dialogue of an entire scene, Shakespeare is topical only out of his superfluity—in an aside, a simile, an image, a flourish, a jest. Whereas the contemporaneous is of the very body of the work of such a writer as Ben Jonson it is with Shakespeare largely a matter of separable accident. From Jonson we can extract compact little character sketches of the stock figures of the age, or scenes that are as precise in their Elizabethanism as a document. Isolate from its context in Shakespeare such a scene as the one in *The Merry Wives of Windsor* where Sir Hugh Evans, the schoolmaster, puts little William Page through his paces for the benefit of his mother, and we do not instinctively exclaim 'How Elizabethan!' but probably 'How delightful!' Mrs Page is a mother with a schoolboy son: 'Sir Hugh, my husband says my son profits nothing in the world at his book...'. The Elizabethan matron is the lady of such a book as *The French Garden*,[1] who gives us both the conscious theory of the age and its somewhat self-conscious contemporary expression when she rebukes her son who gets up late in the morning:

Come hither, friend! I am ashamed to hear that what I hear of you....You have almost attained to the age of nine years, at least to eight and a half, and seeing that you know your duty, if you neglect it you deserve greater punishment than he which through ignorance doth it not. Think not the nobility of your ancestors doth free you to do as you list: contrariwise, it bindeth you more to follow virtue

Ben Jonson put it memorably when he declared that Shakespeare was not of an age but for all time. We are right to feel that he beyond all his fellows escaped more completely from that pressure of immediacy and the contemporaneous that mutes the poetry, constricts the heart, chills the blood and trammels the flight of the imaginative artist—driving him either into the circumscription and delimitation of 'realism', or else into realms of fantastic 'escape'. He is robustly independent of the pressure which drove Sidney into Arcadia, and Dekker to Alsatia. Like all great artists he was less susceptible to pitifulness in the concrete shape of rags and wretchedness, debt and beggary and disease, at his doors, than to the heart of pity. Where a writer like Galsworthy focuses his gaze too narrowly on Mrs Jones the charwoman, Shakespeare gets 'pity' itself—states the thing universally, as in Lear's 'Poor naked wretches!'....

From one point of view, therefore, we are right when we assert that the relation of Shakespeare to the manners and customs and topicalities of his age is matter for the editor of the annotated edition—the stuff of which examiners and examinations are made—of interest to the antiquary, but of little value to the lover of the plays. Maria is not more essentially herself when she compares Malvolio's face, creased into a thousand wrinkles by his efforts to smile, to 'the new map with the augmentation of the Indies'. It added vividness in its own day: but it adds

[1] By Peter Erondelle. For a modern edition see *The Elizabethan Home*, ed. M. St C. Byrne.

nothing to her character. If we leave it out nobody but the one person in a thousand who has seen the map, with its amazing rhumb lines, is any the poorer to-day. It is of little importance that Juliet's burial conforms to Italian and not English custom. It has nothing to do with any so-called Italian atmosphere. There are two reasons why she is borne to the church 'as the custom is' on an open bier. The first—Shakespeare found the detail in his source, Arthur Brooke's poem: the second—some such device was essential to the story.

When everything possible, however, has been urged against antiquarianism, the fact remains that every genuine student of Shakespeare, who wishes to come to grips with the thought of the plays and to realise to the full their complete dramatic values, needs, for this more thorough apprehension, some detailed knowledge of that particular social order which happens to be their general background. It is a fact that the organisation of life in Shakespeare's England differed considerably from ours to-day; and we must understand what those differences are, if we are to know his people as fully as possible, and appreciate the subtler points of their emotional relationships,[1] their behaviour and reactions to each other and to their circumstances. He will sacrifice verisimilitude to the requirements of drama, but throughout he takes for granted the social fabric of his age.

It follows, therefore, that the background of life in the plays is, and at the same time is not, the background of Elizabethan life. As an example—old Capulet is an admirable picture of a testy Elizabethan parent, and his behaviour to Juliet in the matter of the match with Paris reminds us instantly of the perpetually quoted account that Lady Jane Grey gives of her own noble father and mother. The human reality is faithfully portrayed, and at the same time the detail of the portrait is contemporary. If, however, we go on lightheartedly to assume that old Capulet in his behaviour as a 'nobleman' bears any resemblance to an Elizabethan noble of similar standing we shall be hopelessly misled. If we compare him with the genuine article

[1] As, for example, in Malvolio's overheard soliloquy, cf. *infra*, pp. 204, 210.

we realise at once that the intimate 'realistic', or Elizabethan, scenes in which he appears are purely 'romantic', or, if we prefer, untrue to the facts of contemporary noble life. Shakespeare may label Capulet the head of a noble household, who can treat Paris, 'a young Nobleman, Kinsman to the Prince', as his equal, and a proper match for his daughter; but when it comes to a scene like Act IV, Sc. iv, which shows the home life of this supposed nobleman, we realise that the setting is not Verona but Stratford, and that the most likely person to have sat for that very realistic portrait is John Shakespeare, or any of the good burgesses who were William's father's friends. They probably got in the way of all their busy servants and kitchen staff on the occasions of daughters' weddings: but it is quite certain that an Elizabethan nobleman, with his retinue of anything from twenty to eighty gentlemen officers, and from a hundred to five hundred yeomen servants, did not come into personal contact with Antony and Potpan, Peter and Angelica, and did not himself have to issue orders for the quenching of fires and the turning up of tables.[1] In these scenes Capulet is brother to Dekker's jolly shoemaker, Simon Eyre, not to Lord Burghley.

This Capulet instance may be a rather simple and obvious one, but it warns us quite effectively that it will not be safe to assume, on Shakespeare's evidence only, that his 'realistic' scenes can be accepted without question as Elizabethan. There are, indeed, two questions which, with their answers, form an inevitable preliminary to any general consideration of the relation of Shakespeare's plays to the life of Elizabethan England. The first is—does Shakespeare make deliberate differences between the life and manners of plays whose scene is set in England, and those whose scene is set either in some European or some imaginary country? The second is—does he differentiate between the life of his own day, and that of past ages? They are both plain questions with plain answers, but they are all too

[1] Cf. *infra*, p. 206. But see also *De Maisse's Journal* (trans. Harrison and Jones) where Queen Elizabeth herself can be found giving orders for quenching a fire in the Privy Chamber.

frequently confused and complicated by being broken up into such themes as 'Shakespeare's anachronisms', his geographical knowledge, his possible or alleged travels, his knowledge of history, his use of local colour, etc.

Now there is no reason to suppose that Shakespeare got any more dramatic value out of accuracy and inaccuracy than any other dramatist, with a popular audience, in any age. In matters historical and geographical the delights of accuracy, and consequently of inaccuracy, are alike wasted upon the average audience. Whether ancient or Elizabethan, Roman, Venetian or English, the truth about Shakespeare's scenes is that they are all set in the theatre. I do not believe that Shakespeare ever bothered his own imagination or his audience's as to where, in *The Merchant of Venice*, an imaginary Venice ends and his own London begins. Nor can I believe that either he or they ever gave a thought to whether there were or should be differences between life at the Court of Cymbeline and at the Courts of Elsinore or Bohemia or Richard II. In relation to all misleading subdivisions of these questions there is only one simple issue for the dramatist—what 'corroborative detail' out of life, talk, books, will enable his imagined people to live more intensely and credibly for their hour upon the stage?

The dramatist's response to this problem is a twofold one. For the benefit of himself and the more sensitive members of his audience he has congruous allusion. It may mean nothing to the general, but mention of the Rialto and of Antonio's trading ventures gives depth and solidity to the figures of Antonio and Shylock, as Cotsall and 'a good yoke of bullocks at Stamford Fair' give body to Shallow and Silence. Infinitely more useful from a dramatic point of view, however, is familiar reference—the sweeping up into the body of the dialogue of the everyday realities of the Elizabethan background. Thus it is that clocks strike in ancient Rome, Roman Britain and Ephesus: Hector quotes Aristotle, and Pandarus talks of Friday and Sunday: the Ephesians conduct monetary transactions in ducats, marks and guilders, and ancient Britons and Romans dispute over a tribute of £3000. Thus it is that households in Illyria are staffed on strictly Elizabethan lines: that we find the abbess of a nunnery in Ephesus, a nine men's morris in the wood near Athens, and Whitsun pastorals, the hobby horse and Christian burial in pagan Bohemia: that Claudius of Denmark is guarded, very inefficiently, by 'Switzers': and that Pandarus compares the soldiers who pass by after the incomparable Troilus to 'porridge after meat'.

It extends, of course, to his use of names. For the sake of congruity there are Antonios, Orsinos, Antipholuses and Leonatos. But the schoolmaster in Ephesus is called Pinch: Snug, Bottom and the other English mechanicals are found plying their trades in Athens: Elbow, Froth and Mistress Overdone inhabit not Southwark but the stews of Vienna: Dull, Costard and Moth have strayed beyond the Pyrenees to Navarre: Belch and Aguecheek cavort in Illyria: Dogberry and Verges keep the watch in Messina: even Coriolanus speaks of the Roman mob as 'Hob and Dick': and the Gobbos, who are well known in the parish registers of Titchfield—the home of the Earl of Southampton—turn up in Venice.

References to clothing and its accessories are, with a very few exceptions, definitely Elizabethan. Cleopatra has a 'lace' which Charmian has to cut: in the Rome of Coriolanus and the Athens of Timon they wear 'hats', and the conspirators in *Julius Caesar* have their hats pulled about their ears, while Caesar himself 'plucks me ope his doublet'. According to Hamlet they wore the fashionable shoe-rosettes of James's Court at Elsinore, as well as the sixteenth-century chopine: they had new ribbons to their pumps in Athens for the performance of 'Pyramus and Thisbe': Poins wore peach-coloured silk stockings in the London of Henry IV: Falstaff ordered satin for an (Elizabethan) 'short cloak and slops', and thought Mistress Ford would look well in a 'semicircled farthingale', and Doll accused Pistol of tearing 'a poor whore's ruff in a bawdy house'. Chiron in *Titus Andronicus* wears the fashionable Elizabethan 'dancing rapier', the courtier's ornamental weapon; and Shakespeare gives the Tudor rapier to most of his other quarrelsome gentlemen, whether they live in fourteenth-century Verona, twelfth-century Denmark, the turmoil of Yorkist-Lancastrian England, or the mediaeval England of Richard II, Henry IV and Henry V. The plundering Romans carry off from Corioli 'doublets that hangmen would bury with those that wore them'. The fashionable Elizabethan scented glove seems equally popular in pagan Bohemia, where Autolycus sells the yokels 'gloves as sweet as damask roses'; and in Troy Helen swears 'by Venus' glove', while Troilus throws his to Death as a challenge, and takes a glove from Cressida as a love token. In *Coriolanus* matrons fling their gloves to greet the victor of Corioli; and in *Timon of Athens* Alcibiades throws his glove to the senators in token of his friendly intentions.

Food and drink and furniture are all Elizabethan. They pick English wild flowers in the meadows of Bohemia, and English garden flowers in Perdita's rustic garden. Ophelia's flowers are English, as English as the brook with its slanting willow where she drowns herself: and Juliet's corpse is strewn with rosemary, like any properly coffined English maiden's. Titania sleeps on a bank of wild thyme, 'o'er-canopied' with English woodland flowers; and the gardeners in *Richard II* bind up that Tudor newcomer of fruits, the 'dangling apricocks'. And besides this lode of familiar allusion there are complete passages in the dialogue which serve the same purpose. Touchstone's disquisition on the degrees of a quarrel, Mercutio's anatomy of duelling, Hamlet's lecture on actors and acting, are all pure Elizabethan set pieces. Equally, if the talk is of games or dancing, hunting, hawking, bear-baiting, greyhound coursing, or other sport, reference and language are alike that of Shakespeare's own day.

The point of it all is—verisimilitude, actuality. It is also the main point of such peculiarly Elizabethan sketches as Oswald, Osric and Parolles. We may dislike the last, think the second preposterous, and feel the first to be an alien in the world of *King Lear*: but they are all three accurate topical portraits, which must undoubtedly have made Shakespeare's own audience more at home in ancient Britain and at Elsinore. Shakespeare does not handle time and place directly: he translates them into terms of emotional atmosphere. His differentiation between ancient and modern times, and between English, foreign and imagined realms, is not achieved by historical detail or local colour. The Venetian background of *The Merchant of Venice* is negligible, so far as local colour is concerned. It amounts to references to the Rialto, to a gondola and to the 'tranect' or common ferry, to Mantua and Padua and Rome. But if these things are negligible, the emotional atmosphere of Renaissance culture in which the play is set is all-important. The grace, the dignity, and the sweet gravity of the verse, translate the characters from the London-Venice of their creation into that scene of timeless abstraction which is Renaissance feeling.

It is more or less the same with *Cymbeline*, which is not so much given a setting as made decorative in the Renaissance manner. Nominally the scene is Roman Britain and Rome; but Posthumus is a 'gentleman of the bedchamber' to a king who was 'knighted' by Augustus Caesar, and when he leaves for Rome he waves farewell with glove and hat and handkerchief. Imogen packs the 'doublet and hose' for her disguise in a 'cloak-bag', invents for herself a dead master, 'a very valiant Briton' called 'Richard du Champ', and takes service as a 'page' with Caius Lucius. Imagery and oaths have a slight classical flavour; and the atmosphere suggested is that of antiquity as conceived by the Renaissance[1]—left on record in their paintings of classical subjects, and recently in our own time translated on the stage into the visual realities of costume and setting by the Compagnie

[1] The illustrations of the 1577 edition of Holinshed's *Chronicles* should help the student to appreciate this point. A set of some dozen or more 'portraits', in fancy dress, has to be repeated until it has done duty for most of the monarchs from Brute to Harold. Leir, for example, is dressed in the usual Renaissance version of a Roman *lorica* and helmet (cf. the Peacham illustration of *Titus Andronicus*, reproduced in Chambers's *Shakespeare*, I, 312), and his effigy afterwards reappears for Julius Frontinus and Placidius. Duncan is also dressed Roman, though Macbeth and Banquo meeting the Weird Sisters ride as middle-aged Elizabethan gentlemen of sober but good taste and habit. Brute 'kills his father by misfortune' attired in the hunting costume of an Elizabethan gentleman (cf. Turbervile's *Noble arte of venerie or hunting*, 1575) and the same picture afterwards does duty for the slaying of William Rufus. But if Brute turns parricide in Elizabethan garments (p. 10), on the next page he adjusts matters by changing into a reasonably correct Roman tunic and armour to pursue his similarly clad Trojan enemies into a river—which latter plate serves then on p. 440 to illustrate a Scottish battle of 1529. More or less genuine Britons fight adequate (Renaissance) Romans at p. 123, and really good Romans win the battle of Tewkesbury.

des Quinze for their production of the *Viol de Lucrèce*. In sum, neither accuracy nor inaccuracy flaws the atmosphere in which Shakespeare means a play to have its being. In *King Lear* Kent is put in the stocks, Edmund is a sixteenth-century Italianate villain, and paper, holy water, the French disease, Bedlam beggars, etc., are Elizabethan actualities: but not all the Elizabethanism in the world can temper the play's ancient savagery with a contemporary civility. It is a savagery of primitive spirit and primitive passion, not of archaism.

A rapid summary of this kind is in no sense exhaustive, but it serves, at least, to establish a general answer to these general questions concerning the life, manners and scene of the plays. The scene is the stage, and the idiom of life contemporary. With the ground thus cleared only one further warning is necessary. In the following pages an attempt will be made to determine the social standing and the social relationships of certain typical individuals in the plays; but it cannot be too emphatically stated that the greatest circumspection must be used before further attempts are made to base upon the material thus collected for a special purpose general assumptions about Shakespeare's knowledge and ignorance. Shakespeare is not a document: he is a dramatist. We may think it probable that when he drew old Capulet he did not know what life in a noble household was like; but we do not know this for a fact. Every student should take the Folio's list of dramatis personae in *Othello* as a significant warning. In it Iago is described as 'a Villaine', Cassio as 'an Honourable Lieutenant', Desdemona as 'Wife to Othello', and Emilia as 'Wife to Iago'. Here is dramatic and artistic truth; and if, after studying carefully the text of this or any other of the plays and what we know of Elizabethan life, we are still in doubt as to the exact social status of Iago and Emilia or any other character, the only assumption warranted is not one concerning Shakespeare's knowledge and experience, but simply that it does not matter to us, as it did not matter to the dramatist.

In so far as the detail of Elizabethan life and custom differs from the modern, reference to a good annotated edition, or to

Shakespeare's England, will generally clear up most difficulties. Nor need we concern ourselves here with his presentation of 'the people', or of ordinary burgess households in which the social relationships—including that of master and servant—are simple and comprehensible. In *The Comedy of Errors*, *The Merry Wives of Windsor*, and *The Taming of the Shrew* (setting aside the Induction to the last), we have only to deal with the relations between gentlemen, burgesses, work-people, and servants of the yeoman class, all of which are very much as they might be to-day, allowing for a little more exuberance and general heartiness all round. At the same time their 'contemporary' quality has been affirmed and demonstrated often enough to allow us to accept Shakespeare's picture without further question. But for the greater number of the plays, which are set in the Courts and households of kings, nobles and petty princes, the commentators as a whole have given us so little help that there is not in existence any one composite and documented account of this aspect of the Elizabethan background to which the student can be referred. To understand the circumstances and relationships of regal and noble life we have to investigate a social order of which we know very little to-day—an order in which the 'servants' or 'serving-men' are 'the Duke's son preferred page to the Prince, the Earl's second son attendant upon the Duke, the Knight's second son the Earl's servant, the Esquire's son to wear the Knight's livery, and the Gentleman's son the Esquire's serving-man'.[1] We are faced with the task of disentangling Elizabethan and modern notions of 'service', and in consequence we cannot afford to start with the plays themselves. Shakespeare is not a document: and we must establish the facts before we are entitled to question the authenticity of old Capulet's portrait, or to follow up similar investigations into the 'reality' or accuracy of Shakespeare's rendering of this extremely important aspect of contemporary life.

By 'the Court' was meant at once Elizabeth's house, her household, and the seat of government. All the important noblemen of the realm were in attendance at Court for a large part of the year, and the organisation of the household was an extra-

[1] *A Health to the Gentlemanly Profession of Serving Men*, by J. M. (1598).

ordinarily elaborate and complicated affair. The best and most complete account of it is to be found in E. K. Chambers's *Elizabethan Stage* (vol. I). All that can be attempted here is an indication of those aspects and details of Court life and ceremony which are relevant to the study of Shakespeare's plays.

The first thing to realise is that access to the sovereign—except for those in personal attendance—was extremely difficult. It is generally allowed that anyone who had the right to come to Court had the right of access to the Presence Chamber;[1] but if their desire was to speak to the Queen they were as far to seek as ever, unless they could obtain the grant of an audience. We are more accustomed to the amiable and picturesque anecdotes of Elizabeth on progress and on public occasions, staging herself with inimitable glamour and effect as the 'mere English' monarch in the bluff King Hal tradition, whom the meanest of her subjects might approach. But it is very necessary to balance this impression by reading some such account as the one given us by Rowland Whyte[2] of the denials, rebuffs and heart-breaking delays which kept even such great ladies as the kinsfolk and friends of the Earl of Essex from gaining access to the Queen, in order to plead his cause during the period of his disgrace. From Whyte's letters we can also realise not only this jealously guarded privacy of the monarch, but also the elaborate ceremonial with which it was preserved, and the impressiveness that was attached even to the actual progress through the palace of anyone fortunate enough to secure an audience. When the Dutch ambassador, Vereiken, was received in 1600 he was met officially at the gate of the palace, and taken to the Hall. From thence he was conducted through the Council Chamber to the

[1] See *Ordinances*: Household of Charles II: 'All persons of gentlemen of quality and of good fashion, and the gentlemen that attend our great officers and privy counsellors and persons of good quality are permitted to come and remain in the said chamber, and all wives and daughters of the nobility and their women that attend them, may pass through this chamber, and all other ladies of good rank and quality, but not their servants'. The ordinances for the Queen's Privy Chamber in 1627 declare that no one under the degree of a baroness can be admitted, 'unless sworn of the chamber'.

[2] A. Collins, *Letters and Memorials of State*, II, letters of 4 Nov., 29 Nov., 8 Dec. 1599; 3 Mar. 1600; etc.

Great Chamber, which was 'full of ladies and gentlemen' and the guard. He then passed through the Presence Chamber, 'full of great ladies' and 'the fair Maids, attired all in white', from which he was led to the Privy Chamber, where all the Ladies of the Privy Chamber were assembled. Finally he was received by the Queen in the Withdrawing Chamber, in the presence of all the Lords of the Privy Council, and, to complete the effect, 'his followers were suffered to enter in with him'.[1]

The personal attendants of the monarch were the Gentlemen of the Privy Chamber. Henry VIII had eighteen such gentlemen, six of whom were in attendance at once, with two Gentlemen-Ushers and four Grooms of the Chamber to assist them. They were the only persons who were allowed to help the King to dress. His doublet, hose and shoes were brought to the door of the Privy Chamber by the Yeoman of the Wardrobe, where they were taken by the grooms, who, with the ushers, enjoyed the privilege of warming the clothes before they handed them to the gentlemen. Every night the grooms made up pallet beds in the Privy Chamber for two of the gentlemen who were required to sleep there. During the day they had at all times to remain in the Privy Chamber. They were allowed to amuse the tedium of waiting by 'honest and moderate' card-play, dicing, chess and tables, from which they had to desist at once as soon as they were warned of the King's approach.[2]

Under Elizabeth these eighteen gentlemen were retained, but their duties of personal attendance naturally devolved upon the Ladies or Gentlewomen of the Bedchamber and the Privy Chamber, while the housemaid work of the grooms was carried out by four 'chamberers' or chambermaids. Apparently three Ladies of the Bedchamber and five of the Privy Chamber were in attendance at once.[3] There was, of course, tremendous competition for these posts. Not only were the fees good—the gentlemen received £50 and the ladies £33. 6*s*. 8*d*. per annum—but the lucky holders came in for other valuable rewards of service, such

[1] A. Collins, *Letters and Memorials of State*, II, 170.

[2] *Ordinances for the Household made at Eltham*, 1526.

[3] Chambers, *Elizabethan Stage*, vol. I, citing Lansdowne MSS. LIX, f. 43.

as the reversion of profitable leases, and sometimes even large gifts of money.[1] According to one list the total personnel of the Privy Chamber consisted of the Lord Chamberlain, the Vice-Chamberlain, four Knights, the Knight-Marshal, eighteen Gentlemen, four Gentlemen-Ushers, the Groom-Porter, fourteen Grooms, four Carvers, three Cupbearers, four Sewers, four Squires to the Body, four Yeomen-Ushers, four Pages, four Messengers, two Clerks of the Closet,[2] and the Ladies already mentioned. Elizabeth also followed the custom of her sister and of her father's queens in having always in attendance the famous Maids of Honour—six young women of noble or gentle birth, in charge of an older lady known as the Mother of the Maids. Chambers states that the maids did not receive any salary, but in Henry VIII's time at any rate they were paid £10, in addition to their board and lodging.[3] With the kitchen and all the provisioning offices, the wardrobe, the stable, and the rest we need not concern ourselves, but mention should be made of the Gentlemen Pensioners and the Guard. The Pensioners,[4] carrying their gilt battle-axes, formed a guard of honour which escorted the Queen on most occasions. The Guard was the palace guard,[5] whose uniform is still familiar to us as that worn by the 'beefeaters' of the Tower.

The etiquette and ceremonial complications of regal life find but little reflection in the plays. What Shakespeare either did not know, or else deliberately rejected for dramatic purposes, was the circumstance and order of life in a royal household. By ignorance or by design—more probably a mixture of both—he has given us a romantic picture. It was natural that he should seize upon as apt for dramatic purposes the popular aspect of royalty,[6] with which Elizabeth's subjects were well acquainted: Shakespeare and his Queen both possessed a superb sense of the

[1] See especially Calendars of State Papers (Domestic) for the whole reign. For example, in 1594, Lady Scudamore, Gentlewoman of the Bedchamber, received £300 as the Queen's free gift (S.P.O. Dom. 1594, CCXLVIII, May 31st).

[2] Printed in Peck, *Desiderata Curiosa*, and *Ordinances*.

[3] See below, pp. 207–8.

[4] Under Elizabeth this establishment numbered 50.

[5] 100 ordinary yeomen, and 50 extraordinary.

[6] *E.g.* Theseus with the 'mechanicals', Henry V both as Prince and King.

theatre. What is surprising, however, is that he should so entirely neglect the dramatic opportunities offered by the intimate-formal routine of Court life, had he been acquainted with it. *Henry VIII*, in which we must allow for the collaboration of Fletcher, is the only play which exploits it in any way, though the natural dramatic value of this carefully staged remoteness and inaccessibility is enormous.

But Shakespeare will have none of it. Court life in the plays is definitely a homely affair in comparison with Court life at Whitehall. It is accurately Elizabethan—that is, true to the architectural reality of any great Elizabethan house—to take Hamlet through the King's chamber in order to reach his mother's closet; but no monarch at his prayers would ever have been left so (theatrically) unprotected as Claudius. In the circumstances of complete distrust which Hamlet creates for himself by the 'Mouse-trap' play he could not have progressed so far through antechambers and presence chambers without some announcement from the grooms of the Chamber, the gentlemen-ushers, and the gentlemen of the Privy Chamber, let alone the guard! In fact—as Claudius remarked later—'Where are my Switzers?' The Tudors knew a great deal about the divinity that hedged kings, but they took care to reinforce it with normal precautions. The danger of assassination was ever present. We come back to reality in Act IV, Sc. V, when Ophelia is not able to obtain access to the Queen until permission is given and she is brought in by a gentleman-in-waiting.

In general, the way in which anyone in the plays can obtain access to the monarch is a matter of theatrical licence. Messengers should not burst into the royal presence without being announced by gentlemen-ushers. But they rush in gaily in *Cymbeline* (II, ii), in *Hamlet* (IV, vii), in *Antony and Cleopatra* (II, v), in *Richard III* (II, iv), and *Henry V* (II, iv), when no particular dramatic purpose save economy is thereby served. In *Richard II* Aumerle —a man already suspect—rushes wildly into the presence (V, iii), to be pursued to the door a moment later, first by his father, and then by his mother, both of whom shout and clamour for admission until the King unlocks the door. The reasonable stage version of actuality can be seen in *Henry VIII* (III, i), where a gentleman enters to Queen Katharine to crave admission for Wolsey and Cardinal Campeius, who 'wait in the presence', 'great cardinals' as they are. When in Act IV, Sc. ii, divorced and dying, she is burst in upon by a messenger, real dramatic purpose is served by this violation of the decencies:

Enter a Messenger.

Mess. An't like your Grace—
Kath. You are a saucy fellow:
Deserve we no more reverence?
Grif. You are to blame,
Knowing she will not lose her wonted greatness,
To use so rude behaviour; go to, kneel.

In the presentation of regal and noble life Shakespeare bends actuality to his purpose how and when he pleases. His handling of murder is an instance of this. Assassination or the murder of a king in the sixteenth century simply could not be carried out privately, unless it was done by poison.[1] To attack the victim unexpectedly on some public occasion was the only way. We have only to look at all the famous murders of the time to realise this—Henry III of France, Henry of Navarre, the Guise, William the Silent, the Regent Moray, even a simple person like Rizzio. All took place in circumstances of the utmost publicity. When it suits him to do so Shakespeare keeps close to contemporary practice, as in the murder of Claudius: the last scene of *Hamlet* is admirably and accurately contrived. Infinitely the most impressive of all his murder scenes, however, is the murder of Duncan, which is almost completely 'romantic' in its disregard of contemporary circumstance.

Lady Macbeth does her best to provide 'corroborative detail' by explaining how she has drugged the two chamberlains or grooms of Duncan's chamber, so that he sleeps unguarded. That these so-called grooms should have been gentlemen-in-waiting, of the same standing as Macduff, is unimportant.[2] What Mac-

[1] Even poison was a matter of extreme difficulty. Royal and noble food was still 'tasted'. See also G. B. Harrison, *Second Eliz. Journal*, pp. 320–2 for an account of a plan to kill Elizabeth by poisoning the pommel of her saddle.

[2] Cf. *supra*, p. 198 and *infra*, pp. 203, 205–6, 215–17.

beth and his lady would, in reality, have found extraordinarily difficult, would be to get rid of their own ladies and gentlemen-in-waiting and their own grooms, without first going through the ceremony of going to bed.[1] Shakespeare compromises by providing Macbeth with one servant, whom he dismisses—

> Go, bid thy mistress, when my drink is ready
> She strike upon the bell. Get thee to bed.

One servant is a reasonable dramatic symbol for attendance, but unless we dismiss with him all 'realistic' criteria we must remember that—to take only one instance—Lady Macbeth would have found it practically impossible to escape the observation of that extremely alert waiting-gentlewoman of Act v, Sc. i, not to mention the various grooms who would have had to stay up to quench fires and lights and lock up after all the waiting-gentlewomen and gentlemen had gone to bed. It is all very well for Lady Macbeth to tell her husband

> Get on your night-gown, lest occasion call us,
> And show us to be watchers;

but actually the nightgown—which was a dressing-gown or robe—would have been in the care of the Yeoman of the Wardrobe, and when required would have been handed to a gentleman-in-waiting who would have helped his lord to put it on. Macbeth would probably have had no idea where to find his nightgown for himself. Even in a modern household that is well maided and valeted it is often impossible to find a garment without ringing for the servant who gives personal attendance—attendance which still means constant surveillance and attention, but which is absolutely negligible in comparison with what would have been found in any Elizabethan nobleman's household. In fact, if a sixteenth-century monarch is to be privately murdered by a nobleman, circumstances such as those arranged for Evadne in *The Maides Tragedy* are practically the only possibility, if the dramatist is to be forced to consider the 'realities' of every-day life.

[1] Cf. *infra*, pp. 205–6.

The household of an Elizabethan nobleman was organised on the same lines as the Court, though on a somewhat smaller scale. The number of gentlemen-in-waiting and of yeoman servants would naturally vary according to the means of the individual and the state which he desired to keep, but the household officers and the conditions of service were the same in large or small establishments. At the head of every household was the Steward, who was responsible to the master or mistress for the general conduct of affairs, for the provisioning, for keeping an eye on the necessary repairs all over the estate, for the payment of wages, the overlooking of all departmental accounts, and the discipline of the staff. Associated with him as a rule, but of subsidiary importance, were the Comptroller and the Treasurer or Cofferer. In a group by themselves came such persons as Secretaries, Schoolmasters and Chaplains; and in another people whose employment was not strictly within the household, such as a High Steward of Courts, an Auditor, a Receiver-General and a Solicitor—any or all of whom might be needed by a nobleman with large estates to administer. A Master or Gentleman of the Horses was usual in most households, and the rest of the gentlemen-servingmen were as a rule grouped as Gentlemen-Ushers, Sewers, Carvers, Gentlemen of the Chamber and Gentlemen-in-Waiting or Gentlemen Waiters. Beneath all these were the yeomen servants and the grooms belonging to all the different offices, such as ewry, pantry, bakehouse, cellar, kitchen, wardrobe, stables. The laundry was generally staffed by women, and the immediate attendants of the ladies of the household were waiting-gentlewomen and chamberers or chambermaids.

In most noble households in Tudor times the greater number of these gentlemen servants were gentlemen by birth. Many of them possessed independent means, and were the owners of or heirs to estates. It is said of Burghley that 'most of the principal gentlemen in England sought to prefer their sons and heirs to his service', and that he had 'attending on his table' twenty gentlemen, each of whom had £1000 a year 'in possession and reversion'.[1] The treasurer of the Household to Edward Earl of

[1] Peck, *Desiderata Curiosa*, I, 24, 1779.

Derby, who died in 1572, was a knight, Sir Richard Shierborn:[1] the House Steward of Gilbert Talbot, seventh Earl of Shrewsbury, who died in 1592, had previously been senior Fellow of St John's College, Cambridge.[2] The Steward of the fifth Earl of Northumberland, in Henry VIII's time, had three personal servants to attend on him.[3] The Steward of the Earl of Derby ruled an establishment of eighty gentlemen and five hundred yeomen.[2] The Steward of even the most modest household, such as that of Katharine Willoughby, Dowager Duchess of Suffolk, would have at least eighty to a hundred persons in his charge.[4]

From such facts as these it is easy to see that an Elizabethan household steward was a gentleman of considerable importance, occupying a very responsible position, which gave him the exercise of very considerable power, and must probably have called for much discretion and tact. Anthony Browne, second Viscount Montague, in his *Booke of Orders and Rules*[5] for the conduct of his household at Cowdray, gives us a detailed account of the duties of all his servants, and is particularly interesting on the subject of his Steward. The Steward was the chief officer in the house. He dined and supped in the great hall, seated in the place of honour, at his own table, 'and that always in a gown, unless he be booted'. His instructions were, not to 'give place unto any'; and gentlemen strangers who were entertained at the castle ate at his table. The preservation of discipline was in his hands, and the Viscount writes:

I will that in civil sort he do reprehend and correct the negligent and disordered persons, and reform them by his grave admonitions and vigilant eye over them, the riotous, the contentious, and quarrelous persons of any degree...the frequenters of tabling, carding, and dicing in corners and at untimely hours and seasons...The incorrigible persons and wilful maintainers of their outragious misgovernment and unsufferable disorders...whom neither his persuasions, reason itself, nor authority can contain within the limit of their duty: of

[1] J. Nichols, *Illustrations of the Manners and Expences of Antient Times*, 1797.
[2] Calendar S.P.O. Dom. 1591–4, CCXLI, 174.
[3] *The Earl of Northumberland's Household Book*, ed. Bishop Percy, 1770.
[4] *Historical MSS. Commission, Earl of Ancaster's MSS.* p. 459.
[5] *Sussex Archaeological Collections*, vol. VII.

them I will that he give me information, and leave them and their cause to mine own consideration.

The Viscount had his rules read aloud to the assembled household once a year 'about the audit time'. In view of *Twelfth Night* (II, iii, 95 ff.) one might almost imagine that Malvolio or his creator had somehow managed to be present on one such occasion![1]

The Viscount's Gentleman-Usher seems to have been directly responsible, under the Steward, for the detailed organisation of the work and duties of both the gentlemen and the yeomen servitors; or, as the Viscount has it, 'He shall have authority, in civil and kind manner, to command any gentleman or yeoman to do any service that shall be for mine honour'. It was his business to appoint his lordship's carvers and sewers from among the number of his gentlemen, to attend upon visitors in the morning and make all arrangements for their comfort, and to wait upon the Viscount at dinner—'wait', that is to say, in the general sense of overseeing the details of the service. He was commanded, for example, to see that no waiter was allowed 'to carry a dish or attend at my table in doublet and hose only, without either coat, cloak, or some upper garment'.[2]

The Gentlemen of the Chamber attended to the Viscount's personal wants when he rose in the morning and when he went

[1] Those who like to believe that Shakespeare drew from the life may be interested in the following 'possible' connexion between him and this particular document. The dedicatee of *Venus and Adonis* (1593) and *Lucrece* (1594), as well, probably, as the beloved youth of the *Sonnets*, was Henry Wriothesley, third Earl of Southampton. He was born in 1573, and succeeded to the earldom in 1581. His mother was Mary Browne, daughter of the first Viscount Montague. Anthony Browne, born in 1574 (four months later than Southampton), who succeeded his grandfather as second Viscount in 1592, was therefore his first cousin. We have no evidence as to the degree of intimacy that existed between them, but we know that Anthony was brought up at Cowdray, and that Southampton stayed there with his grandfather from time to time. It was quite near to his own home, Titchfield. The old Viscount took a considerable interest in the affairs of his elder grandson, and it is likely that the cousins saw a good deal of each other in childhood and youth. While accepting implicitly the machinery and order of life with which the 'Rules' deal, it is not difficult to imagine that the young Earl might have been amused by the somewhat pompous and self-conscious 'Booke', as written up by his junior in 1595, at the age of twenty-one!

[2] A detailed description of the ceremony of the serving of the Viscount's dinner can be found in the present writer's *Elizabethan Life*, pp. 31, 32.

to bed. The senior amongst them waited upon his 'trencher and cup, at dinner and supper', and acted as a personal attendant wherever he went. The Gentlemen-in-Waiting attended the Viscount and his wife whenever they 'walked abroad', and arranged amongst themselves so that a sufficient number of them were always in attendance in the Great Chamber by 10 a.m. When required by the Gentleman-Usher to do so they acted as valets to guests staying in the house, and in the order of precedence took their place after the Gentlemen of the Horse, who in their turn took place after the Gentlemen of the Chamber.

The Yeoman-Usher was in charge of the Grooms of the Chamber and the Yeomen of the Chamber. He saw to it that they kept the Great Chamber and the dining chambers clean and tidy; and, under the Gentleman-Usher, supervised the serving of the meals. The Yeomen of the Chamber were responsible for the keeping and the proper care of the Viscount's apparel, linen, robes and jewels. They slept in the withdrawing chamber, adjoining the bedchamber, so as to be at hand if required. They brushed carpets, laid fires, and prepared, brushed and laid out the Viscount's wearing apparel for the day. They made the Viscount's bed, and did all necessary housemaid's work. Unlike the housemaid, however, they were also required to attend upon the Viscount when he walked in the park, 'one to carry my cloak; the rest to do mine errands, to take up and make clean my bowls, and the like'. The Grooms did all servants' work in the Great Chamber, such as making the fires, and fetching drink for the meals. The Yeomen of the Chamber, however, were responsible at night for seeing to the quenching of fires and lights and for locking up after everyone had gone to bed.[1]

Even when it is possible to discover the actual names of people who occupied positions in noble Elizabethan households it is generally very difficult to find out anything about them. In consequence, it is almost impossible to be definite and precise as to the exact social standing of a steward or a waiting-gentlewoman

[1] For further details see Note A, p. 215.

or a gentleman-in-waiting. In general we should be right to expect such persons to be of gentle birth, and in the cases of waiting-gentlemen and gentlewomen sometimes of the same social status as their employers. The theory of service was that those of gentle birth were served personally by men and women also of gentle birth. By the beginning of the seventeenth century, however, it is probable that conditions were slightly different from what they had been a hundred years earlier, and that there were more waiting-gentlemen and gentlewomen who were 'gentle' only by virtue of their office than there had been in earlier Tudor times. The old idea was that the proper places for 'goodman Tomson's Jack, or Robin Rush, my gaffer Russetcoat's second son' were 'the one holding the plough, the other whipping the carthorse'; but by 1598 J. M. is complaining that the 'Gentlemanly Profession of Serving Men' is being invaded by these farmers' sons and others of the same class, so that service is no longer the honourable calling it was, and that the real 'gentleman' servant is often hard put to it to secure employment. It is, of course, literary evidence, and must not be too liberally interpreted; but we are probably right to take it as a warning that during Shakespeare's lifetime, the range of birth, means, breeding and character, within this class technically described as 'gentle', may have been considerable.

A few examples will help to illustrate the situation. They belong to the period twenty-five years previous to the birth of Shakespeare, but I believe they are typical for the whole of the century. Honor Grenville—a daughter of the family rendered illustrious by the Elizabethan Sir Richard, amongst others—became by her first marriage the third wife of Sir John Basset of Umberleigh in Devon. Three of her seven children were Anne, Katherine and Phillippa, to each of whom Sir John left a marriage dowry and £3. 16*s*. 4*d*. a year 'for their sufficient finding'.[1] As her second husband Honor married Arthur Plantagenet, Lord Lisle, a natural son of Edward IV, who held various important positions under Henry VIII. In 1537 she managed to secure for Anne the position of maid of honour to Queen Jane Seymour, which carried with it £10 a year in wages

[1] M. A. E. Wood, *Letters of Royal and Illustrious Ladies*, II, 76.

and board and lodging at Court. Anne had to provide her own servant, also the dresses that the Queen considered suitable. Amongst her companions, later in her career, was that poor relation of the Norfolk family, Katherine Howard, who eventually became Henry's fifth queen.[1]

Mistress Katherine Basset had to be content with a less exalted position. Honor's niece by marriage, the Countess of Sussex, one of the Queen's gentlewomen, could not take her into her chamber while she was at Court, 'as she has three women already, which is one more than she is allowed'. She was, however, taken into the household of the Countess of Rutland, another friend of Honor's, who was also a gentlewoman to the Queen. Here she was obviously singled out and treated as a companion by the Countess, but that her normal position in such a household would have been that of a waiting-gentlewoman is obvious from a letter written to Lady Lisle by John Hussey. Lady Lisle had planned that Katherine should go to the household of the Countess of Hertford, and the Earl wrote to say that she would be as welcome to him and his wife as one of his own daughters. Hussey, however, wrote 'I see she is unwilling to leave my lady Rutland, lest being with Lady Hertford *she should be taken but as her woman*, for Lady Rutland does not so use her'. Eventually Katherine became a maid of honour to Anne of Cleves, so that her story throws considerable light upon the position of 'gentlewoman' in a noble house.[2]

With a certain number of facts thus established, on documentary and not literary evidence, we can now return to those of the plays which are set amidst the circumstances of noble life. That Shakespeare's personal knowledge of the life and detail of a noble household grew with the years and by opportunity seems evident. In *Love's Labour's Lost* and *Romeo and Juliet* he portrays vividly enough the young gallant, for whom Southampton and any of his intimates may stand as originals. Mer-

[1] For these and most of the following details see James Gairdner, *Letters and Papers*, vols. for 1537–9.

[2] See Note B on p. 217.

cutio, Romeo, Benvolio, Paris, Tybalt, Biron and the rest are just such gay, witty, hot-tempered, assured young fellows as the typical young nobleman of the day. Old Capulet (*circa* 1591–5) is not just such another figure as the older nobleman, who would most certainly not have been able to tell one of his grooms where to find drier logs for the fire. Leonato of *Much Ado about Nothing* (*circa* 1599) will, however, pass very creditably for what he is—a noble gentleman who can receive the Prince in his house, and can wed his daughter Hero to the Prince's intimate friend, Count Claudio. It is noticeable that on the occasion of this later wedding, in a wifeless household, Leonato does not figure in any such scenes as those in which Capulet so incongruously strayed towards the kitchen. Even when he is shown in contact with Dogberry and Verges, he leaves to them the business of examining the men they have apprehended. Domestic realism is confined to where it properly belongs—the scenes between Hero and Beatrice and their waiting-gentlewomen.

In spite of Charles Lamb and Mr William Poel[1] *Twelfth Night* has in the past frequently suffered by reason of a fairly general ignorance of that aspect of Elizabethan life which is mirrored in its underplot. That neither stage nor study has as yet completely escaped from the bad old tradition is suggested by the examination candidate who wrote 'Malvolio was the clown in *Twelfth Night*, and Maria, who was the maid, along with the other menservants who were nearly always drunk, decided to play a trick on him'. There is still a tendency to regard the former as a fantastic stage butler, and the latter as a cheeky modern lady's maid, with the servants' hall as the setting. In point of fact, however, Olivia's household is one of the most accurately Elizabethan pictures of a noble household that Shakespeare has drawn.

[1] Lamb in his essay *On some of the Old Actors* pointed out that 'We must not confound him [Malvolio] with the eternal old, low steward of comedy. He is master of the household to a great princess: a dignity probably conferred on him for other respects than age or length of service'. But the whole essay should be carefully studied.

Mr Poel has continually, both in precept and by practice, emphasised this and other points which are vitally affected by knowledge of the social background of the age.

Olivia is a Countess, of rank to marry with the ruler of Illyria, Orsino, who is described alternatively as Duke and Count. For a contemporary parallel we might perhaps fix upon a Tudor gentlewoman, who died in 1580, but who was famous in ballad and play and in people's memory until a much later date. The lady in question was Katharine Willoughby, a descendant of the old nobility, who married as her first husband Charles Brandon, Duke of Suffolk, whose third wife had been Mary Tudor, sister of Henry VIII and widow of Louis XII of France. In 1560–2, when living quietly in the country at Grimsthorpe in Lincolnshire,[1] her household—apart from her own family—consisted of some eighty persons, including a Steward, a Comptroller, a Cofferer, a Master of the Horses, three Gentlemen-Ushers, seven Gentlemen-Waiters, and all the usual yeomen and women servants. Olivia's background is just such a household. 'Who of my people', she asks, 'hold Viola in delay?' Malvolio in his day-dream imagines himself summoning her 'officers' about him as if they were his own. Some of her people, Olivia directs, are to have a special care of Malvolio in his supposed madness. Malvolio is just such another careful, grave and dignified gentleman as Viscount Montague's Ideal Steward. Maria is a shrewd, lively and well-educated gentlewoman, who can write as fair a hand as her lady's, and who marries her lady's kinsman when everybody sobers down to normal.[2] Unless we have in our minds some such conception of the decent and well-conditioned household that Shakespeare's audience knew as the reality, we miss half the subtlety—the humour of the topsy-turveydom of Twelfth Night licence introduced into ordinary life. To get the real and deliciously contrived contrapuntal melody of the piece it is essential to let the underplot move to the Twelfth Night tune of the madness of Misrule, while the sentimental theme threads its way through

[1] See *Hist. MSS. Comm.*, *Earl of Ancaster's MSS.*

[2] I do not think we ought to take Sir Toby's description of Maria as 'my niece's chambermaid' literally—meaning what the Elizabethans usually term a 'chamberer'. It would have been quite obvious from her dress that she was *not* a chamberer, so I can only suppose it was more or less equivalent to calling someone's private secretary 'chief cook and bottle washer'.

a lunacy of love. But the play loses if the underplot merely clowns its way along, in the wake of Sir Toby and Sir Andrew. The fantastic fun that as a rule we extract from the gulling of Malvolio gets an abrupt shock at his final exit. There is sharper comedy, more in keeping with that troublesome exit, if we realise that, in Elizabethan fact, the gulling of Malvolio hovers perpetually on the brink of reason, the verge of reality. Katharine Willoughby, Dowager Duchess of Suffolk, married as her second husband Richard Bertie, her Gentleman-Usher! She was one of the romantic figures of the age, and the story of her life was as widely known as Foxe's *Book of Martyrs*—second only to the Bible in its popularity—could make it. Her step-daughter, Frances Duchess of Suffolk, married her Groom of the Chamber, Adrian Stokes; and Lady Mary Grey—daughter of Frances, and step-granddaughter of Katharine—who stood in the direct succession to the throne, actually married the Queen's Sergeant-Porter. 'There is example for it: the lady of the Strachy married the yeoman of the wardrobe.'

Maria brings us at once to the consideration of Shakespeare's waiting-gentlewomen,[1] and the question, Are they the ladies of gentle birth that we should expect to find in such positions? Is Maria of the same social standing as Katherine Basset? Are Maria, Helena of *All's Well that Ends Well*, Nerissa, Emilia, Margaret and Ursula of *Much Ado about Nothing*, all of the same social standing as Anne Boleyn, 'a Knight's daughter', who is waiting-gentlewoman to Queen Katharine in *Henry VIII*? Instinctively, I believe, we put Anne Boleyn and Helena in a class apart, and group the others with such figures as Charmian and Iras, Lucetta, and the unnamed gentlewoman attending on Lady Macbeth, as 'not quite ladies'. This is probably quite wrong and illogical, and is also probably based on ignorance of Elizabethan conditions and a resultant faulty stage tradition.

If we can free our conception of Maria from the twist that stage practice has given to it, we realise that there is nothing in

[1] For a vivid description of some of the duties and of any morning in the life of any waiting-gentlewoman, see Erondelle's *French Garden*, pp. 59–65 of *The Elizabethan Home* (2nd ed. 1930).

the text of the play to impugn her gentility. From the outset she treats Sir Toby and Sir Andrew as her equals, nor is there anything in her behaviour to justify us in considering her as belonging to a different class from Helena. She is sharp-tongued, witty, and high-spirited: Helena's is a sweeter, graver, deeper nature. If Maria is to be condemned as low-life comic-relief, simply because she assists in the practical joke, Sir Toby and Sir Andrew must share her fate. If we dislike the familiar tone of her conversation with the knights, what are we to say of Helena and her conversation with Parolles (*All's Well that Ends Well*, I, i, 118 ff.)? But we accept Helena without question as a gentlewoman; and the Countess of Rousillon treats her as a daughter, as a favoured gentlewoman like Katherine Basset was treated. In fact, to differentiate between Maria and Helena in the matter of social standing and dress is illogical. The real difference is one of character.

This, I believe, is also true of Nerissa, Margaret, and Ursula, and even of Emilia, who is the most difficult case of all. The text gives definite indications, Cassio describing her as 'the gentlewoman that attends the general's wife'. Cassio, Iago and Roderigo are all apparently social equals and 'gentlemen'. It would certainly not be safe to argue that because Bardolph is the only other Lieutenant, and Pistol the only other Ancient or Ensign drawn by Shakespeare, that therefore Cassio and Iago cannot be gentlemen. Emilia's duties as a waiting-gentlewoman are all quite in order. She helps Desdemona to undress, puts her things away, gives her her 'nightly wearing', and is requested

Prithee to-night
Lay on my bed my wedding sheets.

It is perfectly correct for her not to dine with her mistress (*Othello*, III, iii). In all normally regulated Elizabethan households the gentlemen and gentlewomen-in-waiting always dined at their own tables. In spite of these indications, however, it is difficult to feel that Emilia belongs socially to the same class as Helena. Her spirited, outspoken championship of her mistress in the last scenes makes her part extraordinarily 'sympathetic' in Act v—so much so, in fact, that an actress of any quality can sweep an audience off their feet with it: but her theft of the handkerchief, coupled with her altogether unforgivable obtuseness in the matter, offends unbearably.

The (theatrical) problem of the gentleman who is 'no gentleman', and yet is not cast for 'villain', is always a difficult one. In the present instance we can meet it by disregarding the Elizabethan social scheme, taking character as indicative of class, and presenting Emilia so as to give something of the impression of the simple-privileged-retainer—analogous to the Nurse in *Romeo and Juliet*. To differentiate her manner as coarser, her apparel as simpler, and her intelligence and behaviour as on a lower plane, when compared with Helena and Maria, may help to prevent us from feeling that her character is split into two incongruous and irreconcilable halves. On the other hand, I do not for a moment believe that this is the Elizabethan version of the situation, as presented by Shakespeare. It would be a mere concession of the theatre to our unconscious demand for a scheme of ideal values.

We in our own day do not feel that there is anything ambiguous about the social position of such a character as Captain Dancy in Galsworthy's *Loyalties*; and on the Elizabethan stage I have no doubt that Emilia was dressed and presented like Helena and Maria—that is, as an Elizabethan gentlewoman. We can think what we like about her behaviour, but we must not say that *because* she steals the handkerchief *therefore* she cannot be a 'lady', either by birth or upbringing. It is a point which can well be illustrated by a story told in the Acts of the Privy Council,[1] of Sir Roger Manwood, Chief Baron of the Exchequer, who 'took' from 'one Roger Underwood, a very poor man' a chain to which he had apparently taken a fancy—'pretending it to be his own', according to the Privy Council minutes! It took strong measures and several letters from the Privy Council to make the Chief Baron return the chain to its rightful owner.[2]

[1] A.P.C. 1592, XXII, 451.

[2] But in justice to Manwood it must be added that Manningham's *Diary* gives a slightly more creditable version of the affair (see *Diary*, Camden Soc. p. 91).

When handling secondary characters of this kind Shakespeare had two methods. If his dramatic purpose simply required persons occupying a recognised position in the social scheme, we get such sketches as Lucetta, waiting-gentlewoman to Julia; Margaret and Ursula; Lady Macbeth's gentlewoman, and the Queen's woman in *Richard II.* Being first and foremost stock utilities they are true to type. They know their place, because they are their place. On another level altogether works the Shakespeare who is interested in presenting a character, and is distinctly less interested in bothering about details of social status. These other personages are not always sure of their place. Emilia seems to be a case in point; and an even more significant and interesting example is Gratiano, who is obviously conceived first as a character, and only afterwards as someone in a certain social position, and therefore related in a specific way to the other persons of the drama.

When Gratiano first enters with Bassanio and Lorenzo, Salarino's greeting is 'Good morrow, my good *lords*', which gives the momentary impression that here is yet another of Shakespeare's favourite groups of three young men—Biron-Longaville-Dumain, Don Pedro-Claudio-Benedick, Mercutio-Benvolio-Romeo. Gratiano hastens to confirm this impression by monopolising the conversation. He lectures and chaffs Antonio, that 'royal merchant', calls him 'My Antonio', and tells him 'I love thee, and it is my love that speaks'. His tone to Bassanio's 'kinsman', in fact, is the tone of Bassanio's equal, and for this particular scene it is difficult to regard him as anything else. At the lowest computation he is to Bassanio as Benedick is to Claudio. When he next appears, however, it is evident that Bassanio is a 'lord' and that Gratiano is not, although for the moment he keeps up something of the pretence of equality by addressing him as 'Signior Bassanio' (*The Merchant of Venice*, II, ii, 191, 204). After this, however, he slides rapidly down the social scale, gives up being the agreeable rattle that he set out to be, addresses his former companion as 'my lord Bassanio' and 'your lordship'; and by the end of Act IV is obviously nothing more than a gentleman-in-waiting to Bassanio, who has married

Portia's waiting-gentlewoman, and who can be sent to fetch and carry for his lord. In fact, the exigencies of the drama and the necessity of finding a husband for Nerissa, whose status is clear, translate Gratiano from one sphere of life into another. He remains a 'gentleman', but he becomes a serving-man, whereas in Act I he behaves as a character, but not as an Elizabethan gentleman-in-waiting. He begins like Benedick, and ends up like Fabian.

On the basis of the material thus collected and the examples discussed it should be possible for the producer and the student to decide upon the social position of most individuals in the plays. We can, of course, take our cue from Shakespeare and ignore facts, but it is generally wiser for the interpreter to leave that liberty to the creative artist. It will also be wiser not to try to base too much biographical conjecture upon such facts as these. It may be that to the end Shakespeare was to some extent ignorant of the manner of life at Whitehall or Theobalds or Kenilworth or Cowdray. Even if this were true, however, it is perfectly obvious that, like any other playwright in any age, he could have found out most things that he needed or wanted to know. The real value of a knowledge of the social background is twofold. In certain cases, such as *Twelfth Night*, it enables us to interpret more accurately the author's intention. It also enables us to see how, when and where Shakespeare deliberately rejects the actual. If we see this we may also see *why* he rejects it; and that means the rare privilege of yet another glimpse of the artist at work.

NOTE A

A most valuable document to study in conjunction with this pattern household of Viscount Montague's is the list of the servants of Henry Courtenay, Marquis of Exeter, which was made at the time of his execution in 1538.[1] It is valuable because it gives full details about the social status, age, means, wages, and even the accomplishments and personal appearance of most of the members of the household. First on the list come nineteen Gentlemen of the Household. Amongst them there is one William Perpoynte, 'and he is the

[1] Gairdner, *Letters and Papers, Henry VIII*, 1538, II, 755. (S.P. I, 138.)

lady marquess's kinsman and at her finding'—in other words, financially supported by her: one William Seyntlowe, 'son and heir to Sir John Seyntlowe',[1] aged twenty, married to one of Sir Edward Baynton's daughters, and allowed £10 a year by his father. Then there is 'Thomas Sparrow gentleman', the Receiver-General, aged fifty-six, 'very discreet, of good conditions and also of goodly substance'. There is a Thomas Seyntlow, described as 'a tall gentleman and of personage, and shooteth well, with all other honest conditions meet for a gentleman': Thomas Godolphin, aged thirty, unmarried, who is 'diligent in serving about a nobleman, with honest and decent qualities': Richard Buller, 'of a mean stature', who is 'found' yearly by his friends to the amount of £3. 6*s*. 8*d*.: and John Ligh, described as son and heir to Mr Lieghe, the King's Gentleman-Usher.

The gentlewomen who attended upon the Lady Marquess were five in number. It is doubtful if any of them were of the same social standing as the gentlemen. Their ages range from fifty-six to twenty-two: they are all described as unmarried; and one, 'Margaret Brewne', as 'a poor woman, not having many friends'. Anne Browne is described as 'good with the needle, and can play well upon the virginals and lute'.

In the third division of the list come the ten Yeomen and Grooms of the Chamber, including the Barber, who 'is a very good Barber': also an old man of sixty, now quite helpless, who had served the family all his life; and David ap Jenkyn, who 'did always wait upon the lord marquis in his chamber'. Fourteen Yeomen-Waiters and fourteen Yeomen and Grooms of the Stable are also listed, and the Calendar computes the total number of these inferior servants as one hundred and three.

Their wages varied, not only according to the positions held, but apparently also according to their individual needs. Some were 'found' or partially found by their families or friends. Some owned lands. Others had nothing but their wages, livery and keep. The chief Gentlewoman received £3. 6*s*. a year, and the others £2. 13*s*. 4*d*. each.[2] The Schoolmaster received £6. 13*s*. 4*d*., and the Secretary

[1] Sir John Seyntlowe (or St Lowe) was Sheriff of Gloucester 1536–7. For the Northern Rebellion he was to bring from Somerset a troop of 100 men, and he is listed as one of those to attend on the King's own person. In 1536 he was a captain in Ireland, drew wages for 3 grand captains, 3 petty captains and 300 foot. He was one of the gentlemen appointed to meet Anne of Cleves in 1539 (see Gairdner, *Letters and Papers*, 1536–40).

[2] In or about 1589 we find the Lady Mounteagle's gentlewoman receiving £5, and her chambermaid 30*s*., with 30*s*. allowance for livery. Menservants' wages in the same household varied from 40*s*. to £5 and £6, the allowance for livery being in every case 30*s*. (*Hist. MSS. Comm.* No. 55, vol. III, Tresham Papers).

£4. 13*s*. 4*d*. The wages of a Gentleman-in-Waiting seem to have ranged from £6 to £12. The ordinary wage for a Yeoman of the Chamber seems to have been £1. 6*s*. 8*d*. The Yeoman of the Wardrobe had £2; so had the Porter, the three Under-Falconers, and the Chief Baker. The fourteen Yeomen-Waiters had £3. 3*s*. 4*d*. each.

NOTE B

Other helpful details can also be gathered from the Lisle correspondence. We learn, for example, that one of Lord Lisle's land-stewards was anxious for Lady Lisle to take into her service as a gentleman-in-waiting the third son of a certain Sir Peter Philpot. Hussey writes that the father will help to maintain him, that his eldest brother is dead, and the second 'sore sick and not likely to recover; and if he die the third will recover, besides his father's land, 500 marks a year. *If he were once in service means might be found that Mrs Philippa and he might couple together*'. A waiting-gentleman, in fact, might prove a good match for a daughter of the house. On another occasion Hussey writes, 'I have been asked what you will give with Mrs Katherine's marriage'. He has let it be rumoured that her dowry might be 300 marks, but he believes that if Lady Lisle could make it 500 her daughter can secure a real matrimonial 'catch'—Sir Edward Baynton's son and heir—so that 'she will have an heir who can spend 1000 marks a year'. Sir Edward Baynton was one of the favourite courtiers of Henry VIII, vice-chamberlain to three of his queens, and head of a family that traced its descent back to the time of Henry II. One of his sons-in-law, as we have already seen, was Sir John Seyntlowe's son and heir and one of the Marquis of Exeter's gentlemen-in-waiting. Actually Katherine never married the Baynton heir, but the connexions thus established by such details help us to understand the nature of 'service' in the sixteenth century.

Lady Lisle's own gentlewomen varied in rank. At the time of the attainder of John Lord Hussey[1] in 1537 negotiations were on foot for her to take one of his daughters. Although executed for an alleged complicity in the Pilgrimage of Grace, Hussey had been a person of the first importance at Court. His wife was a daughter of the Earl of Kent, and he himself had held, amongst other offices, that of Comptroller of the Royal Household, and that of Chamberlain to Princess Mary. At another time Lady Weston—who had herself been one of the gentlewomen of Queen Katherine of Aragon—recommended

[1] Not to be confused with John Hussey, the Lisles' familiar servant, and agent in England.

Lady Lisle to take the daughter of Christopher More, 'a gentleman which my lord knoweth well'. The only Christopher More of that time who is likely to have been well known to Lord Lisle, was Sheriff of Surrey and Sussex in 1539/40. In the Squires' list of the gentlemen attending on the King who were to meet Anne of Cleves on her arrival in England Christopher More figures as a gentleman who was to ride in a coat of black velvet, with a gold chain, and to bring with him six servants. The gentlewoman herself had been brought up in the household of 'my Lady Boser', had been with Lady Weston for several years, and was strongly recommended by her as capable of waiting upon Lady Lisle or her daughters. She can 'keep your plate or your napery', writes Lady Weston; and as for the daughters of the house, she can 'bring them up well, and can teach them right good manners'.[1]

[1] Wood, *Letters*, II, 80–2.

SHAKESPEARE'S SOURCES

BY

A. L. ATTWATER

THE PRACTICE OF THE THEATRES

(*a*) Collaboration and Revision

In the prologue to *Volpone* Ben Jonson wrote:

> 'Tis knowne, five weeks fully pen'd it:
> From his owne hand, without a co-adjutor,
> Novice, journeyman, or tutor,

and this claim to have written his masterpiece so quickly without assistance emphasises a dominant condition of work in the Elizabethan theatre and a resulting practice. The repertory system and competition between the companies, as well as the limited number of theatre-goers, demanded a regular supply of fresh plays; rapidity of composition was essential, and a natural result was collaboration. Jonson himself admitted, when he published his *Sejanus*, that in that play as acted 'a second Pen had good share', but he replaced the work of his collaborator by his own rather than 'defraud so happy a Genius of his right by my lothed usurpation'. In the collection of plays attributed to the famous partnership of Beaumont and Fletcher there was certainly 'lothed usurpation' of the rights of Massinger and others. But, while title-pages rarely name more than two authors, Henslowe's accounts often show three or four, or even five poets, working together on one play.

The demand for fresh plays might also be satisfied in part by the furbishing up of old ones, but the evidence for such revision is not so straightforward. A statement on the title-page that a play has been 'newly corrected, augmented, and amended' was often made because an imperfect, pirated version was already in the booksellers' shops. On the other hand Henslowe sometimes marked as 'new' a play which had already appeared some years before. *The Spanish Tragedy* is thus marked by him in 1597, and an edition of this play was published in 1602 'with new additions of the Painter's part'. The additions generally held to have been made by Bird and Rowley to Marlowe's *Doctor Faustus* are also substantial. Hamlet says to the First Player:

Can you play *The Murder of Gonzago*?

and then asks:

You could, for need, study a speech of some dozen or sixteen lines, which I would set down and insert in't, could you not?

The Player's ready assent would suggest that he found nothing strange in this proposal. It is reasonably conjectured that some time after Shakespeare's death extra songs and dances for the witches were added to *Macbeth*.

There were many reasons why plays in the stock of a repertory company should be altered from time to time. Topical allusions went out of date and new ones would be needed. Henslowe's accounts record payment to poets for 'mending' their own and other men's plays for performance at Court, and changes in the place of performance or in the personnel of a company might necessitate revision.[1] Customs differed between theatres, and Marston's *Malcontent*, written for performance at the Blackfriars, where there was music between the acts, had to be lengthened for the Globe, where the custom of music was 'not received'.

But these additions and mendings scarcely warrant the assumption that whenever an old play was revived, its style and

[1] The two versions of *King Lear*, IV, vii, in one of which Lear is obviously discovered in bed and in the other 'Enter Leare in a chaire carried by servants', indicate 'mending' either for a performance where no inner stage was available or to make more theatrically effective the playing of the rest of the scene, while in the Quarto of *Othello* Desdemona's song is cut, presumably because the King's Men had, at the time when this version was in use, no leading boy actor who could sing.

structure were drastically altered. Possibly the practice of adapting Elizabethan plays common after the Restoration indicates a survival of an old custom of the theatre, but in a company with a fairly permanent personnel, revision would probably be limited. Burbage would not wish to study a different Hamlet every few years.

(b) The Hunt for Plots

The urgent needs of the theatre encouraged the poets to lay their hands on all likely matter for drama. The more scholarly among them made use of their wide reading. *Tamburlaine* shows that Marlowe's knowledge of history and geography was extensive, and Jonson having inserted in *Catiline* long translated extracts from Cicero's speeches, retorted upon his critics, 'Though you commend the two first acts, with the people, because they are the worst; and dislike the oration of Cicero, in regard you read some pieces of it at school and understand it not yet: yet I shall find the way to forgive you'. Act I contained the ghost of Sylla, prodigies of darkness, groans and fiery lights, and the drinking by the conspirators of the blood of a murdered slave —effects which would appeal to the groundlings, but for which Jonson had the authority of his books. Other dramatists chose more popular sources. Collections of tales such as Painter's *Palace of Pleasure* and Fenton's *Tragicall Discourses* had made the English reader familiar with the Italian novel. *A Mirror for Magistrates* and the Chronicles of Holinshed were an inexhaustible quarry for a national drama, and nobler material treated in a more inspiring way was available in North's translation of Plutarch's *Lives*. Here was God's plenty for the dramatist seeking a plot.

(c) Plagiarism

Such a common stock of reading offered to the dramatists a rapidly available supply of ready-made stories with conventional situations and characters. The hero villain, the braggart captain, the comic constable were any man's material, and some of these characters would, like the Clown, be expected by the audience to conform to the traditions of the old drama. Consequently, with the pressing need for quick production, originality was rare. Moreover, the rivalry between companies often led to the direct imitation by one of what another had made popular. Nor at first did much moral stigma attach to plagiarism. From time to time protest was made, as when R. B. wrote in *Greene's Funeralls*,

Greene made the ground to all that wrote upon him.
Nay more the men that so eclipst his fame
Purloyned his Plumes, can they deny the same?

Nashe, it is true, dignified the theatre with the title of Poets' Hall, but the writing of plays does not at first seem to have been put on the same footing as other literary work. The players bought the poet's play, which then became the property of the company. Jonson, who was laughed at for calling his plays 'Works', took a more serious view of the playwright's standing, and the second earliest use of the word *plagiary* recorded in the *Oxford Dictionary* is in his *Poetaster*. Crispinus (Marston), singing as his own a song by Horace (Jonson), is called 'plagiary', and Demetrius (Dekker) is arraigned as 'play-dresser and plagiary'. Jonson's outlook was exceptional, but his sonnet-epigram on Poet-Ape must have had a basis in contemporary fact and sentiment.

Poore POET-APE, that would be thought our chiefe,
  Whose workes are eene the fripperie of wit,
From brocage is become so bold a thiefe,
  That we the rob'd, leave rage, and pittie it.
At first he made low shifts, would picke and gleane,
  Buy the reversion of old playes; now growne
To 'a little wealth, and credit in the scene,
  He takes up all, makes each man's wit his owne:
And, told of this, he slights it. Tut, such crimes
  The sluggish gaping auditor devoures;
He marks not whose 'twas first: and after-times
  May judge it to be his, as well as ours.
Foole, as if halfe eyes will not know a fleece
From locks of wooll, or shreds from the whole peece.

SHAKESPEARE'S SOURCES

(*a*) Dramatic Material

(i) *Henry VI*

The 'reversion of old plays' has become an obsession with editors and critics of Shakespeare, but since Malone it has been generally held that he may have served his prenticeship as a 'play-dresser', revising and bringing up to date the work of other men. In all the early plays critics have found incongruity of style, crude characterisation and unpleasing matter, which seem not to be explained by immaturity, and parallels with the work of other poets, which go beyond imitation. Somewhat doubtful testimony of the late seventeenth century attributed *Titus Andronicus* to a 'private author', to whose play Shakespeare only gave some 'master-touches', but though no lover of Shakespeare would be sorry for proof that he had no hand in what Dr Johnson called the 'barbarity of the spectacles', it is difficult in the face of Meres's direct statement to acquit him of some considerable share in the play. The epilogue to *Selimus* (1594) ends:

> If this first part, Gentles, do like you well,
> The second part shall greater murthers tell.

It was for these 'gentles' that Shakespeare was writing, and *Titus Andronicus* was a popular play.

It is, however, round Shakespeare's share in the three parts of *Henry VI* that controversy has raged longest. Part I appeared first in the Folio, but versions of Parts II and III were published in quarto, *The First Part of the Contention betwixt the two famous Houses of Yorke and Lancaster* in 1594, *The true Tragedie of Richard Duke of Yorke* in 1595. Although Dr Johnson came to the conclusion that these were piracies, it was commonly held until lately that they represented early versions of plays of composite authorship which Shakespeare afterwards revised, and confirmation of this view was found in Greene's famous attack on Shakespeare, where the line of verse is a parody of

> O tiger's heart wrapp'd in a woman's hide.
> *III Henry VI*, I, iv, 137.

The interpretation put upon Greene's complaint was that Shakespeare, like Jonson's Poet-Ape, had obtained 'the reversion of old plays' by the University Wits and had sprung into fame by dressing them up. It has now been proved that the quartos are 'bad' quartos, giving pirated versions of plays which are more correctly represented in the text of the Folio, and Greene, it is suggested, was attacking a player, who having won his position by speaking the poets' lines—a puppet that spake from their mouths—now had the audacity to bombast out blank verse of his own.[1] Contemporaries seem to have understood Greene's charge as one of plagiarism (see the quotation from *Greene's Funeralls* on p. 222), but the new explanation seems the sounder. There remains therefore only internal evidence of style upon which to determine the question of authorship. The authenticity of all three parts has been doubted since Pope, and in Part I, which might have become associated with the other two, even if it were not by the same author, Malone maintained that except in parts of the Fourth Act, there was 'not a single print of the footsteps of Shakespeare'. A desire to acquit Shakespeare of the denigration of Joan of Arc has been common and natural, but the degeneration of her character is to be found in the chronicles upon which the play is based, and at so early a stage of dramatic development in the Elizabethan theatre it would be unwise to lay too much stress on inconsistent characterisation, especially when it has the warranty of the chronicles. It is also unreasonable to expect a dramatic poet writing for a popular audience to whitewash an enemy alien, of whom the sober chronicler used such phrases as 'all damnablie faithlesse to be a pernicious instrument to hostilitie and bloudshed in divelish witchcraft and sorcerie'. Moreover, when attempts are made to assign the different strands in all three parts to Marlowe, Greene, Peele or other supposed authors, there is no substantial agreement except on two points. One passage of blank verse so mature as to suggest an 'addition' for some late revival (Part II, v, ii, 31–56) is given by all critics to Shakespeare, and most of them seem inclined to attribute the Joan of Arc episodes to

[1] Peter Alexander, *Shakespeare's Henry VI and Richard III*, 1929.

Peele. Support for Shakespeare's authorship of Parts II and III has been increased by the proof that the *Contention* and the *True Tragedie* are pirated versions of these two plays.

(ii) *The Ur-Hamlet*

That Shakespeare began work as a reviser has also been conjectured from other 'bad' quartos. To solve the problems raised by these 'stolne and surreptitious copies' it has been suggested that the pirates had recourse to some old play on which Shakespeare had probably already worked, and for an early dramatic version of the story of Hamlet there is considerable evidence. In 1589, in his preface to Greene's novel *Menaphon*, Nashe wrote:

It is a common practice nowadays amongst a sort of shifting companions, that runne through every Art and thrive by none, to leave the trade of *Noverint*, whereto they were borne, and busie themselves with the indevours of Art, that could scarcely Latinize their neck verse if they should have neede; yet English *Seneca* read by Candlelight yeelds many good sentences, as *Blood is a begger* and so forth; and if you intreate him faire in a frostie morning, hee will affoord you whole Hamlets, I should say handfuls of Tragicall speeches.

Nashe continues with a reference to 'the Kid in Aesop' and a taunt that these 'famished followers' of Seneca have now been driven 'to intermeddle with Italian translations'. The father of Thomas Kyd was a scrivener; Kyd himself had probably translated an Italian treatise just before Nashe wrote this preface. *The Spanish Tragedy*, acknowledged to be Kyd's, was clearly written under Senecan influence and is a play about revenge. The reference to the kid in Aesop may be a punning indication of the person at whom Nashe is aiming his satire. A play *Hamlet* was certainly performed in June 1594, probably by the Chamberlain's Men, and between this date and 1600 there are scattered references to a play or plays on this theme. On these grounds Malone ascribed to Kyd a *Hamlet*, which has since been named the *Ur-Hamlet*. Moreover a German version of the play, *Der Bestrafte Brudermord*, shows obvious kinship with the 'bad' First Quarto, having for example the name of Corambus for Polonius. Parallels with the verse style and diction of Kyd have been traced in Shakespeare's *Hamlet*, and these are more common in the 'bad' quarto; and dramatic difficulties in the play have been attributed to out-croppings of the *Ur-Hamlet*.

But though a fairly strong case can be made out that Kyd wrote a *Hamlet*, and though by careful scrutiny of the texts critics have elaborated theories of a continuity from the *Ur-Hamlet* of Kyd through a series of revisions by Shakespeare and others to the play as it stands in the Folio, the proper verdict is still 'not proven'. The problem of the First Quarto may still be from what sort of an abridgment of Shakespeare it derives, and how much of its peculiarity is to be ascribed to the assistance given to the pirates by an improvising actor with his memory full of tags from parts which he had been playing. Nor have the possibilities and results of shorthand reporting been fully explored.[1] Probably Shakespeare took a story which had already been dramatised and a hero, the outlines of whose character were already known, and treated them in his own way.

(iii) *Old Plays*

Doubt whether Shakespeare was to any great extent an adapter of other men's work is raised by the study of four extant 'old plays', all at some time owned by the Queen's Men, on subjects which he afterwards handled, namely *The Troublesome Raigne of King John*, *The Famous Victories of Henry the Fifth*, *The True Tragedie of Richard the Third*, and *The True Chronicle History of King Leir and his three daughters*.[2] None of these plays bears any textual relation whatever to the corresponding play by Shakespeare. He may have taken from the *True Tragedie* a hint or two such as the hesitation of the second murderer of Clarence, or from *King Leir* that striking piece of stage business when

[1] See *The Tragicall Historie of Hamlet, Prince of Denmarke*, 1603, edited by G. B. Harrison (Bodley Head Quartos); see also articles by W. Matthews, *Modern Language Review* (July, 1932, and January, 1933), on the impracticability of the existing systems of shorthand for reporting plays in the theatre.

[2] *The Taming of the Shrew* is excluded from this discussion owing to the doubt whether *The Taming of A Shrew* is to be regarded as a source play or a 'bad' quarto, and *Measure for Measure*, because Whetstone's *Promos and Cassandra* appears never to have been acted.

Cordelia kneels before Lear asking his blessing and he before her asking her pardon. There is nothing in *King Leir* of Lear's madness, there is no Fool, and the play ends, like Tate's version, with the victory and restoration of Lear. *The Famous Victories* covers the whole range of both parts of *Henry IV* and *Henry V*, and the chief link between it and Shakespeare's work is that the leader of the Prince's disreputable company is Sir John Oldcastle, nicknamed Jockey. He is but a wraith of Shakespeare's Oldcastle-Falstaff, although there is one passage in which he shows a slight trace of Falstaffian unction.

Prince Henry. But heres such adoo now a dayes, heres prisoning, heres hanging, whipping, and the divel and all; But I tel you sirs, when I am King, we will have no such things, if the old king my father were dead, we would be all kings.

Oldcastle. Hee is a good olde man, God take him to his mercy the sooner.

It has been conjectured that between the *Famous Victories*, which may be an abridgment of two plays, and Shakespeare's *Henry IV* and *Henry V* there was an intermediate handling by some other dramatist of the whole story of Prince Hal. It is hard to believe that there was anything between the *Troublesome Raigne* and *King John*. The relation between these two plays is therefore important. It would be rash to generalise from one special instance, but with such confirmation as is afforded by the *True Tragedie*, *King Leir* and the *Famous Victories*, it may be suggested that when Shakespeare took as his source an existing old play, he completely rewrote it rather than dressed it up. Between the *Troublesome Raigne* and *King John* there are few verbal links, and though Shakespeare retained the main structure of the old play, everywhere his work shows signs of a new shaping spirit of art. Episodes are rearranged to achieve a truly dramatic progress towards the climax, character is revitalised, and the language is entirely transmuted. The old play is full of crude anti-papal propaganda; in removing most of this Shakespeare certainly obscured the motive of the monk in poisoning the King. This loose end is evident in the study, but in the theatre the swift following of John's attempt to murder Arthur by his misfortunes and death enables Shakespeare to disguise a *post-hoc* as a *propter-hoc*, and to effect an illusion of tragic consequence. In the old play Faulconbridge is little more than a braggart, incapable of that anger and pity with which Shakespeare ennobles him as he stands over the dead body of Arthur. If *King John* gives any idea of the normal way in which Shakespeare 'mended' old plays, there is no need to trouble much about the nature of the *Ur-Hamlet*, or of the *Jew*, supposed to be at the back of *The Merchant of Venice*.[1]

(*b*) Non-Dramatic Material

(i) *Holinshed*

Shakespeare's art is also revealed in his method of turning into drama the history which he found in Holinshed's Chronicles. Of the early historical plays *Richard II* keeps closest to its source, although the story is transformed by much imaginative invention and by a marked indulgence in the lyric moment, as for instance in the Deposition scene, the elaborate ritual of which derives more from Froissart than from Holinshed. Froissart also tells a story of the greyhound Mathe, who deserted Richard for Bolingbroke, a story which may have given Shakespeare a hint for 'roan Barbary'. For *I Henry IV*, in which Shakespeare perfected his own type of history, he had the *Famous Victories* as authority for Prince Hal's wildness, a theme which is not greatly emphasised by Holinshed. Nor did the chronicles give any help towards the character of the altogether admirable Hotspur, whose age Shakespeare does not scruple to alter to suit the design of his play. What he took from Holinshed was the episode of the Percies' rebellion, drawn to it perhaps by the

[1] To give the *Troublesome Raigne* its due, there is more humanity in Arthur's words after he has thrown himself from the battlements:

> Hoe, who is nigh, some body take me up,
> Where is my mother? let me speak with her,

than in Shakespeare's conceit:

> Oh me! my uncle's spirit is in these stones.

incident of the quarrel over the prisoners, since Essex, a man as covetous of honour as Hotspur, had lately been involved in a curiously similar quarrel with his sovereign. The scene between the Prince and his father Shakespeare transferred from a later date. It seems likely that he intended Part I to be complete in itself, with Prince Hal's 'reformation' established at the battle of Shrewsbury, which Holinshed marks with a marginal caption, '*The valiancy of the yoong prince*'. Part II can be regarded as a hastily written encore, and the increase in Falstaffian matter reveals the cause; it is not surprising that the historical framework, a mere copy of Part I, is not so close to the chronicles, although the King's dying admonition to his son is straight from Holinshed. At Agincourt there was no room for Falstaff, and in *Henry V* Shakespeare's reliance on Holinshed is again considerable, while for the 'command' play, *The Merry Wives of Windsor*, which provided more 'fat meat' for Queen Elizabeth, it is quite reasonably supposed that he dressed up some existing play, which may have been the conjectured *Jealous Comedy*.

Shakespeare's method of using Holinshed was to select some section of the chronicles which gave him a satisfactory framework for his play. Material which expressed motive or which enabled him to reveal or develop character might be shifted from its proper historical setting and added to this nucleus. Material which proved intractable was either abandoned altogether or handled merely by reference. His debt to the chronicles is often to be seen in the marginal captions of Holinshed, such as '*King Richard in utter despaire*', at his landing from Ireland, or '*A guiltie conscience in extremitie of sicknesse pincheth sore*', of Henry IV. For characterisation Holinshed only occasionally breaks his narrative to give a sketch such as that of Queen Margaret, 'This ladie excelled all other, as well in beautie and favour, as in wit and policie; and was of stomach and courage more like to a man than a woman', or of Richard II, 'He was seemelie of shape and favor, & of nature good inough, if the wickednesse & naughtie demeanor of such as were about him had not altered it'.

(ii) *North's* Plutarch

Throughout the later English histories Shakespeare seems to be setting himself the problem of characterisation. These men lived and died, as the chroniclers relate; what manner of men were they? At the moment when he was passing 'from *Henry V* to *Hamlet*' in search of a better instrument for expressing character, biography takes the place of chronicles as his source, and biography which combines the psychology and narrative skill of a Greek philosopher-historian with the vigorous style of a typical Elizabethan. North's *Plutarch* was a collection of heroic portraits with an immediate appeal to the men of Shakespeare's age. Holinshed gave him matter, but rarely suggested the style of his treatment; the mass of verbal borrowing from North tells a different tale.[1] Plutarch, moreover, with the tradition of a great dramatic literature behind him, often writes his biographies in such a way as to suggest tragedy, and Shakespeare accepts from him hints for his own tragic pattern.

In *Julius Caesar* for the scaffolding of his play he still uses the method which he had applied to Holinshed, and takes the last few pages of Plutarch's *Life of Caesar*, beginning at a point where North notes marginally, '*Why Caesar was hated*'. These pages tell the story of Caesar's assassination and the riot which followed his funeral, and then Plutarch comments:

So he reaped no other fruit of all his reign and dominion, which he had so vehemently desired all his life, and pursued with such extreme danger, but a vain name only, and a superficial glory, that procured him the envy and hatred of his country. But his great prosperity and good fortune, that favoured him all his lifetime, did continue afterwards in the revenge of his death, pursuing his murderers both by sea and land, till they had not left a man more to be executed, of all them that were actors or counsellors in the conspiracy of his death.

[1] The extent of this borrowing is much greater in the two later Roman plays, *Antony and Cleopatra* and *Coriolanus*, but it is worth noting that when he returned to Holinshed for parts of *Macbeth*, in the dialogue between Malcolm and Macduff (Act IV, Sc. iii), at a point in the play where dramatic tension is relaxed, and, it may be, Shakespeare's interest, being centred in Macbeth and Lady Macbeth, momentarily flagged, he followed the language of his source almost as closely as in *Antony and Cleopatra* and *Coriolanus*.

There follows briefly the story of Philippi, and of the spirit that appeared to Brutus, saying, 'I am thy ill angel'. Here then in the *Life of Caesar* was the plot for a tragedy of Caesar's death and of his 'spirit ranging for revenge'; Shakespeare fills it out with matter chiefly from the *Life of Brutus*. The *Life of Caesar* gave him his plot, the *Life of Brutus* most of his characterisation. The enigmatic character of Caesar may be due to an attempt to reconcile Plutarch's picture with current opinion of the 'thrasonical', 'hook-nosed fellow of old Rome'; but for Brutus, Portia and Cassius, Plutarch yielded ample matter, even to Portia's inconsistency and the contrast between the characters of Brutus and Cassius—'It is also reported that Brutus could evil away with the tyranny, and that Cassius hated the tyrant'. The closeness of *Julius Caesar* to its source is the strongest argument against the theory that the play represents the work of half a dozen poets at different times.[1]

For *Antony and Cleopatra* Shakespeare begins his borrowing from Plutarch's *Life of Antony*, at a point where the *Life* tells how 'the last and extremest mischief of all (to wit the love of Cleopatra) lighted on him'. Here, though the borrowing is extensive, even to the versification of North's prose in such speeches as Enobarbus' description of Cleopatra's barge, it is the romantic transmutation of what is borrowed, which repays study. Plutarch wrote, 'For they made an order between them, which they called *Amimetobion* (as much to say, no life comparable and matchable with it), one feasting each other by turns, and in cost exceeding all measure and reason'. This idea of luxury Shakespeare has transformed to

> The Nobleness of life
> Is to do thus: when such a mutual pair,
> And such a twain can do't, in which I bind
> On pain of punishment, the world to weet
> We stand up Peerless.[2]

[1] Disintegrators of the canon who have urged that *Julius Caesar* was revised by Ben Jonson have attributed this inconsistency of Portia to Jonson's dislike of political ladies; North, however, thought it worth the caption, '*The weakness of Portia notwithstanding her former courage*'.

[2] The capitals are from the Folio; the emphasis on *Peerless* may reveal an echo of *Amimetobion*.

Shakespeare, however, seems to have felt the need for some such contrast as is provided throughout the play by Enobarbus's dry comments upon Cleopatra and for some other foil to Antony than his rival Octavius, and for this purpose he practically invented the character of Enobarbus, who in Plutarch is little more than a name.

In the same way and for a somewhat similar dramatic purpose the character of Menenius in *Coriolanus* is worked up from very slight material in Plutarch. In this play, though verbal borrowing is perhaps at its greatest, Shakespeare treats history with much more freedom. The details of the political struggle did not interest him, although the political opinions of his hero form a great part of the character as presented in the play. The great scene between mother and son which is the climax of the tragedy comes straight from Plutarch, and there are many references in the *Life* to Coriolanus' love for Volumnia. Plutarch's description of his character is that of a *choleric* man, but at the end of it he notes that the Romans in those days set great store by 'valiantness, which they call *virtus*', to which North's marginal note is '*What this word* VIRTUS *signifieth*'. Coriolanus is Shakespeare's last study of that heroic 'virtue' which the Renaissance loved.

(iii) *The Italian Novel*

The Italian novel and the great mass of romance material available in poems and collections of tales must have made a different appeal to Shakespeare. Here was stuff with which to make patterns, to be altered and mixed at will and as he liked, full of stock ideas of girls disguised as boys or pastoral simplicity. For the comedies before 1600 all these romances gave him what he needed for the centre of his design, a pair of lovers in some interesting or curious adventure; to this he could add whatever his comic invention might create in the persons of Dogberry, Touchstone or Feste, Sir Andrew or Malvolio, and could enrich the whole with music and song. Even the romance itself might, as in *Much Ado about Nothing*, form the tapestry before which a pair of lovers whom he had himself invented could play their wrangling comedy. As he wrote, names and incidents easily passed in his mind from one old tale to another, and his memory offered him all sorts of combinations. The road to Xanadu could not be more phantom-thronged than the voyage to Illyria.

Some of the stories from Italy chosen by Shakespeare for his plots may have been already dramatised. Arthur Brooke in the preface to his narrative poem, *Romeus and Juliet*, wrote that he had seen 'the same argument lately set foorth on stage'. It is, however, unnecessary to assume such an 'old play' as Shakespeare's main source, and the relation between *Romeo and Juliet* and Brooke's poem is sufficiently close to make it clear that Shakespeare made use of this poem rather than the prose version of the tale in Painter's *Palace of Pleasure*. The chief alteration which he makes in the story is his drastic shortening of the time of the action. In the poem, after the secret marriage of Romeo and Juliet,

> The summer of their blisse doth last a month or twaine,

and considerable time elapses after Tybalt's death and Romeo's banishment before the match with County Paris brings the tragedy to its crisis. Shakespeare brings Romeo straight from the marriage at Friar Laurence's cell to the fatal street brawl where Mercutio and Tybalt are slain, and it is only a day or two after his departure into exile that the news of Juliet's death brings him riding hastily back to Verona. The rapidity of action which Shakespeare achieved by this concentration of the whole story into a few days is part of the secret of the play's dramatic effectiveness. In the same way, with the characterisation, the lively variety given to the early part of the play by the figures of Mercutio and the Nurse is Shakespeare's own invention. He found in Brooke a mere hint of the Nurse's comic garrulity, and the character and wit of Mercutio are all his own.

Another romance which came to England from Italy was that mediaeval graft on to the Homeric legend, the love-story of Troilus and Cressida, but by the time that Shakespeare wrote his play on this theme the whole tone of the story had strangely altered. The character of Cressida had much degenerated from that which Chaucer's sympathetic handling had introduced to English readers. The inclusion in the collected editions of Chaucer's works of Henryson's *The Testament of Cresseid* as the concluding book of Chaucer's *Troilus and Criseyde* had made men familiar with the picture of Cressida 'with fleschly lust so maculait' and 'so giglotlike'.[1] She had become a symbol of wantonness and fickleness. Pandarus too had fallen from the gallant and sympathetic friend of Troilus, whom Chaucer portrays, and his name had already added a word to the English language. The Greek heroes had also suffered much denigration. Mediaeval romance was always on the side of Troy, and both Caxton, whose book Shakespeare certainly used, and Lydgate portray Achilles as cruel and unscrupulous, killing both Hector and Troilus by unknightly treachery. Lydgate even blames Homer for setting such high store by Achilles:

> Wherfor, Omer, preyse him now no more.
> Let not his pris thi rial boke difface,
> But in al haste his renoun out arace.

Against this prevailing view Chapman's translation of seven books of the *Iliad* could have prevailed but little at the time when Shakespeare was writing his *Troilus and Cressida*, and those who like Swinburne criticise Shakespeare for 'brutalising' the character of the great Achilles, whom they know from Homer, are forgetting the material on which Shakespeare had to work.

Troilus and Cressida is also an interesting example of Shakespeare's weaving together strands of plot taken from different sources into one continuous story. In this way it is like *King Lear*, *Macbeth*, and *Cymbeline*. He allows himself complete freedom in rearranging episodes which he found in his authorities. The pivot of the war-story is the duel between Hector and Ajax, and this he took from Chapman, but Achilles' love for Polyxena and his traitorous correspondence with the enemy are incidents related by Caxton at a much later stage of the siege. Shakespeare uses them to make more rational the inaction of Achilles. And as

[1] There exists a fragmentary 'plot' of a play on this story in which the words 'Enter Cressida, with Beggers' suggest that the fate of leprosy which Henryson assigns to Cressida was part of the action of this lost play.

always, a reading of his sources gives occasional glimpses of Shakespeare at work. It has been suggested that in Ulysses' complaint that 'the specialty of rule hath been neglected', a theme which appealed greatly to Shakespeare, there is an echo of a speech of Homer's Ulysses, which Chapman translates:

> Nor must Greekes be so irregular
> To live as every man may take the scepter from the king:
> The rule of many is absurd, one Lord must leade the ring
> Of far resounding government.

In Chapman he certainly found the character of the railing Thersites, but there is no clear origin for the stupidity of Ajax. It has been attributed to a simile in Homer describing his stubbornness in battle as like a 'dull mill ass', which the children cannot drive away from the cornfield:

> And still the self-providing asse doth with their weakenes beare,
> Not stirring till his wombe be full, and scarcelie then will stere.
> So the huge sonne of Tellamon amongst the Trojans farde.

But there is another hint in Chapman which may have been more fruitful. After the duel between Ajax and Hector the Greeks hold a feast:

> An Oxe that fed on fyve fayre springs, they fleede and quartred him,
> And then (in peeces cut) on spits they rosted every limb;
> Which neatly cookt they drew it off: worke done, they fell to feast;
> All had inough; but Telamon the king fed past the rest
> With good large peeces of the chyne.

Thersites in his first scene with Ajax calls him a mongrel *beef-witted* lord.[1]

Two comedies, *As You Like It* and *The Winter's Tale*, are straightforward dramatisations of English novels, and both Lodge's *Rosalynde* and Greene's *Pandosto* offered opportunities to exploit the pastoral theme. Lodge gave to his novel the sub-title of *Euphues' Golden Legacy*, and the talk of Shakespeare's courtiers and lovers in Arden has something of the flavour of Lyly's dialogue. The sub-title of Greene's *Pandosto* is *The Triumph of Time*, which in itself is suggestive of what some critics find to

[1] Compare Sir Andrew Aguecheek's excuse when he has been 'put down' by Maria. 'I am a great eater of beef, and I believe that does harm to my wits'.

be Shakespeare's purpose in the later romances, to present dramatically the theme of a reconcilement through the mediation of the younger generation, and it is in keeping with such a purpose that Shakespeare softens somewhat the harsher ending of Greene's story. But again it is not so much what Shakespeare takes from his source as what he adds that gives the plays their particular charm. The forest of Arden would not be the same without Jaques, nor the Bohemian sheep-shearing without Autolycus.

It is, however, significant that, if we except *Hamlet*, which may have come to Shakespeare already dramatised, *Othello* only of the great tragedies of his maturity was based upon a romance. Here the main framework and the chief joints in the story are the same in the play as in Cinthio's novel. Shakespeare's change of the method of killing Desdemona is due primarily to his fundamentally different conception of the Moor's character.[1] In the tale the ensign (Iago) steals the handkerchief from Desdemona, while she is caressing his three-year-old child, but there is nothing about the magic of the handkerchief, a brilliant invention of Shakespeare which enables him to show Othello dominating Desdemona, as during their courtship, by his tales of wonder. The tragic irony of this intimate glimpse into the past was not within the power of the tale-teller. But the real core of the story, the conflict between the Moor's love for Desdemona and the inner villainy of the outwardly pleasing ensign, is in the novel, and the Moor's distress under the ensign's persistent probing is expressed in a number of vivid images. Some of the material is rearranged, and there are additions, as for instance Roderigo, introduced as one means of interpreting the character of Iago. For it is by characterisation chiefly, of which there is but little in the novel, that Shakespeare transforms the story. Here he seems to be putting into his source what in *Julius Caesar* he was drawing out of Plutarch. The creation of Hamlet had intervened between these two plays.

[1] In the novel the Moor and the ensign are mainly concerned to hide all traces of their guilt, which they do by pulling down part of the ceiling upon Desdemona, after Iago has killed her, in order to suggest accidental death.

SHAKESPEARE'S READING

No English translation of Cinthio's tale of the Moor of Venice is known to have existed in Shakespeare's time, but since he quotes Italian in *Love's Labour's Lost*, he may have used the original Italian novel, and several parallels between the play and the novel confirm this conjecture. When the ensign has imparted to the Moor his ingenious plot for the murder of Desdemona, Cinthio writes, 'Piacque al Moro il crudel consiglio', and although Shakespeare has altered all the details of this part of the story, there is in Othello's 'Good, good, the justice of it pleases', evidence that Shakespeare still had the novel clearly in his mind. Shakespeare's knowledge, however, of languages and his general learning have been very much debated. The search for parallel passages in other authors, especially the classics, may have begun on that famous occasion when the worthy John Hales of Eton retorted to Ben Jonson, that if 'Mr Shakespeare had not read the Ancients, he had likewise not stolen anything from them', and undertook to produce on any 'topic finely treated' by any of the classical authors 'something upon the same subject at least as well written by Shakespeare'. Later in reaction against an attribution to Shakespeare of a very wide reading in the classics Richard Farmer wrote his famous *Essay on the Learning of Shakespeare*, in which he asserted that Shakespeare's '*studies* were most demonstratively confined to *nature* and his own language', and that 'the source of a tale hath been often in vain sought abroad, which might easily have been found at home'. Ben Jonson, a good scholar, probably wrote in self-comparison when he allowed to Shakespeare 'small Latin, and less Greek', and Farmer's own immense learning probably caused him to exaggerate his denial of learning to Shakespeare. But his insistence on the necessity for critics of Shakespeare to acquire 'an intimate acquaintance with the writers of the time, who are frequently of no other value', indicated a fruitful line of study, and much of modern research is foreshadowed in his verdict on editors' mistakes: 'The cant of the age, a provincial expression, an obscure proverb, an obsolete custom, a hint at a person or fact no longer remembered, hath continually defeated the best of our guesses'.

The study of books which Shakespeare appears to have used certainly reveals him as a snapper-up of unconsidered trifles. The Anthropophagi, with stories of whom Othello charmed Desdemona, are to be found in Philemon Holland's translation of Pliny's *Natural History* (1601), the devils with whom Edgar communes during his feigned madness in *King Lear* are enumerated in a tract against witchcraft, Samuel Harsnett's *A Declaration of egregious Papist Impostors* (1603), and many other examples of such borrowing of topics and even phrases can be collected. One passage in *The Tempest*, where Shakespeare is making use of Florio's translation of Montaigne, has raised the question how far Montaigne either directly or through Florio influenced Shakespeare. *Hamlet* is the play which suggests most clearly the philosophy of Montaigne, and Florio's translation was not published until 1603, but Shakespeare must have known Florio through the common patronage of Southampton and therefore may have seen some of his work before publication. Possibly, however, such apparent reflection of Montaigne's thought as may be found in Shakespeare may be due to the spirit of the age affecting both of them rather than to the influence of one upon the other.

THE DISINTEGRATION OF THE CANON

Two plays, *All's Well that Ends Well* and *Measure for Measure*, based upon Italian romances and written during the tragic period, while they contain much which only the mature Shakespeare could have written, are uneven and seem to many critics to contain alien matter. Collaboration has therefore been suggested, with Chapman or with one George Wilkins, an obscure novelist and poetaster, whose hand has also been traced in *Pericles*. *Timon of Athens* seems to have been left unfinished by Shakespeare, but its finishers have been variously identified. Certain shows in the plays written after Shakespeare had retired to Stratford have on grounds of style been ascribed to other pens, as for instance parts of *Cymbeline*, especially the vision, and the masque in *The Tempest*. In the middle of the eighteenth century a critic pointed out unusual versification in *Henry VIII*, and much of this is now ascribed to Fletcher. For collaboration between Shakespeare and Fletcher evidence has also been found in *The Two Noble Kinsmen*, in which there is the same mixture of styles and which in the Stationers' Register of 1634 was entered under their names, and there is a still later entry under their names in 1653 of a play now lost, *Cardenio*, probably the *Cardenno* performed by the King's Men in 1613.

On the assumption that Shakespeare started as an adapter of old plays and finished by collaborating with other poets, and that revision and collaboration were established practices in the Elizabethan theatre, scholars have sought over the whole body of his work for traces of revision and of other hands. Investigation has been made both by bibliographical research and by an attempt to be equally scientific in the discrimination of styles. The result of these investigations has been called the Disintegration of Shakespeare.

J. M. Robertson, who carried furthest disintegration by means of the judgment of styles, claimed as his aim 'the scientific solution of the assignment of alien matter to alien hands'. In such an examination all incongruities of language or rhythm, and all inequalities of dramatic technique must be scrutinised, and all parallels to the work of other authors collected. Robertson's conclusions can be summed up in his own description of *A Midsummer Night's Dream* as Shakespeare's 'first, and indeed only complete work'. The bibliographical disintegrators proceed by the study of all the clues which the original texts provide, such as differences of spelling, curious punctuation, passages of verse printed as prose, the wrong lineation of verse, inconsistent speech-headings, the presence of 'mutes' in stage-directions or of actors' names in speech-headings, and all those irregularities which the edited texts conceal. Professor Dover Wilson, in examining on these lines the texts of the fourteen comedies, has only left four to Shakespeare's sole work. In all the rest he finds fragments either of pre-Shakespearian work or of the work of collaborators, and in almost all he argues for abridgment or drastic revision. In *A Midsummer Night's Dream*, the only play left by Mr Robertson to Shakespeare, Professor Wilson, though allowing Shakespeare's authorship, finds at least three strata of composition and revision.

The bibliographical investigation, as it is more objective, should be more reliable than the discrimination of styles, but it can be questioned whether our limited knowledge of the habits of Elizabethan authors with their manuscripts and of Elizabethan compositors with their copy justifies some of the theories based upon the irregularities of the printed text. Shakespeare himself was probably not consistent in his 'foul papers', and something of this inconsistency would remain in his fair copy, and eccentricities of spelling and punctuation would generally be obscured by the conventional practice of scribes and compositors. The ignorance and incompetence of many of the compositors are only too apparent.

How difficult it is to be scientific in the discrimination of styles and how easy to 'lose distinction' is proved by the divergence of opinions on the authorship of *Henry VI*. 'From mere inferiority', wrote Dr Johnson, 'nothing can be inferred; in the productions of wit there will be inequality. Sometimes judgment will err, and sometimes the matter itself will defeat the artist.' J. L. Lowes has shown what strange fragments of a poet's reading may emerge from his subconscious memory, and an overworked actor-dramatist might often fall back on common form. Further, metrical tests are not reliable when applied either to small sections or to admittedly early work in which a poet may be under some dominating influence of the moment or experimenting towards an individual style. Many years after Marlowe's death Jonson preserved the memory of his 'mighty line' and its full influence on the young Shakespeare must be accepted, while in his mature work account must be taken of weariness, lack of interest, haste in composition, or dramatic intention in varying the texture of his verse.

The extent to which disintegration has been carried has produced a natural reaction. The proof of the honesty of Heminge and Condell in the matter of the 'stolne and surreptitious' quartos has certainly given greater authority to the Folio as the canon, but reaction has perhaps gone too far. The study of Shakespeare's manner of handling his known sources removes all doubt of the originality of his genius either in creating characters or in shaping stories to fulfil his dramatic purpose, but orthodox criticism has never been afraid of admitting the presence of alien matter in several plays in the Folio. Ben Jonson retorted upon his Poet-Ape that 'half-eyes' would know

...a fleece
From locks of wooll, or shreds from the whole peece,

and the real answer to the disintegrators lies in demonstrating that undeniable impression of unity and of a characteristic style which distinguishes most of the plays in the Shakespeare canon from those of his contemporaries.

SHAKESPEARE AND THE DRAMA OF HIS TIME

BY

BONAMY DOBRÉE

SHAKESPEARE AND HIS CONTEMPORARIES

THE STATE OF THE DRAMA AT ABOUT 1590

ALTHOUGH every great artist is unique, valuable because he brings what others do not, yet every writer, except when he is deliberately experimenting, works in the idiom of his age. This is especially true in the drama, since it appeals to mass consciousness, and must be readily understood, almost intuitively apprehended. If Shakespeare were a young man now he would not write as he did; his idiom would be derived, say, from Ibsen or Mr Shaw; whereas, living in his own era he probably developed it mainly from Marlowe and Kyd. This, of course, does not refer merely to the derivation or adaptation of lines or thoughts. No doubt if Marlowe had not written in *Faustus*:

> Was this the face that launched a thousand ships
> And burned the topless towers of Ilium?

Shakespeare would not have written of Helen in *Troilus and Cressida*:

> She is a pearl
> Whose price has launched above a thousand ships
> And turned crowned kings to merchants.

But that is only a reference back. What is more radical is the relation of Shakespeare to his dramatic environment (by which is meant chiefly his fellow-dramatists), in the matter handled, in the pattern produced in the handling, and in the medium, that is, the verse and language, employed to produce the effect. And though caution must be employed in treating of so dubious a matter as 'influence', it is possible to make what may be considered at least plausible suggestions.

What we have come to call 'Elizabethan' drama seems to us quite clearly to have been launched on its career between the time Shakespeare was definitely living in Stratford and the time when he was probably writing his first play; but it is a question whether it was so obvious to him that some startling new development was taking place, and that two or three special plays were to come to rank as the original founts. Time, and the loss of a number of dramas, have conveniently simplified the view for us; the map is unrolled, we can see the whole river, and trace it back to its source. It is easy for us to see that Marlowe had discovered, if in somewhat immature form, the way to write dramatic blank verse; that Kyd, besides rivalling Marlowe in this, had shown how a certain type of tragedy might be handled; that Peele had let a rush of fresh air into comedy: but for Shakespeare the view was different. How could one tell, for instance, that it was not Lyly who had set his foot upon the right path? For it must have been a time extremely bewildering to the contemporary would-be dramatist, when different companies, acting to different types of audience, producing various kinds of plays, were competing, or deliberately not competing perhaps, for favour; when men were trying first one thing, then another, often helping each other out, or botching up parts of plays with, apparently, a total disregard of what their partners were trying to do, or, possibly, not noticing that they were doing anything different in kind. It is important, therefore, to look at the state of the drama when Shakespeare wrote, not independently, but with Marlowe and perhaps others, the three parts of *Henry VI* (1590–2).

What, then, were the recent successes by the writers who were, apparently, in the way of enlarging the scope of the drama and drawing the public, and were making it a medium in which a man conscious of great powers could work? There was Lyly, but it is likely that we can safely reject him as an early influence on Shakespeare, not so much because his plays, say *Campaspe* (1584) and *Endimion* (1588), were written for boy players, as that their scope was obviously so much more restricted than that of their successors, their pretty artificiality far too limiting for the emotions it was now plain could be expressed in the theatre. Lyly certainly did much to free the drama, but the four playwrights who seem to have given the impetus to the main movement are Marlowe, Kyd, Greene, and Peele, of whom the first two are the most important.

Marlowe, Kyd, Greene, and Peele

It cannot be said that Marlowe's *Tamburlaine* (1587), *The Jew of Malta* (1589), or *Dr Faustus* (1592), are good plays from the point of view of construction; Marlowe's main contribution in these works was to show that the whole force of Spenserian loveliness could be adapted to stage purposes, and to make blank verse a far readier medium for stage speech than it had ever been before. He made the rhetorical unit (not the prosodic one) three stresses, as in 'And ride in triumph through Persepolis', abandoning the five of such early experiments as *Gorboduc* (1561), or *Jocasta* (1566). And if in *Tamburlaine* he brought the emotions of the exterior sensuous universe into the realm of the drama, itself a tremendous achievement, in *Dr Faustus* he approached the moral problem of choice. Further, in *The Jew of Malta* he showed that the kind of speech he loved to use, the rhythms he delighted to employ, need not be restricted in their use to heroically romantic subjects. All the time, also, he was feeling his way to greater dramatic effects; in *Dr Faustus*, the naïve progress of *Tamburlaine*, which reads like a narrative poem, was being relieved by dramatic lights and shadows, just as the famous apostrophe to Helen already quoted replaced the quite undramatic statement in *Tamburlaine*:

> Helen (whose beauty summoned Greece to arms
> And drew a thousand ships to Tenedos).

The movement of *The Jew of Malta*, even, is distinctly more complex, though all three plays belong to the type of art that borders on caricature. It was not till *Edward II*, also 1592, that he really revealed his potentialities as a dramatist, for though that play also is somewhat trudgingly straightforward in its progress, the structure of emotions built up in the spectator (which is really in the last analysis what dramatic structure means) begins to approach the more complex dramatic form. His verse in the last play, if perhaps not so gloriously enraptured as in his earlier work, is a far more supple instrument, and it is astonishing to find the poet of the somewhat monotonous rhythm of *Tamburlaine* achieving:

Base Fortune, now I see that in thy wheel
There is a point, to which when men aspire,
They tumble headlong down: that point I touched,
And seeing there was no place to mount up higher,
Why should I grieve at my declining fall?
Farewell, fair queen; weep not for Mortimer
That scorns the world, and as a traveller
Goes to discover countries yet unknown.

The personal problem that Marlowe was solving was that of turning the impassioned lyricist into a dramatic poet.

Kyd's contribution is far harder to analyse, but it is equally fundamental; for popular as Marlowe's plays were, they were outdone in the general mind by *The Spanish Tragedy* (*circa* 1588). The play is important, firstly because it was a drama of contemporary life, showing that the subject of plays need not be removed in time to give them dignity or aesthetic value; and secondly, because it stood in the forefront of the long line of Senecan dramas, introducing not only the obvious Senecan counters such as revenge and ghostly apparition, but also the Stoic moral stamp, and the sententious utterance, from which even Shakespeare himself was not free. Far more important, however, than either of these things, it showed what could be done in deepening the emotions, in attaining that poignancy of horror which was to attain its extreme in Webster. It was the blackness, not the glory of tragedy, that Kyd brought into the realm of drama, a blackness made darker by enlisting thought to reinforce the emotions. Thought itself as a major element was to be exhibited at its purest only perhaps by Chapman, but by introducing it in a way that Marlowe never touched, nor, possibly, thought of, Kyd, by the necessity new material imposes upon technique (technique being the means by which material is handled), still further freed blank verse. Such lines as:

> Eyes, life, world, heav'n, hell, night, and day,
> See, search, show, send some man, some means that may...

show an advance which is startling in the otherwise not too varied setting of Kyd's usual rhythm. There is one further possibility that Kyd indicated, even if only in embryonic form which it was left to Shakespeare to bring to full ripeness, namely the development of character through action and the interaction of events upon the soul.

Greene's contribution indicated no advance in material, for he seems to have taken his cue from Marlowe; nor did he make verse more subtle or complex. Such lines as:

> Daphne, the damsel that caught Phoebus fast,
> And locked him in the brightness of her looks,
> Was not so beauteous in Apollo's eyes
> As is fair Margaret to the Lincoln Earl...

are, with hundreds of other passages, sheer Marlowe. What Greene did, however, was to intermingle the distant grandeur of Marlowe with the nearness of everyday. The setting of *A Looking Glasse for London and England* (1590), written with Lodge, may be Nineveh in the days of Jonah, but the prose scenes in the inns, the lawcourts, or the streets, mirror Elizabethan London; and if *Frier Bacon and Frier Bongay* (*circa* 1590) is set in the time of Edward III, the Fressingfield of that play is the Suffolk of Queen Elizabeth. And moreover his mingling of everyday homely comedy with stateliness and royalty gave an added freedom, and provided its actors with good material, just as did the introduction of comic scenes in the historical drama. In these three playwrights, then, are to be seen the main movements of the drama when Shakespeare began to write, the importance of Peele being mainly that, in *The Old Wives Tale* (*circa* 1592), he introduced satirical criticism of the popular drama of the day, and thus gave the latter a lightness, and some of the saving grace of humour, which brought it out of the region of the pedantic. These writers made it clear that a playwright was free to experiment in any direction that he chose, provided, of course, that he pleased the public.

Exterior Influences: Popular Taste, the Plague, the Theatres. Dekker and Heywood

So far we have treated of those aspects of the drama that might be expected to engage the attention of an artist who wished to enter himself in the fraternity, namely material and handling: but now we must turn to what would attract the business man as being likely to succeed with the public. What, in brief, the adventurers so far named did, was to establish in popular favour the chronicle play, the historical play, tragedy (especially on Senecan lines), and realistic romantic comedy. The playwrights eagerly took from each other hints for what would tickle the palate of the audience; thus Greene and Peele followed up *Tamburlaine* with *Alphonsus King of Arragon* (*circa* 1587), and *The Battell of Alcazar* (1589): Peele was to follow up *Edward II* with *Edward I* (1593), again introducing comic episode, while Greene had produced *James IV* in 1591. Since necromancy had proved popular with *Frier Bacon and Frier Bongay*, it appeared again in *Faustus*; and so on. Thus Shakespeare was to make his entry in the three parts of *Henry VI*, chronicle plays; and in *Titus Andronicus* (1593–4), a horror tragedy of the Italo-Senecan stamp. It was not until after these that he was to take a hint from Lyly, partly in adapting the material, namely that of high comedy, partly in the use of prose, and still more in the use of punning and quibbling in such plays as *The Two Gentlemen of Verona*, *Love's Labour's Lost* (both 1593–4), *Much Ado about Nothing* (1598–9), and down to as late as *As You Like It* (1599–1600), though Lyly's actual dramatic method has vanished in the last two. Lyly, then, seems to have been a later influence, a harking back as it were to material which had been allowed to lie fallow. To begin with, Shakespeare must be classed with the group which numbered Marlowe, Kyd, and Greene, for he worked with their material and by their methods, besides using much the same sources.

The break in theatrical activity caused by the plague in 1593–4 affected the playwrights mainly as it altered the organisation of the companies; for from then, for some years, players and playwrights were banded into the rival camps of the Admiral's Men and the Lord Chamberlain's Men. Thus if one group scored a success, the other was quick to outdo it. For instance, when the Admiral's Men attracted crowds with Munday's lost play of *Robin Hood* (1598), the Chamberlain's Men replied with another play of romantic forest life, namely *As You Like It.* What the change meant to Shakespeare was that he was solidly fixed with a permanent company, acting for it, writing plays for it, rewriting its old stock, such as (perhaps) *The Taming of the Shrew,* which he did in 1593–4, collaborating with other writers attached to it, and thus living in intimate contact with them. Whether he got more stimulus from his friends or from his rivals can only be a matter of conjecture.

Until Ben Jonson produced *Every Man in His Humour* with Shakespeare's company, with Shakespeare acting in it, in 1598, no new star likely to change the course of things appeared on the horizon. Heywood and Dekker, yes; but both are comparatively minor, and their most important work was not produced until after this date. Heywood's original contribution to the drama was, of course, the domestic tragedy of *A Woman Kilde with Kindnesse* (1604), which at any rate did not much affect Shakespeare except for what hand he may have had in *A Yorkshire Tragedy.* Dekker's *The Shoemaker's Holiday* may have been acted before this time—it was printed in 1599—but there is no reason to suppose that the 'homely realism' of the 'lovable, elusive child of nature' would have been any different from what it was had Shakespeare never written (he derives, rather, from Greene), or that the rollicking fun had any effect on Shakespeare. It is then to Jonson that we must look for the next important point in the history of 'Elizabethan' drama.

Jonson: The Humours: Stage Speech

One of the few certain things we know about Shakespeare is that he had many discussions, 'wit contests', with Jonson: at least to doubt Fuller's report is to carry scepticism too far. Besides, on the face of it, the thing is so likely. How far the two were intimate friends is another question, just as dubious as the determination of the degree of hostility that existed between them during the theatrical war which was soon to come. But that the two actor-playwrights should not have discussed their craft is unthinkable. The two men were, perhaps, as different in character as two men can be, as distant as they were in their dramatic aims; but genius recognises genius, and both could meet on the common ground of a passionate love of poetry. That Jonson was at all affected by anything Shakespeare said is highly improbable; though he was the younger man, he was far too deeply trenched in his theories and opinions, too endowed with a thick carapace of obstinacy, to budge one inch. Jonson would no doubt be irritated at the attitude of a man so careless about many things which he thought of supreme importance, and who, though he did so brilliantly well, might so easily do better. He was to do better, but whether because of anything he learnt from Jonson can only be guesswork.

The matters of fundamental importance which any two literary men would naturally discuss are structure and diction; but at the moment of their meeting over Jonson's play in which Shakespeare acted, the matter most to the front would be the theory of the 'humours'. The theory itself may be regarded as an exaggerated statement, phrased in mediaeval medico-psychological jargon, of what takes place in the rendering of all comic characters from Plautus to Meredith, namely the abstraction of certain socially harmful qualities to make fun of. It suited Jonson's devastatingly satirical turn of mind to conceive that

> . . . some one peculiar quality
> Doth so possess a man, that it doth draw
> All his affects, his spirits, and his powers,
> In their confluctions, all to run one way:

it was not usually to his purpose to show a character in whom the elements (choler, melancholy, phlegm, and blood) were so mixed that anyone might stand up and say 'This was a man'. And whereas he was concerned to create a closed world in which the 'humour' characters might act with perfect consistency, Shakespeare, we suppose, was concerned to show men who moved as readily in the world of life as they did upon the stage. Moreover, the theory of humours (which Chapman, possibly, had set upon the boards in 1597 in *An Humerous Dayes Myrth*, and which was in the air, as we see from the writers of 'characters', who were about to be numerous) soon transcended itself. Volpone, Morose, Sir Epicure Mammon, become tremendous symbols of evil, just as Tartuffe does; they are no longer to be laughed at. What concerns us here, however, is how far the theory may have affected Shakespeare. It is, of course, impossible to say; but at the time it is not beyond the bounds of likelihood that the theory did cause him to sharpen his pen, to tighten up his technique, when dealing with such figures as Malvolio (*circa* 1602) (the humour of pride), or some of the passages of *Troilus and Cressida* (1601–2). Jaques is clearly a humour of melancholy. It is possible to regard Angelo in *Measure for Measure* (1604–5) as a humour which breaks down, as though, perhaps, to mark the weakness of the theory when applied to three-dimensional life. Shakespeare's association with Jonson we can legitimately suppose to have been fairly close for a year from the summer of 1598, and it is possible to argue that his increased interest in character for its own sake from that date was due to the stimulus of the theory of humours; but Shakespeare's character-drawing is so distinct from Jonson's that it is equally possible to argue that his later portrayals are due to his natural development and his final maturity.

Where mechanical structure is concerned, Jonson's influence on Shakespeare seems to have been nil; we do not associate Shakespeare with classical form. But Jonson's diction suggests possibilities which, however, it is not within the province of this chapter to argue. Jonson, with that conscious development of his art which characterises him, seems to have been trying to work out a perfect form of stage speech, learning no doubt from Shakespeare's experiments in Marlovian blank verse, rhymed couplets, the quatrain, and prose, as also from the quatrains of the author of *Selimus*, and the speeches, almost in sonnet form, of Daniel in his *Cleopatra* (1593). He seems to have been feeling for an instrument as far from 'normal' blank verse as it was from ordinary prose, so that the verse and the prose, though still distinguishable, appear to have come closer together till they have much the same inflexions.[1] The question is not one of prosody, but of oratory, for the problem in dramatic writing is to discover a medium which will be flexible, fast or slow as you wish, bringing the stress on the right word so that the actor can make no mistakes, and so phrasing your speech that it will be easy for an actor to make it audible to a large audience, possibly out of doors. Not only the sensitiveness of the ear has to be considered, but the capacity of the lung.

If we look at Jonson's verse and prose the progress is plain enough. The verse of *Volpone* (1605), the opening speech of which has so strong a flavour of *The Jew of Malta*, still has the ring of Marlowe:

> Thy baths shall be the juice of July-flowers,
> Spirit of roses and of violets,
> The milk of unicorns, and panther's breath
> Gathered in bags, and mixed with Cretan wines.
> Our drink shall be prepared gold and amber....

But when we come to *The Alchemist* (1610), there is a markedly different rhythm, as far removed from any iambic measure as it is from any other regular stress-spacing:

> Nor shall you need to libel 'gainst the prelates,
> And so shorten your ears against the hearing
> Of the next wire-drawn grace. Nor of necessity
> Rail against plays, to please the aldermen
> Whose daily custards you devour; nor lie
> With zealous rage till you are hoarse...,

[1] It is my private opinion that Shakespeare worked on much the same lines: see my *Histriophone* (Hogarth Press, 1923).

as verse, in fact, admirable stage speech, which to say and to hear is not far different from the prose of *The Silent Woman* (1609):

> By my integrity, I'll send you over to the Bank-side; I'll commit you to the master of the garden, if I hear but a syllable more. Must my roof be polluted with the scent of bears and bulls, when it is perfumed for great ladies? Is this according to the instrument when I married you? that I would be princess, and reign in mine own house; and you would be my subject and obey me?

a prose which seems all the time to be bordering on verse, as the verse, without being prose, seems to hover all the while on the edge of the 'other harmony'. That Jonson wrote this prose especially as a stage instrument (as all good playwrights do), and not because it was the way natural to him, is immediately obvious if we read any of his prose descriptions of a masque, or *Discoveries*.

The same process seems to have been adopted, not arrived at, by Middleton, Tourneur, and Webster. In these, and later in Massinger, even in Shirley (though not in the invertebrate stuff poured out by Fletcher), we find verse admirably suited to the stage, but often prosodically abominable. It is hardly distinguishable from the prose, which would itself be worthless except as a stage instrument.

The War of the Theatres: the Boy Players: Accession of James I

Shakespeare's first connexion with Jonson seems to have been short-lived, whatever may have happened in later years; for hardly had they met than there broke out the war of the theatres, in which they were on opposite sides. The main quarrel was between Jonson on one side and Dekker and Marston on the other, Jonson's stage contributions being *Cynthia's Revels* (1600–1) and *Poetaster* (1601), while the other side produced *Histrio-Mastix* (1598 or 1599) and *What You Will* (1601) by Marston, and *Satiro-Mastix* (1601) by Dekker. The quarrel was made all the more possible by the re-emergence at about this time of the boy companies, which vied in popularity with the two main ones, whose commanding position had not been altered by the growth of two or three others towards the end of the decade. The part Shakespeare took in the war remains obscure: all that we have to go upon is the sentence in *The Returne from Pernassus II* (Christmas 1601) which runs: 'Oh, that Ben Jonson is a pestilent fellow; he brought up Horace giving the poets a pill, but our fellow Shakespeare hath given him a purge that made him bewray his credit': which may mean either that Shakespeare showed how to write classical tragedy, such as *Julius Caesar* (1599–1600), without eternal classical allusions, and so put Jonson to shame: or that he had a hand in a lost play in which a close-stool was a property; or that he meant to portray Jonson when he drew Ajax in *Troilus and Cressida* (1601–2), a doubtful conjecture. The importance of the war to the student of the drama, as opposed to the student of the history of the drama, is not very great; but that it quickened the critical sense of the dramatists as regards their own work, and stimulated the actors, is probable from Shakespeare's 'little eyases' reference in *Hamlet.* Nor did the reappearance of the boy companies, at both Whitefriars and Blackfriars, seem to make any essential difference in the type of play being written in the tradition which time has shown to be the main one. It is true that such a play as Daniel's *Philotas*, acted by the Children of the Chapel, would have fared badly out of doors; but that *West-Ward Hoe* or *Eastward Hoe*, *The Silent Woman*, or *The Widdowes Teares* needed the indoor atmosphere is at least doubtful; and if *The Roaring Girle* could stand daylight, we may well ask why *The Dutch Courtezan* should demand candles. *The Malcontent*, indeed, was acted both by the Children of the Chapel and by Shakespeare's company. The theatre for which a play was written did, of course, sometimes make a slight difference to mechanical technique, but not to the essential dramatic structure.

The accession of James I no doubt to some extent altered the outlook of the dramatists; but whatever effect it had on plays was at first only on the surface, though the effect it had on the actors was more important. They became more official, were exalted to being the Queen's Men, Prince Henry's Men, and so on, Shakespeare's own company becoming the King's Men. More varied were the developments which took place in the private theatres, developments rather by the side of the main current than in it; but this can only be mentioned here, not discussed.

Chapman, Marston, Middleton

It is more to the point to study the dramatists who had made their appearance at the end of the century, not because they had much or any effect on Shakespeare—it is, rather, the other way about—but because they developed farther than Shakespeare did certain aspects of the drama in which they specialised, using material which he was content to handle as side issues in his wider sweep. The greatest of these is no doubt Chapman, the nearest approach to a 'metaphysical' poet in the drama of the time. It is not only that such sentences from *Bussy D'Ambois* (1604) as:

> I'll make th'inspired thresholds of his court
> Sweat with the weather of my horrid steps

smack of metaphysical 'wit', but that with him we are conscious of the 'emotional apprehension of thought'. To put it crudely, Hamlet's or Macbeth's thought is born of their emotion; but in such passages as this which follows from *The Tragedie of Charles Duke of Byron*, the thought *is* the emotion:

> Oh of what contraries consists a man!
> Of what impossible mixtures! vice and virtue,
> Corruption and eterneness at one time,
> And in one subject, let together, loose!
> We have not any strength but weakens us,
> No greatness but doth crush us into air:
> Our knowledges do light us but to err...,

while all through his plays, Chapman seems to be wrestling with a question of unity, of how man is 'to join himself with th'Universe'. Just as it was Marlowe's problem to turn a lyrical poet into a dramatist, and to capture the delicious world of sense for the drama, so it was Chapman's to turn the metaphysical poet into a writer of plays, and to capture for the drama the realm of philosophy. Had he not largely succeeded in doing so, his work would have as little importance in the main current as so lovely a thing as Daniel's *Philotas* (1604), which could not live outside the walls of a private theatre. As it is, his work would seem to rank (one must be dubious till one has seen him acted) with any of his contemporaries, except Shakespeare's, even, one would say, by the side of Jonson's: for if *The Widdowes Teares* (*circa* 1606) is not great comedy, comedy which topples over into tragedy, then there is no meaning in the phrase.

As distinct in his own manner when working alone, and at his best, is Marston, for it is he who most clearly exhibits harsh and satiric (not crude) realism, and directly critical comedy, such as we never get at any length in Shakespeare, if at all. Dekker, in a sense, is realistic enough, but his realism is always touched by a delicate and joyous fantasy; Jonson, at his most characteristic, is not realistic at all: he created the objects of his satire. But Marston's world is not Jonson's. The objects of the former's somewhat savage attacks are individuals rather than synthetic concepts of mankind, at least when he is most himself. He can denounce terrifically, as in *The Malcontent* (1604), and one wonders whether Timon of Athens was not familiar with the speeches of Andrugio in *Antonio and Mellida* (1599): but his contribution was to lash the crying follies of his time, not of all time, as Jonson did. *The Dutch Courtezan* (1603–4) is his triumph. It can be said that he developed the Beatrice-Benedick scenes of Shakespeare, but it is more illuminating to realise that he forestalled the comic dramatists of the next age. Crispinella is a Restoration heroine, and many Restoration writers, Congreve himself among them, borrowed from her speeches. 'My stomach o' late stands against kissing extremely': 'A husband generally is a careless, domineering thing, that grows like coral, which as long as it is under water is soft and tender, but as soon as it gets his branch above water is presently hard, stiff, not to be bowed but burst'—those are sentiments commonly uttered by heroines of plays in Charles II's reign. His world indeed, rasping, bustling, though very much of his time, is more like that of Wycherley than of any of his contemporaries; and although he might say in the prologue to this play 'We strive not to instruct but to delight', the moralist is plain in the whole development of the play, except in the amusing 'gulling' scenes of Cockledemoy and his dupes.

Again we must distinguish between the realism of Middleton and that of Marston or of Dekker. At first sight *A Trick to Catch the Old One* (*circa* 1605), or *A Chast Mayd in Cheapeside*, has the same quality of contact with life, the gritty, vociferous, tumultuous life of Jacobean London as Marston's plays. But Middleton was doing more than achieve immediate truth to life that he might satirise it; he was aiming at a more general moral truth, and the strange figure of Moll Cutpurse in *The Roaring Girle* (1610) is a solid character built up on self-abnegation. His qualities are more obvious in his tragedies, which came later, such as *Women Beware Women*, and especially *The Changeling* (1623), which show him imbued with a sense of the conflict between good and evil, though perhaps but for Shakespeare he would not have been able to probe so deep as he did. At all events he is an important figure in the drama of his day, especially as he collaborated so often and so willingly; but for that very reason he is hard to decipher. It may be (as Swinburne said) as profitable to research into the natural history of snakes in Iceland as to discuss the supposed obligation of Shakespeare to Middleton or of Middleton to Shakespeare in the witch scenes in *Macbeth* and *The Witch*: and Dugdale Sykes showed that what of Middleton we may find in *Timon of Athens* does not much affect Shakespeare; but one would like to be certain what part Middleton took in Dekker's *The Honest Whore* (*circa* 1605), what part Dekker in *The Roaring Girle*, and what Middleton owed to Rowley in *The Changeling*, though the central part is undoubtedly due to the former. But whatever his collaborations may have been, we can assert that without Middleton Jacobean drama would not be what it is.

Trend of the Drama at about 1610: Courtly and Masque Influence. The King's Men at the Blackfriars. Beaumont and Fletcher

By the end of the first decade of the seventeenth century the drama had begun to take a different trend. In the theatre itself the boy actors had disappeared, and the King's Men had removed to Blackfriars. But more important was the effect, now fully felt, of the companies having become definitely Court companies, with more markedly courtly audiences. What these wanted was not so much profound art, which implies thought and a sense of values; nor great poetry, which demands attention; but amusement, a certain easiness of approach which need not be honoured with the name of cynicism, and clear limpid verse without much backbone to it. They got all these things. Almost miraculously, it would seem, the gods sent Beaumont and Fletcher, especially Fletcher, to give them romantic drama (romantic being here used in opposition to realistic) which was neither comedy nor tragedy, but an evening's entertainment. Their taste was for plays with plenty of unexpected incident, strange happenings, and characters that it required no imagination to grasp. The result was a prettification of the drama; even tragedy from Beaumont and Fletcher, such as *The Maides Tragedy* (1608), was prettified; the sentiments are 'literary' in the bad sense of the word, 'poetic' in the same bad sense, 'poetry' being added as a 'beauty', instead of being the life-blood of the whole thing. One has only to glance at Middleton, Marston, Chapman, Jonson, let alone Shakespeare, to be struck with the sickly unreality, emotionally speaking, of *The Faithfull Shepherdesse* (1608–9) or of *Philaster* (1610), and the superficiality of the comedy which might be exemplified by Fletcher's later play *The Spanish Curate* (1623). Hand in hand with the weakening of the idea went the softening of the verse, not only in the matter of metrical fibre, as in the constant use of the double ending, but in the absence of probing utterance, of flame-like epithet, of compelling image. It is true that the fiery plays of Webster were to follow, perhaps Tourneur's *The Atheist's Tragedie* (1607–11), and Chapman's *The*

Revenge of Bussy D'Ambois (*circa* 1611), but these were not plays that told. Webster did add something to the realm of drama, namely the emotion of emotion itself, just as Marlowe had brought in the emotion of sensuousness, and Chapman the emotion of thought; but he seems to indicate the finality of a period rather than a renewed sprouting. It was, then, the romantic plays that held the stage, and it is often supposed that it was to conform with the new departure that Shakespeare wrote *Cymbeline* (1609–10), *The Winter's Tale* (1610–11) and *The Tempest* (1611–12).

Shakespeare as Part of His Time

It has been the object of this chapter to suggest that to appreciate Shakespeare fully it is essential to read his contemporaries, to see if and where, when he used the same kind of material as they did, he bettered them, to realise which aspects he left alone or barely touched, and to see to what extent he was part and parcel of his time, and how far he transcended it. To what degree he was influenced by his collaborators, how much effect he had on them, is a dubious matter, but it is none the less fascinating and important for that. It is unlikely that after *Hamlet* Shakespeare was much influenced by what others around him were doing, for by the time a man of his stature has attained maturity he knows what he wants to do, and which are the aspects of life he feels it important to deal with.

To say, then, how far Shakespeare led or followed the movements of his time is a question that it is very difficult to answer. It is clear that in his early years he was content to allow his pen to be guided; he was apprenticed, so to speak, to Marlowe, Kyd, Lyly, Greene, and perhaps others, taking his good things where he could find them, transforming them into what he wished, standing out from the very beginning as a separate voice, though one which it is not always easy to distinguish when he sang in parts with others. In his great period, from *Hamlet* (1601) to *Timon of Athens* (1608), he stands single; whatever it may have been that made him write his great tragedies, whether despair or a Nietzschean over-fullness, he was intent to write them in his own way, a way which no one could follow. This is not to say that he was ever unready to seize new ideas, nor that others did not gain much from his example, but this does not mean that he originated or followed a movement. Indeed on one outstanding point, the treatment of the revenge motive, his work appears to have had no effect, for its disintegration in *Hamlet* put no stop to the theme in all its crudeness, as we see from Chapman and Tourneur.

During his master period he was concerned with his own vision, investigating, as a strong man does, the utmost horrors of life, following an instinct of supreme health which for some inexplicable reason has sometimes, as in the case of *Measure for Measure*, been stigmatised as 'morbid'! But in his final phase, when he had worked out what was in him, he seems indeed to have written to meet a demand, though there is nothing improbable in the author of the *Dream* wishing to write *The Tempest* for his own gratification. Moreover, he was not a great original thinker; there is no need for a great artist to be so; he must be a profound thinker, but that is a different thing. Besides, the mind of a great artist is highly individual; it works in ways not to be apprehended by lesser mortals, and to try to class Shakespeare with a group, or to attach a group to him, is waste of time. Imitators he had; Fletcher imitated him perhaps; but imitators invariably copy only the inessential, which is all that they can copy. There are parallelisms both in theme and words between *Cymbeline* and *Philaster*—which of them has the precedence in time is not determined; but the emotional, the poetic structure of the plays, is utterly different.

It is this striking difference of Shakespeare from his contemporaries which makes such critics as William Archer[1] raise him to the heights to despise the rest, an opinion apparently shared by Landor. Unfortunately, Archer, while blaming what he regarded as the hideous disorder, moral and technical, of the Elizabethans, did not explain why he accepted exactly the same moral horrors and technical anarchy (this is his view) in Shake-

[1] *The Old Drama and the New: passim.*

speare. Shakespeare, as far as sources, plots, treatment, and so on go, is superficially the same as any one else in his period; he used the same idiom, he erred exactly as the others did, on Archer's count. What then is there in him to bring about that 'evaporation of all disagreeables', to use Keats's phrase, which makes him eternal, while the others have, for all public purposes, been forgotten? It is this seeming paradox that makes it important to study his contemporaries, even his successors, especially perhaps Massinger, to see the emotional units, which apparently were real to the Elizabethans, becoming counters. The truth is, of course, that what is important in an artist of any sort, is not his subjects, but what he brings to them. Shakespeare's fellow-writers are undoubtedly worth reading for their own sakes: some of them pierced here and there beneath the skin of their own time, but none so generally as Shakespeare. Though he was a craftsman, doing his work after the manner of the other craftsmen of his time, he was intent (as some of the others were) to objectivise his own vision; his vision, however, happened to be comprehensive; and what is more, he had the personality of a genius in poetic expression. The conclusion is commonplace, but it is all the same true: the interest grows when we come to try to analyse the genius. And it is in doing this that a knowledge of his contemporaries is most helpful.

SHAKESPEARE'S TEXT

BY

A. W. POLLARD

The following editions of plays and poems by Shakespeare were published prior to the collected edition of his plays in the Folio of 1623. The text of editions marked * is notably abridged and corrupt.

1593. Venus and Adonis. *R. Field.* Entered on Stationers' Register: April 18th. Dedicated to the Earl of Southampton. Reprinted: 1594, (1595 ?), 1596, 1599 (2 eds.), (1602 ?), "1602" (three later reprints so dated to avoid censorship), 1617, 1620.

1594. Lucrece. *R. Field.* Entered: May 9th. Dedicated to the Earl of Southampton. Reprinted: 1598, 1600 (2 eds.), 1607, 1616.

1594. The most lamentable Romaine tragedie of Titus Andronicus. (Anon.) *J. Danter, sold by E. White & T. Millington.* Entered: February 6th. Reprinted: 1600, 1611.

*1594. The first part of The Contention betwixt the two famous houses of Yorke and Lancaster. (Anon.) *T. Creede for T. Millington.* Entered: March 12th. Reprinted: 1600, and again in 1619 with '*The True Tragedie*' as 'The Whole Contention betweene the two famous houses, Lancaster and Yorke'. A memorial abridgment of a text of *II Henry VI* not greatly differing from that of the Folio.

*1595. The true tragedie of Richard Duke of Yorke. (Anon.) *P. S[hort] for T. Millington.* Reprinted: 1600 and again in 1619 with 'The first part', as *The Whole Contention.* A memorial abridgment of a text of *III Henry VI* not greatly differing from that of the Folio.

*1597. An excellent conceited tragedie of Romeo and Juliet. (Anon.) *J. Danter.*

1597. The tragedie of King Richard the Second. (Anon.) *V. Simmes for A. Wise.* Entered: August 29th. Reprinted 1598 (2 eds.), 1608 with additions to the Parliament scene (two issues), 1615.

1597. The tragedy of King Richard the Third. (Anon.) *V. Sims for A. Wise.* Entered: October 19th. Reprinted: 1598, 1602, 1605, 1612, 1622.

1598. The history of Henrie the Fourth: with the battell at Shrewsburie. (Anon.) *P. S[hort] for A. Wise.* Entered: February 25th. Reprinted: (Newly corrected by W. Shake-speare) 1599, 1604, 1608, 1613, 1622.

1598. A pleasant conceited comedie called Loues labors lost. Newly corrected and augmented by W. Shakespere. *W. W[hite] for C. Burby.* (Probably preceded by an unauthorised version similar to the *R. and J.* of 1597.) Not entered till 1607.

1599. The most excellent and lamentable tragedie of Romeo and Juliet. Newly corrected, augmented and amended. (Anon.) *T. Creede for C. Burby.* Reprinted in 1609 and without date (two issues, one with Shakespeare's name).

1600. The second part of Henrie the Fourth. *V. S[ims] for A. Wise and W. Aspley.* Entered: August 23rd. Two issues.

1600. A Midsommer Nights Dreame. *For T. Fisher.* Entered: October 8th. Reprinted with same date in 1619.

1600. The most excellent historie of the Merchant of Venice. *J. R[oberts] for T. Heyes.* Entered: July 22nd, 1598 and October 28th, 1600. Reprinted with same date in 1619.

1600. Much adoe about Nothing. *V. S[ims] for A. Wise and W. Aspley.* 'Staied' August 4th (1600). Entered: August 23rd.

*1600. The cronicle history of Henry the Fift. *T. Creede for T. Millington and J. Busby.* 'Staied' August 4th (1600). Entered: August 14th. Reprinted in 1602 and (with the false date 1608) in 1619.

*1602. A most pleasaunt and excellent conceited comedie, of Syr Iohn Falstaffe, and the Merrie Wives of Windsor. *T. C[reed] for A. Johnson.* Entered and assigned January 18th. Reprinted 1619.

*1603. The tragicall historie of Hamlet, Prince of Denmarke. *[V. Sims] for N. L[ing] and J. Trundell.*

1604. The tragicall historie of Hamlet, Prince of Denmarke. Newly imprinted and enlarged. *J. R[oberts] for N. L[ing].* Entered to Roberts July 26th, 1602. Part of the edition dated 1605. Reprinted 1611 and without date.

1608. Mr. William Shak-speare: his true cronicle historie of the life and death of King Lear and his three daughters. *for N. Butter and are to be sold at the signe of the Pide Bull.* Entered to N. Butter and J. Busby November 26th, 1607. Reprinted with same date in 1619.

1609. The late and much admired play, called Pericles, Prince of

Tyre. By William Shakespeare. *For H. Gosson*, 1609. Two issues. Entered to E. Blount May 20th, 1608. Reprinted 1611 and 1619.

1609. The Historie of Troylus and Cresseida. As it was acted by the Kings Maiesties seruants at the Globe. Written by William Shakespeare. *Imprinted by G. Eld for R. Bonian and H. Walley*. Reissued with title-page cut away and replaced by a half sheet (two leaves) with new title (*The Famous Historie of Troylus and Cresseid*, etc.) and an address beginning: Eternall reader, you haue heere a new play, neuer stal'd with the Stage. Entered to J. Roberts February 7th, 1603; to R. Bonion and H. Walleys January 28th, 1609.

1609. Shake-speares Sonnets. Never before imprinted. *G. Eld for T. T[horpe] to be solde by J. Wright*. (Another issue with only '*to be solde by J. Wright*'.)

1619. (Reprints by W. Jaggard for T. Pavier.) 'The Whole Contention betweene the two famous houses (etc.). *For T. P.*', followed, with continuous 'signatures', by *Pericles, Prince of Tyre. Printed for T. P.* 1619 and seven other reprints (with distinct signatures), all bearing a device with motto 'Heb Ddieu Heb Ddim' owned in 1619 by William Jaggard, but some with their original imprint and date, known to have been bound together variously arranged: *A Yorkshire Tragedie, Printed for T. P.* 1619; *Merry Wives. Printed for Arthur Johnson*, 1619; *The Merchant of Venice, Printed by J. Roberts*, 1600; *A Midsummer nights dreame. Printed by J. Roberts*, 1600; *King Lear. Printed for Nathaniel Butter* 1608; *Henry V. Printed for T. P.* 1608; *Sir John Oldcastle*. Written by William Shakespeare. *London, printed for T. P.* 1600.

Owing to the volumes containing these plays having been broken up whenever they came to be sold the dates earlier than 1619 were accepted as correct, and the reprint of *The Merchant of Venice* was generally regarded as the First Edition.

1622. The tragœdy of Othello, the Moore of Venice. *N. O[kes] for T. Walkley*. Entered: October 6th, 1621.

There is no evidence that Shakespeare ever read the proofs of any edition of his plays or poems except the first of *Venus and Adonis* and *Lucrece*, the personal dedications of which to his patron the Earl of Southampton entitle us to believe that he took an active part in their publication. It is probable that his annoyance at the appearance of incomplete and mangled versions of *Love's Labour's Lost* (conjectured to have been printed in or about 1597), *Romeo and Juliet* (1597) and *Hamlet* (1603) caused his fellow-actors to supply for publication the authentic texts preserved in the quartos of *Love's Labour's Lost* (1598), of *Romeo and Juliet* (1599), and of *Hamlet* (1604). But until he himself and his learned friend Ben Jonson conferred on them prestige the unclassical plays presented in the public theatres were scarcely reckoned as literature. Many of them were patched together by three or four authors of little standing or reputation, who demanded payment for them in instalments during the few weeks in which they were being written.[1] Even as late as 1616 it was considered a presumption on the part of Jonson to issue a volume of plays as his *Works*. Shakespeare was then dead, and it is idle to speculate whether, if he had lived a few years longer, emulation of Jonson might have given us a First Folio which he had personally revised.

In the 'Address to the Reader' in the Folio of 1623 there is an often quoted allusion to the stolen and surreptitious copies with which readers had previously been abused. It is important to remember that the most challenging of these surreptitious editions, the *Hamlet* of 1603, disappeared absolutely from view until a copy was discovered in 1823 by Sir H. E. Bunbury at Barton, bound with other quartos. Thus when the serious study of Shakespeare's text began in the eighteenth century the allusion of the Folio editions to stolen and surreptitious copies had to be explained without it. The unhappy explanation accepted was that all the early quarto editions were being denounced in these terms, notwithstanding the recognition by Malone that the texts of several of the first editions in quarto were demonstrably better than those printed in 1623. In his *Shakespeare Folios and Quartos*, published by Messrs Methuen in 1909, the present writer argued that the passage as to the badness of previous editions, when literally interpreted, did not involve a condemnation of more than *some* ('diverse') of the previous editions, and that its claim

[1] We read much of these impecunious playwrights in the accounts kept from February 1592 to 1603 by Philip Henslowe, a Sussex man, who settled in Southwark before 1577 in the employment of an estate manager (whose widow he married) and acquired much house property and land. He took part in building the Rose theatre in Southwark in 1587, and had an interest also in the Fortune in Cripplegate. He acted as a middleman between the players and playwrights, and entered in his 'diary' notes of his dealings with both.

Mar. Is it not like the King?
Hor. As thou art to thy ſelfe,
Such was the very armor he had on,
When he the ambitious *Norway* combated.
So frownd he once, when in an angry parle
He ſmot the ſleaded pollax on the yce,   Polack
Tis ſtrange.
Mar. Thus twice before, and iump at this dead hower,
With Marſhall ſtalke he paſſed through our watch.
Hor. In what particular to worke, I know not,
But in the thought and ſcope of my opinion,
This bodes ſome ſtrange eruption to the ſtate.
Mar. Good, now ſit downe, and tell me he that knowes
Why this ſame ſtrikt and moſt obſeruant watch,
So nightly toyles the ſubiect of the land,
And why ſuch dayly coſt of brazen Cannon
And forraine marte, for implements of warre,
Why ſuch impreſſe of ſhip-writes, whoſe ſore taske
Does not diuide the ſunday from the weeke:
What might be toward that this ſweaty march
Doth make the night ioynt labourer with the day,
Who is't that can informe me?
Hor. Mary that can I, at leaſt the whiſper goes ſo,
Our late King, who as you know was by Forten-
Braſſe of *Norway*,
Thereto prickt on by a moſt emulous cauſe, dared to
The combate, in which our valiant *Hamlet*,
For ſo this ſide of our knowne world eſteemed him,
Did ſlay this Fortenbraſſe,
Who by a ſeale compact well ratified, by law
And heraldrie, did forfeit with his life all thoſe
His lands which he ſtoode ſeazed of by the conqueror,
Againſt the which a moity competent,
Was gaged by our King:
Now ſir, yong Fortenbraſſe,
Of inapproued mettle hot and full,

B 2   Hath

Hamlet I, i, 58–96. From the surreptitious quarto of 1603.

Hora. Stay, ſpeake, ſpeake, I charge thée ſpeake. *Exit Ghoſt.*
Mar. Tis gone and will not anſwere.
Bar. How now *Horatio*, you tremble and looke pale
Is not this ſomthing more then phantaſie?
What thinke you-ont?
Hora. Before my God I might not this belieue,
Without the ſencible and true auouch
Of mine owne eies.
Mar. Is it not like the King?
Hora. As thou art to thy ſelfe.
Such was the very Armor he had on,
When he the ambitious *Norway* combated,
So frownd he once, when in an angry parle
He ſmot the ſleaded pollax on the ice.
Tis ſtrange.
Mar. Thus twice before, and iump at this dead houre,
With martiall ſtauke hath he gone by our watch.
Hora. In what perticular thought, to worke I know not,
But in the groſſe and ſcope of mine opinion,
This bodes ſome ſtrange eruption to our ſtate.
Mar. Good now ſit downe, and tell me he that knowes,
Why this ſame ſtrikt and moſt obſeruant watch
So nightly toiles the ſubiect of the land,
And with ſuch dayly coſt of brazon Cannon
And forraine marte, for implements of warre,
Why ſuch impreſſe of ſhip-writes, whoſe ſore taske
Does not deuide the Sunday from the weeke,
What might be toward that this ſweaty haſt
Doth make the night ioynt labourer with the day,
Who iſt that can informe mee?
Hora. That can I.
At leaſt the whiſper goes ſo; our laſt King,
Whoſe image euen but now appear'd to vs,
Was as you knowe by *Fortinbraſſe* of *Norway*,
Thereto prickt on by a moſt emulate pride
Dar'd to the combat; in which our valiant *Hamlet*,
(For ſo this ſide of our knowne world eſteemd him)
Did ſlay this *Fortinbraſſe*, who by a ſeald compact
Well ratified by lawe and heraldy

Hamlet I, i, 51–87. From the 'good' quarto of 1604 (1605).

that good texts had been substituted in the Folio for these restricted the criticised texts to the 1597 Quarto of *Romeo and Juliet* (with probably a lost edition of *Love's Labour's Lost* of the same year), the 1600 Quarto of *Henry V*, the 1602 of *The Merry Wives of Windsor* and the 1603 of *Hamlet*. The argument in 1909 was supported by some contentions of doubtful validity, and needed supplementing, but it sufficed to gain for the phrases 'good quarto' and 'bad quarto' a definite place in the bibliography of Shakespeare.

The segregation of the 'bad' quartos into a class by themselves led to an intensive study of them, which has produced important results. The discredit for their production had previously been thrown on unscrupulous booksellers, supposed to have sent shorthand writers to the theatre to take down what they could of a play, their notes being afterwards patched together by a hack editor, despite the very great doubt as to whether shorthand in the reign of Queen Elizabeth was sufficiently developed to make piracy of this kind possible. Two famous allusions by Thomas Heywood[1] to piracies by means of shorthand notes, which may be good evidence for what was happening at the time (1605–8) of which he was writing, were taken as proof of what was happening several years earlier, and this view is still widely held in Germany.

On the other hand as early as 1880 in his preface to the facsimile of the 1603 *Hamlet* Dr Furnivall had pointed out that the accuracy of the speeches of Marcellus and Voltemar suggested the use of 'some parts bought or got from actors', and in 1900 in the Oxford reprint of the *Merry Wives of Windsor* (1602) Dr W. W. Greg (following H. C. Hart in the 'Arden' edition) had singled out as suspicious the excellence of the speeches of the Host of the Garter Inn. In 1923, in his *Two Elizabethan*

[1] In a prologue written in 1632 for a revival of his *If you know not me you know nobody, or the Troubles of Queen Elizabeth* asserting (of the quarto of 1605) 'Some by Stenography drew The plot: put it in print: (Scarce one word trew:)', and in the preface to his *Lucrece* (1608). There is some reason to believe that as to the first he was mistaken, the play appearing to be rather a memorial reconstruction by actors in it than produced by stenography. But by 1608 stenography must be admitted, and it has been seriously maintained that the quarto *King Lear* of that year was produced in this way.

Stage Abridgments, Dr Greg further argued that the printed text of Greene's *Orlando* (1594) could not be explained by any theory of successive corruptions by copyists, but must be due to the efforts of actors stranded in the provinces to reconstruct from memory a makeshift text of a play not in their repertory. In 1923 also Mr Crompton Rhodes in his 'tercentenary study' of *Shakespeare's First Folio* put forward (p. 83) a similar solution of the problem with courageous precision:

The only simple explanation of the four quartos is that (i) (each) was a prompt-book used by the strolling players, (ii) each was prepared by some actor who had played a part in Shakespeare's play in the Lord Chamberlain's Company in London, (iii) the basis of each version was this accurate part, the rest being constructed from memory, most fully in scenes where he had played, (iv) the traces of shorthand in certain plays is due to the pirate's dictation to a confederate, (v) the abridgment was less deliberate than determined by his failure of memory, (vi) the versions (except possibly *The Merry Wives*) were subsequent to the Folio versions, (vii) the stationers were not at all concerned in the piracy, but only in the printing.

At the back of Mr Rhodes's statement lay his knowledge that Sheridan's plays had been pirated in some such way in the eighteenth century (a parallel which Sheridan's contemporary George Steevens had adduced, but not pressed), and his own personal experiences of how plays can be 'vamped' by strolling actors. Not all upholders of an explanation of this kind would agree that the chief constructor had his own written part with him, but some such theory has obtained considerable acceptance in England, though not much as yet among foreign students.

The substitution of the theory of reconstruction from memory for that of shorthand notes has enabled Mr Peter Alexander to add to the four 'bad quartos' already mentioned those printed in 1594 and 1595 under the titles *The Contention betwixt the two famous houses of Yorke and Lancaster* and *The True Tragedie of Richard Duke of Yorke*. In these he finds, not, as Malone had argued, the first drafts, mainly by other hands, of the plays printed in the Folio as *The Second* (*Third*) *Part of King Henry VI*, but imperfect and mangled versions of a text of these plays differing originally very slightly from that of the Folio. Students who accept the memorial reconstruction explanation of the badness of the quartet, *Romeo and Juliet*, *Henry V*, *The Merry Wives of Windsor* and *Hamlet*, generally accept it as applying also to these two additions. Mr Alexander's revival on similar lines of a contention, first put forward by S. Hickson in *Notes and Queries* in 1850, that *The Taming of A Shrew*, printed in 1594, is a perversion rather than a source of Shakespeare's *The Taming of the Shrew*, and not an earlier play on which *The Shrew* was based, has not won so much support.

Even while it had been most fashionable to denounce all the quarto texts as 'stolne and surreptitious' the experience of editors had extorted admissions that some of these texts were good enough to have been printed from Shakespeare's manuscript or a careful copy of it. It must be supposed that they regarded all the good quartos as 'stolne' and all the bad ones as 'surreptitious', though if 'stolne' is to be taken as implying physical thefts of the 'books' of plays from the theatre it is strange that no attempt was made to explain how these were carried out over a long period of years. A study of the Entries of Plays in the Stationers' Registers[1] given by F. G. Fleay in Table IV of his *Chronicle History of the Life and Work of W. Shakespeare* (1886), or of the similar table of Printed Plays by Sir E. K. Chambers (*Elizabethan Stage*, vol. IV, Appendix L), supplies clues which those acquainted with the theatrical history of the period can interpret. In the years 1586–9 there are no entries of plays; in the four years 1590–3 only five; in 1594 twenty-three, with seven more in the next year; in the four years 1596–9 eleven; in 1600 nineteen, with nine more in 1601; in 1602 and 1603 six. The peak figures for 1594 and 1600, with their respective aftermaths in the following year, must be traced mainly to sales by the only possessors of numerous play-books, the companies for which plays were written. As to why sales were so high in these

[1] Entry on the Register kept by the Stationers' Company was required by its rules and secured to the enterer the exclusive right to print the book so entered. See Note at end of this chapter.

particular years Sir E. K. Chambers has offered neater explanations than those I had myself advanced, viz. that 'in 1594 the companies were reforming themselves after a long and disastrous spell of plague, and in particular the Queen's, Pembroke's and Sussex's men were all ruined, and their books were thrown on the market', while for the second large batch of sales 'reason might be found in the call for ready money involved by the building of the Globe in 1599 and the Fortune in 1600' (*Eliz Stage*, III, 184). It may also be noted that the putting on sale of the 'bad quartos' already enumerated was almost certainly responsible for the appearance not only of the good quartos by which they were severally replaced, but also for those of *Richard II* and *Richard III* of 1597, *Love's Labour's Lost* (1598) and *The Merchant of Venice*, *A Midsummer Night's Dream*, *Much Ado about Nothing*, and *I and II Henry IV*, which together contributed five entries to the peak of 1600. In their uncertainty as to what mangled versions of their stock plays might be put into print Shakespeare's company may well have thought it better to take what money was offered for the right to publish a good text in each case than to withhold publication at the risk of being forestalled by the appearance of mangled and imperfect ones.

It would thus seem that down to the end of the reign of Elizabeth and a little later all the 'bad quartos' of plays by Shakespeare should be regarded as patched up in the provinces from memory by actors who had played in them in town, and sold on their return to printers or stationers who asked no questions; and all the good quartos as honestly purchased from the company which had acquired them to act in London. What was the probable character of these good texts? In earlier protests against the prevailing pessimism on this point I was content to argue from what we know as to the history of plays by other dramatists that there was a 'high probability' that *some* of them were printed from Shakespeare's own autograph manuscripts. In the absence, however, of evidence to the contrary there is a strong *a priori* argument that this is likely to have been the case as regards each individual play; for if there was no playhouse transcript then Shakespeare's autograph had no competitor, while if a fair copy had been made in the playhouse, this would certainly have been regarded as the better manuscript to keep; and thus again the autograph becomes the probable source of the good quarto.

Have we any Shakespeare autograph by which this probability can be tested? In 1916 Sir Edward Maunde Thompson, who for many years before he became Director of the British Museum had been Keeper of its Department of Manuscripts and had made himself a great reputation as a palaeographer, after contributing a chapter on Shakespeare's autograph signatures to *Shakespeare's England*, produced a more exhaustive monograph entitled *Shakespeare's Handwriting* (Oxford: at the Clarendon Press, 1916). In this he revived with greater authority and discrimination a theory broached mainly on literary grounds in 1871 by Richard Simpson in a paper entitled 'Are there any Extant Manuscripts in Shakespeare's handwriting?' contributed to *Notes and Queries* (Fourth Series, vol. VIII), claiming that certain scenes in a manuscript play on Sir Thomas More in the Harleian collection at the British Museum were in Shakespeare's autograph. The play had been edited for the Shakespeare Society by Alexander Dyce in 1844, and, shortly before Thompson began his study, had been reproduced in collotype by J. S. Farmer in 1910 and edited in 1911 for the Malone Society by Dr W. W. Greg, who carefully distinguished all the five different hands found in it, while contenting himself with a rather wistful reference to Simpson's attribution to Shakespeare of hand D.

Thompson's argument for Shakespeare's authorship of the three pages was further developed in his contribution to *Shakespeare's Hand in the Play of 'Sir Thomas More'* (Cambridge University Press, 1923), in which he justified his 'general impression' (a recognised process in palaeography, of which he was specially a master) from the use simultaneously both in the signatures and the three pages of the same alternative forms of *a*, *e*, *h*, *k* and *p*, also of some exceptional forms, notably a peculiarly spurred *a*. His contentions were challenged in *The Booke of 'Sir Thomas*

Moore': a bibliotic study (New York, 1927), by Dr Samuel A. Tannenbaum, an able *advocatus diaboli*, who without denying the possibility of the identity of the two hands argued that the balance of evidence was against it. On the other hand Dr Greg, who had also closely checked and criticised Thompson's arguments, summed up the position in two articles in *The Times Literary Supplement* (November 24th and December 1st, 1927) with the three propositions:

1. The palaeographical case for the hands of S(hakespeare) and D being the same is stronger than can be made out for their being different.
2. The hand of S. is more nearly paralleled in D than in any other dramatic document known to us.
3. Setting S. aside, it can be shown that D was not written by any dramatist of whose hand we have adequate knowledge.

If the decision of the authorship of the three pages rested exclusively on palaeographic evidence, these propositions would not amount to proof, as against the possibility of an unknown writer. But in *Shakespeare's Hand in the Play of 'Sir Thomas More'* Professor J. Dover Wilson strengthened the argument by showing that the handwriting of the three pages helped to explain the misprints in the quartos and Folio, while he also worked out a similar argument based on spelling. He had grasped the fact that the printers of Shakespeare's day, on whom much unmerited scorn has often been cast, played a great part in simplifying and normalising the uncouth spellings of the sixteenth century. It seems natural, indeed, that being used to the simpler spelling of the university-trained clergy (who provided them with so much work in printing sermons and treatises) they should substitute this for the more archaic and individual spellings which came to them in other manuscripts. Thus where these archaic or individual spellings crop up now and again in print they must be debited to authors and not to the compositors. Wilson's theory has been tested by application to the few cases where an author's manuscript is available for comparison, and is now generally accepted. His success in finding in 'good' early

Shakespeare quartos parallels to all the archaic spellings in the three pages of *Sir Thomas More* was a new contribution to the proof of Shakespeare's authorship of them. To most students, however, the final proof probably lies in the masterly paper by Professor R. W. Chambers on 'The Expression of Ideas—particularly political ideas—in the "Three Pages" and in Shakespeare', since reinforced by his article 'Some Sequences of Thought in Shakespeare and in the 147 lines of "Sir Thomas More"' in the *Modern Language Review* for July 1931. Under Dr Chambers's guidance we can find in these lines a combination of three characteristics of Shakespeare which should be decisive: (i) a uniquely passionate conception of the necessity of respect for order and degree, which is most fully worked out in the great speech of Ulysses in *Troilus and Cressida*, I, iii, 75–137; (ii) a sympathetic understanding of the workings of uneducated minds, which can find humour in the strange logic evolved in crowds, as in the Jack Cade scenes in *II Henry VI*; (iii) a conviction that the most excited crowd can be swayed by oratory of the right kind, as in the first scene of *Coriolanus*, and the Forum scene in *Julius Caesar* (III, ii). In fact Shakespeare had a technique of his own for crowd scenes, and a technique of his own in developing the argument for order and authority, and this technique,[1] in which the same phrases and ideas tend to recur, is so peculiar to himself that when, between *II Henry VI* at one end of the nineties and *Julius Caesar* and *Troilus* at the other, it is found in 1596 or a little earlier, in three autograph pages contributed to the play of *Sir Thomas More*, in a handwriting admittedly of the same kind as Shakespeare's, and unlike that of any of his known contemporaries, and with slightly archaic spellings, all of which recur sporadically in good texts of his plays, it seems pedantic to refuse to acknowledge that the contributor must have been Shakespeare himself.[2]

[1] And also, as Professor Spurgeon has shown (*Rev. of Eng. Studies*, VI, 257), a very individual use of imagery.

[2] It should be noted that, in addition to the 147 lines on three pages which have been specially investigated, one further speech by More, 22 lines (Addition III) beginning 'It is in heaven that I am thus and thus', has also been claimed as Shakespeare's.

What do these three pages in Shakespeare's autograph tell us as to how he wrote his plays? In the first place they may be claimed as confirming the witness of his fellow-actors Heminge and Condell, in their address 'To the Great Variety of Readers' in the Folio of 1623, in which they wrote: 'His mind and hand went together: And what he thought, he uttered with that easinesse, that wee have scarse received from him a blot in his papers'. On two of the pages the ink has spread with the course of years so that they are not easy to read, but there are no noticeable blots, and the third page is beautifully clear, save for two and a half lines and an interlining heavily erased by the bookkeeper, who added an interlining of his own. As he wrote the other 144 lines, Shakespeare eighteen times struck out a word, or the beginning of a word, immediately after he had written it, following on at once with his second thought. Two of these corrections (ll. 72 and 79) indicate a slight pause, for in each case after writing 'yor' he began to repeat the word (with 'y' and 'yo') before he added the substantive. Possibly we should find further evidence of pauses in the strange gaps in some words ('fo rbid', l. 96; 'o ffyc', l. 98; 'th' offendo r', l. 123; 'count ry', l. 126).[1] On the other hand in five lines he was thinking quicker than he could write, and we find him setting down a word, or part of one, prematurely (l. 35 'ar', l. 37 'but', l. 102 'le' of 'lent', l. 107 'ar', l. 129 'why yo^{u}'). In nine other places the correction denotes a change of mind, and in another two he seems to have been troubled with his minims, beginning to write 'number' with 'mu' (l. 51) and writing 'in' instead of 'no' (l. 95). Six other corrections were not (or not necessarily) made immediately, being additions or substitutions by interlineation or in the margin. But, more especially in the first and second pages, the general impression is of a quick hand and a quicker brain, the five words prematurely written being specially noteworthy. It should be observed also that, while only two minim mistakes (one of them—'in' for 'no'—perhaps a doubtful

[1] This curious trick, rather than the loose locking of the quarto (suggested by Professor Dover Wilson) may explain the 'vene we' for 'venewe' in *Love's Labour's Lost*, v, i, 56.

The Addition (D) to the Play of *Sir Thomas More*, lines 126–140

what Country by the nature of yor error
ſhoold gyve you harber go you to ffraunc or flanders
to any Jarman pvince, ~~to~~ ſpane or portigall
nay any where ~~why you~~ that not adheres to Jngland
why you muſt neede be ſtraingers, woold you be pleaſd
to find a nation of ſuch barbarous temper
that breaking out in hiddious violence

whett their deteſted knyves againſt yor throtes
ſpurne you lyke dogge, and lyke as yf that god
owed not nor made not you, nor that the elamente
wer nct all appropriat to ~~their~~ yor Comforte.
but Chartered vnto them, what woold you thinck

instance) were corrected, there are six others (four with a stroke too few and two with a stroke too many) which were allowed to pass. These slips also probably denote speed.

On the other hand in ll. 112–14 this quick writer and thinker by an unassimilated interlineation ('in in to yor obedienc') over l. 113, neglect of capitals and punctuation and writing a line and a half continuously, so puzzled the bookkeeper that he linked the first five words with the previous sentence and struck out, not only the interlineation, but the original two and a half lines, filling the gap with four words of his own devising, 'tell me but this'.[1] The passage suggests that the bookkeeper in Shakespeare's theatre may have done considerably more harm to the text of the plays than editors have guessed!

If Valentine Sims or any other reputable Elizabethan printer had been given the three pages of the 'More' manuscript to print, what would he have been likely to make of them? His compositor might have been puzzled by the absence of *e* final in 'straing' (strange) l. 8, 'offyc' (office) l. 98, 'ffraunc' (france) l. 127, the gaps we have noticed in a few words, the uncertain use of minims and the very scanty punctuation, which is most defective at the ends of lines and least at the breaks in them. He would, of course, have had to follow the bookkeeper in omitting the two and a half lines needlessly struck out, and printing his silly little insertion. But on the whole it may fairly be said that while the handwriting is in places difficult enough to make a compositor careful, it offered no insuperable obstacles to correct printing. At the same time if, with the help of the proof-corrector, he had set up any thirty lines of the 147 on these pages with only a single error, and that often of only a

[1] What Shakespeare left (besides the interlineation) was apparently:

to kneele to be forgyven
is safer warrs, then ever yo^u can make 112
whose discipline is ryot; why even yor hurly
cannot proceed but by obedience [.] what rebell captaine
as mutynes ar incident, by his name
can still the rout [?] who will obay a traytor[?]

The italicised words are those for which the bookkeeper substituted 'tell me but this'.

single letter, I think he would hardly be considered to have done badly. Now this, or possibly a little less than this, is the average of error in the play which in 1597, after entry on August 29th on the Stationers' Register[1] 'by appointment from Master Warden Man', was published with the title:

> The Tragedie of King Richard the second. As it hath beene publikely acted by the right Honourable the Lorde Chamberlaine his Seruants...Printed by Valentine Simmes for Androw Wise, and are to be sold at his shop in Paules church yard at the signe of the Angel.

This, unless we are to except the *Titus Andronicus* of 1594, which is usually thought to have only been 'touched' by Shakespeare, was the first play wholly by him to be printed in a 'good' quarto.[2] It was reprinted twice in 1598 and subsequently in 1608 and 1615. If we follow its history we shall get a fair idea both of the standard of goodness attained in a good text and of what might happen to it by way first of deterioration and subsequently of restoration.

The printing of *Richard II* in 1597 started badly, since (on nine different pages and on the front or back of eight different sheets) no fewer than seventeen misprints were not corrected until part of the total number of copies which formed the edition had been printed off. This happened again when *King Lear* was being printed, and the different states in which some of the sheets were found led for a time to a belief that they belonged to two different editions.

The First Quarto of *Richard II* and the two reprints of the following year (1598) suffered also from the omission, whether by order of the licenser or from fear of trouble, of 165 lines (IV, i, 154–318, 'May it please you, lords...by a true king's fall') usually called the 'Deposition scene'. The omission was inaccurately supplied, probably from a shorthand report, in the quartos of 1608 and 1615, and accurately in the Folio of 1623.

The First Quarto and its successors have no division into acts, nor are the scenes marked by headings; they usually, but not

[1] For the importance of these entries see Note at the end of this chapter.

[2] See p. 267.

always, end with the word *Exeunt*, denoting a clear stage. When several characters leave, but the scene is continued, this is often indicated by the word *Manent* (or *Manet*) with the names of those who remain.

The play of *King Richard the Second* as printed in this first quarto contains 2581 lines. The editors of the (old) *Cambridge Shakespeare* edited by J. Glover (vol. I), W. G. Clark (vols. II–IX) and W. A. Wright (1863–6) (second ed. by W. A. Wright, 1891) rejected sixty-nine of its readings, in addition, of course, to mere typographical flaws, or on an average one reading in every 37·4 lines. I should myself reverse the verdict in a few cases, and about a dozen others might fairly be reckoned as matters of spelling. A majority of the rest are errors in a single letter or transpositions. Most of the errors are obvious at sight, and all but twenty (including some of the doubtful ones) were corrected anonymously in printing offices before the end of the seventeenth century.

Unfortunately while almost every printer corrected some of the mistakes of his predecessor, every printer added some, mostly more, of his own.

Valentine Sims, who did so well in the first edition, corrected fourteen errors in his second (1598) and added 123 new ones. In his third edition (also printed in 1598) he corrected eight of the original errors and partly corrected another, and three of the newer ones, but added thirty-five. In 1608 in a new edition printed by W. W. (William White) for Matthew Law, who had acquired the copyright in 1603, three errors were corrected (two original and one later) and eighteen more introduced, the text also being enlarged by an imperfect report of the lines omitted in the previous editions. In 1615 White corrected one of his own mistakes, and introduced thirty-eight others. Finally the Folio of 1623 corrected 145 errors and added just 100.[1] The fact that

[1] Compare with this analysis of the textual history of a play for which the Folio printer used a late quarto Professor Dover Wilson's calculation that in printing from the only quarto of *Love's Labour's Lost* the Folio printer corrected 117 errors, reproduced 59 and added 137. In the similar case of *Much Ado about Nothing* Professor Wilson from among 141 Folio variants from the single Quarto only accepts seventeen!

the Folio prints about three times as many errors in *Richard II* as the First Quarto needs to be emphasised in condemnation of the fairly numerous handsome editions of Shakespeare in which the Folio text is followed throughout; but it should not lead to pessimism as to the text of plays in which the Folio is based on a manuscript copy. Valentine Sims, who introduced 123 new errors in the Second Quarto (correcting fourteen old ones) was the same printer, and may have been employing the same compositor, who had set up the First Quarto the year before, with sixty-nine. It is quicker to print from print because the compositor, instead of spelling out his copy, can take in a whole line at a glance, and in the two minutes occupied by setting up the seven or eight words in a decasyllabic line one or more of those he carries in his head may insensibly be altered before he puts them into type. In setting up from manuscript the compositor would take fewer words at a time, and, as there is no reason to suppose that Jaggard's standard was lower than that of Sims, we may hope that in the previously unprinted plays for which the Fclio is the sole authority, the average accuracy was as high as in the First Quarto of *Richard II*, i.e. one error, often insignificant, in a little over thirty lines.

Readings first found in any quarto after the first[1] cannot be attributed to the intervention of the author, but must be regarded as good or bad emendations, or misprints. The recurrence in the Folio of a reading found for the first time in one of the late quartos throws on an editor the task of deciding whether it is a good emendation confirmed by the prompt-copy, or a bad emendation, or a printer's error, left uncorrected in the (usually late) quarto used as copy when the Folio was being printed. In the second or third case the repetition in the Folio of an error or peculiarity of spelling or any similar detail becomes evidence as to the quarto edition used as copy for the play in which it occurs. In this way it has been shown that the 1598 Heyes Quarto was used as copy for the Folio text of *Love's*

[1] There is a possibility, where only a few copies of a first edition are extant, that a second edition may preserve a correction made in some copies of the *editio princeps*, of which none now survives.

Our deerest *Regan*, wife to *Cornwell*, ſpeake?

Reg. Sir I am made of the ſelfe ſame mettall that my ſiſter is,
And prize me at her worth in my true heart,
I find ſhe names my very deed of loue, onely ſhe came ſhort,
That I profeſſe my ſelfe an enemie to all other ioyes,
Which the moſt precious ſquare of ſence poſſeſſes,
And find I am alone felicitate, in your deere highnes loue.

Cord. Then poore *Cord.* & yet not ſo, ſince I am ſure
My loues more richer then my tongue.

Lear. To thee and thine hereditarie euer
Remaine this ample third of our faire kingdome,
No leſſe in ſpace, validity, and pleaſure,
Then that confirm'd on *Gonorill*, but now our ioy,
Although the laſt, not leaſt in our deere loue,
What can you ſay to win a third, more opulent
Then your ſiſters.

Cord. Nothing my Lord.

Lear. How, nothing can come of nothing, ſpeake (againe.

Cord. Vnhappie that I am, I cannot heaue my heart into my mouth, I loue your Maieſtie according to my bond, nor more nor leſſe.

Lear. Goe to, goe to, mend your ſpeech a little,
Leaſt it may mar your fortunes.

Cord. Good my Lord,
You haue begot me, bred me, loued me,
I returne thoſe duties backe as are right fit,
Obey you, loue you, and moſt honour you,
Why haue my ſiſters husbands if they ſay they loue you all,
Happely when I ſhall wed, that Lord whoſe hand
Muſt take my plight, ſhall cary halfe my loue with him,
Halfe my care and duty, ſure I ſhall neuer
Mary like my ſiſters, to loue my father all.

Lear. But goes this with thy heart?

Cord. I good my Lord.

Lear. So yong and ſo vntender.

Cord. So yong my Lord and true.

Lear. Well let it be ſo, thy truth then be thy dower,
For by the ſacred radience of the Sunne,

King Lear, I, i, 69–111. From the Quarto of 1608.

Our deerest *Regan*, wife of *Cornwall*?

Reg. I am made of that selfe-mettle as my Sister,
And prize me at her worth. In my true heart,
I finde she names my very deede of loue:
Onely she comes too short, that I professe
My selfe an enemy to all other ioyes,
Which the most precious square of sense professes,
And finde I am alone felicitate
In your deere Highnesse loue.

Cor. Then poore *Cordelia*,
And yet not so, since I am sure my loue's
More ponderous then my tongue.

Lear. To thee, and thine hereditarie euer,
Remaine this ample third of our faire Kingdome,
No lesse in space, validitie, and pleasure
Then that conferr'd on *Generill*. Now our Ioy,
Although our last and least; to whose yong loue,
The Vines of France, and Milke of Burgundie,
Striue to be interest. What can you say, to draw
A third, more opilent then your Sisters? speake.

Cor. Nothing my Lord.

Lear. Nothing?

Cor. Nothing.

Lear. Nothing will come of nothing, speake againe.

Cor. Vnhappie that I am, I cannot heaue
My heart into my mouth: I loue your Maiesty
According to my bond, no more nor lesse.

Lear. How, how *Cordelia*? mend your speec ah little,
Least you may marre your Fortunes.

Cor. Good my Lord,
You haue begot me, bred me, lou'd me.
I returne those duties backe as are right fit,
Obey you, Loue you, and most Honour you.
Why haue my Sisters Husbands, if they say
They loue you all? Happily when I shall wed,
That Lord, whose hand must take my plight, shall carry
Halfe my loue with him, halfe my Care, and Dutie,
Sure I shall neuer marry like my Sisters.

Lear. But goes thy heart with this?

Cor. I my good Lord.

Lear. So young, and so vntender?

Cor. So young my Lord, and true.

Lear. Let it be so, thy truth then be thy dowre:
For by the sacred radience of the Sunne,

From the Folio of 1623.

Labour's Lost, the 1600 (the only quarto) for *Much Ado about Nothing*, the 1608 Quarto with sheets H and K in an uncorrected state for *King Lear*, the 1609 Quarto for *Romeo and Juliet*, the 1611 Quarto for *Titus Andronicus*, the 1619 Jaggard Quarto with false imprint and date (1600) for *A Midsummer Night's Dream*. In most, possibly all, of these cases the copy of the quarto used for this purpose must be supposed to have been taken to the theatre, and there corrected with the aid of whatever was being used as a prompt-copy (for *A Midsummer Night's Dream* possibly a marked copy of the Quarto of 1600), and then given to the printer. He, poor man, had to be content with what was thus given him, without asking for further help from the theatre, and is fairly frequently found tinkering out of his own head and tinkering wrongly.[1]

Where no quarto was available for reprinting, if two manuscripts were kept at the theatre the printer would naturally be given the one considered the worse, which might be, as in *Henry V*, *Coriolanus* and *Antony and Cleopatra*, Shakespeare's original manuscript, in preference to a fair copy made for the use of the prompters and marked with his notes. If only one copy existed, possibly because Shakespeare's autograph had been clear enough to use as a prompt-copy, this would be specially transcribed for the printer, as may have been the case with *As You Like It*, *Julius Caesar* and *Twelfth Night*. If there were no prompt-copy in existence it has been suggested independently by Professor Dover Wilson and Mr Crompton Rhodes, that the text of a play may have been reconstructed from the 'parts' given to individual players, with the aid of the 'plot', or schedule of the successive scenes and of the actors in each of

[1] A well-known example is in *I Henry IV*, v, iii, 11:

> 1598 Q: I was not born a yielder, thou proud Scot.
> 1613 Q: I was not born to yield, thou proud Scot.
> Folio: I was not born to yield, thou haughty Scot.

So again, *Richard III*, I, i, 65:

> 1597 Q: That tempers him to this extremity.
> Later QQ: That tempts him to this extremity.
> Folio: That tempts him to this harsh extremity.

I have already used these examples elsewhere, but there are others!

them, hung up in the theatre for each actor to know when to go on the stage. Such an origin would account for the absence of stage directions and the massing of the names of all the actors present in a scene at the head of it, found in *The Two Gentlemen of Verona*, *The Merry Wives of Windsor* and *The Winter's Tale*. But this theory has been hotly contested.

As the first collected edition of Shakespeare's plays the Folio of 1623 acquired no small prestige, and it is perhaps not surprising that in the three reprints of 1632, 1663–4 and 1685 the same cumbrous form was retained. Each reprint can be proved to have been printed from its immediate predecessor, and to have corrected some obvious errors in it, while adding new ones of its own. Little work has been done on them, for the excellent reason that any results obtained must be concerned only with the history of the text and can hardly contribute to its further improvement. In his edition of *Romeo and Juliet* in 1859 Tycho Mommsen suggested that an unknown corrector of the Second Folio attempted to improve the rhythm; in 1902 Mr C. Alphonso Smith maintained that it was with syntax that the editor was concerned. The only serious examination of this Folio known to me was contributed by Professor Allardyce Nicoll to the *Studies in the First Folio*, by members of the Shakespeare Association (1924) in a section entitled 'The Editors of Shakespeare from First Folio to Malone'. In this he discredits the existence of any general principle in the changes made, but (i) attributes to the printer's reader the modernisation of spelling and also the correction of the colloquial usages of 'who' and 'whom' and of the dropping of the final *t* in the second person singular of verbs after *d* and *t*, and of the use of singular verbs with plural substantives, both in the text and the *Exit* and *Manet*, for *Exeunt* and *Manent* of some stage directions. In six plays, *I Henry VI* (22 improvements), *Romeo and Juliet* (17), *II Henry VI* (11), *III Henry VI* (8), *Titus Andronicus* (7), *The Winter's Tale* (7), he finds traces (ii) of the student of metre who had attracted the attention of Tycho Mommsen. Another haphazard reviser (iii) interested himself in the stage directions of most of the comedies (but *not* of *Much*

Ado about Nothing, *The Merchant of Venice*, *A Midsummer Night's Dream* or *Twelfth Night*), and also (iv) with five tragedies (*Titus Andronicus*, *Troilus and Cressida*, *Romeo and Juliet*, *Hamlet*, and *Antony and Cleopatra*) in which he sedulously set right the forms of Greek and Latin proper names. Probably the authors of improvements (ii) and (iv) were amateurs who placed the notes they had made for their own amusement at the disposal of the printer. The total of the improvements made is considerable.

The Third Folio is notable for having added as an afterthought to the thirty-six plays of its predecessors that of *Pericles*, which had been printed in quarto in 1609, and as a second afterthought (distinguished by the sheets of this addition having yet another set of 'signatures') six other plays, two of which, *The London Prodigall* (1605) and *A Yorkshire Tragedy* (1608), had borne 'Written by William (or W.) Shakespeare' on their titles while he was still at work in London, and three others, *Locrine* (1595), *Thomas Lord Cromwell* (1602 and 1613) and *The Puritane* (1607), more innocently, the initials W. S. The sixth, *Sir John Oldcastle* (1600), had no assertion of this kind, and the names of its real authors 'Mr Monday, Mr Drayton, and Mr Wilson and Hathway' happen to be inscribed in Henslowe's *Diary* as receivers of £10 in payment for the First Part and in earnest of the Second. In their texts both this Third Folio and its successor in 1685, the Fourth, are reported as following the course of correcting some old misprints and making new ones, with modernisation of the spelling.

So far the text had been in the hands of printers, with possibly some help from readers of Shakespeare among their friends. In 1709 after the clumsy Fourth Folio (a taller volume than its predecessors by nearly an inch, and somewhat wider) had held the market for twenty-four years, appeared the first modern edition, printed in six volumes, crown octavo, with an engraved frontispiece to every play, showing a scene apparently as the artist thought it might be represented on the contemporary stage, and edited by Nicholas Rowe, himself a successful dramatist. If we may judge from the very useful lists of readings accepted by modern editors appended by Professor Dover Wilson to his facsimiles of single plays from the First Folio (Faber and Faber), quantitatively Rowe had no rival except the team of improvers of 1632, with Theobald as a not too bad third. For *Macbeth* he heads the list with sixteen emendations, including a change of a single letter in I, vii, 47, which gives us Macbeth's

> I dare do all that may become a man,
> Who dares do more, is none,

where the Folio reads unhappily 'Who dares *no* more'! So again in II, i, 56–8 Macbeth's imprecation stands in the Folio

> Thou sowre and firme-set Earth
> Heare not my steps, which they may walke, for feare
> Thy very stones prate of my where-abouts,

and it was Rowe who turned 'which they may walke' to 'which way they walke', leaving it, however, to Capell to transmute 'sowre' into 'sure'. Rowe also in IV, iii, 235 lets Malcolm comment on Macduff's outburst 'This tune goes manly', where the Folio for 'tune' reads 'time'. Whether he was right in I, iii, 97–8 in reading

> ...as thick as hail
> Came post with post

for the Folio's

> ...as thick as Tale
> Can post with post,

modern timidity may feel less than certain. The most famous emendation in all Shakespeare's text, Theobald's 'and a' babld of green fields', for 'and a table of greene fields', continued to excite doubts until scholarship was assured of Shakespeare's frequent colloquial use of *a* for *he*, of the approximate identity of 'babld' with 'table' in an English hand of Shakespeare's day and the frequency with which, like other poets, he dropped the *e* in the *ed* of a past participle.

Pope in his *Shakespeare* (1725) paid special attention to rhythm and punctuation and might be ranked high among Shakespeare's editors had he not relegated passages he disliked to the margin, and even omitted some offending lines altogether.

Capell by his special study of the early quartos became the last of the prolific improvers. After him it is rare to find any of the other notable eighteenth-century editors, Johnson, Steevens or Malone, contributing more than a single accepted emendation in a play. In the nineteenth century new emendations did not altogether cease (some meddlers produced sheaves of them), but as succeeding editors sedulously omitted them from their texts their only result was to increase the tediousness of footnotes. Misprints are occasionally made by a compositor who has struggled with an ill-written word letter by letter, and these may be solved by a knowledge of Shakespeare's vocabulary and checked by a knowledge of his handwriting; thus misprints of this kind are still from time to time being corrected. But when an impatient bookkeeper struck out two and a half lines of Shakespeare's text and inserted a half-line of his own, or when a word was omitted in the corrected copy brought from the theatre to the printer of the Folio and the printer had to supply it out of his head, no knowledge of Shakespeare's handwriting will avail to recover what Shakespeare wrote, and it is perhaps well to prefer the old error to choosing between rival modern conjectures. Yet other bad readings may well have originated in slips of Shakespeare's own making, and these also may be beyond correction. Thus a perfect text of his plays is unattainable, yet it may well be doubted whether the texts now circulating would not have seemed to Shakespeare miracles of correctness; and there is little evidence that their shortcomings in any way obstruct enjoyment and appreciation of his genius.

The great edition of the nineteenth century was the *Cambridge Shakespeare* of 1863–6, built up (among the books which Capell collected and bequeathed to Trinity College, Cambridge) by editors of marvellous patience and great learning. Their patience was perhaps too great, for their notes are burdened by too copious a record of second-rate conjectures which they might well have ignored. But their services to scholarship were very great, and through the simultaneous issue of the 'Globe' edition (1864) produced the nearest approach to a standard 'Shakespeare' there has ever been. Their own achievement, however, prompted a new start, which took form in the really useful spadework which underlay the eccentricities of the New Shakspere Society, in the facsimiles of Shakespeare quartos superintended by F. J. Furnivall and the valuable prefaces contributed to several of them by P. A. Daniel. In the present century these have been followed by the Oxford Facsimile of the First Folio by collotype and Messrs Methuen's of all four Folios by photozincography, and quite recently by the delightfully handy facsimiles of ten separate Folio texts by Messrs Faber and Faber. Scholars to-day, wherever these helps are available, are as well off as Clark and Wright were amid the Capell books at Trinity College. With a knowledge of Shakespeare's handwriting and spelling added to the student's equipment new work can still be done, more than three centuries after the issue of the First Folio, and how interesting that work can be is seen in *The New Shakespeare* edited by Professor J. Dover Wilson. This is easily the most exciting ever printed, and one which has benefited not only by modern helps to emendation but perhaps even more, on the conservative side, by the completion of the *Oxford English Dictionary*, which often unties knots without the surgery of conjecture.

NOTE

The Stationers' Company of London had been formed out of two earlier companies in 1464, and from early in the sixteenth century printers are known to have belonged to it. On May 4th, 1557, it was incorporated by a royal charter, with privileges which gave the government almost complete control over the book trade. Only members of the Company were allowed to print, and every book licensed had to be entered on the Company's register. The procedure for licensing was cumbrous until 1586, when an order of the Star Chamber placed it in the hands of the Archbishop of Canterbury, who on June 30th, 1588, issued a list of his authorised deputies. All regulations for licensing tended to weaken in quiet times, and it is probable that the master and wardens sometimes exceeded their powers of acting as licensers for unimportant books, but in 1599 there was another return to stringency with an order that 'Noe English historyes be printed excepte they bee allowed by some of her Maiesties privie Counsell; (&) that noe playes be printed excepte they be allowed by suche as have aucthoritie'. In 1607 the authority for licensing plays was vested in the Master of the Revels, *ex officio*, the Master in that year being Edmund Tilney, an old man in bad health, who was soon after succeeded by his nephew and deputy Sir George Buc. In May 1622 Buc in turn was succeeded, owing to ill health, by Sir John Ashley or Astley, whose deputy, Sir Henry Herbert, held the office till 1642, and again after the Restoration. It was the licenser's duty to see that no play was acted which was politically dangerous, or offensive to the home government or to the ambassadors of friendly Courts; also from 1606 to eliminate profane oaths or the irreverent use of the name of God. Hence the frequent substitution of 'Heaven' in the Folio of 1623 where earlier texts print 'God'.

By their formation into a Company with a monopoly of printing for the whole of England, save for what was produced by the University Presses at Cambridge (from 1583) and Oxford (from 1585), the London Stationers were protected from outside competition, and their own regulations obliged them to respect the rights of the member to whose name a book was entered in its register, the fee for entrance being at first 4*d*., afterwards 6*d*., for each book. No provision was made for safeguarding the rights of anyone not a member of the Company. The nobleman, as whose servants a company of players held their right to act in public, would be their natural protector in such matters; but we do not hear of these patrons being called on for help. When, however, in 1619 William Jaggard printed, among other books to which he gave false dates (see p. 265), an edition of *The Merchant of Venice* which had been entered in 1600 to Thomas Heyes, while Thomas's son Laurence successfully established his rights in the book by appeal to the Stationers' Company, the players (it has been plausibly conjectured) procured from the Lord Chamberlain, the Earl of Pembroke and Montgomery, a letter to the Master and Wardens (to which his brother and successor referred in a similar letter of his own in June 1637) bidding them take order for the stay of further impressions of any of the plays or interludes of His Majesty's Servants without their consent; and this intervention seems to have had considerable effect.

The protection offered to its members by the Company of Stationers sometimes took strange forms. Dr Greg (*The Library*, 4th ser. VI, 47–53) has made it probable that in 1592 Abel Jeffes, having printed at some date before August of that year a 'bad' quarto (no longer extant) of *The Spanishe Tragedie*, by registering it, on October 6th, some time after publication, was able to induce the Stationers'

Company to confiscate a 'good' text printed by Edward White, presumably with the leave of the players who owned it, so that White could only use his rights in his text by engaging Jeffes to print it for him to publish. On this precedent, if *The First Part of the Contention* be accepted as a 'bad' quarto of *II Henry VI*, the registration of it by T. Millington on March 12th, 1594, which seems to have carried with it protection for its continuation, *The True Tragedie of Richard Duke of Yorke*, published the following year, would have stood in the way of Shakespeare's company replacing it by a better text; and the registration of the bad *Henry V* by T. Pavier on August 4th (1600), and of *The Merry Wives of Windsor* by J. Busby with transfer on the same day to Arthur Johnson, had a like effect. On the other hand Danter's timidity in not registering the 'bad' *Romeo and Juliet* of 1597 enabled the players to replace it by the edition of 1599, and the entry of *Hamlet* by James Roberts in 1602 kept the road clear for the issue of the good quarto of 1604, though it did not prevent the issue of the 'bad' one of 1603. No reason is known why, instead of calling on the Stationers' Company to confiscate the 1603 edition, Roberts took his own better text to the publisher of it! Students of these matters must be prepared to live and learn, for they are not quite cleared up yet.

NOTE ON THE FACSIMILES

The reproduction facing p. 274 is from Harley MS. 7368 in the British Museum, being taken from the block made for *Shakespeare's Hand in the Play of 'Sir Thomas More'* (Cambridge University Press, 1923). Note the immediate deletions in ll. 128, 129, proving it an autograph, the absence of punctuation at the ends of lines (save after 137), the *m* for *un* in 140, and the space between the fifth and sixth letters in 'count ry' (l. 126).

The facsimiles between pp. 266–7 and 278–9 are from British Museum copies of the *Hamlet* quartos of 1603 and 1605 and *Lear* (1608). In the 1603 quarto note the excellence of the text when Marcellus is speaking and the mislining and omissions in the subsequent speech by Horatio. The 1605 quarto gives a good text, probably from Shakespeare's manuscript, though, if so, the compositor may have marred it by glances at that of 1603. In the *Lear* quarto note the mislinings and omissions which cause it to be suspected as a report, probably by shorthand. Opposite are shown the corresponding lines from the recto and verso of sig. qq 2 of the Folio of 1623. Note that the half-line 'to loue my father all' is omitted from the Folio, and that 'speec ah little' shows the accidents which could occur in passing a page through the press.

SHAKESPEARIAN CRITICISM

I. FROM DRYDEN TO COLERIDGE

BY

T. S. ELIOT

I do not propose in this brief sketch to offer a compendium of all that has been written about Shakespeare in three languages in the period I have to cover. For that the reader may turn to Mr Augustus Ralli's *History of Shakespearean Criticism* (Oxford: 2 volumes). The purpose of a contribution on 'Shakespeare Criticism' to such a volume as this, as it seems to me, should be to provide a plan, or pattern, for the reading of the principal texts of Shakespeare criticism. Such a vast amount there is, such a sum of Shakespeare criticism increasing every day at compound interest, that the student of Shakespeare may well wonder whether he should consume his time over Shakespeare criticism at all. The first step, therefore, in offering a scheme of Shakespeare criticism is to give a reason why the student of Shakespeare should read what has been written about him. The second step is to make points of emphasis to show why he should read certain things first, and other things second; rather than occupy himself industriously reading everything that has been written about Shakespeare with equal attention and in perfect chronological order.

Why then, to begin with, should we read all that has been written about Shakespeare, in three hundred years, merely because we want to understand Shakespeare? Should we not rather just soak ourselves in the poetry and drama of Shakespeare, and produce our own opinions, unaided and unencumbered by antiquity, about Shakespeare? But when a poet is a great poet as Shakespeare is, we cannot judge of his greatness unaided; we need both the opinions of other poets, and the diverse views of critics who were not poets, in order to help us to understand. Every view of Shakespeare is an imperfect, because a partial, view. In order to understand these views, we need something more than a good memory. In order to make a pattern of Shakespeare criticism, we need to have some conception of the function of criticism. It is quite impossible to make anything of the history of Shakespeare criticism, unless we can come to some understanding of criticism in general. We have first to grasp what criticism is, and second to grasp the relation between literary and philosophical criticism on the one hand, and literary and textual criticism on the other. With the history of textual criticism, with our increasing knowledge of Shakespeare, of his times, of his texts, of his theatre, I am not to be concerned; but I am concerned with (among other things) the general formulation of the relation between our literary criticism and our scholarly knowledge. In the history of the criticism of Shakespeare which is primarily or strictly literary and dramatic there is a certain 'progress', but only such progress as is possible as a result of the improved texts, the increased knowledge about the conditions of the Elizabethan stage, about the life of Shakespeare himself, and about the times in which he lived. Otherwise, it would be imprudent to say that we are approximating towards a final goal of understanding, after which there will be nothing new to be said; or retrospectively, to assume that A. C. Bradley's criticism of Shakespeare is 'better' than that of Dryden. Shakespeare criticism will always change as the world changes.

This point is really a very simple one, and easy to accept when our eye is on the history of criticism in general; but when we are confining our attention to the history of the criticism of a single great poet like Shakespeare, it is easy to slip into a different assumption. We find it difficult, of course, to believe that the view of Shakespeare to be taken 100 years hence can be very different from our own. On the other hand, we are inclined to assume that the criticism of Shakespeare written before the nineteenth century is less illuminating than that written since. Neither assumption is quite true. There is undeniably an aspect in which early criticism may be seen as the substructure of that of the nineteenth century. We have to admit that the fuller understanding of Shakespeare's greatness came slowly, just as it comes slowly, I believe, in the life of the individual reader. But Shakespeare criticism cannot be appreciated without some understanding of the time and of the place in which it is written, without allowing for its nearness or remoteness in place or time from the object, and for its inevitable development in the future. The views of Shakespeare taken by different men at different times in different places form an integral part of the development and change of European civilisation during the last 300 years. Furthermore, in this study we should, I think, take an attitude which is represented by the popular word *Gestalt* or, as we might say, 'pattern'. That is, we should not begin by the attempt to decide which Shakespeare critics are most illuminating, and ignore the rest; what we have to study is the whole pattern formed by Shakespeare criticism from his own time to ours. In tracing this pattern, certainly, we must study some critics more closely than others, and we may for practical purposes select certain critics who serve to determine the main outline of the pattern; but it should be the whole pattern rather than the individual critic, in which we interest ourselves.

For this reason I shall not attempt, in this space, a compendious history of the subject. I shall simply select certain critics, according to the principle I have indicated above, and leave the reader to fill in the gaps by his own reading. There are obvious points of triangulation. First, there is the testimony of Shakespeare's contemporaries, of which, making due allowance for personal bias, that of Ben Jonson may be our specimen. Second, there is the criticism of the age of Dryden, regarding which, again, we make due allowance for the singular individual genius of Dryden. This is a period in which there is still a criticism of the *acted* play (as Pepys's *Diary* attests); when—so far as the distinction holds—there is still dramatic as well as literary criticism; it is still a period in which criticism is directly in simple relation to the object, in contrast with modern criticism which is necessarily as much in relation to other criticism as to the work of Shakespeare itself. In the time of Pope and his contemporaries we feel at once the greater distance of time between the critic and the object, and we begin to feel that criticism has already to take account of criticism as well as of the object criticised. (This period, by the way, has been somewhat maligned: there is no period in which Shakespeare has not been treated with the greatest respect.) Against this, we must offset the critical views of the French in the eighteenth century, where we find, not so much the conflict of one dramatic type with another, as the conflict of English drama with a critical theory which was *not contradicted* by French practice. The French views of the eighteenth century—for example those of Voltaire, Diderot and La Harpe—have again to be compared with the other French views of the nineteenth century—as those of Taine and Victor Hugo. Meanwhile we find English criticism modified, during the later part of the eighteenth century, by the development of the sentimental attitude. English criticism of the greater part of the nineteenth century is very largely a development from the work of Coleridge, Lamb, Hazlitt and De Quincey; amongst these the influence of Coleridge is very much the most significant; and the explanation of Coleridge is partly found in the German critical thought of the latter part of the eighteenth century.

The student of Shakespeare criticism will be aware of all these views and developments, will endeavour to appreciate their appropriateness each to its place and time, their relations to each other, their limitations of time and cultural sympathy, and will consequently recognise that at different places and times criticism has different work to do. The contemporary of the poet has both obvious limitations and obvious advantages; he is too near to the object to see it clearly or in perspective; his judgment may be distorted by enthusiasm or prejudice; on the other hand he enjoys the advantage of a freshness unspoilt by generations of other men's views. The later critic has both to try to see the object as if for the first time, without the direction of the criticism which has intervened; and also, as I have said, previous criticism is itself a part of the object of his criticism. Hence the critic's problem becomes for every generation more complicated; but also, every generation has a better opportunity for realising how complicated the problem is. At one time, the critical task may be the elaboration of a kind of criticism already initiated; at another, its refutation; at another, the introduction of a new theory, that is to say the exposition of an aspect hitherto overlooked; or again, it may be to combine and to display the pattern afforded by the diverse voices. And in this Shakespeare pattern everything laudatory must find a place, when it is a true praise not previously sounded; and everything derogatory too, even when blunted by misunderstanding, so long as it evinces the temper of an age or a people, and not merely a personal whim.

Of the contemporary comment upon Shakespeare it is that of Ben Jonson which is best remembered and most quoted; and with justice, as Jonson not only had the finest critical mind of his day, but as a dramatist and poet is of so different a kind from Shakespeare that his opinion has a peculiar interest. We may incline to think that Shakespeare's contemporaries underestimated his accomplishment, and were blind to his genius; forgetting that greatness is in a sense the result of time. It has again and again been illustrated that the opinion of contemporaneity is imperfect; and that even when it shows intelligent appreciation and enjoyment, it is apt surprisingly to elevate some quite insignificant figure above a very great one. Our opinions of our own contemporaries will probably seem grotesque to the future. I believe that if I had lived in the seventeenth century, it is quite likely that I should have preferred Beaumont and Fletcher to Shakespeare; though my estimate of their difference to-day is enough to satisfy the most fanatical Shakespearian. What I wish to do is to remove the *stigma* of being a contemporary, and to deprecate the complacency which attaches to being a member of posterity.

And I certainly do not mean to confound all distinctions, or to allow easily all opinions to be right. Whenever Dryden mentions Shakespeare, Dryden's opinion must be treated with respect. To understand his view of Shakespeare we must read *all* of his critical writing. And in particular, in weighing Dryden's opinions, we must spend some time over his collocation of Shakespeare and Fletcher, we must try to come to a point of understanding at which we *see* why it was natural and proper for him to make this frequent parallel and comparison. That is not so much a matter of wide reading or scholarship, although we must make ourselves very familiar with the plays of Fletcher, and with the plays, as well as the criticism, of Dryden: it is a matter of the exercise of the critical imagination. There are critics who are definitely wrong-headed. Thomas Rymer was a man of considerable learning, and not destitute of taste, when he left his taste to look after itself; but a false theory of what the drama should be, of what he *ought* to like, came very near to paralysing that function altogether, and made him the butt of his own and subsequent times. Nevertheless, I believe that the falsity of his dramatic theory, and the absurdity of the conclusions he drew from it, have had the unfortunate effect—as the extremity of false theorising is apt to do—of sometimes confirming people in their own false opinions merely because they assured themselves too confidently that whatever Rymer did not believe must be right.

As soon as we enter the eighteenth century we feel a change in the atmosphere of criticism; and in reading the criticism itself we are aware that Shakespeare is beginning to be more read than seen upon the stage. Addison calls attention to a point of detail (the crowing of the cock in *Hamlet*) which has probably, we feel, struck him rather in the reading than at a performance; the attention of the eighteenth-century critic in England is rather on the poetry than on the drama. The observations of Pope are of value and interest, because they are by Pope. If other eighteenth-century critics are to be read, it is not so much for their individual contributions, but as a reminder that there was no period in which Shakespeare fell into neglect. There is indeed some development. Shakespeare begins to be written about in greater detail and at greater length, and apart from any more general discussion of the drama; he is, in the eighteenth century, gradually *detached* from his environment, from the other dramatists, and from a time which had become unfamiliar. And it may be mentioned, though this is outside my province, that during the eighteenth century the standard of scholarship and editorship was rising. But the major part of eighteenth-century criticism down to Johnson, and almost all the French criticism of Shakespeare during this period, strike me as unprofitable reading unless we enlarge our interests. The criticism of Shakespeare at any epoch is a most useful means of inducting us into the way in which people of that time enjoyed their contemporary poetry; and the approval which they express of Shakespeare indicates that he possessed some of the qualities that they cultivated in their own verse, and perhaps other qualities that they would have liked to find there. A study of the opinions of Voltaire, La Harpe and Diderot about Shakespeare may help to increase our appreciation of Racine; it is quite certain that we can never make head or tail of these opinions unless we do enjoy Corneille and Racine. And I do not mean merely a polite acquaintance with their plays, or a fluent ability to declaim their verse; I mean the immediate delight in their poetry. That is an experience which may arrive late in life, or oftener not at all; if it comes—I am speaking, of course, of Anglo-Saxon experience only—it is an illumination. And it is far from corrupting our pleasure in Shakespeare, or reducing our admiration. Poetry does not do these things to other poetry: the beauty of one kind only enhances the lustre of another.

To pass from Dryden to Johnson is to make the journey from one oasis to another. After the critical essays of Dryden, the Preface to Shakespeare by Samuel Johnson is the next of the great pieces of criticism to read. One would willingly resign the honour of an Abbey burial for the greater honour of words like the following, from a man of the greatness of their author:

The poet, of whose works I have undertaken the revision, may now begin to assume the dignity of an ancient, and claim the privilege of established fame and prescriptive veneration. He has long outlived his century, the term commonly fixed as the test of literary merit. Whatever advantages he might once derive from personal allusions, local customs, or temporary opinions, have for many years been lost; and every topic of merriment, or motive of sorrow, which the modes of artificial life afforded him, now only obscure the scenes which they once illuminated. The effects of favour and competition are at an end; the tradition of his friendships and his enmities has perished; his works support no opinion with arguments, nor supply any faction with invectives; they can neither indulge vanity, nor gratify malignity; but are read without any other reason than the desire of pleasure, and are therefore praised only as pleasure is obtained; yet, thus unassisted by interest or passion, they have passed through variations of taste and changes of manners, and, as they devolved from one generation to another, have received new honours at every transmission.

What a valedictory and obituary for any man to receive! My point is that if you assume that the classical criticism of England was grudging in its praise of Shakespeare, I say that no poet can ask more of posterity than to be greatly honoured by the great; and Johnson's words about Shakespeare are great honour.

Johnson refutes those critics—and only Johnson could do it—who had thought that Shakespeare violated propriety, here and there, with his observation that Shakespeare's 'scenes are occupied only by men, who act and think as the reader thinks that he himself should have spoken or acted on the same occasion'. But a little further Johnson makes another most remarkable (but not sufficiently remarked) observation, to which several subsequent editors and publishers, even to our own time, seem to have paid not sufficient deference:

The players, who in their edition divided our author's works into comedies, histories, and tragedies, seem not to have defined the three kinds by any very exact or definite ideas.

To those who would divide periods, and segregate men, neatly into classical and romantic groups, I commend the study of this sentence, and of what Johnson says afterwards about the relation of the tragic to the comic. This Preface to Shakespeare was published in 1765, and Voltaire, still writing ten years and more after this event, was maintaining an opposite point of view. Johnson saw deeper than Voltaire, in this as in most matters. Johnson perceived, though not explicitly, that the distinctions of tragic and comic are superficial—for *us*; though he did not know how important they were for the Greeks; for he did not know that they sprang from a difference in ritual. As a poet—and he was a fine poet—Johnson is at the end of a tether. But as a critic—and he was greater as critic than as poet—Johnson has a place comparable to that of Cowley as poet: in that we cannot say whether to classify him as the last of one kind or the first of another. There is one sentence which we may boggle over. Johnson says:

> In tragedy he (*i.e.* Shakespeare) often writes, with great appearance of toil and study, what is written at last with little felicity; but, in his comic scenes, he seems to produce, without labour, what no labour can improve.

This is an opinion which we cannot lightly dismiss. Johnson is quite aware that the alternation of 'tragic' and 'comic' is something more than an alternation; he perceives that something different and new is produced. "The interchanges of mingled scenes seldom fail to produce the intended vicissitudes of passion'. '*Through all these denominations of the drama Shakespeare's mode of composition is the same.*' But why should Johnson have thought that Shakespeare's comic parts were spontaneous, and that his tragic parts were laboured? Here, it seems to me, Johnson, by his simple integrity, in being wrong has happened upon some truth much deeper than he knew. For to those who have experienced the full horror of life, tragedy is still inadequate. Sophocles felt more of it than he could express, when he wrote *Œdipus the King*; Shakespeare, when he wrote *Hamlet*; and Shakespeare had the advantage of being able to employ his grave-diggers. In the end, horror and laughter may be one—only when horror and laughter have become as horrible and laughable as they can be; and—whatever the conscious intention of the authors—you may laugh or shudder over *Œdipus* or *Hamlet* or *King Lear*—or both at once: then only do you perceive that the aim of the comic and the tragic dramatist is the same:

they are equally serious. So do the meanings of words change, as we inspect them, that we may even come to see Molière in some lights as a more serious dramatist than Corneille or Racine; Wycherley as equally serious (in this sense) with Marlowe. All this is suggested to me by the words of Samuel Johnson which I have quoted. What Plato perceived has not been noticed by subsequent dramatic critics; the dramatic poet uses the conventions of tragic and comic poetry, so far as these are the conventions of his day; there is potential comedy in Sophocles and potential tragedy in Aristophanes, and otherwise they would not be such good tragedians or comedians as they are. It might be added that when you have comedy and tragedy united in the wrong way, or separated in the wrong way, you get sentiment or amusement. The distinction between the tragic and the comic is an account of the way in which we try to live; when we get below it, as in *King Lear*, we have an account of the way in which we do live.

The violent change between one period and another is both progress and retrogression. I have quoted only a few sentences from Johnson's Preface to Shakespeare; but I think they represent the view of a mature, if limited, personality. The next phase of English criticism of Shakespeare is prefaced from Germany. I must add, however, that the influence of German criticism upon English at this point can easily be exaggerated. It is in no wise to belittle the value of this criticism, if we affirm that there was rather a similarity of outlook, and a natural sympathy between the German and the English mind, in approaching Shakespeare, which we do not find with the French critics. It would be rash to assert that the German mind is better qualified to appreciate Shakespeare than is the French; but one less comprehensive generalisation I believe can be made. For the French mind, the approach to Shakespeare has normally been by way of a comparison to Corneille and Racine, if not to Molière. Now for the Frenchman the plays of his classical age are primarily, to this day, plays to be acted; and his memories of them are of the theatre at least as much as of the library. For the Englishman of the nineteenth century the plays of Shakespeare have been dramatic poems to be read, rather than plays to be seen; and for most of us to-day the great majority of the plays are solely literary acquaintances. Furthermore, the French have always had this background of their own great dramatic achievement. But the Germans have never had this background of native authority in the drama; their acquaintance with Shakespeare was formed in the study; and until the reputation of Goethe was firmly established throughout Europe they had no native dramatic author with whom to compare him. For these reasons alone, without any rash generalisations about the Gallic and the Teutonic mind, we should expect the German attitude to be more sympathetic.

But the kind of criticism which arises rather from reading than from attendance at the theatre arose in England spontaneously. The first striking example of this sort of criticism, a remarkable piece of writing which deserves meditation, and which commands our respect whether we agree with its conclusions or not, is Morgann's Essay *On the Dramatic Character of Sir John Falstaff* (1777). For the case which Morgann attempts to make out, I refer the reader to Morgann himself. My point is that Morgann's essay is the first conspicuous member of a long line of criticism dealing with the characters of the personages in the plays, considering not only their actions within the play itself, but inferring from their behaviour on the stage what their general character is, that is to say, how they would behave in other circumstances. This is a perfectly legitimate form of criticism, though liable to abuses; at its best, it can add very much to our enjoyment of the moments of the characters' life which are given in the scene, if we feel this richness of reality in them; and at its worst, it becomes an irrelevance and distracts us from our enjoyment of the play.

The first of the great German critics, Lessing, tended to make of Shakespeare almost a national issue, for he it was who affirmed that English literature, and in particular Shakespeare, was more congenial than French literature and drama to the German taste. The German critics in general insist upon the naturalness and fidelity to reality of Shakespeare's plays. Herder, a critic of considerable understanding, begins to appreciate the existence of something like a poetic pattern, in calling attention to the fitness between the passions of the personages and the scenery in which these passions are enacted. But what interests me in this place is not a detailed valuation of the opinions of the German critics of this period—not even the opinions of the Schlegels and Goethe—but a consideration of the general tendency of their opinions. Neglecting the circumstances in which the plays were written—and indeed the historical information was not available—and paying little attention to their dramatic merits, the Germans concentrated their attention chiefly upon the philosophical significance of character. They penetrate to a deeper level than that of the simple moral values attributed to great literature by earlier times, and foreshadow the 'criticism of life' definition by Arnold. Furthermore, it is not until this period that an element of 'mystery' is recognised in Shakespeare. That is one of the gifts of the Romantic Movement to Shakespeare criticism, and one for which, with all its excesses, we have reason to be grateful. It is hardly too much to say that the German critics and Coleridge, by their criticism of Shakespeare, radically altered the reflective attitude of criticism towards poetry.

The writings of Coleridge upon Shakespeare must be read entire; for it is impossible to understand Shakespeare criticism to this day, without a familiar acquaintance with Coleridge's lectures and notes. Coleridge is an authority of the kind whose influence extends equally towards good and bad. It would be unjust to father upon him, without further ceremony, the psycho-analytic school of Shakespeare criticism; the study of individual characters which was begun by Morgann, to the neglect of the pattern and meaning of the whole play, was bound to lead to some such terminus, and we do not blame Morgann for that. But when Coleridge released the truth that Shakespeare already in *Venus and Adonis* and *Lucrece* gave proof of a 'most profound, energetic and *philosophic* mind' he was perfectly right, if we use these adjectives rightly, but he supplied a dangerous stimulant to the more adventurous.

'Philosophic' is of course not the right word, but it cannot simply be erased: you must find another word to put in its place, and the word has not yet been found. The sense of the profundity of Shakespeare's 'thought', or of his thinking-in-images, has so oppressed some critics that they have been forced to explain themselves by unintelligibles.

I have not spoken of Hazlitt, Lamb and De Quincey; that is because I wished to isolate Coleridge as perhaps the greatest single figure in Shakespeare criticism down to the present day. In a conspectus like the present, only the most salient points can be more than mentioned; and Hazlitt, Lamb and De Quincey, for my present purposes, do but make a constellation about the primary star of Coleridge. Their work is chiefly important as reinforcing the influence of Coleridge; though De Quincey's *Knocking on the Gate in Macbeth* is perhaps the best known single piece of criticism of Shakespeare that has been written. But for the student of Shakespeare criticism, the writing of all of these men is among those documents that are to be read, and not merely read about.

II. FROM COLERIDGE TO THE PRESENT DAY

BY

J. ISAACS

The eighteenth century was the age of Shakespeare idolatry, with Garrick's Shakespeare Jubilee, and Daniel Webb's typical remark in 1762: 'the most extraordinary genius, that our country, or, perhaps, any other has produced'. The later history of Shakespeare criticism is a reflection of the history of human movements of thought, or of the particular pattern of thought in each country on which he has impinged. The growth of romanticism swept Shakespeare forward as an unwitting leader in the campaign against Cartesian mechanism. In Germany, Russia and France he became part of the movement. Herder and Goethe in Germany, Pushkin and Bielinski in Russia, Stendhal and Hugo in France, all bear critical testimony to the progress of the romantic movement under his banner. In Germany and Russia the period of the romantic movement is the 'Hamlet-period', in which the character of the Shakespearian figure becomes a mirror and symbol of the national growing-pains. Friedrich Gundolf's *Shakespeare und der deutsche Geist* (1911) is a penetrating history of the German mind and civilisation in terms of its awareness and assimilation of Shakespeare. The pre-romantic legacy, with Maurice Morgann, William Richardson and Thomas Whately, was an overwhelming belief in Shakespeare's power as a creator of living and plausible characters. The romantic legacy, with Coleridge, Hazlitt and Schlegel, was an insistence on Shakespeare as a creative and original genius whose contribution was to be measured and traced. Kantian, Schellingian and other currents induced a philosophical tendency towards unity of conception and interpretation. Wordsworth, as early as his brilliant *Essay Supplementary to the Preface of 1815*, acknowledged, to Coleridge's annoyance, the German superiority in recognising that 'the judgment of Shakespeare in the selection of his materials, and in the manner in which he has made them, heterogeneous as they often are, constitute a unity of their own, and contribute all to one great end, is not less admirable than his imagination, his invention, and his intuitive knowledge of human nature'.

Once the chronology of the plays had been established in its main outlines, the task of tracing Shakespeare's growth to maturity, his summits of achievement, and in general the pattern of his creative career, was facilitated. The task was attempted simultaneously in England and Germany, but reached special heights under the impulse of the unifying philosophical approach. In England, William Spalding, Charles Knight and Henry Hallam, and in Germany Hermann Ulrici and G. G. Gervinus, were the chief builders of a Shakespeare whose pattern of growth could be traced in well-marked successive periods. In David Masson in 1865 we get the first glimpses of the sentimental 'final mood of reconciliation' theory. Dowden's *Shakspere: His Mind and Art* (1875) is the first book in English to give anything like a unified and rounded picture of the whole achievement of the dramatist. Dowden and Furnivall went all out on the 'four period' doctrine, and though their sentimentality and their belief in Shakespeare's doctrine of female sweetness and purity soon earned the label of gush from more sober critics, it is this sentimental picture which still too largely holds the field in orthodox circles. In 1864 Rümelin's *Shakespeare Studies by a Realist* incurred the powerful scorn of the reinforced sentimentalists, but was the forerunner of a serious change in critical orientation. Hand in hand with sentiment concerning Shakespeare's female characters, but in keeping with the scientific movement of the later century, went hard-headed investigation into the statistics of Shakespeare's versification, and exact measuring of his artistic processes. The Shakespeare idolatry of the eighteenth century was a pleading for the recognition of his creative genius: the idolatry of the nineteenth century was an employment of his genius as an excuse for the investigation of the important red herring of the moment, whether character study, creative unity, periodising, verse processes, chronology, ethics, dramatic technique, or, at opposite poles of homage, critical bibliography and the poet's personality. After the romantic period, in which criticism was frequently produced by poets, the study of Shakespeare's poetry with any degree of critical intensity was rare. Ten years after Dowden's sentiment came R. G. Moulton's science in *Shakespeare as a dramatic artist. A popular illustration of scientific criticism* (1885), a direction followed later by G. P. Baker and, with a difference, by Quiller-Couch.

One of the chief critical occupations of the nineteenth century, and in part of the twentieth century, was the building up of a picture of Shakespeare's personality. In their different ways Dowden, Brandes, Frank Harris, and even James Joyce in the brilliant debate in *Ulysses*, have attempted the task. The mere attempt implies the possession of a predisposing conception that tends to make Shakespeare an amateur philosopher's plaything. The most aggressive title in this field, though kindly meant, is C. H. Herford's *The normality of Shakespeare, illustrated in his treatment of love and marriage* (1920). The chief monument of this tendency lies in A. C. Bradley's magnificent, influential and dangerously side-tracking studies, written, as it were, in the margin of Hegel.

I take it that the true objects of Shakespeare criticism are (*a*) to give a picture of the author by tracing his treatment of material so far as it is conscious, or eliciting his unconscious processes without imposing an autobiography of the critic upon the victim of his inquiries; (*b*) to give the pattern of the man and dissect for admiration the beauties he produces, the complexity and explosive force of the poetry, and the deploying and juxtaposition of the characters. From this point of view the examination of the growth of character-study is instructive. In the eighteenth century Morgann, in proving that Falstaff was no coward, believed in Shakespeare's characters 'rather as historic than dramatic beings'. Coleridge, among other views, held that Shakespeare created a character 'by conceiving any one intellectual or moral faculty in morbid excess and then placing himself, thus mutilated and diseased, under given circumstances'. Such a doctrine was a transition from the eighteenth century method to the romantic conception of the creative and conscious genius. Furnivall's platonic affairs with Shakespeare's heroines indicate a characteristic divorce of head and heart. Bradley took *The Rejection of Falstaff* into philosophical regions. With the waning of philosophical idealism, the new realism, though not always the new science, treated matters differently. The new science was seen in Dr Ernest Jones's *The Œdipus-complex as an explanation of Hamlet's mystery* (1910), reissued in the more receptive post-war year of 1922. This is the last flicker of the Richardsonian method, but employs all the subtleties of the new Freudian technique of psycho-analysis. Apart from the initial fallacy, which is Morgann's fallacy, the justification of the method lies in its attempt to add to our information concerning Shakespeare's choice of material and his adventures among motives. The psycho-analytical technique as applied to Coleridge by J. L. Lowes in *The Road to Xanadu* is valuable because the evidence is available, *i.e.* the patient gives his replies, but we know nothing about Shakespeare except what we can learn from his behaviour; but according to this theory his plays *are* his behaviour, and therefore a valuable set of clues to his interests, passions, tensions, thoughts, complexes of association, and even the objects of his affection or hate. The new realism turned to less subtle and less debatable sources for dealing with character. G. A. Bieber, under the influence of Schücking, discussed the 'melancholy type', as it pervaded Elizabethan society, for light on Hamlet, and Lily B. Campbell explored the physiological psychology of the age in order to establish Shakespeare's automatic equipment for dealing with character. E. E. Stoll, the most powerful and illuminating of the American school of realists, and L. L. Schücking, the penetrating author of *Character Problems in Shakespeare's Plays*, have both turned to the evidence of the plays and above all of contemporary dramatic conventions for their proofs. They have established the fact that soliloquies are to be taken at face value, that statements made by one character about another are to be believed, that Elizabethan ghosts were real to the audience, and with a score of similar positions have overturned the whole system of romantic character study.

The new realism has tried to isolate and display, not the Romantic Shakespeare, nor the Victorian Shakespeare, but the Elizabethan Shakespeare. The present tendency of Shakespeare criticism is to face the author squarely rather than dodge him by excursions into philosophy, history or ethics. One of the great pioneers of this approach, and one of the most balanced of worshippers, was Sir W. Raleigh, who in his 1907 study boldly spoke of the brothel scene in Pericles 'which no pen but his could have written', and speaking of *Measure for Measure* as Shakespeare's nearest approach to the direct presentation of a moral problem, concluded that there was no single character through whose eyes we can see the question and situation as Shakespeare saw them. The new realism also owes much to the diverse shock-tactics of T. S. Eliot, and of G. Bernard Shaw, once a member of Furnivall's New Shakspere Society. Valuable work is being done by H. B. Charlton in viewing Shakespeare's early plays in the light of Renaissance critical conceptions of drama and the European picture of romance in Elizabethan times. A pertinent approach, and one likely to endure by its relevance, is the transference of investigation from the study to the theatrical laboratory by H. Granville-Barker.

The study of Shakespeare's poetry is at last coming into its own, and firm materials for criticism, though only materials as yet, are being assembled by such students of imagery as Edmund Blunden, George Rylands, Elizabeth Holmes and Caroline Spurgeon. It is a strange comment on the history of Shakespeare criticism that during 300 years no serious study, and, apart from Coleridge's brilliant asides, no serious attempt even at a study of Shakespeare's poetical processes has been made. That poetry cannot be isolated from the history of the other arts has long been a commonplace on the Continent, and one important line of inquiry has been hinted at. Some decades ago Heinrich Wölfflin revolutionised European art history by a reasoned distinction between Renaissance and Baroque art. The first person to apply this distinction to the study of Shakespeare was the dean of German literary history, Oskar Walzel, in *Shakespeares dramatische Baukunst*, fittingly enough in the *Shakespeare-Jahrbuch* of the Tercentenary year 1916.

Ralli's chronological summary of Shakespeare criticism gives a terrifying notion of the extent of the material; the present short sketch endeavours in summary form to indicate the main tendencies and to relate them to larger movements of mind in the period covered.

SHAKESPEARIAN SCHOLARSHIP

BY

J. ISAACS

SHAKESPEARE scholarship is of vast extent and complexity. It is concerned in its major operations with (*a*) the establishment of the text, (*b*) its transmission, (*c*) its elucidation, (*d*) the canon, (*e*) chronology, (*f*) the study of sources, (*g*) the biography of the author, (*h*) his manipulation of material, (*i*) his mental processes, (*j*) his versification, (*k*) his reading, (*l*) his poetical imagery, (*m*) his relation to the literary movements of his time, (*n*) his relation to individual contemporaries, (*o*) his reputation, (*p*) his influence at home and abroad, (*q*) the historical and political background, (*r*) the social background, (*s*) the intellectual background, scientific and philosophical, (*t*) the linguistic background, (*u*) palaeography, (*v*) iconography, (*w*) the theatrical background, (*x*) the specific conditions of performance, (*y*) the author's dramatic technique, and (*z*) the pattern of his growth. The *select* bibliography by Ebisch and Schücking contains over 4000 items, and the present outline is a first attempt to cover the whole field of scholarship from Langbaine to the twentieth century.

The seventeenth century did little more than hint. Dryden in *An Essay of Dramatick Poesie* was aware of the existence of problems of language, versification, learning, sources, and biography, but the time was not yet ripe for action. Fuller and Aubrey made jottings for the life of Shakespeare. The much maligned Rymer started two hares, the discussion of Shakespeare's dramatic method by comparison with a specific source, and the publication, in his *Fœdera*, of a contemporary document containing Shakespeare's name. Gerard Langbaine in 1688 and 1691 valuably conducted the first systematic search for the sources of the plays.

The eighteenth century is our creditor for a hundred things in method and achievement. From Rowe to Malone there is an unbroken continuity of text, good, bad, and indifferent. Rowe in 1709 first made Shakespeare accessible in octavo, he used the 1685 folio, modernised it into readability, paid minimum homage to quarto collation, although he possessed a few quartos and a Second Folio, compiled lists of Dramatis Personae, completed the division into acts and scenes, marked exits and entrances, in certain plays marked the location of scenes, and gave the first formal life of the author, incorporating traditions and anecdotes. Pope in 1725 printed from Rowe's text, collated more quartos, made personal and arbitrary corrections and rejections, indicated more completely the location of scenes, and extended scene division to the French method of a new scene for each new character. In the 1728 edition he printed a list of 29 quartos he used or knew of. According to Malone, the unknown editor of the Second Folio and Pope were the two great corrupters of Shakespeare's text. Theobald, maligned, despised, insulted and pillaged for over a century, was rehabilitated by Lounsbury, Churton Collins and R. F. Jones. His *Shakespeare Restored*, 1726, demolished Pope's edition and formed a landmark in commentary. His edition of 1733 makes him the great pioneer of serious Shakespeare scholarship. He too used his predecessor's text, but following Bentley's methods, treated Shakespeare as a corrupt classical text to be restored by the aid of all available knowledge. He possessed a large collection of quartos, was the first editor with an extensive and serious knowledge of Elizabethan and earlier literature, and had sufficient languages to read many of the original sources. He studied Shakespeare minutely, formulated his metrical and grammatical practice, and illustrated and corrected the text from the known procedure of the author himself. He was the first to point to Shakespeare's use of North's *Plutarch*, to draw attention to an existing translation of the *Menæchmi* of Plautus, and to trace Shakespeare's reading and use of Holinshed. He turned to the earliest texts and restored readings without need of conjecture. His certain conjecture and method may be seen at its best in the note on the *weyward* sisters in *Macbeth*: his brilliant conjectural emendation, however much assailed, in 'a' babbled of green fields': his making sense of nonsense in the prologue to *Troilus and Cressida*. He made pioneer advances, without consolidating them into treatises, in the study of authorship, chronology and sources. He was the first to allude to *The True Chronicle History of King Leir*, the first to use *The Famous Victories of Henry V*, and had heard of Lodge's *Rosalynde*. Professor Karl Young pays him the tribute that 'in a surprising number of specific instances he furnished fresh information and suggestions that ought to have guided his successors to far greater industry, and to far less disparagement of their guide'. Unquestionably Theobald is the first giant of Shakespeare scholarship.

Accurate scholarship lagged for some while. One of the worst editions was that of Sir Thomas Hanmer, 1743–4, based on Theobald's text, which went so far as to omit a scene of *Henry V* 'improper enough as it is all in French, and not intelligible to an English audience', and emended Cassio 'a fellow almost damn'd in a faire Wife' to 'damn'd in a fair phyz'. Warburton in 1747 insulted Theobald, but used his text and much of his material, while introducing some of the wildest emendations in our history. He was seriously taken to task by Thomas Edwards in his *Supplement*, 1746, and in his later *Canons of Criticism*. The contribution of Dr Johnson has been seriously exaggerated by misinformed piety. Perspective has been distorted by the attribution to him of many of Theobald's discoveries and much of Theobald's pioneer method. His *Miscellaneous Observations on the Tragedy of Macbeth* in 1745 contained proposals for an edition. His prospectus of 1756 is an admirable summary of principles and methods proposed before him, and followed by later editors, but his edition of 1765 based on Warburton's text was avowedly undertaken for money, and as Hawkins says in his *Life* 'neither in the first place did he set himself to collect early editions of his author, old plays, translations of histories, and of the classics, and other materials necessary for his purpose, nor could he be prevailed on to enter into that course of reading, without which it seemed impossible to come at the sense of his author'. He did not even make adequate use of Charlotte Lennox's *Shakespear Illustrated* (1753–4), the first published collection of Shakespearian source material for some twenty-two plays, to which he himself had contributed a dedication. The faults of his edition are atoned for by his magnificent critical preface and comments on individual plays, by his pioneer recognition that only the first of the folios has textual authority, and by the later additions of Steevens, the second of the eighteenth century giants.

With Steevens and Capell began a new era, the quarto era. In 1766 George Steevens reprinted twenty of the quartos from Garrick's collection in four volumes. The stage directions are not tampered with, nor added to, there are no localisations, no added act or scene divisions, and the title-pages are reasonably exact. He included *King Lear* and the *Sonnets*, and the longest list of old editions hitherto compiled, including 'nine seen by nobody he knows'. Edward Capell, who had been collecting quartos since 1744, and had spent twelve years in preparation, sent the first sheets of his edition to press in 1760, and began publication in 1768. This edition is a dividing line in textual history, and Capell is one of the neglected major scholars of the century, partly because of the strangeness of his style, but mainly because, rather than print an ugly page, the results of his laborious and minutely accurate collation of quartos remained unpublished (except for a section issued in 1774), until 1783 (two years after his death) in the three massive quartos of his *Notes and Various Readings* and *The School of Shakespeare*. The editor's dedication of this work accused Steevens of systematic plagiarism of Capell's 1768 edition. Steevens certainly used Capell, but his powers were such that he had no need to. All editors and commentators of this period were quick to take hints, and pursue suggested inquiries. Steevens was one of the most learned in Elizabethan matters, an alert, shrewd and skittish scholar, enlivening his later editions with obscene annotations fathered facetiously on two respectable clergymen who had incurred his enmity. He took over Dr Johnson's edition, supplied the missing scholarship and industry, and in 1773 issued a ten-volume edition, containing richer illustrative material from contemporary literary sources than had previously been assembled, which in its 1778 revision is one of the landmarks of Shakespearian scholarship. From the 1760's onward scholarship moved with lightning pace. An example will show most clearly the interlocking of scholars and new fact. In 1766 Thomas Tyrwhitt in an anonymous pamphlet of textual conjecture, *Observations and Conjectures upon some passages of Shakespeare*, was the first to mention Meres's *Palladis Tamia.* In 1767 Richard Farmer used Meres incidentally in his rich mine of background information, the *Essay on the learning of Shakespeare*. In 1768 Capell used him for purposes of dating, and also quoted an entry in the Stationers' Register. In 1778 Steevens published the first extensive transcript of relevant Shakespeare entries from the Stationers' Register 'through the kindness of Mr Longman of Pater-noster Row, who readily furnished me with the three earliest volumes', and this immediately precedes Malone's epoch-making *Attempt to ascertain the order in which the plays attributed to Shakespeare were written.* But meanwhile Capell had been at work on the same problem and with the same materials, and in the neglected storehouse of his *Notes and Various Readings* (vol. II, p. 183), printed during 1779 and 1780 but held up until 1783, is found a discussion of the order and time of writing, based on internal evidence, Meres, and an 'Extract from the Books of the Stationers' Company, communicated by Mr S. Draper, Partner with the Tonsons' and on p. 185 a chronological table of the plays. As Mr Draper seems to give up publishing about 1765, we have a pretty picture of parallel efforts in an age of scholarly rivalry and bad feeling. The extent to which material was becoming available can be measured by examining the vast prolegomena to Steevens's 1778 edition, with its extract from *The Gull's Hornbook*, the drawing of the exterior of the Globe, the list of ancient translations from classic authors (partly compiled by Richard Farmer, who had contributed a substantial appendix to the 1773 edition), the reprints of prefaces to earlier editions, the facsimiles of Shakespeare's Will and signature, the notes to Langbaine by Oldys, the extracts from the Stationers' Register, the list of ancient editions (amplifying Pope's, Theobald's, Warburton's, Capell's and Steevens's earlier lists of quartos), extracts from Shakespeare criticism, and other valuable matter.

At the beginning of his *Attempt* in 1778 Malone sums up the position of scholarship. 'All the ancient copies of his plays, hitherto discovered, have been collated with the most scrupulous accuracy. The meanest books have been carefully examined, only because they were of the age in which he lived, and might happily throw a light on some forgotten custom, or obsolete phraseology: and, the object being still kept in view, the toil of wading through *all such reading as was never read*, has been cheerfully endured, because no labour was thought too great, that might enable us to add one new laurel to the father of our drama. Almost every circumstance that tradition, or history has preserved relative to him or his works, has been investigated, and laid before the public.' Malone was to add almost as much again, and to show that by comparison the study of Shakespeare was, as it is again to-day, an almost untouched field. His industry is incalculable. Capell is said to have transcribed the whole of Shakespeare ten times. Malone's annotations in any book from his library are profuse and almost always relevant (*e.g.* his copy of Capell in ten volumes in the British Museum, re-collated throughout, with copious insults, in 1781). In 1780 he published a supplementary two volumes to Steevens, containing the *Poems*, the doubtful plays from the 1664 Folio, a first sketch of his pioneer *Historical account of the rise and progress of the English stage*, and numerous annotations. In 1790 he issued his edition in ten volumes, with revisions of his chronology and stage-history, and vastly increased illustrative material; and he and Steevens are the chief builders, with Reed and the youngest Boswell, of variorum editions. Johnson—Steevens—Reed in twenty-one volumes, 1803, is the First Variorum; Johnson—Steevens—Reed in twenty-one volumes, 1813, is the Second Variorum; and Malone—Boswell in twenty-one volumes, 1821, is the Third Variorum, and in these are summarised and incorporated the body of eighteenth-century scholarship.

Apart from this almost apostolic succession of editions, with their concomitants of emendation and illustrative material, the eighteenth century opened up fields of research in almost every direction known to later scholarship. As early as 1729, J. Roberts in a pseudonymous *Answer to Mr Pope's Preface to Shakespeare* published a sketch of the old actors, and discussed, in four categories, the 'copy' for the Folio. In 1779 Steevens supervised the publication of *Six Old Plays* used by Shakespeare. In 1768 Richard Warner in *A letter to Mr Garrick* gave a specimen of a remarkable proposed glossary illustrated from vast reading in literature contemporary with Shakespeare. His note on 'the word occupy' in *II Henry IV* is an admirable example. In 1790 the Rev. Samuel Ayscough, F.S.A., compiled the first extensive *Index* or concordance, still in use on the reference shelves of the British Museum. The study of Shakespeare's verse started with Theobald, received valuable discussion in Capell's posthumous *Principles and Construction of Shakespeare's Verse*, and as early as 1756, in the sixth edition of T. Edwards's *Canons of Criticism*, Richard Roderick noted the verse peculiarities of *Henry VIII* which were to loom so large in the 'verse-test' movement. Shakespeare's grammar was investigated by Theobald, and classified in summary rules by John Upton in 1746. The punctuation of Shakespeare was worked out on historical lines by George Chalmers in 1797 in his *Apology for the believers in the Shakespeare Papers*. The biography was explored by William Oldys in the missing notes left unarranged at his death in 1781, and Malone made the extensive additions which were codified by Alexander Chalmers in 1809 in time for the intensive onslaught of the nineteenth century. Capell in 1768 had suggested the necessity of 'a brief history of our Drama, from its origin down to the Poet's death: even the stage he appear'd upon, its form, dressings, actors should be enquir'd into, as every one of these circumstances had some considerable effect upon what he compos'd for it', and Percy, Malone and Chalmers built this up, with the aid of those like Dodsley, Hawkins and Reed, who were publishing remains and documents of older drama, and of Warton who was clarifying the perspective of English poetry. It is to Steevens and Malone that we first owe the Henslowe papers, the Dulwich 'plots', the Revels Accounts, Sir Henry Herbert's Office Book, and the first facsimiles of Shakespeare's signatures. The study of the canon was pursued by a dozen authors from Pope and Theobald to Malone, who printed the Apocrypha in 1780. Comparative studies of Shakespeare's usage with that of other dramatists owe much to Theobald, Warner, Steevens, Capell and Malone, and even the vagaries of the historical and topical allusion school can be paralleled in James Plumptre's *Observations on Hamlet...being an attempt to prove that he designed it as indirect censure on Mary Queen of Scots* (1796). Even the habit of public lecturing on Shakespeare was a product of the eighteenth century, and the first ascertainable lecture was given by Charles Macklin, who, in the *Public Advertiser* for November 21st, 1754, proposed to lecture, beginning the next day, 'upon each of Shakespear's Plays, to consider the Original Stories from whence they are taken, the Artificial or Inartificial Use, according to the Laws of the Drama, that Shakespear has made of them. His Fable, Moral, Character, Passions, Manners, will likewise be criticised, and how his capital Characters have been acted heretofore, are acted, and ought to be acted...The First Lecture will be on HAMLET'. Twenty years later William Kenrick, the critic of Dr Johnson's 'ignorance or inattention', offered a course beginning with *Henry the Fourth.* One of the most important and neglected anticipations of the latest scholarship was an offshoot of the psychological study of Shakespeare, and is to be found in Walter Whiter's *Specimen of a Commentary on Shakespeare...on a new principle of criticism derived from Mr Locke's Doctrine of the Association of Ideas*, 1794. Whiter took Locke's statement, 'Ideas, that in themselves are not at all of kin, come to be so united in some men's minds, that it is very hard to separate them; they always *keep in company*, and the one no sooner at any time comes into the understanding, but its *associate* appears with it; and if they are more than two which are thus united, *the whole gang* always inseparable shew themselves together', and 137 years before Dr Caroline Spurgeon's study of *Iterative Imagery* noted the recurrent association of candy and fawning dogs.

In the variorum editions from 1803 to 1821 the nineteenth century found a kind of Chinese wall preventing exploration of earlier scholars. After Coleridge's new and rounded picture of Shakespeare there was less pioneer stone-breaking and road-making, and more consolidation of fields won. In 1790 Malone had said, 'When our poet's entire library shall have been discovered, and the fables of all his plays traced to their original source, when every temporary allusion shall have been pointed out, and every obscurity elucidated, then, and not till then, let the accumulation of notes be complained of. I scarcely remember ever to have looked into a book of the age of Queen Elizabeth, in which I did not find somewhat that tended to throw a light on these plays'. A floodlight was thrown by Francis Douce's remarkable *Illustrations of Shakespeare* in two volumes, 1807 (*e.g.* 'Dagonet in Arthur's Show') and the same year saw the first type-facsimile of the First Folio, said to be supervised by Douce. The eighteenth century had been an age of individuals, and usually well-to-do individuals. The nineteenth century was to see the triumph of corporate and organised research. In 1840 the first Shakespeare Society was formed by J. P. Collier with the aid of a council including G. L. Craik, A. Dyce, J. O. Halliwell (aged twenty), Charles Knight and Thomas Wright. The chief contributors to its papers were J. P. Collier, Peter Cunningham, J. O. Halliwell and J. N. Halpin. Its list of publications is huge and of the first importance, including Peter Cunningham's *Revels Documents*, 1842; Dyce's edition of *Sir Thomas More*, 1844; J. P. Collier's *Henslowe's Diary*, 1845; and J. P. Collier's *Extracts from the Registers of the Stationers' Company*, 1848, as well as a host of plays, mediaeval and Elizabethan, and much background matter. Individual editions of the works continued to be produced by S. W. Singer and J. P. Collier. J. O. Halliwell's much neglected Folio Edition is still valuable for its rich archaeological illustrations. Delius produced a valuable selective edition, and Dyce's second edition was adorned with an excellent glossary, scrupulously acknowledging previous achievement, and on such words as 'sack' making important additions. The great landmark of the mid-century is the *Cambridge Shakespeare* of Clark, Glover and Wright in 1863–6, which in the 1891–3 revision is almost the standard text of to-day. Its rigorous system of collation was facilitated by Capell's superb bequest of quartos to Trinity College. Furness's New Variorum Edition from 1871 provided a new labyrinth of commentary and illustration. Furnivall's important introduction of 1877 prefaced a one-volume edition of Delius, and later editions of value include Appleton Morgan's *Bankside Shakespeare* from 1886, issued by the New York Shakespeare Society, and printing quartos and Folio side by side, Sir Israel Gollancz's popular *Temple Shakespeare* (1894–1922), the co-operative *Arden Shakespeare* from 1899 to 1924 under the general editorship of W. J. Craig and R. H. Case, selected plays edited by G. S. Gordon, and by H. J. C. Grierson, and from America the *Tudor Shakespeare* by W. A. Neilson and A. H. Thorndike, and the co-operative *Yale Shakespeare* by W. L. Cross and Tucker Brooke.

The main divisions of nineteenth-century scholarship are indicated by Furnivall in his enthusiastic preface to the *Leopold Shakespeare*, 1877, 'the great defect of the English school of Shakspereans is their neglect to study Shakspere as a whole.... This subject of the growth, the oneness of Shakspere, the links between his successive plays, the light thrown on each by comparison with its neighbour, the distinctive characteristics of each Period and its contrast with the others, the treatment of the same or like incidents etc. in the different Periods of Shakspere's life—this subject, in all its branches, is the special business of the present, the second school of Victorian students...as antiquarian illustration, emendation, and verbal criticism—to say nothing of forgery, or at least, publication of forg'd documents—were of the first school'. The old Shakespeare Society had come to an end in 1853 as a result of J. P. Collier's forgeries, and in 1872 F. J. Furnivall founded his New Shakspere Society which lasted until 1894. Its strength lay in the meetings and discussions recorded in its valuable series of *Transactions*. The two Victorian giants, in their different ways, were J. O. Halliwell(-Phillipps) and F. J. Furnivall. Halliwell worked with tremendous industry, either alone or in societies, accumulating library after library of Shakespeariana, sold or given away after sucking out the Shakespearian lore. His list of publications great and small is appalling. He edited for the Shakespeare Society the 'First Sketches' of *II and III Henry VI* and *The Merry Wives of Windsor*. His Folio edition of the works is a mine and storehouse of information. He explored and published the Stratford records, he compiled a dictionary of Old English plays, and a glossary of obsolete English. His successive accumulations of material for Shakespeare's life culminated in the two-volume *Outlines* of 1887 containing all the documents then known. He published a list of visits of the London theatrical companies compiled from the records of seventy English towns, and even a dictionary of misprints in Elizabethan volumes, of surprising interest and value. He issued a minute photographic facsimile of the first Folio in 1876, and between 1862 and 1871 issued forty-eight volumes of lithographic facsimiles of the quartos. Probably no single worker of the nineteenth century contributed more material for the study of Shakespeare.

Furnivall was more of a team-leader and benevolent task-master. His passion for Shakespeare appears in every line that he wrote. He began as a Chaucerian expert, but a Shakespearian amateur, and the *Leopold* preface admirably explains his processes. The New Shakspere Society is popularly identified with the furious aridity of the verse-tests and Furnivall's reputation has suffered on that account, but his intention was to use these in the service of aesthetic criticism and the establishment of the order of Shakespeare's growth as an artist. The history of the verse-tests under Furnivall is fully given, in richly personal tones, in his introduction to Gervinus's *Commentaries* written in 1874, and in his introduction to the *Leopold Shakespeare* of 1877. Nothing could be less mechanical than his position. 'Don't turn your Shakspere into a mere arithmetic-book, and fancy you're a great critic because you add up a lot of rymes or end-stopt lines, and do a great many sums out of your poet. This is mere clerk's work; but it is needed to impress the facts of Shakspere's changes of metre on your mind, and to help others, as well as yourself, to data for settling the succession of the plays. Metrical tests are but one branch of the tree of criticism....No one test can be trusted; all must be combined and considered, and us'd as helps for the higher aesthetic criticism'. Apart from a neglected observation by Richard Roderick published in 1758, the first use of verse-tests was made, in the interests of the study of chronology, by Malone in his famous *Attempt* (first issued in 1778, revised in 1790, and in its final form in the 1821 variorum). He used the Rhyme test, and the unstopped or run-on line test. In 1833 William Spalding, at the age of twenty-four, published his brilliantly analytical *Letter on Shakespeare's authorship of 'The Noble Kinsmen', and on the characteristics of Shakespeare's style.* (Reprinted by Furnivall in 1876.) This is the real foundation of the whole business. But for the N.S.S. the beginning was James Spedding, whose article *Who wrote Henry VIII?* in the *Gentleman's Magazine*, August 1850, initiated the quantitative method. Charles Bathurst's *Remarks on the differences of Shakespeare's versification in different periods of his life*, 1857, and G. L. Craik's *The English of Shakespeare*, 1856, extended the inquiry. Independently in England and Germany the Rev. F. G. Fleay and Professor Hertzberg were working out their tests. Hertzberg published before Fleay, and Furnivall at first was not aware of Fleay's activities, but when the Society started almost all its earliest meetings were devoted to Fleay, and at the first meeting Fleay produced his Metrical Table. Fleay was an erratic thinker, and Furnivall later said, 'His theories when not confirming former results should be lookt on with the utmost suspicion'. The latest forms of the tables are given in Furnivall's two prefaces, but the method was soon forgotten in England, though in Germany some valuable work has been done by Hermann Isaac (Conrad) in the *Shakespeare-Jahrbuch*, 1896, and the *Preussische Jahrbücher*, 1905.[1]

Furnivall also directed the issue of *Allusion Books*, reprints of background material such as William Harrison's *England*, and

[1] The appendix in E. K. Chambers's *William Shakespeare*, II, 397, gives important bibliography and tabular material.

above all a valuable series of quarto reprints with stimulating prefaces by himself, P. A. Daniel, Dowden and others, in which minute comparisons were made and students encouraged to work on the original materials. These quartos and Booth's almost impeccable 1864 type facsimile of the first Folio popularised and advanced first-hand textual study. The *Transactions of the N.S.S.* contain valuable documents such as Dr Forman's notes on plays he had seen, discussion of natural history imagery, of Elizabethan England and the Jews, and Richard Simpson's discussion of political and historical relations of the plays, a problem approached by G. Chalmers, H. P. Stokes and Lilian Winstanley, and more recently by G. B. Harrison in his *Elizabethan Journals*. The total activity of the New Shakspere Society was an outcome of the scientific fever of the later half-century, and Furnivall's conclusion is instructive. 'The study of Shakspere's work must be made...natural and scientific, and in the order of the maker's making, and I claim that the method I have pursued is that of the man of science, comparison, noting of differences, and identities of expression, subject, character, mood and temper of mind; and that this method and its result do bring a fresh element of certainty into the order of Shakspere's plays, and the groups into which they fall.' That this scientific detachment was accompanied by the prevailing sentimentality towards *Shakespeare's Heroines* does not detract from its historical value.

Something must be said of the German contribution. This was ultimately the outcome of the earlier Romantic movement in which Shakespeare was used as a pawn in the intellectual fight against France, and as a philosophical ally in the anti-Cartesian campaign. Lessing, Wieland, Herder and Goethe in their different fashions brought him on to the map, but A. W. Schlegel's superb translation between 1797 and 1810 of seventeen plays, completed by Tieck later, presented Germany with a living dramatist in modern speech, and removed most of the antiquarian difficulties which had held up English appreciation. Schlegel and Coleridge simultaneously devoted attention to Shakespeare as a whole, as a creative genius. Tieck was a great student of Elizabethan drama, as well as of the theatre. Hegel had used Shakespeare as part of his philosophical and aesthetic system, and the first serious attempts to present Shakespeare as a whole were made by Germans, Hermann Ulrici in 1839 and 1847, and G. G. Gervinus in 1849 and 1850. This is so marked that it can be truthfully said, and it was emphatically said by Furnivall in his prospectus of the New Shakspere Society, 'It is a disgrace to England, that...no book by an Englishman exists which deals in any worthy manner with Shakspere as a whole', and this was true until Dowden's *Shakspere: His Mind and Art*, 1875, which acknowledged a heavy debt to the Germans. In scholarship Karl Simrock's *Die Quellen des Shakespeare in Novellen, Märchen und Sagen*, 1831, was the first collection of sources published anywhere since Charlotte Lennox's in 1753–4. (J. P. Collier followed with his *Shakespeare's Library*, 1843, W. C. Hazlitt later, and Sir I. Gollancz in 1907 with his *Shakespeare Classics*.) Delius issued his *Shakespeare Lexicon* in 1852 and his study of Elizabethan theatrical conditions in 1853. His text, first issued in 1854, was chosen by Furnivall for the *Leopold Shakespeare*. The tercentenary in 1864 produced effects in two opposite directions. Gustav Rümelin issued his 'realist' counterblast to Shakespeare idolatry and the *Deutsche Shakespeare-Gesellschaft* was founded. Its sixty-eight Yearbooks form a series of concentrated and unbroken scholarship (even in war-time) to which there is no exact parallel in any English-speaking country.[1]

The end of the eighteenth century saw the need of a study of the history and conditions of the theatre. Malone's 1790 investigation laid the foundations, and J. P. Collier's three-volume *History* of 1831 is one of the great early landmarks. In Germany Tieck, inspired by the Alabaster *Roxana* print first republished in 1825, prepared a reconstruction of the Fortune Theatre, the

[1] German scholars have contributed to every serious branch of Shakespeare scholarship, and Ebisch and Schücking's *Bibliography* indicates the specific contributions of such men as Aronstein, Bolte, Brandl, Brotanek, Albert Cohn, Creizenach, Eckhardt, Elze, Rudolf Fischer, Wilhelm Franz, Gaedertz, Gundolf, Hermann Isaac, Wolfgang Keller, Leon Kellner, Koeppel, Leo, Loening, Otto Ludwig, Morsbach, Sarrazin, Alexander Schmidt, Schücking, Sievers, Viëtor, Walzel, and Max J. Wolff.

first attempt of its kind. His influence on German stage practice was profound. In England 1844 saw the first attempt, under Planché, to produce a play in the Elizabethan manner. It was *The Taming of the Shrew*, done before curtains, without scenery, and with locality boards. Delius was concerned with stage conditions and contemporary stage directions, but the great impetus came with the publication of the Swan drawing in K. T. Gaedertz's *Zur Kenntnis der altenglischen Bühne*, 1888. This was taken up by scholars everywhere, and Genée, Brodmeier, Wegener, Neuendorff and Creizenach in Germany, and G. F. Reynolds, W. J. Lawrence, William Archer, V. Albright, T. S. Graves, A. H. Thorndike, J. Q. Adams, C. W. Wallace, Lily B. Campbell, together with A. Feuillerat all contributed fact and theory to build up the picture presented in E. K. Chambers's monumental *Elizabethan Stage*, 1923. Of outstanding merit, in their different approaches, are the contributions of G. F. Reynolds, of W. J. Lawrence, of William Poel and the Elizabethan Stage Society, and above all of W. W. Greg in his *Henslowe's Diary* (1904 and 1908), and his indispensable *Documents of the Elizabethan Playhouse*, 1931. The present writer has endeavoured to pursue new paths in *Shakespeare as Man of the Theatre* and *Production and Stage Management at the Blackfriars Theatre*. The most valuable application of theatrical knowledge to the criticism of the plays is in H. Granville-Barker's exhaustive *Prefaces to Shakespeare*, 1927 and 1930.

The eighteenth century, in Theobald and Upton, was concerned with problems of grammar, but no formal study was written until E. A. Abbott's *Shakespeare Grammar*, 1869. Continental scholars contributed much. Wilhelm Franz's *Shakespeare-Grammatik*, 1898–1900, is the standard work. Henry Bradley, Wyld and Jespersen have illuminated Shakespeare's linguistic practice. Wilhelm Viëtor, Zachrisson, Ekwall and Sievers have built up Shakespeare's pronunciation, following in the wake of A. J. Ellis, 1867–89, and using the old grammarians reprinted by Brotanek. Percy Simpson (1910) and A. W. Pollard have revolutionised the study of punctuation, and George Gordon's *Shakespeare's English* (1928) is the best short discussion of vocabulary. The study of Shakespeare's language has been facilitated by a host of glossaries and concordances. In 1790 S. Ayscough's *Index* was the first comprehensive concordance; 1822 saw Nares's *Glossary*, and 1845 Mrs Cowden Clarke's *Complete Concordance*. Nares was valuably enlarged by Halliwell and Wright in 1859. Dyce's valuable glossary appeared in 1864, and 1874 produced A. Schmidt's indispensable *Shakespeare Lexicon*. J. Bartlett's standard *Concordance* appeared in 1894, and the most recent and valuable publications are C. T. Onions's *Shakespeare Glossary* (1911) and Skeat and Mayhew's *Glossary of Tudor and Stuart Words* (1914).

On the borderline of scholarship and aesthetics lies the newly fashionable study of imagery on psychological principles. Walter Whiter opened the subject in 1794. William Spalding had some penetrating remarks in 1833. Halpin and the old Shakespeare Society, and Furnivall and the New Shakspere Society, were not unconcerned with processes and with specific fields of imagery, but not until the present century, largely in the wake of the fashion for Donne and the Metaphysicals, did the problem become acute. In 1918 (published 1924) H. W. Wells made a penetrating analysis of Elizabethan *Poetic Imagery*; G. Rylands's *Words and Poetry* (1928) was a sensitive study. Elizabeth Holmes in 1929 published *Aspects of Elizabethan Imagery*; Edmund Blunden in *Shakespeare's Significances* (1928) brought a poet's knowledge of processes to the imagery of *King Lear*. G. Wilson Knight in *The Wheel of Fire*, 1930, *The Imperial Theme*, 1931, and *Shakespeare's Tempest*, 1932, made stimulating if not always acceptable suggestions, and Caroline Spurgeon has tackled the problem methodically and as a whole by means of card indexes, and has issued samples of her findings in *Leading motives in the Imagery of Shakespeare's Tragedies*, 1930, and *Shakespeare's Iterative Imagery*, 1931. Of considerable value is the renewed attention given to the psychological background of Shakespeare's plays. The pioneer was Richard Loening in his *Ueber die physiologischen Grundlagen der Shakespeareschen Psychologie* in the *Shakespeare-Jahrbuch* for 1895, followed by S. Singer in the *Jahrbuch* for 1900. More recently a brilliant band of American scholars, including M. W.

Bundy, Hardin Craig, Ruth L. Anderson, Lily B. Campbell and W. W. Lawrence, have contributed materially to our understanding of Elizabethan conceptions of physiological psychology and their significance in interpreting the plays. American scholars have also contributed largely to the study of the relations between Shakespeare and his contemporaries. A. H. Thorndike's *Influence of Beaumont and Fletcher on Shakespeare*, 1901, was of pioneer importance, and his *Relations of Hamlet to Contemporary revenge plays*, 1902, and E. E. Stoll's *Marston and the Malcontent Type*, 1906, and his *Hamlet: An historical and comparative study*, 1919, provide the best type of comparative study. Rounded pictures of Shakespeare are still scarce, but outstanding works include R. M. Alden's *Shakespeare*, 1922, J. Q. Adams's *Life of William Shakespeare*, 1923, Sidney Lee's valuable and standard repository *A Life of William Shakespeare*, E. K. Chambers's exhaustive survey of problems *William Shakespeare*, 2 volumes, 1930, and Walter Raleigh's brilliant sketch, 1907. George Brandes's *William Shakespeare*, 1896, despite its many faults did much for Shakespeare on the Continent, and the German lives by A. Brandl and by Max J. Wolff have perhaps been unjustly neglected in this country.

The last direction of research is the bibliographical, and here the results have been brilliant and spectacular. In *Notes and Queries*, one of the most valuable nineteenth-century repositories of minor Shakespeare scholarship, on July 1st, 1871, Richard Simpson asked, *Are there any extant MSS in Shakespeare's handwriting?* and was the first to suggest that part of *Sir Thomas More* was in Shakespeare's autograph. 'The way in which the letters are formed is absolutely the same as the way in which they are formed in the signatures of shakespeare', and on September 21st, 1872, James Spedding said, 'To know what kind of hand Shakespeare wrote would often help to discover what words he wrote'. Henry Bradley in 1906 suggested 'that the conjectural criticism of Elizabethan texts has hitherto taken far too little into account the peculiarities of the handwriting of the period....It would be a considerable help to textual critics if some one would compile a judiciously classified list of the kinds of mistakes most frequently met with in the original editions of sixteenth century works'. Since then the stream has grown in force, and through Sir E. M. Thompson's *Shakespeare's Handwriting*, 1916, *Shakespeare's Hand in the Play of 'Sir Thomas More,'* 1923, and W. W. Greg's careful edition of the play in 1911 conviction has grown to support specific and detailed study of the text in the light of known peculiarities of Elizabethan handwriting, and with the collaboration at different points of Hilary Jenkinson, R. B. McKerrow, A. W. Pollard and W. W. Greg, *The New Shakespeare* (1921–), under the textual direction of J. Dover Wilson, is examining afresh all disputed and many undisputed readings. The main direction of bibliographical investigation, however, is concerned with the copy for the printer, and the transmission of the text. The problem emerged in the pioneer work done by A. W. Pollard, W. W. Greg and W. J. Neidig in clearing up the mystery of *Certain false dates in Shakespearean quartos* (*The Library*, 1908). A. W. Pollard, the Dean of living bibliographers, in *Shakespeare Folios and Quartos*, 1909, *A New Shakespeare Quarto, Richard II*, 1598 (1916), *Shakespeare's Fight with the Pirates*, 1917 and 1920, and *The Foundations of Shakespeare's Text*, 1923, has revolutionised the study of the transmission of the text, and instituted valuable categories of 'Good and Bad Quartos', of the highest promise for future research. The full story of the adventure still remains to be published by Dr Pollard. The Bibliographical Society, and the Malone Society (1907) have both ensured the success of the bibliographical method, and the new Oxford edition of the works by R. B. McKerrow will embody all the findings.

The eighteenth century was the great age of pioneers working in a virgin forest of text, annotating it, and opening up fields of scholarly research under the direction of a growing idolatry and furor. The nineteenth century is so richly strewn with monographs and learned articles that the paths, when they can be seen, are found to be, in the main, the work of journeymen, often inspired journeymen it is true, contributing each his portion to the cleaning up of the text, the formation of a picture of Shakespeare the dramatist, and his relations with the age he lived in. The century was so confused by conflicting loyalties to ethical and scientific positions that much of its most valuable work was achieved in spite of the times. During the last fifty years a growing realism of attack has produced a vast quantity of new pioneer work revising the whole field, working at first hand on neglected or misunderstood documents, questioning old orthodoxies with the higher criticism of intensive and minute bibliographical inquiry, and, in effect, throwing the whole mass of Shakespeare scholarship once more into the melting-pot. These minuter studies are in danger of obscuring the general picture of Shakespeare's achievement, but in three directions at least, the text, the theatre, and the poetry, there are signs of concentrated attack of the highest promise for the desired synthesis. It would seem as though the future of Shakespeare scholarship lies in the organisation of new co-operative methods. A systematic stock-taking of what has already been achieved will indicate much of what remains to be done. The new objectivity of research to-day is particularly favourable to such methods. By proper allocation and apportionment of tasks between the Shakespeare Association of England, the Shakespeare Association of America, and the German Shakespeare-Gesellschaft, and by organised University seminar work on specific problems, many of the projects at present beyond the individual's capacity could be brought to fruition. We need a complete picture of Elizabethan authorship, patronage, literary groupings, publication, etc., on the lines suggested by Sheavyn, Evelyn Albright and McKerrow: we need a real survey of Shakespeare's predecessors and the evolution of the earlier drama: we need, surprisingly enough, a satisfactory history and classification of Elizabethan drama as a whole: we need the full truth about the growth of Renaissance drama, and an exact account of Shakespeare's own theatrical practice and how far it conforms with or differs from the common behaviour of the time: we want to know about the inn-yards and the Academic Drama (a volume of translations from the Latin would in itself acquire merit): we need a full study of Shakespeare's language, his powers and paths of creation, and his processes of imagery in chronological evolution: we need a systematic comparison of all Shakespeare's writings with their source materials, and a concise account of the findings: we need a clear intellectual history of the Elizabethan and Jacobean ages. All these, and a hundred other practical and realisable tasks still remain to be completed, and not until they have been settled can we hope for a satisfying and scholarly account of 'The Mind and Art of Shakespeare'.

SHAKESPEARE IN THE THEATRE FROM THE RESTORATION TO THE PRESENT TIME[1]

BY

HAROLD CHILD

PUBLIC stage-plays were prohibited by Parliament in September 1642. The prohibition was far from effectual; and one way of getting round it was the performance, under pretence of rope-dancing and the like, of 'drolls', that is, extracts from plays or abbreviations of plays. Among these may have been the *Merry Conceits of Bottom the Weaver*, published with others in 1673. But the theatrical events of the Interregnum have little direct bearing on the subsequent history of Shakespeare. The first play by Shakespeare to be acted after (or perhaps just before) the Restoration was apparently *Pericles*, staged in the spring or summer of 1660 at the Phoenix or Cockpit playhouse in Drury Lane by a company of young players collected by John Rhodes, a bookseller, who had formerly been wardrobe keeper at the Blackfriars Theatre. Of this company Betterton (then, perhaps, twenty-five years old), who had been apprenticed to the bookselling, was a member, and soon a notable one. Another company, chiefly composed of old players of King Charles I's days, was acting at the Red Bull playhouse in Clerkenwell, and a third was set up by William Beeston at the playhouse in Salisbury Court, Whitefriars. Any Shakespeare which these companies acted must have been performed as near as possible in the pre-

[1] No account has been taken in this chapter of productions outside the United Kingdom.

Rebellion manner—whatever that may have become. The changes came in gradually, and began with a restriction on the freedom of the drama. In August 1660 an order was issued for a grant to Thomas Killigrew and Sir William D'Avenant of exclusive power to create two companies of players and to build two theatres; and this restriction was scarcely affected by a grant to George Jolly of power to keep a 'nursery' of young players. By November D'Avenant had formed his company, called the Duke's, chiefly out of Rhodes's young men, but without the best of them, Kynaston; and Killigrew formed the King's Company chiefly out of the old actors, but adding to them Kynaston. A few dates may here be useful. *November 8th*, 1660: the King's Company moved from the Red Bull to Gibbons's tennis-court in Vere Street, where the Stoll picture-house now stands. *June* 1661: the Duke's Company opened its new theatre in Lincoln's Inn Fields. *May* 1663: the King's Company moved to its new theatre (sometimes called the first Drury Lane) between Brydges Street and Drury Lane. 1671: the Duke's Company opened its new and grand theatre in Dorset Garden, Salisbury Court. *January 25th*, 1672: the first Drury Lane was burned down, and the King's Company moved for a time into the Duke's old theatre in Lincoln's Inn Fields. *March 2nd*, 1674: the second Drury Lane, built by Wren, was opened by the King's Company. *November* 1682: the two companies, amalgamated into one, began to act at Drury Lane. 1695: Betterton and others seceded from Drury Lane and set up in a new theatre in Lincoln's Inn Fields. 1705: this company moved to the great new theatre built by Sir John Vanbrugh in the Haymarket. 1708: the two companies again amalgamated and acted at Drury Lane. 1710: Betterton died.

On December 12th, 1660, a royal warrant gave D'Avenant the exclusive right to the performance of *The Tempest*, *Measure for Measure*, *Much Ado about Nothing*, *Romeo and Juliet*, *Twelfth Night*, *King Henry VIII*, *King Lear*, *Macbeth*, and *Hamlet*, and two months' right in *Pericles*. On August 20th, 1668, another warrant gave the Duke's *Timon of Athens*, *Troilus and Cressida*, and *King Henry VI*; and on January 12th, 1669, the King's were granted

The Winter's Tale, *King John*, *King Richard II*, *The Two Gentlemen of Verona*, *The Merry Wives of Windsor*, *The Comedy of Errors*, *Love's Labour's Lost*, *A Midsummer Night's Dream*, *The Merchant of Venice*, *As You Like It*, *The Taming of the Shrew*, *All's Well that Ends Well*, *King Henry IV*, *King Richard III*, *Coriolanus*, *Titus Andronicus*, *Julius Caesar*, *Othello* (called *The Moor of Venice*), *Antony and Cleopatra*, and *Cymbeline*. D'Avenant, that is, having first pick, chose four tragedies that were likely to be popular, only four comedies (on three of which he certainly, and on the fourth probably, had designs) and, in *King Henry VIII*, the most spectacular of the histories. The King's Company, being mainly composed of old actors, would not be very ill-content with the old ways. D'Avenant, ever an innovator, had new ideas. He expressly asked for a warrant of December 12th, 1660, for the purpose of 'reforming' the plays named in it and 'making them fit' for his company, and he soon showed what he meant.

On August 24th, 1661, Pepys went to Lincoln's Inn Fields ('the Opera', he calls it) and there saw *Hamlet, Prince of Denmark*, done with scenes very well. On February 18th, 1662, he saw at the same theatre *The Law against Lovers*, 'a good play and well performed, especially the little girl's...dancing and singing; and were it not for her, the loss of Roxalana would spoil the house'. Here already are two new factors to consider, scenes and women-players.

It was not, in all probability, D'Avenant at his 'Opera', but Killigrew with his old actors in Vere Street, who first brought upon the public stage professional actresses. On December 8th, 1660, he produced *Othello*, with Mrs Hughes as Desdemona and Mrs Rutter as Emilia. But D'Avenant's theatre was the first to foreshadow the incalculable change which this meant in the presentation of Shakespeare. Mr Granville-Barker has pointed out how Shakespeare took advantage of the convention of his time to avoid—even in *Romeo and Juliet* and in *Antony and Cleopatra*—direct sex-appeal, and to give his women-characters insight and humour, a quick wit and a shrewd tongue instead. The introduction of actresses—especially in a period of great sexual freedom and in a theatre more directly than before under the favour of a licentious Court—showed a lack in Shakespeare which the Restoration people very quickly tried to fill. Hence 'the little girl' in *The Law against Lovers* (which, in spite of its title, was a Shakespearian work). She is only a pert little piece, of no importance to the play; but she is a very early example of that exploitation of femininity which was to lead to some surprising liberties with the plays of Shakespeare, and to continue even into the nineteenth century. And already we find Pepys lamenting the absence of a certain actress, Roxalana, the beautiful Mrs Davenport, who had lately been lured off the stage by a mock-marriage with a nobleman.

Hamlet was 'done with scenes very well'; and once more we are on the edge of a difference—not yet great but destined to become so—between the playing of Shakespeare before and after the Interregnum. Before the closing of the playhouses the public stage had been learning from the masques about spectacle and the decoration of drama; and D'Avenant, whose *Salmacida Spolia* (1640) was the last of the royal masques, produced some time in 1656 in a room behind Rutland House, Aldersgate Street, his 'opera', *The Siege of Rhodes*, which had 'scenes in prospective'. These scenes consisted of permanent side-wings painted to represent rocks and cliffs, and of shutters, or flats, which could be run together and changed, in sight of the audience, to make different backgrounds. There was no attempt at creating the illusion that what the audience saw was not a stage setting but a real place. The old hangings had been replaced by pictures, that was all; and the pictures were framed within a proscenium. The stage still projected a long way in front of the proscenium; and, although the inner stage of the pre-war days had been increased in size and in importance, the art of acting was still largely the art of declamation and gesture on an open platform with the audience on three sides of it. Yet the implications of the change were important. In the first place, the complete and definite localisation of the scene had at least begun. For a century and more the changing of a scene would go on taking place in sight of the audience by the drawing back of the flats, while a player, standing at ease on the fore-stage, would see, say, his library walls disappear and himself thus transferred from his home to anywhere else that the dramatist might please; but the idea of localisation was at work, and was to lead to much difficulty and violence in the production on a localised stage of so loosely localised and occasionally unlocalised a drama as Shakespeare's. Secondly, the idea of scenery and of spectacle as things to be cultivated for their own sakes was transferred from the masques (specially composed for such purposes) to drama that had been written for very different purposes; and the implication was that that drama might be sacrificed at pleasure to the claims of scenery and spectacle.

It was, however, by no means only the new toys they had to play with—actresses, painted scenes and mechanical devices—which induced the men of the Restoration to tamper with the drama of Shakespeare. They had their principles. D'Avenant, at any rate, had; and during his lifetime (he died in 1668) the treatment of Shakespeare at his theatre was determined by these principles more than by the presence of actresses and much more than by the desire for scenic display. The King's Company went on playing Shakespeare abbreviated but not adapted—with one exception. That exception was a rough, coarse version of *The Taming of the Shrew*, called *Sauny the Scot*, attributed to Lacy, who himself played Sauny (Grumio). This prose play, with its new fifth act and very homely humour, suggests something botched up for surreptitious performance after the war was over and Lacy, a lieutenant in the King's army, had returned to civil life. But this sort of treatment was the very opposite of D'Avenant's. D'Avenant has been called 'almost a prude'. To him Shakespeare was an author who needed not coarsening but refining, especially in his comedies. Let us agree at once (with *The Tempest* shortly to come under notice) that some of the Restoration refinement can make our own stomachs turn; but there is evidence in Pepys that Shakespeare's comedies, as they stood, seemed to that age 'silly'; and that in comedy and tragedy alike, they believed they could improve him by means of what they had learned from Ben Jonson and from France. D'Avenant and his followers were half-hearted and inconsistent.

They did not always observe the unities of time and place, nor always keep tragedy and comedy apart, nor always avoid violent action on the stage. But they strove for symmetry of plot and balance of persons and consistency of character; they tried to make the action easy to follow, and every word of the dialogue comprehensible and strictly to the point. They tried to polish and to regulate; and Shakespeare, himself a valiant adapter, would probably have admitted them right in principle, and laughed, or sworn, at the havoc they made of his poetry, his fancy, the range and freedom of his thought and knowledge. It was scarcely their fault they did not know when to let well alone. The record by Downes that Betterton was coached in *Hamlet* by D'Avenant, who had seen the part acted by Taylor, who had succeeded Burbage in it, seems to imply a care for the pure tradition; and *Hamlet*, in fact, was only pretty drastically cut, especially in the long speeches. Yet even in *Hamlet* D'Avenant could not let the diction alone. He must needs alter it even in the passages marked for omission on the stage. But any journalist who has had to 'reform and make fit' other people's articles will understand how his pen took charge.

Like Garrick (and like Mr J. M. Robertson) D'Avenant had a true reverence for Shakespeare, though belief in it is sorely tried by three of his productions. Pepys's 'little girl' was acting Viola, a character in *The Law against Lovers*, in which D'Avenant ran together *Measure for Measure* and Benedick and Beatrice out of *Much Ado about Nothing*. The refining hand is plainly visible. The language is trimmed and tamed, and prose is turned into blank verse. The low comedy characters are cut out. And Angelo is made respectable: he was only testing Isabella's virtue before he should proclaim his honourable love for her. D'Avenant's *Measure for Measure* was thus changed from tragi-comedy into comedy as D'Avenant understood it. His *Macbeth* shows still more strongly his desire for balance and for consistency. Macbeth and Lady Macbeth are both more whole-heartedly and simply evil than in Shakespeare; and to balance the evil pair there must be a consistently good pair, Macduff and Lady Macduff. The Porter must go, since this is a tragedy. At the end all the poetry is cut out of Macbeth's part; and as for the diction, it is hard to say whether D'Avenant's rhymed couplets or his blundering blank verse are less like the Shakespeare they replace. But they are certainly more refined.

> The divell damne thee blacke, thou cream-fac'd Loone:
> Where got'st thou that Goose-looke?

says the Folio.

> Now Friend, what means thy change of countenance?

says D'Avenant. But not even refinement can explain the change of

> After Lifes fitful Feuer, he sleepes well,

into

> He, after life's short feavor, now sleeps; Well.

Yet the play would doubtless go with a bang in performance (it held the stage till Garrick ousted it); and it was not at first all overlaid with spectacle, as it was to be in 1672. There was, indeed, a good deal of trap-door and flying-machine stuff for witches and ghosts, and the supernatural part was, in general, purged of mystery and revealed in the clear light of acrobatics; but it was not the desire to 'operatise' the play in that sense which led to the chief of D'Avenant's rewriting. Nor was it so even with that very nasty piece of 'refinement', the version of *The Tempest* produced at Lincoln's Inn Fields in November 1667. The idea was D'Avenant's; and at the root of it lies the old desire for balance, consistency and trimness. The execution must be mainly Dryden's, partly because he said so, partly because that great man could be a very nasty writer and D'Avenant was never that, and partly because (with due weight given to his *Troilus and Cressida*) Dryden was too good a poet to tinker needlessly with Shakespeare's verse as D'Avenant did; and on the whole this *Tempest* is freer from that vice than the *Macbeth* or *The Law against Lovers*. But all the mystery, the charm, the wisdom have been sacrificed to symmetry, to consistency and to the 'love-interest' which from now on asserts itself more and more in adaptations from Shakespeare. Miranda (who had never seen a man) and Ferdinand must be balanced by Hippolito (who had never seen a woman) and Dorinda, another daughter for Prospero. Caliban must have a sister, Sycorax, who makes amorous advances to 'Trincalo', and even Ariel must have 'a gentle Spirit for his Love', named Milcha, whose only use is to dance with him at the close. The cast (as usual in these adaptations) is cut down, but the comedy of the sailors (made much 'lower' comedy than before) is retained. The whole is the capital example of the difference between the two conceptions of dramatic form. The Restoration (and the men that followed upon it) honestly thought that they were refining the rough work of an artless genius.

D'Avenant, no doubt, loved spectacle and the devices of stagecraft. His production of *King Henry VIII* was splendid with costumes, processions and 'shows' (or tableaux, as we might call them) of massed figures—some of them, no doubt, painted in perspective. But meanwhile the King's Company in Vere Street and at Drury Lane were staging other than Shakespearian plays with even greater splendour; and it was after D'Avenant's death in 1668 and the opening in November 1671 of the theatre in Dorset Garden, which he had projected, that Betterton, now in fact in control, went to lengths in this respect at which even D'Avenant might have hesitated. It was in April 1674 that Dorset Garden staged Shadwell's alteration of D'Avenant and Dryden's *Tempest*, in which (though the changes in the book are not great) the intention is frankly not drama but entertainment by music, spectacle and dancing.

Now the turn of the tragedies had come. It has been suggested that this was partly because the years 1678–82 were full of political anxiety; and that then, as round about 1715 and in other internal crises, the theatre sought wisdom from Shakespeare's tragedies, especially from *Coriolanus* and from *King Richard II*. This does not, however, altogether explain the rush of rehandling Shakespeare, in all degrees from almost total rewriting to adaptive alteration, which in those years involved half a score of the tragedies. Perhaps Rymer's book on *The Tragedies of the Last Age* (1678) had some influence; but before that was published Dryden had, in *All for Love*, taken a Shakespearian theme, that of *Antony and Cleopatra*, and written on it a play which exemplified his views of dramatic construction, especially in the matter of balance of characters. This play was produced at Drury Lane in 1677–8. At the same theatre in 1678 Ravenscroft made *Titus Andronicus* more horrible than the original. In that year also Dorset Garden saw Shadwell's workmanlike version of *Timon of Athens*, with a strong love-interest added, and not too much bother about the rules, and Dryden's still more workmanlike *Troilus and Cressida*, a regular tragedy, with characters so consistent and elevated that Cressida is a faithful and ill-used heroine. In 1679–80 Otway's *Caius Marius*, packing *Romeo and Juliet* off into the most unhomelike exile in ancient Rome, first allowed Juliet (Lavinia) to wake before Romeo (Marius junior) is dead, thus setting a fashion which prevailed into the nineteenth century. And, probably in December 1680, we come upon him whom a good critic has called not the villain but the clown of the piece, Nahum Tate. His *King Richard II* (quickly suppressed by authority, and vainly revived as *The Sicilian Usurper*), with its uxorious hero, its whiffs of the 'love-and-honour' essence of heroic tragedy, its low-comedy York and the trick table which robbed the imprisoned monarch of his victuals, was acted at Drury Lane; it was the other house that early in 1681 put on his adaptation of *King Lear*, which, giving Cordelia a lover in Edgar, cutting out the Fool, and arranging a happy ending with Lear alive and Cordelia married, kept Shakespeare's *King Lear* from the stage till Edmund Kean's day. What Tate thought he was doing to improve *Coriolanus* when, at Drury Lane in 1681–2, he turned it into *The Ingratitude of a Commonwealth* is harder still to discern; and the increased love-interest, with suicide, attempted rape and other dainty devices, could not make a success of the clumsy and untidy piece, even with its first hearers. There remain to be mentioned Crowne's two pretty workmanlike adaptations from *King Henry VI*, both acted at Dorset Garden in 1680 and 1681: *Henry VI, The First Part*, and *The Misery of Civil War*; and an adaptation by D'Urfey of *Cymbeline*, acted at Drury Lane at a date uncertain, under the title of *The Injur'd Princess*, which trims up Shakespeare's play and adds a nice little new plot which includes the exhibition on the stage of an attempted rape and the putting out of Pisanio's eyes.

After 1682, when rivalry between the two houses was stilled by the amalgamation and Betterton found himself in possession of the King's Company's repertory as well as of his own, the rush of new versions ceased, although the political incentive had not been withdrawn. The next notable adaptation was not seen for ten years; and then Betterton went further than D'Avenant had ever done in making a fine show of music and machines. *The Fairy Queen* was a version of *A Midsummer Night's Dream* produced at the Dorset Garden house in 1692. Purcell's music endears its memory; but what its first audiences enjoyed more was the scenery and the spectacle. The extant descriptions of the scenery show that by this time the public stage was surpassing all that the masques had done. If this 'opera' achieved only half that it aimed at, it must have been a triumph of ingenuity in the use of shutters or flats, cut-out wings and scenes, back cloths, running water and much else. It is only fair to note that the text was not very grievously knocked about. The dialogue was tamed a little, and there was some re-arrangement of scenes to make room for all the music, dancing and spectacle, in which monkeys and Chinese persons and properties had a place. Though too costly to make much profit, the show was a great success; and it tipped the scales heavily against simplicity in the production of Shakespeare's comedies. Between 1695 and the death of Betterton in 1710, more of the same sort of thing was produced by him at Lincoln's Inn Fields and the new theatre in the Haymarket. In 1699 came *Measure for Measure*, probably arranged by Charles Gildon, which, throwing overboard not only all the comic characters but also all D'Avenant's interpolations from *Much Ado about Nothing*, goes back towards the original and presents a compact play, short enough to leave plenty of room for the masque and other spectacular and musical additions. In 1701 came *The Jew of Venice*, by George Granville, Lord Lansdowne. Because Shylock was played by Dogget, it has been supposed that Granville made the part purely comic; but there is no warrant for that in the text of his version. His Shylock is not so far from Shakespeare's as the rest of the play; once more we have a trimmed, debased and neatly jointed action, with room in it for a great masque. Very much worse was Charles Burnaby's dull and vulgar version of *Twelfth Night*, called *Love Betray'd* (Lincoln's Inn Fields, 1703), altered to make room for a masque that was never presented. Meanwhile, for Drury Lane John Dennis had prepared his tedious and dirty perversion of *The Merry Wives of Windsor*, called *The Comical Gallant* (1702). Finally, one very famous adaptation of a tragedy belongs to this period, Colley Cibber's *King Richard III*, produced at Drury Lane in 1700 and maintained on the stage whole or in part until very recent times. Cibber's work is not to be lightly condemned. It is a hodge-podge of several of the Histories; much of the added dialogue is flat and poor, and there is some 'love-interest' and some added violence. But Cibber's Richard is a finer part for a 'star' than Shakespeare's, and his whole play is first-rate 'theatre'.

Othello, *Julius Caesar*, *King Henry IV*, *Hamlet*—these four were left unmangled, save for some reasonable cutting. For the rest, the age had set an example of altering Shakespeare, and that example was pretty consistently followed till within living memory. But in the next era, in which the leading theatre was chiefly under the management of Wilks, Dogget, Colley Cibber, Barton Booth and Steele in various combinations, a physical change was made of an importance which few can have then foreseen. In order to make the pit bigger, Rich, the manager of Drury Lane, cut off some of the fore-stage. The more open the platform, the more chance there was for a drama of a free and fluid structure. The more the play was pushed back towards and behind the proscenium arch, the more need there was for a new technique in production; and henceforth there was a continuous series of attempts (culminating in the theatre of Beerbohm Tree) to fit Shakespeare not (as Dryden, D'Avenant and their like had) into new critical rules, but into a stage for which his plays were not written.

The period between Betterton and Garrick was, on the whole,

a good time for Shakespeare. The Opera (as Vanbrugh's theatre had become) in the Haymarket, by putting on spectacular productions, was relieving Shakespeare and the drama of that liability; and when, in the seventeen-twenties, Rich started pantomime at Lincoln's Inn Fields and Drury Lane followed suit, the relief was even greater. It seems possible, indeed, that scenically Shakespeare was kept rather short. At Drury Lane his plays were mounted decently, but they were not pampered. It speaks all the better for the age that so many of them were in favour. The Restoration versions prevailed for the most part; but Lincoln's Inn Fields played Shakespeare's *Coriolanus*, not Tate's, and revived several other plays which had been neglected. And the period was not prolific in new adaptations. In 1716 two people made farces out of the Sly business in *The Taming of the Shrew*, and a musician made a comic masque out of the clowns in *A Midsummer Night's Dream*. In 1719 Drury Lane staged a very bad version of *Julius Caesar*, and also (not without an eye on the Pretender and the '15) a dismal sort of cold shape made by Dennis out of *Coriolanus* and called *The Invader of his Country*; and Lincoln's Inn Fields (politics again) tried Theobald's *King Richard II*, with a new love-interest in it. Aaron Hill dandified *King Henry V*, and there were others; but these feeble versions, in the best of which 'refinement' seems the only purpose, did not last, whereas the Restoration versions for the most part did. The last years of the period showed a decided swing back towards Shakespeare. In 1737 or thereabouts *King Richard II*, without either Theobald or Tate, and *King Henry V*, with all the comic characters put back, were played at Covent Garden (the new theatre opened in December 1732). And in 1740–41 came Macklin—Macklin who dressed *Macbeth* in Scottish garments; who restored at Drury Lane Shakespeare's *Merchant of Venice*, and, rescuing Shylock from low comedians like Griffin, presented what his age, at any rate, accepted as 'The Jew that Shakespeare drew'—a monster of malevolence and cunning. It has been suggested that to Macklin's influence was due also the restoration at Drury Lane of Shakespeare's *As You Like It* and *Twelfth Night*. The movement back to Shakespeare was well on its way when Garrick took the town by storm. The productions had interpolated music (by Arne and other good composers), and dances between the acts; but spectacle was not a rival of drama, and the notion of 'improving' Shakespeare by the rules was weakening fast.

Then came Garrick, bursting into fame at an unlicensed, unfashionable theatre, Goodman's Fields, which in 1740–41 had put on *The Winter's Tale* and *All's Well that Ends Well*, showing how the vogue of Shakespeare's comedies had spread in the first half of the century. Garrick came in on the crest of the wave of Shakespearian study by more or less competent pre-Johnson editors, and in the dawn of the 'return to nature' which heralded the romantic movement. As actor, there can be little question of his influence for good. If it be true that, when Benedick said, 'Hang me in a bottle like a cat and shoot at me', Garrick described in pantomime every step in the process, he would have to do it with extraordinary brilliance and swiftness of gesture not to be considered by modern taste a fussy player with little sense of proportion; and in Abel Drugger and other parts he was capable of irrelevant clowning. On the other hand, Davies's description of his Hamlet is alone enough to prove that by his power and range of personal expression he substituted representation for the fine old formal declamation of Quin and the others, and paved the way for the romantics, Edmund Kean, even Edwin Forrest and Junius Brutus Booth. In staging, too, he worked reforms. It is no longer believed that he introduced footlights; but in France he learned a good deal about lighting, which he used. He engaged good scene-painters (among them De Loutherbourg, whom, however, he apparently never allowed to paint a single scene for Shakespeare); and in 1765 gave their work a fair chance of being seen by banishing the audience from the stage. He brought back the decency and trimness of setting which had declined since Cibber and his friends were fresh at Drury Lane; and before the end of his long reign he had carried forward the movement (begun at least as far back as Aaron Hill) towards appropriate period and place in costume—his *King Lear* of 1776, for instance, was 'judiciously habited in old

English dresses', or, at any rate, what the critic of the *London Chronicle* took for such. And, 'star' though he was, the testimony of Mrs Clive and others seems to show that he at least had an inkling of a play as a single work of art, and of his players as parts of a whole, not merely as support for himself. Finally, he gave Shakespeare an enormous vogue, and set him up on a pedestal; and it was not all his fault (since many of the best critics of his time admired his taste) that, when we look at the pedestal, we see at the top not Shakespeare but a Roubiliac convention of Shakespeare. He played a great deal of Shakespeare, with the great tragedies (except *Julius Caesar* and *Coriolanus*), five of the comedies and two of the histories very frequently in the bill. And he did much to restore the purity of the text to the stage. His *Macbeth* (1744) had a brand-new dying scene for Macbeth, but it cut out the D'Avenant stuff about Lady Macduff. He restored, very nearly in their true form, *Coriolanus* (1754), *The Tempest* (1757), *Antony and Cleopatra* (1759), and *Cymbeline* (1761)—Posthumus being one of his best parts. He brought back some of Shakespeare (especially of his language) into *Romeo and Juliet* (1754), though Otway's notion of a dying scene between the lovers in the tomb held on till Kemble; into *King Lear* (1756)—but not very much; and into *Timon of Athens* (1771). But he made, or caused to be made, little entertainments out of *A Midsummer Night's Dream*, and *The Taming of the Shrew*, and a neat little pastoral out of *The Winter's Tale*, and he had *The Two Gentlemen of Verona* thoroughly reformed and made fit. None of this is very bad; but Garrick did what not even Dryden had dared to do: he laid hands on the structure and the story of *Hamlet*. That was in 1772, when his head had been more than a little turned by the adulation with which Paris had backed up London's willingness to believe him a great critic as well as a great actor; and his defiance of Voltaire had almost compelled him to prove that Shakespeare (with a little help from David Garrick) was not really a vulgar barbarian. It was, in fact, from Voltaire himself, in *L'Appel à toutes les nations de l'Europe*, that Garrick took much of his scheme for improving *Hamlet*. The result was never printed; but Professor

Odell has collected all the available accounts of it, contemporary and later, and these strongly suggest that, besides cutting out the grave-diggers and otherwise obliging Voltaire, Garrick did indeed alter the play 'in the spirit of Bottom the Weaver' and make his own part 'fatter' than it was. But he acted it so well that his version lived on, to be taken up by Henderson in 1777. The worst effect of Garrick as a whole was that he lent his great reputation as a student and champion of Shakespeare to the notion that Shakespeare was raw material, to be worked up by anyone who thought himself clever enough. That example was eagerly followed by Tate Wilkinson, for instance, and the provincial theatres which were growing in scope and importance. And with Drury Lane leading the way, no wonder Covent Garden and the Haymarket (let Theophilus Cibber rage against Garrick as he might) felt free to alter *Romeo and Juliet*, *King John*, *Cymbeline* and *Coriolanus* as they pleased. But it was at Covent Garden that George Colman, in 1763, restored a good deal of Shakespeare, in place of a good deal of Tate, to *King Lear*.

After Garrick's retirement in 1776, it is best to hurry on to John Philip Kemble. Kemble could not do his best while he was managing Drury Lane for Sheridan, the old house from 1780 to 1793, and the new, and much enlarged, house from 1794 to 1802; yet it was for the big stage of the new house that he ordered of William Capon the obviously very romantic scenery which (possibly taking a lesson from what De Loutherbourg had done for *The Tempest* in 1777) brought the production of Shakespeare a long step nearer the later idea of illusion. Mrs Siddons had very lately discarded the old tragedy-queen head-dress and hoops for a more appropriate garb; and in the opening production of *Macbeth* the witches shared with the new scenery the attempt to express the romantic, the sinister, the supernatural. As manager of Covent Garden from 1803 till it was burnt in 1808, and again of the new house from 1808 till his retirement in 1817, Kemble pretty steadily carried forward a treatment of Shakespeare which combined the historic sense with what is now called stylisation. He went some way towards dressing the characters of Hamlet and Macbeth in the clothes which he thought they would have worn. His scenery was 'stock', and used for many different plays; and so long as the proscenium doors, with the windows over them, were put to important use in the action of the play (the windows were abolished in the new Covent Garden) no real illusion was possible; yet it seems clear that the scenery was intended for more than a mere painted setting. The acting of John Kemble himself—yes, and of the divine Sarah Siddons also—might seem retrograde Quinwards from the quick naturalism of Garrick; it must indeed necessarily have been formalised and simplified by the ever increasing size of the playhouse. Yet it fitted into his dramatic scheme; and his very care to give names to the smallest of the characters left unnamed by Shakespeare joins with all that can be known of his work to imply that he saw, even better than did Garrick, each play as a whole, and tried to give each its proper artistic expression. Moreover, when he had his way, he produced a great deal of Shakespeare; and though the public taste and the size of the theatre forced him to spend a great deal of money on spectacular productions that were not Shakespeare, he mounted Shakespeare always well and sometimes superbly. The worst that can be said against him was that he had too little respect for the text. It would not be kind to hold up against him the first intrusion of the opera-making Reynolds (*A Midsummer Night's Dream*) in 1816, when his hold on things had weakened; but he brought back Dorinda and Hippolito into *The Tempest* after Garrick had ousted them; he played Tate's *King Lear*, Garrick's *Romeo and Juliet*, and other such versions. We must remember that all the time he was trying to interpret by one technique plays written for another; and credit him with having put back a good deal of the original into *Measure for Measure* and *The Merchant of Venice* among others; and his acting versions show no conceit about the rules and very little distortion merely in order to make room for star-acting or for scenic display. This was a good time for Shakespeare; and if John Kemble could have had his way it would have been a better. A large number of his plays were in regular performance. He had outlived in the theatre all the other dramatists of his time except

Massinger, and his text, though still cut and distorted, was at least getting free of other people's words.

But with John Kemble's retirement all stability seemed to be lost, and the success of Edmund Kean in and after 1814 brought in new factors and new dangers. Kean was no pedantic improver; he wanted to play *King Lear* as Shakespeare wrote it; and Elliston at first not only prevented him but also staged so fine a storm that it blew the King out of notice. But whether with or without Elliston or Bunn to manage or mismanage him, Kean was not the man to act Shakespeare consistently and with due care for each play as a whole. He was the first of the great stars—the *virtuosi*, who treated Shakespeare (as some modern executants treat Beethoven) as a means for the exhibition of themselves. Even Hazlitt, his great admirer, begged for fewer 'glancing lights, pointed transitions, and pantomimic evolutions'; and Lewes records his 'sacrifice of the character to a few points'. He was the first and greatest of the romantics, who professed to uphold Nature against convention, and after him came others, Junius Brutus Booth, Edwin Forrest, Barry Sullivan, Fechter—men whose tendency was to exploit the part at the expense of the play and to try and do in the part something that no one had done before. Kean came, moreover, just when there were more opportunities for wandering stars than there had been before. Rivalry and restriction had combined to make the two 'patent' houses so big that, as a contemporary said, a 'national theatre' seemed to mean a theatre large enough to hold the nation, and the very difficulty of keeping them up gave chances to the unlicensed 'minor' theatres. Even before 1843, when Drury Lane and Covent Garden lost their exclusive rights, it was possible for a star-actor to go from theatre to theatre in London, as well as in the provinces, sure of some sort of a company to make a background for him.

Into this instability Macready was not strong enough to bring order. He had not the temperament for a manager; and his obstinacy in frequently changing his bill robbed his Shakespearian work of its best chances with the public. But in his brief spells at Covent Garden (1837–8) and at Drury Lane

(1841–3) he brought back Shakespeare's *King Lear* (even including the Fool, though he, perhaps prudently, gave the part to a girl), *Coriolanus*, and *The Tempest*; and he mounted these and other plays like a student and a gentleman. But now the theatre has to face an old trouble in an exaggerated form. In the eighteen-twenties at Covent Garden Charles Kemble, with Planché's help, had gone far towards historical accuracy in costume and setting. In 1837, at the Haymarket, Benjamin Webster practically abolished the fore-stage. In 1840 at Covent Garden Charles Mathews and Madame Vestris (with Planché and the Grieves to help) got some sort of homogeneous Hellenicism into a beautiful production of Shakespeare's (not Garrick's nor Reynolds's) *A Midsummer Night's Dream.* Macready's own productions, especially his *King John* in 1842, were both splendid and scholarly. We have, then, on a 'picture' stage, strictly localised and made as realistic as possible (it is now some two centuries since the live sparrows in *Rinaldo* at the Opera, but only half a century before the live rabbits in *A Midsummer Night's Dream* at Her Majesty's), an elaborate scenic production; and the scenic devices were still so clumsy (as, indeed, they remained till the present century) that though, with the help of 'front cloths', an act might be run through without undue delay, each act would have its 'full set' and these took time to shift. Moreover front cloths at last came to be thought too conventional, and multiplied full sets meant delay within the acts as well as in the intervals between them. The action of the plays, therefore, came to be broken by frequent intervals; and the text to be cut and rearranged to save superfluous scene-changing, and to make the play fit into the time. And if there was (as there nearly always was) a ballet or a grand procession as well, the play had to be cut still shorter. Shakespeare had scarcely won his right to be staged not only with splendour but with fitness and realism when the scenery declared itself once more not his friend but his rival and foe. Already some of the critics were beginning to ask for 'an occasional preference of the suggestive to the actual'; and in 1844 there came a queer, lonely, prophetic act of recognition of the danger. In the course of his remarkable rule at the Haymarket (1837–53) Benjamin Webster (Planché at his elbow) staged *The Taming of the Shrew* as Shakespeare wrote it, complete, before hangings, without scenery, and in the nearest he could get to the Elizabethan manner.

To this muddled, unstable time two men put an end. Charles Kean (with his wife, Ellen Tree), who had given notable productions of Shakespeare at the Haymarket in 1848, produced at the Princess's Theatre in 1850–59 a famous series of elaborate and scholarly Shakespearian revivals. At Sadler's Wells from 1844 to 1862, and at the Queen's and other theatres afterwards, Samuel Phelps produced all Shakespeare's plays except *King Richard II*, *King Henry VI*, *Troilus and Cressida* and *Titus Andronicus*. But whereas Kean's manner of production compelled much cutting and some rearranging of the text, Phelps's simple staging left him free to secure what he most wanted, and that was the play as near as possible in its original state. Kean played Cibber's, not Shakespeare's, *King Richard III*, and put back Locke's music and the singing witches (which Phelps cut out) into *Macbeth*; and some of his suggestions for *King Richard II* strongly suggest the *Savonarola* of Savonarola Brown. This was to be the tradition that came down through Irving to Tree. The ideal of Phelps was that which mainly inspired the Benson Company and (at any rate till recently) the Old Vic.

Between the era of Kean and Phelps and that of Irving there is little worth note. Covent Garden had dropped out; at Drury Lane, with Chatterton struggling bravely on (1863–79), and at the Haymarket under Buckstone (1853–78), it was the star actors and actresses, English and foreign—Barry Sullivan, Helen Faucit, Fechter, Adelaide Neilson, Edwin Booth, Stella Colas, Ristori, Salvini—rather than the plays that drew audiences. With Irving under Bateman (1871–8) at the Lyceum, a great new star-actor, indeed, arose; but with Irving as his own manager (1878–1902), and especially during the earlier years, stability, fashion, popularity and style came back to the presentation of Shakespeare, although comparatively few of the plays were staged. Irving's position was strong and peculiar. He was a star (which Charles Kean never was), and an individualist; but his acting was as far as possible from the impressionistic display of the romantics. He had a good notion of a play as a single whole; and, though he was forced by his scenery to compress and rearrange, he did nothing so wanton in alteration as Augustin Daly did afterwards. He loved splendour and beauty, and was careful to get the most eminent painters (in days when painters could be very eminent indeed) to design for him; and he liked to fill out the play with significant action (Shylock's return from the supper at Bassanio's to his empty house is a good example); yet his taste, instinctively austere, saved him from the extravagances to which Tree was driven, partly by nature and partly by his desire to go one better than Irving. Only, perhaps, in his version of *Hamlet* did Irving alter the play so as to enhance his own part, and only in *Macbeth* did the prevalent desire for music in the plays send him back to bad old models—in this case to the flying and singing witches (with new music by Sullivan). Other producers of Shakespeare on the same lines—Wilson Barrett, Mary Anderson, Forbes-Robertson, Daly—were committed to some degree or other of compression and alteration. Of these Daly was far the most wanton. Mary Anderson's doubling of Hermione and Perdita was not so disturbing to the play as it sounds, since all she needed to do was to make someone else play Perdita in the last scene. Best of all was Forbes-Robertson's *Hamlet* (1897), which always kept in Fortinbras and began by keeping the scene between Polonius and Reynaldo, and the return of the Danish ambassadors. Realism of setting also brought with it a naturalism in acting (much encouraged by the example of Fechter in 1860) and especially in the speaking of verse, under which the great characters dwindled. Perhaps they dwindled a little more still after the visit of the Saxe-Meiningen company (1881) had brought animated stage-crowds into favour.

Meanwhile, F. R. Benson and his company were on tour, acting as many of Shakespeare's plays, and as much of each as they could, with as simple a setting as they dared. At Stratford-upon-Avon in the spring of 1906 they acted all the Histories;

and during a short season at the Lyceum in 1900 they did *Hamlet* whole. The playgoers—even the critics—did not take to it. Still less did they take to the revolutionary productions of Mr William Poel, who, chiefly in the declining years of Irving and the heyday of Tree, staged for the Elizabethan Stage Society continuous performances of Elizabethan drama without scenery. The critics had begun to complain of too much scenery; but no scenery at all, no stars in the cast, and the strain of listening to a new (or very old) and musical speaking of the poetry, 'with its consonantal swiftness, its gradations sudden or slow into vowelled liquidity, its comic rushes and stops, with, above all, the peculiar beauty of its rhymes'—this was rather too much. Nevertheless, the leaven worked. This almost purely archaistic method of staging, which presents Shakespeare through the technique for which his plays were designed, has been adopted elsewhere—notably at the Maddermarket Theatre in Norwich; but its greatest service has been to familiarise the theatre with the advantages of continuous and loosely localised performance of the plays according to Shakespeare's own dramatic plan. In the Granville-Barker productions at the Savoy Theatre (1912–14) the core of that idea was combined, on a stage extended in front of the proscenium, with a cautious, fastidious use of representation in scenery—a combination which has since been adopted by other producers. Scenic device, and especially the pictorial use of light, has so greatly improved of recent years that there is no reason why the two methods should not be used together, so that Shakespeare could be acted with Elizabethan freedom and fluidity and also with the pictorial beauty and the temporal and spatial definition which audiences enjoy. At present the age shows signs of wanting merely to find some way of playing Shakespeare that has never been tried before. Shakespeare is acted in modern dress; all in black and white; on a stage that is all staircase; so lighted that no faces can be seen; and tricks are played with the construction and the tone of plays every whit as daring as those of Tate or of Cibber. Some of these experiments have led to the acting of plays not often acted; and any method that will expose new beauties or even excite new interest in

Shakespeare is to be so far commended. But the best possible base for all experiment would be a strong and active tradition built up on the understanding that Shakespeare, as playwright, knew what he was about. The maintenance of that tradition is too much to ask of the theatre as at present conducted.

READING LIST

NOTE

THESE reading lists were compiled by the original contributors to provide illustrations and extensions of their studies. They are here reprinted without alteration; but other books on the particular subjects have of course been published since 1935, and for these the reader is referred to the *Cambridge Bibliography of English Literature*, *Volume V* and to the *Concise Cambridge Bibliography of English Literature.*

THE LIFE OF SHAKESPEARE

ELTON, C. I. *W. Shakespeare, his Family and Friends.* 1904.
Collects and sets forth the facts and documents bearing on Shakespeare's genealogy and connexions.

RALEIGH, SIR W. *Shakespeare.* 'English Men of Letters Series.' 1907.
A masterly biographical study.

BEECHING, H. C. *William Shakespeare, player, playmaker and poet.*
A judicious summary, in short compass, of Shakespeare's life and work.

NEILSON, W. A. and THORNDIKE, A. H. *The Facts about Shakespeare.* 1913.
Useful for reference.

HERFORD, C. H. *A Sketch of recent Shakespeare Investigation.* 1923.
Also useful for reference.

ADAMS, J. QUINCY. *A Life of William Shakespeare.* 1923.
A useful life, correlating the facts of Shakespeare's biography with the history of the Elizabethan stage.

LAMBORN, E. A. G., and HARRISON, G. B. *Shakespeare, the Man and his Stage.* 'The World's Manuals.' 1923.
A first-rate compendium of information; invaluable as a handbook and as an introduction to study of Shakespeare.

LEE, SIR S. L. *A Life of William Shakespeare.* Latest revised and enlarged edition. 1925.

The standard work on the subject until superseded by the work of E. K. Chambers.

BAILEY, J. *Shakespeare.* 1929.

An admirable study.

CHAMBERS, SIR E. K. *William Shakespeare.* 1930.

The most complete and authoritative work on Shakespeare, fully documented, indispensable for all advanced study.

WILSON, J. DOVER. *The Essential Shakespeare; a Biographical Adventure.* 1932.

A stimulating reconstitution of Shakespeare's life and work.

HARRISON, G. B. *Shakespeare at Work* [1592–1603]. 1933.

An interpretation and reconstruction of Shakespeare's life and its background, national and theatrical, during the reign of Elizabeth.

J. W. M.

THE THEATRES AND COMPANIES

CHAMBERS, SIR E. K. *The Mediaeval Stage.* 2 vols. 1913.

CHAMBERS, SIR E. K. *The Elizabethan Stage.* 4 vols. 1923.

An encyclopaedic study of all matters dealt with in this chapter, in which the facts are set forth and may be examined independently.

FEUILLERAT, A. *Documents relating to the Office of the Revels.* In Bang, *Materialen*, XXI, 1908, and XXIV, 1914.

Collections and reproductions of documents bearing upon performances at Court under Edward VI, Mary and Elizabeth, with valuable indices and notes.

WELSFORD, ENID. *The Court Masque.* 1927.

SIMPSON, PERCY and BELL, C. F. *Designs by Inigo Jones for Masques and Plays at Court.* 1924.

The information contained in the former of these two may be supplemented by the admirable set of drawings of Masques, *décors* and costumes reproduced, with descriptions, in the latter.

BASKERVILL, C. R. *The Elizabethan Jig.* 1929.

BOAS, F. S. *University Drama in the Tudor Age.* 1914.

MOORE SMITH, G. C. *College Plays performed in the University of Cambridge.* 1923.

These monographs contain the information available upon important special aspects of the stage and drama. Much yet remains to be done in the field of the academic stage in the later part of the period.

GREG, W. W. *Henslowe's Diary,* and *Henslowe Papers.* 3 vols. 1904–8.

Collections and reproductions, with commentary, of original documents from Dulwich College bearing upon Henslowe's theatrical transactions.

GREG, W. W. *Dramatic Documents from the Elizabethan Playhouses.* 2 vols. 1931.

Reproductions, with exhaustive commentary, of all classes of surviving stage documents of the age of Shakespeare, such as 'platts', actors' parts, MS. plays and prompt copies.

GREG, W. W. *Elizabethan Literary Autographs.* 3 parts. 1925–32.

Part I of this work contains specimens of the handwriting of Elizabethan dramatists, with commentary, transcript, and brief biographies.

FURNIVALL, F. J. (editor). *Shakespeare Quarto Facsimiles.* 1885–91.

LEE, SIR S. L. (editor). *Mr William Shakespeare's Comedies, Histories and Tragedies.* 1623.

A collotype facsimile of the First Folio.

GREG, W. W. (editor). Malone Society Reprints. 1907 ff.

FARMER, J. S. (editor). Tudor Facsimile Texts. 1907–13.

In these sets of facsimile reproductions of printed and MS. plays, stage directions may be studied as found in the original texts of Elizabethan plays.

THORNDIKE, A. H. *Shakespeare's Theater.* 1916.

ADAMS, J. Q. *Shakespearean Playhouses.* 1917.

LAWRENCE, W. J. *The Elizabethan Playhouse and Other Studies.* Series 1 and 2, 1912 and 1913.

LAWRENCE, W. J. *Pre-Restoration Stage Studies.* 1927.

LAWRENCE, W. J. *The Physical Conditions of the Elizabethan Public Playhouse.* 1927.

The first two of these works are general studies of the history and structure of the theatres. Dr Lawrence, in his pioneer work, has collected and discussed the evidence upon a wide variety of problems of the stage.

MURRAY, J. T. *English Dramatic Companies*, 1558–1642. 2 vols. 1910.

HILLEBRAND, H. N. *The Child Actors.* 1926.

BALDWIN, T. W. *The Organization and Personnel of the Shakespearean Company.* 1927.

NUNGEZER, EDWIN. *A Dictionary of Actors.* 1929.

These four books contain historical and biographical material concerning Elizabethan actors and theatrical companies.

NOTE

No complete treatment of the history of the stage during the later Jacobean and Caroline ages has yet been written, Sir E. K. Chambers having fixed 1616, the year of Shakespeare's death, as terminating his study. Many of the books listed above, however, cover parts of this later period in special aspects. A still later period is dealt with in J. L. Hotson's *Commonwealth and Restoration Stage* (1928).

Information is gradually being gathered to prepare the way for an exhaustive treatment of the post-Elizabethan age, as also to supplement what is known of Shakespeare's time. New knowledge is being gained piecemeal from the intensive study of literary and documentary sources, from State records and from records of courts of law.

Current views concerning the staging of plays may well be modified in time, and a number of problems remain for further consideration. We have, after all, to deal with the individual possibilities of a variety of theatres at different stages of a long period of development, in a hundred years of theatrical history.

The history of the companies, again, has left room for controversy, due to the instability of the organisation of most of them, with consequent splitting up, temporary coalitions and movements of groups from one company to another.

Very little is known concerning the inn-yard theatres of London, their methods of production and their history. And few indeed are the positive facts known about the immense field of the stage and drama in the provinces during the period.

Finally, we may yet hope for further information upon the lives and careers of dramatists, actors and organisers of the theatre of Shakespeare's time, if not of Shakespeare himself, upon whom diligence has been perhaps too exclusively concentrated in the past.

C. J. S.

SHAKESPEARE'S DRAMATIC ART

In the list below I have noted books which I myself constantly consult. It makes no pretence, of course, to being comprehensive.

EDITIONS OF THE PLAYS

The Furness 'Variorum', 23 vols. containing 21 plays and the poems, published at intervals since 1871. Each volume contains a large accumulation of textual notes and history and of critical extracts. But as this is eclectic rather than selective it needs using with judgment.

The 'Arden' edition, 1899–1924 (a play to a volume). A variety of editors; the value of their work also varying greatly, from excellence to mediocrity. But the scale, scope and format make it a good edition for the student.

Nine of the plays in separate volumes edited by Professor George Gordon, 1912. A suitable edition for the inexpert but keen reader, with its trenchant and scholarly introductions and its explanatory notes.

The new Cambridge edition, 1921– a play a volume. Textually edited by Professor Dover Wilson and therefore of prime importance to the student. Sir Arthur Quiller-Couch has written introductions to the comedies considered as drama and literature.

Bradley, A. C.

Shakespearean Tragedy. 1904.

Studies of *Hamlet, King Lear, Othello* and *Macbeth.*

Bradley, A. C.

Oxford Lectures on Poetry. 1917.

Contains a study of *Antony and Cleopatra.*

Coriolanus—the British Academy Shakespeare Lecture for 1912; republished in *A Miscellany.* 1929.

Analyses of the plays in the light of their chief characters, unsurpassed for sympathetic perception.

Chambers, Sir E. K.

The Elizabethan Stage. 4 vols. 1923.

Chapters xvi–xxi, which deal with the theatres themselves and the staging, are indispensable to the student.

CHAMBERS, SIR E. K.

William Shakespeare. 2 vols. 1930.

This has taken its place as the most authoritative and fully documented statement of what is known of the man and the circumstances in which he worked; besides which, it summarises and evaluates the results of the scholarship devoted to the work itself.

LAWRENCE, W. J.

The Elizabethan Playhouse and Other Studies. Series I, 1912; Series II, 1913.

Pre-Restoration Stage Studies. 1927.

The Physical Conditions of the Elizabethan Public Playhouse. 1927.

Shakespeare's Workshop. 1928.

These, together with many still uncollected papers, are a storehouse of information and provocative argument about the practical conditions of the Elizabethan and Jacobean stage.

MACKAIL, J. W.

The Approach to Shakespeare. 1930.

The title describes the book; it shows the reader and spectator a road which should take him, if he will travel it sensitively, into the very heart of the plays and their beauty.

MOULTON, RICHARD G.

Shakespeare as a Dramatic Artist. 1885. Third edition, revised and enlarged, 1906.

The pioneer work of a penetrating and powerful mind; particularly valuable for its elucidation of the scheme of a play and its characters.

QUILLER-COUCH, SIR ARTHUR.

Shakespeare's Workmanship. 1918.

A series of stimulating lectures upon the art of the plays; full of illuminating, if sometimes disputable, observation; admirably directed to their original purpose, which was to rouse an undergraduate audience to a lively interest in Shakespeare.

RALEIGH, SIR WALTER.

Shakespeare. 'English Men of Letters Series.' 1907.

A brilliant—or better, a radiant—and very individual appreciation of the plays and of what is known of the man. Not impeccable either in statement or judgment; but this is only the defect of its quality.

STOLL, EDGAR ELMER.

Othello. 1915.

Hamlet. 1919.

Shakespeare Studies. 1927.

STOLL, EDGAR ELMER.

Poets and Playwrights. 1930.

The Tempest. 1932.

Art and Artifice in Shakespeare. 1933.

'Objective' studies of the plays, seen more particularly in the light of contemporary literature and ideas. Valuable in themselves and as valuable as a corrective to the work of the 'mystic' school.

GRANVILLE-BARKER, HARLEY.

Prefaces to Shakespeare, Series I, II and *III.* 1927, 1930, 1937.

Detailed studies of (I) *Love's Labour's Lost, Julius Caesar, King Lear*; (II) *Romeo and Juliet, The Merchant of Venice, Antony and Cleopatra, Cymbeline*; (III) *Hamlet*—done from the point of view adopted in this chapter.

H. G.-B.

SHAKESPEARE THE POET

WYNDHAM, GEORGE. *The Poems of Shakespeare.* Edited with an introduction and notes. 1898.

A useful and valuable edition. Some parts of the introduction may be thought too romantic by modern taste.

BEECHING, H. C. *The Sonnets of Shakespeare.* With an introduction and notes. 1904.

Sensible, illuminating, complete. An important suggestion is made as regards the abstract way of writing in some later sonnets.

KELLETT, E. E. *Suggestions.* Ch. IV. 1923.

Pursues Coleridge's observation of the evolution of Shakespeare's metaphors.

NOBLE, RICHMOND. *Shakespeare's Use of Song.* 1923.

A detailed study of the dramatic significance of the songs.

GORDON, G. S. *Shakespeare's English.* S.P.E. Tracts, No. XXIX. 1928.

This all too brief pamphlet is essential for the understanding of the vocabulary.

BLUNDEN, EDMUND. *Shakespeare's Significances.* 1929.

A poet reveals the concealed meanings, the hints and overtones in *King Lear.*

RYLANDS, GEORGE H. W. *Words and Poetry.* 1930. Part II may serve to supplement some paragraphs in this chapter.

RYLANDS, GEORGE H. W. *English Poetry and The Abstract Word.* English Association Studies, vol. XVI. 1930.

SPURGEON, CAROLINE F. E. *Leading Motives in the Imagery of Shakespeare's Tragedies.* 1930.

SPURGEON, CAROLINE F. E. *Shakespeare's Iterative Imagery.* British Academy, vol. XVII. 1931.

The first results of Miss Spurgeon's classification of all the images; similar to the work of Mr Wilson Knight but independent of it and extremely interesting.

MURRY, JOHN MIDDLETON. *Shakespeare's 'Dedication'.* 'Countries of the Mind.' Second series. 1931.

KNIGHT, G. WILSON. *The Wheel of Fire.* 1930.

A new interpretation of Shakespeare based upon a study of the imagery. This idea of the poetic symbolism of Shakespeare is pursued farther (perhaps too far) by the same author in *The Imperial Theme,* 1931, and *The Shakespearian Tempest,* 1932.

G. R.

SHAKESPEARE'S VOCABULARY

BRADLEY, HENRY. *Shakespeare's English.* 'Shakespeare's England.' Vol. II, ch. XXX. 1917.

Remains the most compendious and generally useful review of the Shakespearian form of Elizabethan English. Opinion on some points of phonology has, however, been modified since 1917 and no phonetic notation is used.

WYLD, H. C. *A History of Modern Colloquial English.* Ch. IV. 1921.

Traces the process of standardisation and stresses the courtly side of 'good' English (written and spoken) in the late Elizabethan period.

BOARD OF EDUCATION. *The Teaching of English in England.* 1921.

Ch. II deals with the subject historically and illustrates very cogently and succinctly the neglect of English studies in Tudor schools.

GORDON, G. S. *Shakespeare's English.* S.P.E. Tracts, No. XXIX. 1928.

Stresses freedom of Elizabethan speech. Full and vivid illustration of 'language-making' in Shakespeare and his contemporaries.

McKnight, G. H. *Modern English in the Making.* 1928.
Chs. vi to xi inclusive offer a stimulating and admirably illustrated account of the influences at work in Elizabethan English.

Willcock, G. D. *Shakespeare as a Critic of Language.* Shakespeare Association Lecture. 1935.

G. D. W.

SHAKESPEARE AND MUSIC

Chappell, W. *Old English Popular Music.* Revised by H. E. Wooldrodge. 2 vols. 1893.

Bond, R. Warwick. *The Works of John Lyly.* 1902.

Lawrence, W. J. *The Elizabethan Playhouse and other studies.* 1912.

Cowling, G. H. *Music on the Shakespearean Stage.* 1913.
Information on music in pre-Shakespearian Drama and on the practical details of the Elizabethan stage.

Arkwright, G. E. P. 'Elizabethan Choirboy Plays and their Music.' *Proceedings of the Musical Association,* 1914.

Scholes, P. A. 'The purpose behind Shakespeare's use of music.' *Proceedings of the Musical Association,* 1917.

Bridge, J. F. *Shakespearean Music in the Plays and early Operas.* 1923.

Noble, Richmond. *Shakespeare's Use of Song.* 1923.

Dent, E. J. *Foundations of English Opera.* 1928.

Naylor, E. W. *Shakespeare Music.* 1928.
A useful collection of songs and instrumental pieces of Shakespeare's time arranged for use in the performance of the plays.

Baskervill, C. R. *The Elizabethan Jig.* 1929.
A full account of the jig, with the texts, in whole or part, of thirty-five of them.

Naylor, E. W. *Shakespeare and Music.* 1931.
The best guide to Shakespearian music and to the musical allusions in Shakespeare's poems and plays.

Galpin, F. W. *Old English Instruments of Music.* 1932.

Gibbon, John Murray. *Melody and the Lyric.*
Covers wider ground, but contains many specimens of the songs and dances available for the Elizabethan Drama.

E. J. D.

THE NATIONAL BACKGROUND

STOW, J. *Annales, or a General Chronicle of England.* First printed in 1592; continued by others to 1631.

A most important contemporary record of events of all kinds.

CAMDEN, WILLIAM. *The History...of Elizabeth, late Queen of England.* 1615 (Latin), 1631 (English).

An excellent history of the reign by one who had access to first-hand information.

WINWOOD, SIR R. *Memorials of Affairs of State in the reigns of Queen Elizabeth and King James.* 3 vols. 1725.

A large collection of letters and state documents which came into the hands of Sir Ralph Winwood, for many years English ambassador in France.

STRYPE, J. *Annals of the Reformation.* 1709–31.

STRYPE, J. *Life of Archbishop Whitgift.* 1718.

An important collection of papers, chiefly concerned with ecclesiastical matters.

COLLINS, A. *Letters and memorials of State...from the originals at Penshurst Place.* 1746.

Include many news-letters written from Court to Sir Robert Sidney. Sometimes known as the *Sidney Papers.*

BIRCH, T. *Memoirs of the reign of Queen Elizabeth.* 2 vols. 1754.

Extracts from the correspondence of Anthony Bacon, private secretary to the Earl of Essex.

NICHOLS, J. *The Progresses and Public Processions of Queen Elizabeth.* 2 vols. 1788; new ed. 3 vols. 1823.

NICHOLS, J. *Progresses, Processions and Magnificent Festivities of King James the First.* 4 vols. 1828.

Reprints of records and contemporary accounts of Court ceremonies. Most useful and illuminating, especially the *Progresses of King James.*

HARINGTON, SIR JOHN. *Nugae Antiquae.* Edited by T. Park. 1804.

Includes many of Harington's letters.

CHAMBERLAIN, J. *Letters...during the reign of Queen Elizabeth.* Edited by Sarah Williams. 1861.

Contemporary letters of gossip, 1597–1603. Later letters of Chamberlain are to be found in Winwood's *Memorials* and Birch's *James I.*

SPEDDING, J. *The Life and Letters of Francis Bacon.* 1861.
Particularly valuable for the Essex affair, but touching public life at all points.

GARDINER, S. R. *History of England,* 1603–1642. Vols. 1 and 2. 1893 (revised).
An admirable guide to the history of the reign of James I.

HAWARDE, W. *Les Reportes del Cases in Camera Stellata,* 1593–1609. Edited by W. P. Baildon. 1894.
A barrister's notes of Star Chamber cases.

DASENT, J. R. *Acts of the Privy Council,* 1900 etc.
The minutes and letter-books of the Council.

CHEYNEY, E. P. *A History of England from the Defeat of the Armada to the Death of Elizabeth.* 1913, 1926.
A full history of these years, with chapters on such subjects as the law courts, administration, parliament, local government.

HARRISON, G. B. *An Elizabethan Journal,* 1591–1594. 1928.

HARRISON, G. B. *A Second Elizabethan Journal,* 1595–1598. 1931.

HARRISON, G. B. *A Last Elizabethan Journal,* 1599–1603. 1933.
A day by day account of the things most discussed.

NEALE, J. E. *Queen Elizabeth.* 1934.

Calendars of State Papers Domestic.

Calandars of State Papers. Relating to Ireland.
Abstracts and summaries of documents of all kinds preserved in the Public Record Office, London.

Calandar of the Manuscripts of the Marquis of Salisbury preserved at Hatfield House.
Abstracts and summaries of the many papers collected by Lord Burghley and his son Robert Cecil, afterwards Earl of Salisbury.

G. B. H.

THE SOCIAL BACKGROUND

I. MODERN WORKS

RALEIGH, SIR W. *Shakespeare's England.* 2 vols. 1916.

BYRNE, M. ST CLARE. *Elizabethan Life in Town and Country.* Second edition, 1933.
Both essential for *general study* of social life; special reference should be made to their bibliographies.

WILSON, J. DOVER. *Life in Shakespeare's England.* 1911.
Selections from contemporary material, mostly literary.

BYRNE, M. ST CLARE. *The Elizabethan Home.* Second edition, 1930.
Selections from the conversation manuals of Hollyband and Erondelle: invaluable for their pictures of domestic life in both noble and citizen households.

HARRISON, G. B. *England in Shakespeare's Day.* 1928. 'English Life in English Literature Series.' No. 3.

II. CONTEMPORARY DOCUMENTS, LETTERS, ETC.

The correspondence between Lady Honor Lisle and others, calendared and largely transcribed in *Calendar of State Papers; Henry VIII;* 1537–1539. Some of these letters have been printed by M. A. E. Wood in vols. II and III of *Letters of Royal and Illustrious Ladies*, 1846. These, however, should be read under reference to their originals.

A List of the Marquis of Exeter's Servants. P.R.O. (S.P.I. 138).
For a shortened and not entirely accurate transcript see *Calendar of State Papers: Henry VIII:* 1538, vol. II, p. 755.

A Booke of Orders and Rules of Anthony Viscount Montague in 1595. *Sussex Archaeological Collections.* Vol. VII. 1854.

The Earl of Northumberland's Household Book. Ed. Bishop Percy.

Ordinances for the Royal Household from Edward III to William and Mary. Ed. Nicholas Carlisle, for the Society of Antiquaries. 1829.
The items of most use in the present connexion are: (1) *Articles Ordained by King Henry VII for the Regulation of his Household.* (2) *Ordinances for the Household made at Eltham,* 1526. (3) *Queen Elizabeth's Annual Expense, Civil and Military.* (4) *The Booke of Household of Queen Elizabeth in the 43rd year of her reign.* (5) *Ordinances of the Household of King James I,* 1604. (6) *The Establishment of Prince Henry,* 1610.

Letters, accounts, inventories, etc. calendared in Publications of the *Historical Manuscripts Commission.*

HARRISON, WILLIAM. *Description of England,* 1587. Ed. Furnivall for New Shakspere Society. *Selections from: Elizabethan England;* ed. L. Withington: Scott Library.

RYE, W. B. *England as Seen by Foreigners.* Contemporary opinions, collected and edited, 1865.

NICHOLS, J. *Progresses...of Queen Elizabeth.* 2 vols. 1788; new ed. 3 vols. 1823.

See also sources cited in footnotes.

M. ST C. B.

SHAKESPEARE'S SOURCES

FARMER, RICHARD. *An Essay on the Learning of Shakespeare.* 1767. Reprinted in vol. I of the Boswell-Malone Variorum Edition of the Works. 1821.

A discussion of the extent of Shakespeare's reading, especially of Greek and Latin authors.

MALONE, E. *Dissertation of Henry VI.* Printed in vol. XVIII of the Boswell-Malone Variorum Edition.

The first detailed discussion of the authenticity of the three parts of *Henry VI.*

HAZLITT, W. C. (editor). *Shakespeare's Library.* Second edition, 1875.

The most complete collection of the 'plays romances novels poems and histories employed by Shakespeare in the composition of his works'.

FLEAY, F. G. *Shakespeare Manual.* 1876.

FLEAY, F. G. *Life and Work of Shakespeare.* 1886.

Fleay can be counted as the first 'disintegrator', but his evidence and his conclusions should be carefully tested in the light of recent research.

SKEAT, W. W. *Shakespeare's Plutarch.* 1892.

Contains North's translation of Plutarch's Lives of Coriolanus, Julius Caesar, Brutus, Antony, Octavius, and extracts from the Lives of Theseus and Alcibiades. There is also an edition of the Lives of Coriolanus, Julius Caesar, Brutus and Antony, edited by R. H. Carr (1906). In both these books the marginal captions are printed.

BOSWELL-STONE, W. G. *Shakespeare's Holinshed.* 1896. Reprinted in I. Gollancz, *The Shakespeare Classics.* 1907.

A book of relevant extracts from the Chronicles, arranged with editorial comment under the headings of the different plays. There is also an edition of the Chronicles for the reigns of Richard II, Henry IV and Henry V, edited by R. S. Wallace and A. Hansen (1923). In both these books the marginal captions are printed.

BOAS, F. S. *The Works of Thomas Kyd.* 1901.

Kyd's claim to the authorship of the *Ur-Hamlet* is discussed in the introduction. See also R. B. McKerrow, *The Works of Thomas Nashe*, vol. IV (1908), pp. 449–52.

GOLLANCZ, I. (editor). *The Shakespeare Classics.* 1903–13.

This series of reprints includes *Rosalynde, Pandosto, Apollonius and Sylla, Romeus and Juliet*, Plautus' *Menaechmi, The Taming of A Shrew, The Troublesome Raigne, King Leir*, and two volumes of those parts of North's Plutarch which Shakespeare used.

GREG, W. W. *Henslowe's Diary. Vol.* I, *The Text: Vol.* II, *The Commentary.* 1904, 1907.

The most valuable document for the study of the problems of collaboration and revision.

ANDERS, H. R. D. *Shakespeare's Books.* 1904.

Intended to serve as an introduction to a new edition of Hazlitt's *Shakespeare's Library*, contemplated by the Deutschen Shakespeare-Gesellschaft; it contains much useful matter suggesting the extent and variety of Shakespeare's reading.

MACCALLUM, A. W. *Shakespeare's Roman Plays and their Background.* 1910, reprinted 1925.

The most detailed study of Shakespeare's use of Plutarch, but see also G. Wyndham, *Essays in Romantic Literature* (1919).

STOLL, E. E. *Hamlet, An Historical and Comparative Study.* 1919.

ROBERTSON, J. M. *The Problem of Hamlet.* 1919.

BROCK, A. CLUTTON. *Shakespeare's Hamlet.* 1922.

WALDOCK, A. J. *Hamlet.* 1931.

These four books illustrate the way in which aesthetic criticism of this play has been affected by the theory that Shakespeare's *Hamlet* was 'superposed upon much cruder material which persists even in the final form' [T. S. Eliot, *Hamlet and His Problems*, in *Selected Essays* (1932)].

WILSON, J. DOVER (editor with SIR A. QUILLER-COUCH). *The New Shakespeare.* 1921– .

Prof. Dover Wilson's theories, methods and conclusions can best be studied in the notes, especially the 'Note on the Copy', to the plays published in this edition.

CHAMBERS, SIR E. K. *The Elizabethan Stage.* 4 vols. 1923.

CHAMBERS, SIR E. K. *William Shakespeare.* 2 vols. 1930.
Indispensable for reference on all the points raised in this chapter. Ch. VII of *William Shakespeare,* 'The Problem of Authenticity', is the fullest judicial treatment of the problems of revision and collaboration and of the theories of the disintegrators. See also the same author's British Academy Lecture, *The Disintegration of Shakespeare* (1924, reprinted in *Aspects of Shakespeare,* 1932).

POLLARD, A. W. (and others). *Shakespeare's Hand in the Play of 'Sir Thomas More.'* 1923.
An important study of an existing playhouse manuscript, which shows obvious signs of both revision and collaboration.

GAW, A. *The Origin and Development of* 1 *Henry VI.* 1926.
The fullest treatment of the problem of the authorship of this play, but its conclusions are affected by the theory put forward by P. Alexander.

CHAMBRUN, C. L. de. *Shakespeare, Actor Poet.* 1927.
An argument that Shakespeare was strongly influenced by Montaigne through Florio.

ALEXANDER, P. *Shakespeare's Henry VI and Richard III.* 1929.
A convincing argument that the two parts of the Contention are examples of 'bad quartos'.

ROBERTSON, J. M. *The Genuine in Shakespeare, A Conspectus.* 1930.
Robertson's summary of the conclusions of his investigations; his methods, however, do not lend themselves to summary treatment. They can be studied at greater length in the five volumes of his *The Shakespeare Canon* (1922–32) and in *Literary Detection, A Symposium on Macbeth* (1931).

A. L. A.

SHAKESPEARE AND THE DRAMA OF HIS TIME

LAMB, CHARLES. *Specimens of English Dramatic Poets who lived about the time of Shakespeare.* 1808.

THORNDIKE, ASHLEY H. *The Influence of Beaumont and Fletcher on Shakespeare.* 1901.

GAYLEY, CHARLES MILLS. *Representative English Comedies.* 1903. Introduction. (For the Shakespearian Comedies.)

SWINBURNE, A. C. *The Age of Shakespeare.* 1908.

THORNDIKE, ASHLEY H. *The Facts about Shakespeare.* 1913.

GAYLEY, CHARLES MILLS. *Francis Beaumont, Dramatist.* 1914.

SWINBURNE, A. C. *Contemporaries of Shakespeare.* 1919.

LUCAS, F. L. *The Works of John Webster.* 4 vols. 1927. Introduction in vol. 1.

SYKES, H. DUGDALE. *Sidelights on Elizabethan Drama.* 1928.

SISSON, CHARLES J. *The Elizabethan Dramatists, except Shakespeare.* 1928.

BOAS, F. S. *Christopher Marlowe; A biographical and critical study.* 1940.

CLARK, ARTHUR MELVILLE. *Thomas Heywood.* 1931.

ELIOT, T. S. *Selected Essays.* 1932.

BOAS, F. S. *An Introduction to Tudor Drama.* 1933.

B. D.

SHAKESPEARE'S TEXT

The Cambridge Shakespeare. First Edition, edited by J. GLOVER, W. G. CLARK, and W. ALDIS WRIGHT. 1863–6. Second and third editions, edited by W. ALDIS WRIGHT. 1867 and 1891.

The first edition marked a great advance over previous work both in the soundness of its text and the full, though not complete, collations. It is generally preferred to the later editions.

Facsimiles of the First Folio.

Shakespeare as put forth in 1623. A reprint of Mr. William Shakespeares Comedies, Histories, & Tragedies published according to the True Originall Copies. London, printed by Isaac Iaggard and Ed. Blount, 1623, and reprinted for Lionel Booth, 1864.

A marvellously accurate 'type-facsimile'. Cheaper and handier to work with than the Oxford collotype facsimile of 1902 or the photo-zincographic one of Messrs Methuen (1910), though it cannot, like these, be used for detective work such as that of Mr E. E. Willoughby on *The Printing of the First Folio* (1932). All three facsimiles are out of print. Facsimiles of the Folio text of ten plays, with a note and collations by J. Dover Wilson, have been published by Messrs Faber and Faber.

Shakspere Quarto Facsimiles. Executed under the superintendence of F. J. Furnivall. 43 vols. 1885–91.

The facsimiles in photozincography by C. Praetorius, and photolithography by W. Griggs are not entirely trustworthy, owing to careless retouchings; but they remain indispensable for advanced students, more especially those with introductions by P. A. Daniel.

POLLARD, A. W. *Shakespeare Folios and Quartos: a study in the bibliography of Shakespeare's plays,* 1594–1685. With 37 illustrations. 1909.

Popularised the distinction between 'Good' and 'Bad' quartos.

POLLARD, A. W. *Shakespeare's Fight with the Pirates and the problems of the transmission of his text.*

The Sandars Lectures on Bibliography, 1915; first printed in *The Library*; published by Alex. Moring, 1916; Second edition, revised with an introduction (Cambridge University Press). 1920.

THOMPSON, SIR E. MAUNDE. *Shakespeare's Handwriting; a Study.* 1916.

The first expert examination of the handwriting of the 'More' Fragment with full-sized facsimiles.

WILSON, J. DOVER. Textual Introductions to *The Tempest* and other volumes of 'The New Shakespeare'. 1921, etc.

CHAMBERS, SIR E. K. *The Elizabethan Stage.* 4 vols. 1923.

Vol. III, ch. XXII, pp. 157–200, The Printing of Plays. Vol. IV, Appendix L, pp. 379–397. Printed Plays (a chronological abstract of plays printed or entered for printing in the Stationers' Register, 1558–1616).

GREG, W. W. *Two Elizabethan Stage Abridgements; 'The Battle of Alcazar' & 'Orlando Furioso'; an essay in critical bibliography.* 1923.

Argument for bad text having arisen from memorial reconstruction rather than shorthand notes.

POLLARD, A. W. *The Foundations of Shakespeare's Text.* Annual Shakespeare Lecture of the British Academy. 1923.

Reprinted in *Aspects of Shakespeare.* 1933.

Shakespeare's Hand in the Play of 'Sir Thomas More'. Papers by ALFRED W. POLLARD, W. W. GREG, SIR E. MAUNDE THOMPSON, J. DOVER WILSON and R. W. CHAMBERS, with the text of the Ill May Day Scenes edited by W. W. GREG. 1923.

CROMPTON RHODES, R. *Shakespeare's First Folio; a study.* 1923.

Includes chapters on The Company of Stationers; The 'Pavier' Shakespeare [i.e. the volume of 1619]; The Unblotted Papers; and 'Divers stolne and Surreptitious Copies'.

Studies in the First Folio. Written for the Shakespeare Association in celebration of the First Folio tercentenary. 1924.

The introduction by Sir Israel Gollancz and papers by J. Dover Wilson on 'The Task of Heminge and Condell'; by R. Crompton Rhodes on 'The First Folio and the Elizabethan Stage'; by W. W. Greg on 'The First Folio and its Publishers'; and by Allardyce Nicoll on 'The Editors of Shakespeare from First Folio to Malone', are all of value for the text.

McKerrow, R. B. *An introduction to Bibliography for literary students.* 1927.

Part I discusses the make up of books; part II, bibliographical evidence as to order of editions and date; copy, proofs, proof-corrections and cancels; part III, treatment of copy by compositors.

Tannenbaum, S. A. *The Booke of 'Sir Thomas Moore'; a bibliotic study.* 1927.

Arguments against Shakespeare's authorship of the 'three pages'.

Greg, W. W. *Principles of Emendation in Shakespeare.* Annual Shakespeare Lecture of the British Academy. 1928.

Reprinted in *Aspects of Shakespeare.* 1933.

Chambers, Sir E. K. *William Shakespeare; a study of facts and problems.* 2 vols. 1930.

Vol. I, ch. IV, pp. 92–125, The Book of the Play; ch. V, pp. 126–167, The Quartos and the First Folio; ch. VI, pp. 168–204, Plays in the Printing House; ch. IX, pp. 275, 498, Plays of the First Folio; ch. X, pp. 499–515, Plays Outside the First Folio. I. Sir Thomas More.

Chambers, R. W. 'Some Sequences of Thought in Shakespeare and in the 147 lines of "Sir Thomas More".' *The Modern Language Review*, vol. XXVI, No. 3, pp. 251–80. July, 1931.

Greg, W. W. 'The Function of Bibliography in Literary Criticism illustrated in a study of the text of "King Lear".' *Neophilologus*, vol. XVIII, pp. 241–62.

McKerrow, R. B. *The treatment of Shakespeare's Text by his earlier editors*, 1709–1768. Annual Shakespeare Lecture of the British Academy. 1933.

A. W. P.

SHAKESPEARIAN CRITICISM

JUSSERAND, J. J. *Shakespeare in France under the ancien régime.* 1899.
An interestingly written and informed account of the reception and criticism of Shakespeare in France.

LOUNSBURY, T. R. *Shakespeare and Voltaire.* 1902.
A discussion of the eighteenth-century view of Shakespeare in France.

SMITH, D. N. *Eighteenth-Century Essays on Shakespeare.* 1903.
The pioneer collection of early prefaces and critical essays, with a useful introductory survey.

WARNER, B. *Famous Introductions to Shakespeare's Plays.* 1906.
A slightly different selection, published in America.

ROBERTSON, J. G. 'Shakespeare on the Continent.' *C.H.E.L.* vol. v. 1910.
A masterly sketch by an expert in comparative literature of Shakespeare's reception and influence in Europe.

BALDENSPERGER, F. *Esquisse d'une histoire de Shakespeare en France.* 1910.
An intelligent essay on the history of literary taste in France.

GUNDOLF, F. *Shakespeare und der deutsche Geist.* 1911.
A brilliant survey of German intellectual history as affected by Shakespeare.

HIRONDELLE, A. *Shakespeare en Russie.* 1912.

SMITH, D. N. *Shakespeare Criticism.* 1916.
A useful selection of criticism during several centuries.

HERFORD, C. H. *A Sketch of recent Shakespearean Investigations.* 1923.
A packed and philosophical survey of Shakespearian criticism from 1893 to 1923.

YOUNG, KARL. *Samuel Johnson on Shakespeare.* 1924.
A well-informed and carefully ordered account of the eighteenth-century concern with the reality of characters.

STOLL, E. E. *Shakespeare Studies, historical and comparative in method.* 1927.

BABCOCK, R. W. *The Genesis of Shakespeare Idolatry.* 1931.
A valuable account of the growth of the enthusiasm for Shakespeare during the eighteenth century.

Ralli, A. *A History of Shakespeare Criticism*. 2 vols. 1932.
Useful for its summaries of criticism—but does not give the picture of the evolution of criticism its title would lead one to expect. (See a pertinent and severe criticism by L. L. Schücking, *Beiblatt zur Anglia*, April, 1933.)

J. I.

SHAKESPEARIAN SCHOLARSHIP

Furnivall, F. J. Preface to G. G. Gervinus's Commentaries. 1875.

Furnivall, F. J. Preface to the Leopold Shakespeare. 1877.
A concise statement of the Mid-Victorian position—and account of the verse tests—by the director-general of Shakespeare research in the nineteenth century.

Smith, D. N. *Eighteenth-Century Essays on Shakespeare*. 1903.
Gives much material indispensable in estimating the work of early editors.

Warner, B. *Famous Introductions to Shakespeare's Plays*. 1906.
A further selection of editorial matter.

Lounsbury, T. R. *The Text of Shakespeare*. 1906.
A detailed and valuable account of the work of early editors.

Herford, C. H. *A sketch of recent Shakespearean Investigations*. 1923.
A very useful summary of scholarship from 1893 to 1923.

Simpson, P. *The Bibliographical Study of Shakespere*. Oxford Bibliographical Society, vol. 1, part 1. 1923.
An exact account of the newer methods in textual criticism.

Greg, W. W. *Principles of Emendation in Shakespeare*. 1928.
An acute and stimulating discussion of textual scholarship.

Smith, D. N. *Shakespeare in the Eighteenth Century*. 1928.
Contains an account of the contributions of eighteenth-century scholars to the study of Shakespeare.

Jackson, A. 'Rowe's Edition of Shakespeare.' *The Library*. 1930.
A useful bibliographical account of Rowe's edition and a concise statement of his achievement.

Babcock, R. W. *The Genesis of Shakespeare Idolatry*, 1766–1799. 1931.
Includes a detailed survey of the growth of Shakespeare scholarship in the second half of the eighteenth century.

McKerrow, R. B. *The treatment of Shakespeare's Text by his earlier editors*, 1709–1768. 1933.

A careful and fresh stocktaking of eighteenth-century editorial activity—by the editor of the forthcoming Oxford Variorum text.

J. I.

THE STAGING OF SHAKESPEARE

Genest, John. *Some Account of the English Stage.* 1832.

A record, compiled from play-bills and other sources, of the productions at the London theatres and some others, with criticisms and commentaries.

Stephen, Leslie and Lee, Sir Sidney. *Dictionary of National Biography.* 1885, etc. (in progress).

For lives of the players, etc., and sources from which they were taken.

Irving, Sir Henry and Marshall, Frank A. *The Works of William Shakespeare.* Second edition. 1906.

Commonly called The Henry Irving Shakespeare. Contains a stage history of each play.

Odell, George C. D. *Shakespeare from Betterton to Irving.* 2 vols. 1921.

A history of the adaptation and staging of Shakespeare. A useful introduction to the study of the subject.

Quiller-Couch, Sir Arthur and Wilson, J. Dover. *The New Shakespeare.* 1921, etc. (in progress).

Each volume includes a stage history of the play to which it is devoted.

Summers, Montague. *Shakespeare Adaptations.* 1922.

Gives the texts of *The Tempest or the Enchanted Island* by D'Avenant and Dryden; *The Mock-Tempest or the Enchanted Castle*, by T. Duffett, and *The History of King Lear* in the version by Nahum Tate, with a long introduction and notes.

Nicoll, Allardyce. *Dryden as an Adapter of Shakespeare.* 1922.

A Shakespeare Association pamphlet of great value.

Nicoll, Allardyce. *A History of Restoration Drama* 1660–1700. 1923.

Nicoll, Allardyce. *A History of Early Eighteenth Century Drama* 1700–1750. 1925.

Nicoll, Allardyce. *A History of Late Eighteenth Century Drama* 1750–1800. 1927.

NICOLL, ALLARDYCE. *A History of Early Nineteenth Century Drama 1800–1850.* 1930.

A comprehensive and well-documented account of the subject, in which the history of Shakespeare on the stage is seen in its relation to the drama as a whole.

NICOLL, ALLARDYCE. *The Development of the Theatre.* 1927.

Contains some useful notes on staging and costume, with many illustrations.

SPENCER, HAZELTON. *Shakespeare Improved; the Restoration Versions in Quarto and on the Stage.* 1927.

The title sufficiently describes the scholarly work of research, which is invaluable to the student.

HOTSON, LESLIE. *The Commonwealth and Restoration Stage.* 1928.

Another work of original research, useful as giving the theatrical background, but not greatly concerned with Shakespeare.

[DOWNES, JOHN.] *Roscius Anglicanus.* Ed. by Montague Summers. 1928.

An Historical Review of the Stage from 1660 to 1706, written by the Book-keeper and Prompter of the Duke's Company. First published in 1708. Mr Summer's edition has many pages of explanatory notes.

Collections of play-bills, newspapers and prints: especially the Burney Collection of prints in the British Museum, and the Gabrielle Enthoven Collection of play-bills and other documents in the Victoria and Albert Museum.

H.C.

APPENDICES

APPENDIX I

COMPARATIVE TABLE OF THE AGE AND DRAMATIC ACTIVITY OF SHAKESPEARE AND HIS CONTEMPORARIES

Each dot represents a year. The years of dramatic production are denoted by *. Conjectural dates of birth and death are marked †

Munday b. 1553†	d. 1633
Lyly b. 1554†	d. 1606
Peele b. 1557†	d. 1596
Greene b. 1558	d. 1592
Kyd b. 1558	d. 1594
Chapman b. 1560†	d. 1634
Marlowe b. 1564	d. 1593
SHAKESPEARE b. 1564	d. 1616
Middleton b. 1570†	d. 1627
Heywood, T. b. 1570†	d. 1641
Jonson b. 1572	d. 1637
Dekker b. 1572†	d. 1632†
Day b. 1574	d. 1640†
Marston b. 1575†	d. 1634
Fletcher b. 1579	d. 1625
Beaumont b. 1584	d. 1616

APPENDIX II

A CHRONOLOGICAL TABLE

THE following chronological table covering Shakespeare's working years shows (*a*) some important national and theatrical events; (*b*) the date of publication of some important books; (*c*) approximate date of the first production of the most important plays during Shakespeare's career; (*d*) the dates of their first publication. The evidence for (*c*) and (*d*) will be found principally in Sir E. K. Chambers's *Elizabethan Stage* and *William Shakespeare: a study of facts and problems*. It is seldom possible to date the first appearance of a play exactly: before 1595 and after 1605 the margin of error may be as much as five years. Nor is there general agreement on the dates of Shakespeare's earliest and latest plays: some scholars would date the first as early as 1587. Plays which may be dated with some precision are marked ‡.

	Events	Books published
1587	Execution of Mary Queen of Scots Funeral of Sir Philip Sidney	
1588	Defeat of the Spanish Armada Robert, Earl of Leicester, died	Greene's *Perimedes*
1589	A Parliament held The Portugal Voyage Duke of Guise and Henri III murdered Civil war in France	Hakluyt's *Voyages* Greene's *Pandosto* and *Menaphon*
1590	Sir Francis Walsingham died	Lodge's *Rosalynde* Spenser's *Faerie Queene*, Bks 1–3 Marprelate controversy
1591	Hacket's treason The loss of the 'Revenge' Proclamation against Jesuits and seminaries	Harington's *Orlando Furioso* Sidney's *Astrophel and Stella* Spenser's *Complaints*
1592	Scottish Witchcraft trials Greene died The Great Carrack captured Edward Alleyn marries Henslowe's step-daughter	Greene's *The Conny-catching pamphlets*: *Groatsworth of Wit* Nashe's *Piers Penniless* Constable's *Diana* Chettle's *Kind Hart's Dream*
1593	Parliament held Marlowe killed Plague stops playing	VENUS AND ADONIS Drayton's *Idea* Daniel's *Delia* Chapman's *Shadow of Night*: *The Phœnix Nest* Hooker's *Laws of Ecclesiastical Polity*
1594	Plague till summer Playing reorganised: the Admiral's Men at Rose; Chamberlain's at Theatre Kyd died	LUCRECE *Willobie his Avisa* Nashe's *Jack Wilton*

Plays first produced	Plays published
1 Tamburlaine *Alphonsus of Aragon* *Galathea*	
Endimion *II Tamburlaine*	
Spanish Tragedy *Jew of Malta* *Friar Bacon* *Midas* *Mother Bombie*	*Rare triumphs of Love and Fortune*
Looking Glass for London *Love's Metamorphosis*	*Three Lords and three Ladies of London* *I and II Tamburlaine*
Orlando Furioso *James IV* *The Woman in the Moon*	*Endimion* *I and II Troublesome reign of King John*
Dr Faustus *Edward II* *I, II, III Henry VI* RICHARD III TITUS ANDRONICUS	*Arden of Faversham* *Spanish Tragedy* *Galathea* *Midas*
Massacre at Paris *Dido, Queen of Carthage* TAMING OF THE SHREW COMEDY OF ERRORS TWO GENTLEMEN OF VERONA LOVE'S LABOUR'S LOST	*Edward II* *Edward I*
John a Kent ROMEO AND JULIET	*Orlando Furioso** *Knack to Know a Knave* TITUS ANDRONICUS *Looking Glass for London* *I Contention York and Lancaster* *Taming of a Shrew* *Pedlar's Prophecy* *Famous Victories of Henry V* *James IV* *Friar Bacon* *King Leir* *David and Bethsabe* *Jew of Malta* *Wounds of Civil War*

* The probable explanation of the sudden increase in printed plays in 1594 is that the companies were so disorganised by the plague that they raised money by selling their MSS.

	Events	Books published
1594 (*cont.*)		
1595	Riots in London Ralegh's Guiana Voyage Last expedition of Drake and Hawkins (both died)	Spenser's *Amoretti* Sidney's *Defence of Poesy* Southwell's *St Peter's Complaint*
1596	Calais captured by Spaniards The Cadiz expedition	Harington's *Metamorphosis of Ajax* Lodge's *Wit's Miserie* Spenser's *Faerie Queene*, Bks 4–6; *Four Hymns* Drayton's *Mortimeriados* Davies's *Orchestra*
1597	The Islands Voyage A Spanish armada wrecked A Parliament held	Bacon's *Essays* (1st version) Hall's *Virgidemiarum* Deloney's *Jack of Newbury* and *Gentle Craft*
1598	Rebellion and disaster in Ireland The Queen boxes Essex's ears Lord Burghley died Philip II of Spain died The 'Theatre' demolished	Marlowe's *Hero and Leander* Chapman's Trans. of *Iliad* (7 books) Meres's *Palladis Tamia* Marston's *Scourge of Villainy*
1599	Spenser died Essex in Ireland Satires burnt Chamberlain's Men occupy new 'Globe' Invasion scare Essex fails in Ireland and returns in disgrace Children of Paul's begin playing	Hayward's *Henry IV* THE PASSIONATE PILGRIM Davies's *Nosce teipsum*
1600	Mountjoy in Ireland Kempe's dance to Norwich Alleyn builds 'Fortune' theatre	*England's Helicon* Exorcism controversy

Plays first produced	Plays published
	Cobbler's prophecy
	Four Prentices of London
	True Tragedy of Richard III
	Locrine
	Fair Em
	Battle of Alcazar
	Selimus
	Dido, Queen of Carthage
Midsummer Night's Dream	*George a Greene*
Richard II	*Old Wives' Tale*
	Woman in the Moon
	Knack to Know an honest man
	Edward III
	True tragedy of Richard Duke of York
Blind Beggar of Alexandria ‡	
King John	
Merchant of Venice	
Humorous Day's Mirth ‡	Richard II
Isle of Dogs (lost) ‡	Richard III
The Case is altered	Romeo and Juliet
I Henry IV	
I and II Robert, Earl of Huntingdon	I Henry IV
Englishmen for my money	Merchant of Venice
Every Man in his Humour ‡	*Blind Beggar of Alexandria*
Two Angry women of Abingdon	Love's Labour's Lost
Pilgrimage to Parnassus ‡	*Mucedorus*
II Henry IV	
Much Ado about Nothing	
Shoemaker's Holiday ‡	*I and II Edward IV*
Every Man out of his Humour	*Warning for fair women*
I Sir John Oldcastle ‡	*Humorous day's mirth*
Histriomastix	*Two angry women of Abingdon*
Antonio and Mellida	*Alphonsus of Aragon*
Antonio's Revenge	
The Old Law	
Old Fortunatus ‡	
I Return from Parnassus ‡	
Henry V ‡	
As You Like It	
Julius Caesar ‡	
Blind Beggar of Bethnal Green ‡	*Old Fortunatus*
Patient Grissell ‡	*Patient Grissell*
Merry Wives of Windsor	*Every man out of his humour*

	Events	Books published
1600 (*cont.*)	The Gowry conspiracy Children of Chapel begin playing at Blackfriars East India Company formed	
1601	Essex's rebellion and execution The 'War of the Theatres' Siege of Ostend begun Spanish expedition lands in Ireland A Parliament held: the agitation concerning monopolies	Catholic controversy Holland's Translation of Pliny
1602	Tyrone defeated in Ireland Spaniards surrender Biron's conspiracy	Campion's *Observations on Art of English Poetry* Deloney's *Thomas of Reading*
1603	Tyrone submits QUEEN ELIZABETH DIED ACCESSION OF JAMES I Chamberlain's Men become King's Men Plague stops playing Ralegh and others tried and condemned Renewed vogue of Court masques	Davies's *Microcosmos* Dekker's *Wonderful Year* Daniel's *Defence of Rhyme* Florio's Translation of Montaigne's *Essays* James I's *Dæmonology* (London ed.)
1604	Hampton Court Conference End of Siege of Ostend James's first parliament Peace with Spain	
1605	Act to expel Jesuits and seminary priests	Bacon's *Advancement of Learning*

PLAYS FIRST PRODUCED	PLAYS PUBLISHED
TROILUS AND CRESSIDA	*Alarum for London*
	Maid's Metamorphosis
	HENRY V
	MUCH ADO ABOUT NOTHING
	I and II Sir John Oldcastle
	II HENRY IV
	Jack Drum's Entertainment
	MIDSUMMER NIGHT'S DREAM
Cynthia's Revels	*Love's Metamorphosis*
Poetaster	*I and II Robert, Earl of Huntingdon*
Satiromastix	*Shoemaker's Holiday*
Blurt Master Constable	*Dr Faustus*
What You Will	*Cynthia's Revels*
II Return from Parnassus	*Every Man in his Humour* (1st version)
HAMLET	
Gentleman Usher	*Antonio and Mellida*
Sir Thomas Wyatt ‡	*Antonio's Revenge*
TWELFTH NIGHT ‡	*Satiromastix*
	Poetaster
	MERRY WIVES OF WINDSOR
	Blurt Master Constable
	Thomas Lord Cromwell
Woman Killed with Kindness ‡	HAMLET (Q 1)
Hoffman	
Sejanus	
The Phœnix	
Dutch Courtesan	*Malcontent*
All Fools	*I Honest Whore*
Malcontent	HAMLET (Q 2)
Wise Woman of Hogsdon	
Monsieur D'Olive	
Law Tricks	
Bussy D'Ambois	
I and II Honest Whore	
Westward Hoe	
ALL'S WELL THAT ENDS WELL	
MEASURE FOR MEASURE	
OTHELLO	
The Fawn	*Sejanus*
Eastward Hoe ‡	*Fair Maid of Bristow*
Northward Hoe	*When you see me, you know me*

	Events	Books published
1605 (*cont.*)	Gunpowder plot	
1606	Gunpowder plotters executed State visit of King of Denmark	Dekker's *Seven Deadly Sins of London*
1607	Renewed troubles in Ireland Virginia colonised Riots over enclosures A great frost	
1608	Children at Blackfriars disbanded King's Men take over the private playhouse Notorious pirates executed	
1609	Jonson's *Masque of Queens* at Court Truce in the Netherlands The Oath of Allegiance administered	Dekker's *Belman of London* (?) Fletcher's *Faithful Shepherdess* n.d. Dekker's *Gull's hornbook* Shakespeare's Sonnets

PLAYS FIRST PRODUCED	PLAYS PUBLISHED
I and II If you know me not	*Dutch Courtesan*
Trick to catch the old one	*I If you know me not*
	Eastward Hoe
	All Fools
	London Prodigal
	I Jeronimo
Whore of Babylon	*II If you know me not*
Sophonisba	*II Return from Parnassus*
Woman Hater	*Gentleman Usher*
Volpone	*Sir Giles Goosecap*
Isle of Gulls ‡	*The Fawn*
Rape of Lucrece	*Sophonisba*
Family of Love	*Wily Beguiled*
MACBETH	*Monsieur D'Olive*
KING LEAR	*Isle of Gulls*
Knight of the Burning Pestle	*Westward Hoe*
Travels of three English Brothers	*Whore of Babylon*
Humour out of breath	*Fair Maid of the Exchange*
Atheist's Tragedy	*Phœnix*
ANTONY AND CLEOPATRA	*Michaelmas Term*
CORIOLANUS	*Woman Hater*
TIMON OF ATHENS	*Bussy D'Ambois*
	Cupid's Whirligig
	Travels of three English Brothers
	Miseries of enforced marriage
	Puritan
	Northward Hoe
	What You Will
	Revenger's Tragedy
	Devil's Charter
	Volpone
	Woman Killed with Kindness
	Sir Thomas Wyatt
Faithful Shepherdess	*Trick to catch the old one*
Philaster	*Family of Love*
Maid's Tragedy	*Merry Devil of Edmonton*
Charles, Duke of Biron‡	KING LEAR
Appius and Virginia	*Law's Tricks*
PERICLES	*Humour out of breath*
	Yorkshire Tragedy
	Rape of Lucrece
	Tragedy of Biron
	A mad world, my masters
	Dumb Knight
	PERICLES
Epicœne	*The case is altered*
Bonduca	*Every Woman in her humour*
Woman is a weathercock	*Two maids of Moreclack*

	Events	Books published
1610	The plantation of Ulster Henri IV murdered A great drought	
1611	Carr made Viscount Rochester James quarrels with Parliament	A.V. Translation of Bible Chapman's Translation of *Iliad* completed Donne's *Anatomy of the World*
1612	Sir Thomas Overbury poisoned in the Tower Robert Cecil, Earl of Salisbury, died Prince Henry died	Skelton's Translation of *Don Quixote*
1613	Marriage of Princess Elizabeth The Essex divorce suit The Globe Theatre burnt	Drayton's *Polyolbion* Browne's *Britannia's pastorals*

1616 Death of William Shakespeare

1619 Jaggard's 'False folio' published

1623 The First Folio published

Plays first produced	Plays published
The Alchemist	*Histriomastix*
The Revenge of Bussy D'Ambois	
The Roaring Girl	
If it be not good, the Devil is in it	
CYMBELINE	
King and no King	*Ram Alley*
Catiline	*Atheist's Tragedy*
Chaste maid in Cheapside	*The Golden Age*
Amends for Ladies	*Catiline*
The Golden Age	*May Day*
The Silver Age	*The Roaring Girl*
THE WINTER'S TALE	
TEMPEST	
The Brazen Age	*The Alchemist*
The White Devil	*Woman is a weathercock*
	Christian turned Turk
	Widow's Tears
	The White Devil
	If it be not good
The Duchess of Malfi	*The Revenge of Bussy D'Ambois*
Honest Man's Fortune	*The Silver Age*
The Iron Age	*The Brazen Age*
TWO NOBLE KINSMEN	*Insatiate Countess*
HENRY VIII	*Knight of the Burning Pestle*

APPENDIX III

A NOTE ON PRICES IN SHAKESPEARE'S TIME

BY A. V. JUDGES

It is not uncommon to find in text-books and monographs dealing with particular periods a friendly footnote or so to the effect that currency values at such and such a date can readily be comprehended by multiplying monetary expressions by a suggested figure in order to produce the modern equivalent in purchasing power. Thus to discover the fall in the value of a sterling unit between the reign of Elizabeth and our own day we are told to multiply it by some such figure as 8 or 10. We may well be suspicious of these attempts to cut a quick way through the highly complicated question of comparative price levels, for it is common knowledge that prices in general were rising throughout Shakespeare's lifetime and that they have been fluctuating even more wildly during the last twenty years. But the short-period instability of values is the least serious of our difficulties, for it can be taken into account by the statistician.

There are three main reasons for holding that prices during Shakespeare's lifetime and those of to-day will not yield themselves to satisfactory treatment side by side. The first is that the whole range of transactions in economic life was then distributed as to the relative amounts and the relative values of commodities on a scheme so unlike that with which we are familiar to-day that, lacking a sufficient number of similar items whose prices we may compare, we are without the means of constructing a general price ratio; even approximate results are unattainable. There can be no question of 'weighting' a price index with so many unlikes in the field.

The second reason is that goods passing under the same names then as now are apt to vary from ours in regard to function, or content, or weight and so on, or durability, sometimes in all four respects. In considering such common objects or services as the sheep, the poor man's loaf, an article of woollen underclothing, the day's work of a labourer, we are faced with variations of one kind and another wide enough to lead in each case to legitimate differences of opinion as to the proper mode of comparison to be adopted.

The third reason is that the expenditure of individuals in all classes was arranged on a budgetary system not at all in conformity with modern practice. We, for instance, undoubtedly spend a smaller part of our incomes on food and drink and probably less on clothes. We have a far more complex scale of requirements, of alternative uses, of alternative sources of supply. Moreover, except in the case of very bulky commodities like coal, we are far less disturbed by a variation of prices between one locality and another. The prices of many of our purchases are determined and rendered more stable by conditions of cheap international transport. Another factor in the construction of the modern retail price is the large portion taken by the middleman. In Shakespeare's day, as often as not the retailer was the producer or had played a large part in the production of the wares offered for sale; the price historian is not always in a position to disentangle wholesale from retail prices.

On the whole, values expressed in pounds, shillings and pence have risen in the last three centuries. And we are justified in believing that the money incomes received by people in all walks of life in the time of Elizabeth and James I would be less useful to them if they had to make their purchases at to-day's prices. No doubt, with the whole scale of values re-arranged, they would make their purchases differently; even so they would still be much poorer. Thus we can say that they would be less well housed, less well dressed, less well fed and served, but we cannot say how much less of each, for the advance in prices, as may be demonstrated, has been remarkably uneven. Let us take by way of example some individual commodities that yield themselves more readily than most to comparison.

Taking the retail average in the south-east of England in the last six months of 1933 as 100, the following figures appear to be indicated as an average in the same area during the last thirty years of Shakespeare's life. They are at best only approximate.[1]

Beef	17	Eggs	20
Mutton	20	Candles	125
Butter	50	Heavy woollen cloth (medium quality)	117
Cheese (low quality)	37	Household coal (London, wholesale)	46
English wheat (wholesale)	117		
Rabbits	28		

[1] Thanks are due to the promoters of the *English Price History*, shortly to appear, for some data which have been used in preference to the figures given in Thorold Rogers's *History of Agriculture and Prices*.

INDEX